New Directions in German Studies
Vol. 36

Series Editor:
IMKE MEYER
Professor of Germanic Studies, University of Illinois at Chicago

Editorial Board:

KATHERINE ARENS
Professor of Germanic Studies, University of Texas at Austin

ROSWITHA BURWICK
Distinguished Chair of Modern Foreign Languages Emerita, Scripps College

RICHARD ELDRIDGE
Charles and Harriett Cox McDowell Professor of Philosophy,
Swarthmore College

ERIKA FISCHER-LICHTE
Professor Emerita of Theater Studies, Freie Universität Berlin

CATRIONA MACLEOD
Frank Curtis Springer and Gertrude Melcher Springer Professor in the
College and the Department of Germanic Studies, University of Chicago

STEPHAN SCHINDLER
Professor of German and Chair, University of South Florida

HEIDI SCHLIPPHACKE
Associate Professor of Germanic Studies, University of Illinois at Chicago

ANDREW J. WEBBER
Professor of Modern German and Comparative Culture, Cambridge University

SILKE-MARIA WEINECK
Grace Lee Boggs Collegiate Professor of Comparative Literature
and German Studies, University of Michigan

DAVID WELLBERY
LeRoy T. and Margaret Deffenbaugh Carlson University Professor,
University of Chicago

SABINE WILKE
Joff Hanauer Distinguished Professor for Western Civilization and
Professor of German, University of Washington

JOHN ZILCOSKY
Professor of German and Comparative Literature, University of Toronto

A list of volumes in the series appears at the end of this book.

Authors and the World
Literary Authorship in Modern Germany

Rebecca Braun

BLOOMSBURY ACADEMIC
NEW YORK • LONDON • OXFORD • NEW DELHI • SYDNEY

BLOOMSBURY ACADEMIC
Bloomsbury Publishing Inc
1385 Broadway, New York, NY 10018, USA
50 Bedford Square, London, WC1B 3DP, UK
29 Earlsfort Terrace, Dublin 2, Ireland

BLOOMSBURY, BLOOMSBURY ACADEMIC and the Diana logo are
trademarks of Bloomsbury Publishing Plc

First published in the United States of America 2022
This paperback edition published 2024

Copyright © Rebecca Braun, 2022

For legal purposes the Acknowledgements on p. ix constitute
an extension of this copyright page.

Cover design by Andrea F. Bucsi
Cover image: Lois at the typewriter by Michael Kent, courtesy of the artist

All rights reserved. No part of this publication may be reproduced or
transmitted in any form or by any means, electronic or mechanical, including
photocopying, recording, or any information storage or retrieval system,
without prior permission in writing from the publishers.

Bloomsbury Publishing Inc does not have any control over, or responsibility
for, any third-party websites referred to or in this book. All internet addresses
given in this book were correct at the time of going to press. The author and
publisher regret any inconvenience caused if addresses have changed or sites
have ceased to exist, but can accept no responsibility for any such changes.

A catalog record for this book is available from the Library of Congress.

Library of Congress Cataloging-in-Publication Data

Names: Braun, Rebecca, author.
Title: Authors and the world : literary authorship in modern Germany / by Rebecca Braun.
Description: New York : Bloomsbury Academic, 2022. |
Series: New directions in German studies ; vol. 36 | Includes bibliographical references and index. |
Summary: "Reconstructing literary practice across the last 75
years of carefully contextualized German history, this study provides a
new ontology of authorship: how literature is created by people and why
this matters to the wider world"– Provided by publisher.
Identifiers: LCCN 2022005835 (print) | LCCN 2022005836 (ebook) |
ISBN 9781501391026 (hardback) | ISBN 9781501391064 (paperback) |
ISBN 9781501391033 (epub) | ISBN 9781501391040 (pdf) | ISBN 9781501391057
Subjects: LCSH: German literature–20th century–History and criticism. |
German literature–21st century–History and criticism. | Authorship. | LCGFT: Literary criticism.
Classification: LCC PT134.A85 B73 2022 (print) |
LCC PT134.A85 (ebook) | DDC 830.9/009–dc23/eng/20220512
LC record available at https://lccn.loc.gov/2022005835
LC ebook record available at https://lccn.loc.gov/2022005836

ISBN: HB: 978-1-501-3910-26
PB: 978-1-5013-9106-4
ePDF: 978-1-5013-9104-0
eBook: 978-1-5013-9103-3

Series: New Directions in German Studies

Typeset by RefineCatch Limited, Bungay, Suffolk

To find out more about our authors and books visit www.bloomsbury.com
and sign up for our newsletters.

For my parents

Contents

List of Figures x
Acknowledgements xi
Note on Translations xiii

Introduction: Rethinking Goethe's World Literature
   through Questions of Authorship 1
1 Four Modes of Authorship across the German
   Twentieth Century 25
2 The Exemplary Creator: Modelling Authorship in
   Post-War West Germany 71
3 The Exemplary Pedagogue: Alternative Foundations
   for Belonging in the German Democratic Republic 113
4 Mediating Authorship in Berlin and Frankfurt, 1959–1989 151
5 After the Death of the Author: The Rise of the Utopian Mode,
   1988–2018 193
6 New Collaborations: Models of Transnational Authorship in
   Contemporary German-speaking Europe 233
In Conversation: Ulrike Draesner: On Creating Contexts
   for Literature 259
In Conversation: Olga Martynova: On Living in Multiple
   Literary Worlds 275
In Conversation: Ulrike Almut Sandig: On Collaborating
   across Media, Genres and Countries 299

Bibliography 325
Index 337

Figures

2.1 The 'Verlagscollage', undated. Fritz J. Raddatz is at the base, Ledig above him carries the Chief Financial Officer Kurt Busch on his shoulders, the Head of Distribution Karl Hans Hintermeier to his right and Edgar Friedrichsen, Head of Production, to his left. Reproduced courtesy of Rowohlt Verlag. 108

4.1 Dust jacket of the co-authored novel, *Das Gästehaus* (Berlin: LCB, 1965). Reproduced courtesy of the Literarisches Colloquium Berlin. 163

4.2 Still taken from *Das literarische Profil von Berlin*: Kurt Neuburger tells of his work fostering younger talent in the Kreuzberg Literature Workshop, surrounded by aspiring male authors and beer. Reproduced courtesy of the Literarisches Colloquium Berlin. 178

4.3 Still taken from *Das literarische Profil von Berlin*: Uwe Johnson speaks of the value of literature in contemporary Berlin, pictured in his home in front of a large map of the city and against the background noise of Tempelhof airport. Reproduced courtesy of the Literarisches Colloquium Berlin. 179

5.1 Main home page of the website www.3668ilfpetrow.com. Reproduced courtesy of Daniela Weirich and Felicitas Hoppe. 227

5.2 Detail from the multi-media blog on www.3668ilfpetrow.com, including a photograph by Jana Müller. Reproduced courtesy of Jana Müller and Felicitas Hoppe. 229

5.3 Landing page of the website www.3668ilfpetrow.com. Reproduced courtesy of Daniela Weirich and Felicitas Hoppe. 230

Acknowledgements

The research underpinning this work was generously funded by a Leverhulme Early Career Fellowship and an AHRC leadership fellowship, held at the Universities of Liverpool and Lancaster respectively. I would not be in academia today without the opportunities this funding afforded me.

Collections held at the Stiftung Archiv der Akademie der Künste, Berlin, the Literaturarchiv, Marbach, and the Literaturarchiv Sulzbach-Rosenberg have repeatedly inspired new points of departure for my work. I am particularly indebted to the kindness shown to me by Michael Peter Hehl in helping me find my way around uncatalogued materials on my visit to Sulzbach-Rosenberg and continuing to make further materials and intellectual exchange available to me from afar. I am also very grateful for the friendliness shown by staff who helped me out with licences at the Literarisches Colloquium Berlin and the Rowohlt Verlag.

Writing up this book has taken far longer than I could ever have imagined at the outset. Friends and colleagues intervened at just the right moment with enthusiasm, practical advice, and onward encouragement: Aleida Assmann, Susan Bassnett, Tobias Boes, Laura Bradley, Timothy Brennan, Mary Cosgrove, Karen Leeder, Andrew Piper, Ritchie Robertson, Maria Roca Lizarazu, Gisèle Sapiro, Benedict Schofield, and Emily Spiers. I have also benefitted from extremely supportive heads of department and faculty at Liverpool and Lancaster as I balanced this research with a number of other projects, not to mention life circumstances: Charles Forsdick and Eve Rosenhaft at Liverpool, Robert Crawshaw, Olga Gomez Cash, Simon Guy, and Birgit Smith at Lancaster. The writers Ulrike Draesner, Olga Martynova, and Ulrike Almut Sandig each entered very generously into the spirit of this book and helped me find a way of ending it that felt right.

During the latter part of my research, I drew fresh inspiration from the Institute for Social Futures, founded by the late John Urry and Linda

Woodhead at Lancaster University in 2016 and latterly co-directed by Richard Harper. The ISF has greatly influenced the onward development of my literary thinking and underlying belief that authors matter to the world in ways that have not always been well captured by conventional literary scholarship.

Finally, my children have never known me to be not writing this book. It has been something of a silent older sibling to them that would occasionally burst in upon their lives and snatch my attention for an unknown amount of time. Thank you to them for tolerating its wicked ways. Harald, you have helped me keep it all together: my thanks, and more, to you.

Note on Translations

I am grateful to Elspeth Dale for providing preliminary translations of the conversations with Olga Martynova and Ulrike Almut Sandig. Unless otherwise indicated, all other translations are my own.

Introduction Rethinking Goethe's World Literature through Questions of Authorship

How do authors relate to the wider world in which they live and work? What are the mechanisms that make one bestselling author famous well beyond her lifetime while another sinks without trace while still alive? And where does literature fit in a society's attempts to understand itself? These are just some of the questions that any study of literature's broader social importance must consider. Authors are both literary positions within a text – its putative point of origin and/or the guarantee that a work has been created with some kind of meaning or purpose in mind – and real people with lives and thoughts of their own, who can remain quite independent from the web of literary traditions into which their work is incorporated, and who can matter to their peers in other ways. French literary theory, from Roland Barthes' 'death of the author' and Michel Foucault's recalibrated 'author-function' in the late 1960s to Jérôme Meizoz' 'literary posture' of the 2000s, has given us a core vocabulary for thinking through how this author-in-the-world corresponds to the author-in-the-text. Meanwhile Pierre Bourdieu's sociological work on 'the field of cultural production' provides a conceptual framework for understanding diverse human drivers behind the broader literary sector under nineteenth- and twentieth-century capitalism.[1] Yet authors – and authorship – also roam far more widely than is even allowed for by the broadly defined parameters of language and

---

[1] Roland Barthes, 'The Death of the Author', in Roland Barthes, *Image, Music, Text*, trans & ed. Stephen Heath (London: Fontana, 1977), pp. 142–8; Michel Foucault, 'What is an Author?', in Michel Foucault, *The Essential Works of Foucault 1954-1984*, vol 2, ed. James Faubion (London: Penguin, 2000), pp. 205–22; Jérôme Meizoz, *Postures littéraires: Mises en scène modernes de l'auteur* (Geneva: Slatkine, 2007); Pierre Bourdieu, *The Field of Cultural Production: Essays on Art and Literature*, ed. Randal Johnson (Cambridge: Polity, 1993); Pierre Bourdieu, *The Rules of Art* (Cambridge: Polity, 1996).

society set out by these post-structuralist approaches. They appear on TV and radio shows and in YouTube clips, they create multiple print, sound and visual text types, they lecture in universities and fill writer's residencies in small towns, they write about historical and contemporary events in both the literary review and main political sections of newspapers, they work with people in schools, prisons, hospitals and container ships.[2] All this happens alongside their core business of writing novels, poems and short stories. At the same time, these literary texts appear online, in libraries and bookshops, but they also make their way, in excerpted form, onto city transport systems, mugs, shopping bags, T-shirts and museum walls, as well as into outdoor public spaces, street furniture and end-of-year company reports.

Germany provides a particular cultural setting through which to grasp this expanded phenomenon of authorship. Defined since the eighteenth-century Enlightenment period as the 'Land der Dichter und Denker' (land of poets and philosophers) and held together throughout both the nineteenth and twentieth centuries as a 'Kulturnation', a cultural and implicitly a 'cultured' nation or set of nations, the German-speaking lands have a long history of generating intellectual figureheads who can represent world-leading cultural achievement even as the political balance-sheet falls short. Countless parks and places of education are dedicated to Goethe and Schiller, while 'Literaturhäuser' (literature centres) profiling contemporary writers and writing, along with 'Dichterhäuser' (authors' homes open to the public) commemorating the dead and their work, have spread across regional towns and cities since the 1980s.[3] As if to cement literature's place in the national consciousness, the first major national museum dedicated to twentieth- and twenty-first century literature, the 'Literaturmuseum der Moderne' (Museum of Modern Literature) in Marbach, opened in 2006. It unites diverse literary memorabilia and authorial estates from across German-speaking Europe and garnered further high cultural approval when it scooped the Royal Institute of British Architects' Stirling Prize in 2007. Furthermore, if valuing literature and promoting those who create it is measured in the number of literary awards, then Germany beats all international comparison, with a staggering 180 serious prizes awarded in the early twenty-first

---

[2] Just to back up some of these more exotic locations: Ilka Scheidgen reports how Gabriele Wohmann read in prison, *Gabriele Wohmann: Ich muss neugierig bleiben: Die Biografie* (Lahr: Kaufmann, 2012), p. 151, while Felicitas Hoppe spent a year travelling around the world on a container ship with the proceeds of her first literary prize.

[3] Bodo Plachta, *Dichterhäuser* (Darmstadt: Thiess, 2017).

century, where the next most generous European country, France, counts a mere fifty or so significant awards.[4]

Yet alongside the ostentatious public promotion of certain authors and their work that reaches back into the Goethe period, there is also a long history of writers being politically side-lined (Jakob and Wilhelm Grimm, Heinrich Heine), culturally stuck in a backwater (Heinrich von Kleist, Annette von Droste-Hülshoff), financially unable to make a living for a large part of their writing lives (Heine again, Theodor Fontane) – and this all before the National Socialist book burnings, political misappropriation, and flight into exile of a significant proportion of the authors in the first part of the twentieth century who would subsequently count as either canonical or otherwise laudably Germanic.[5] If the subsequent post-war decades go some way towards redressing the dismissal and/or deformation of authors as citizens with a stake in the world into which they are born, the underlying soil of this rather troubled 'cultural Heimat' is by no means easy to till.[6] Late twentieth-century German-language authors have found themselves trying to lay down their own aesthetic and intellectual roots within, if not across, the divergent furrows of a culturally specific, retrospectively focused political catastrophe on the one hand (the Holocaust) and an emergent global neoliberal market that threatens to monetize everything on the other. In fact, it is the very challenge of staking out a position within such a mixed cultural landscape that makes the expanded case studies in authorship provided by German-language writers of the twentieth and twenty-first centuries so compelling.

This book is about these diverse places and practices for literature, captured through the actions of the people who have created it over the last seventy-five years and the way they have in turn been created by their life and times. In this respect, it builds rather more on the combined 'socio-criticism' and 'literary sociology' of Meizoz and Bourdieu than on the theories of authorship routinely associated with Barthes and

---

[4] For more detail on these figures, see Rebecca Braun, 'Prize Germans? Changing Notions of Germanness and the Role of the Award-Winning Author into the Twenty-First Century', *Oxford German Studies*, 43.1 (2014), 37–54.

[5] Particularly interesting recent studies of these phenomena include W. Daniel Wilson, *Der Faustische Pakt: Goethe und die Goethe-Gesellschaft im Dritten Reich* (Munich: dtv, 2018); Lynne Tatlock, ed., *Publishing Culture and the "Reading Nation": German Book History in the Long Nineteenth Century* (Rochester, NY: Camden House, 2010).

[6] I use the term 'cultural Heimat' to designate the intangible intermingling of German-language cultural achievement and questions of national identity and belonging. See Rebecca Braun, '1967-2007: The Gruppe 47 as a Cultural Heimat', *German Quarterly*, 83:2 (2010), 212–29.

Foucault.[7] At the same time, it draws in crucial Germanic place-led points of reference that have been repeatedly absent from recent scholarship addressing the German-language literary sector and which are central to allowing for the non-human aspects of authorship. Notably, 'world literature' in its early nineteenth-century coinage as Goethe's 'Welt-Literatur' is, as I shall go on to argue, a foundational term for the contemporary study of all literature because it demands the inclusion of the 'real world' within any discussion of literary exchange and/or the creation of compelling alternative literary worlds – issues which Martin Heidegger, Ernst Bloch and Theodor Adorno can all help parse for practical application. My own understanding of such 'literary worlds' chimes with Leslie Adelson's work on the value of the literary imagination as a distinct form of social practice, as well as Eric Hayot's discussion of the concept and its broader significance for literary studies.[8] Adeslon argues that literary texts can challenge conventional understandings of time and space through the enhanced ways of thinking and linking that underpin the imaginative worlds they create, and as a result they have the potential to change the way people perceive and act in the real world.[9] Yet Adelson's argument about the power of this literary space is one pitched primarily at an abstract, cognitive level, and very much applied to the contemporary 'transnational' moment, while Hayot's similarly conceptual discussion aims in the first instance at redrawing the boundaries for classifying and studying texts.

My entry point, by contrast, is through the actual people and the wider practices of making literature in real places over a chronological period that is long enough to trace change, without being so long as to become difficult to survey in a meaningful manner. Accordingly, my starting premise is that the first and most important concrete step towards understanding how literature works as a powerful cognitive phenomenon that affects wider social processes is to think again about the practices of authorship, both literary and sociological, that underpin it. For in thinking about how literature relates to the world, we are also thinking about the physical places in which it can appear as well as the mental spaces it can open up, about the different drivers, both human and non-human, that will determine what 'the literary' looks like, and

---

[7] For discussion of these terms and the distinctions between them when it comes to authorship, see 'Littérature, histoire et sciences sociales: travailler "par cas". Un échange entre Paul Aron et Jérôme Meizoz', *Revue italienne d'études françaises* (online), 7 (2017).

[8] Eric Hayot, *On Literary Worlds* (New York: Oxford U. P., 2012).

[9] See Leslie A. Adelson, 'Literary Imagination and the Future of Literary Studies', *Deutsche Vierteljahresschrift*, 89.4 (2015), 675–83.

about the material and sociological norms that influence whose voice gets heard and which figures are more likely to be cast as representative when placing literary activity within a broad public setting. All of this combines to make for a multiplicity of really experienced worlds within what we ordinarily think of as the 'real world' circumstances of publishing.

An expanded concept of authorship as a grounded and ultimately collaborative activity, which I will set out in detail over the following pages and then trace through the rest of my study, opens up all these issues. Literary critical discussion of authorship in the primarily textual-discursive sense headed up by Barthes and Foucault has so far cast it as one individual point of authority read in and through the text, whether grasped biographically, functionalized through the distinctions of narrative theory, or deconstructed through postmodern notions of performativity. The ontology of authorship that I offer in this study, by contrast, allows for the fact that literary texts are the product of material and cognitive processes in and around people and therefore both inhere in the much wider world and unfold new and different versions of the world. As a result, they have an accordingly diverse and ever more diversifying relationship to authority. These texts have this power not by some kind of literary magic, but by the way real people who live in real places with real hopes and needs engage with them, and this as part of an iterative process. My ontology of authorship allows us to see that authors are both an integral part of this much wider 'real world' network and are immediately relativized by it. They can actively promote patterns of seeing or ways of behaving in collaboration with other people and things and also be wholly co-opted by these other actors, who may not even be human, into quite different discourses in society. This in turn directly impacts back on how literary history unfolds, including the way literature is written in the first place.

The interlinked questions of literary agency and authorial intent are accordingly both located in the biographical individual and extend far beyond her. This poses a significant challenge to any study of authorship that wants to conclude something tangible about its broader effects for the evolution of literature on the one hand and society on the other but must now shuttle back and forth between the two in a way that risks becoming circular. I have addressed this by developing the notion of discrete 'modes of authorship'. These provide common ground in terms of expressing agency and intent but also allow for differing perspectives and conflicting kinds of use. A mode of authorship, as I develop in detail in chapter one, refers to the attitude that accompanies that act of authorship and allows it to be seen, whether this underlying attitude resides in the biographical author, in any of the other individuals engaging with the author and/or her work, or indeed in the way material objects or historical traditions align around the act of authorship. I have established four principal modes of authorship across the twentieth and twenty-first centuries that drive both the production and reception of literature in Germany: the celebratory, commemorative, satirical and utopian modes. While these modes can be intuited from the way in which authors write or other interpreters engage with them, they are not necessarily consciously adopted by either an author or her interpreter. Rather, they emerge precisely from the way the work and its author are placed (or place themselves) in a broader context, whether this context is physical or intellectual. Furthermore, the different modes of authorship we can subsequently discern tend to moderate and inflect one another, often with at least two present to differing degrees at any one point in time.

An author is therefore unlikely deliberately to write in a particular mode, and a critic is unlikely wholly to cast her in another, but the iterative processes underpinning authorship will latently draw upon several of the different modes from the limited set that the deep-reaching historical and material parameters of all cultural activity have made available. What is concrete, by contrast, are the models that both authors and their many interpreters consciously adopt. By this, I am referring to popular images such as the Romantic writer in his garret, or the Enlightenment man of science and letters developing his work in a royal court. In the case of post-war Germany, the model of authorship most obviously performed has been that of the public intellectual, or politically committed writer. All too often, however, attempts to understand these models have taken public interventions (political speeches, essays, newspaper polemics) to be the acts that count, with the literary texts largely just reflecting the views that an author has expressed elsewhere or reacting in a straightforward way to recent political events. This book sets out to introduce far greater nuance into our understanding of how authorship unfolds in both literature and the world. Crucially, I do so by returning to the rich ground of literary texts and looking again, more carefully, at how authorship unfolds both within and around them. Accordingly, the chapters that follow trace the shifting modes of authorship, which in turn drive shifting models of authorship, in the changing contexts of West, East and reunified Germany. All of this is painted against the relatively stable larger backdrop of dominant narratives of place and belonging that have determined German cultural history of the last two hundred years. Taken together, my chronological case studies in German authorship open up a new way of seeing who engages with literature, how, where, and with what potential for changing the world. The result is a new reading of contemporary German literary history – but also a new way of reading *any* literary history, once one has become sensitized to the underlying modes and models of authorship that drive it.

Gabriele Wohmann answers Johann Wolfgang von Goethe: Placing Literature in the World

The case of Gabriele Wohmann (1932–2015) allows us to unpack further the underlying ontology of authorship that the rest of this book develops. Wohmann, whose first short story was published in 1957, received multiple prizes and scholarships for her fiction (notably the 1971 Bremen Literature prize and the 1988 Hessen Culture Prize), held guest lectureships in Augsburg and Mainz, achieved considerable recognition for her radio plays and TV films (the German Record Prize in 1981), was awarded the Distinguished Service Medal of the Federal Republic of Germany in 1980, and was chosen to accompany Helmut Kohl as one of two cultural representatives on his state visit to Indochina and New Zealand in 1988 (the other was the artist Otto Herbert Hajek).[10] In literary review essays from across the 1970s, the established critics and poets Georg Hensel and Karl Krolow underscored both the literary celebrity and the Prussian work ethic of their neighbour on the Darmstädter Rosenhöhe (the 'Rose Heights' in Darmstadt, home to a number of writers and artists): they would glimpse her at work early in the morning or see a light still burning late at night through the large glass windows of her study, and spy her routinely disappearing off in taxis to literary readings or other promotional events around Germany and its bordering countries. With reporters regularly visiting her at home and often commenting admiringly on her slender frame and charming manners, there is the distinct sense throughout the 1970s and into the 1980s that Wohmann, as both a writer and a woman, had the world at her feet.[11]

Yet despite the generally acknowledged success of her popular work that provides sharp-eyed insights into the life of the Federal Republic from the 1960s right through to the first decade of the twenty-first century and spans multiple genres and media, Wohmann has since become a marginal figure in German literary history. Wohmann herself suggests one nascent reason for this in her 1990 TV autobiopic, *Schreiben*

---

[10] Brief further information on her state visit is available in Scheidgen, *Gabriele Wohmann*, p. 198.
[11] Karl Krolow, 'Gabriele Wohmann', in Thomas Scheuffeln, ed., *Gabriele Wohmann: Materialienbuch* (Darmstadt: Luchterhand, 1977), pp. 7–16; Georg Hensel, 'Portrait Gabriele Wohmann', in Scheuffeln, ed., *Gabriele Wohmann*, pp. 31–8, first published as '"Ich bin da einfach reingeraten", Die Schriftstellerin Gabriele Wohmann, porträtiert von ihrem Nachbarn Georg Hensel', in *Die Weltwoche*, Zürich, 12.07.1972.

müssen: Ein elektronisches Tagebuch (Having to write: An electronic Diary), which she wrote and produced, and which aired on the public TV channel ZDF. Reflecting on the tendency in the newspaper literary review sections to focus on her work ethic because she once ironically labelled herself a 'graphomaniac', she observes: 'Ich gelte als übermäßig fleißig, Vielschreiberin – das verdirbt den Ruf, bei Deutschen'[12] (I count as unnaturally hard-working, a woman who writes a lot – that ruins your reputation, with Germans). Historically speaking, this is certainly the case, with prolific nineteenth- and early twentieth-century women writers like E. Marlitt, Marie-Luise Kaschnitz and Vicky Baum repeatedly discounted by the scholars and literary critics who shaped the national literary canon, seemingly by dint of being too popular.[13] Similar lines of rejection can be traced through the academic response to Wohmann, evident not least in the 'Autorenbücher' volume. Günter Häntzschel, who finds little to admire in her emphasis on the everyday woes and angst of unexceptional characters packaged in more and less accessible forms, first characterizes her readership as a rather niche set of upper middle-class Germans who want something that looks sufficiently complex to be literature but is not offensive, and then explains her success to be purely the result of her ability to reproduce the mentality of this readership in her writing. Both the author and her many readers are disregarded in one fell swoop.[14] A further reason for summary dismissal would also appear to be her early inclusion in school textbooks, which Wohmann drily remarks in 1996 resulted in a lot of letters from school children and 'das apodiktische Germanistenurteil'[15] (the apodictic judgement of scholars of German literature). Such absolute dismissal of a body of work that bears many striking similarities to that of the (still) widely acknowledged Martin Walser, but happens to be written by a woman who sells well and is accessible for younger readers, itself speaks volumes about the German literary sector. As Ulrike Draesner expands in her conversation with me at the end of this study, the very term 'Vielschreiberin' (a woman who

---

[12] Gabriele Wohmann, *Schreiben müssen: Ein Arbeitstagebuch* (Frankfurt a.M.: Luchterhand,1991), p. 15.
[13] See Lynne Tatlock, 'The Afterlife of Nineteenth-Century Popular Fiction and the German Imaginary: The Illustrated Collected Novels of E. Marlitt, W. Heimburg, and E. Werner', in Tatlock, ed., *Publishing Culture and the "Reading Nation"*, pp. 118–52.
[14] Günter Häntzschel, Jürgen Michael Benz, Rüdiger Bolz & Dagmar Ulbricht, *Gabriele Wohmann* (Munich: Beck, 1982), p. 140.
[15] Discussed and quoted in Sigrid Mayer & Martha Hanscom, *Critical Reception of the Short Fiction by Joyce Carol Oates and Gabriele Wohmann* (Rochester NY: Camden House, 1998), pp. 11–12.

writes a lot) encapsulates a deep-seated rejection of women in the canonizing literary institutions, both publishing houses and academe, and is still in evidence in present-day practices. Although a man can also be dismissed with the same root word (Vielschreiber), feminizing the judgement makes it all the more lethal. The dominant celebratory mode, in other words, that underpins all promotion of writing often excludes female authors by multiple means even as it appears to allow them in, with choice phrases making these acts of exclusion visible.

In many ways, however, Wohmann is already at least a decade ahead of all this. An alternative playful pass at self-deprecation in her 1972 interview with Georg Hensel shows a refined ability to reflect ironically on interpersonal dynamics and the literary sector's own policing of what counts as literature at any given time. Here, Wohmann is captured playing the coquette writer who knows she has a media reputation for indiscretion, and thus that some kind of intimate revelation is expected of her. She chooses to take the literary biographical route, rendered below in Hensel's reported speech:

> Über ihre Mutter ist sie mit den Lichtenbergs verwandt, der Familie des Darmstädter Aphoristikers, und über ihren Vater, dessen Mutter eine Textor war, mit der Familie von Goethes Mutter und also mit Goethe – eine so erlauchte literarische Abstammung kann heutzutage doch nur imageschädigend sein, oder?[16]

> [Through her mother she is related to the Lichtenbergs, the family of the writer of aphorisms from Darmstadt, and through her father, whose mother was a Textor, with the family of Goethe's mother, and therefore with Goethe – such a hallowed literary genealogy these days is disastrous for your image, surely?]

Although only presented in jest, the idea that Wohmann may have the 'wrong' kind of literary biography for late twentieth-century Germany because she is directly related to the now unfashionable fathers of the modern literary canon opens up a vista onto the world of literature that goes well beyond humour. It highlights the significance of networks, not just in terms of locating writers as knowing certain

---

[16] Hensel, 'Portrait Gabriele Wohmann', p. 35. This genealogy is partially repeated in the opening paragraphs of Ilka Scheidgen's official biography of Wohmann, which point to her maternal links to Georg Christoph Lichtenberg (1742–1799) and the Darmstadt theologian and playwright Ernst Elias Niebergall (1815–1843), but do not mention any paternal link to Goethe: *Gabriele Wohmann*, p. 9.

people or being affiliated with certain literary or socio-political movements, which is the superficial humour in her remark, but also in terms of creating the very sense of what an author is and how this might vary over time. Here, we are encountering two latent, intermingled modes of authorship – the satirical and the celebratory – and can see how they inflect the way that multiple people who engage with a writer and her work (including the author herself) cast the significance of it all.

In this understanding, literary networks cohere as much around dominant attitudes as around people. Places, objects, communications media, and intellectual concepts can all play just as important a role as human beings, and the networks can spread well beyond the conscious purview of the individual author. The work of Bruno Latour provides an important reference point here. He has developed his own take on actor-network-theory (ANT), which is one of the key conceptual approaches underpinning Science & Technology Studies in the Social Sciences. In it, he not only stresses the importance of building up a picture of so-called 'social' phenomena by 'following the actors themselves', i.e. tracing the web of connections that is formed from both human and non-human influences shaping a particular object of study, and, in so doing, creating the 'social context' around it. He also insists on pausing over the way different manifestations of this 'social context' can directly affect whatever is being mediated:

> Even though the question seems really odd at first – not to say in bad taste – whenever anyone speaks of a 'system', a 'global feature', a 'structure', a 'society', an 'empire', a 'world economy', an 'organization', the first ANT reflex should be to ask: 'In which building? In which bureau? Through which corridor is it accessible? Which colleagues has it been read to? How has it been compiled?'[17]

Latour draws particular attention to the physical places or other forms of tangible embodiment in which abstract phenomena gain some kind of anchor in the real world, whether this is through their traceability to a set of individuals, the buildings that have housed (literally and metaphorically) the relevant structures underpinning them, or another abstract set of actions for conceptualizing a modus operandi that itself determines how these phenomena will exist. In elucidating all of these factors, he is interested in pinpointing the multiple mediators that, in his terminology, do not just carry a message from one point to another,

---

[17] Bruno Latour, *Reassembling the Social: An Introduction to Actor-Network-Theory* (Oxford: Oxford U. P., 2005), p. 183.

but actively leave a trace on it, changing it and themselves often also being changed as they do so. It might not seem intuitive to claim that things can express an attitude, but Latour's work encourages us to see how exactly this can be the case, with real tangible results for authorship.

Wohmann's documentary film invites deliberate reflection on the networks radiating out from her authorship along just these lines. It is notable, for example, that numerous scenes are shot in a Jewish cemetery near her home. As we will see in later chapters, shots of gravestones figure highly in documentaries about literature as grasped through authors' biographies and are often used directly to create a certain literary lineage or broader sense of cultural importance for the film's principal topic. While this kind of ancestry generally invokes canonicity, it is striking that Wohmann, the daughter of a protestant pastor and longstanding member of the established writers' group, the Gruppe 47, places her living author persona in the Jewish cemetery, the space historically reserved in Central European cultures for the outsider, minority figure.[18] Furthermore, while this kind of manipulation of place can be interpreted as stage-managed by Wohmann the film director, other elements piece together connections and inferences independently of direct scene-setting.

The question of what, when and where her professional friends eat during the course of a typical working day, for example, naturally reoccurs across several of the interviews as part of the basic fact checking Wohmann is undertaking. At the same time, these conversations are themselves often accompanied by the social conventions of a cup of coffee and a slice of cake, while the film crew as a whole are captured at the beginning and the end sifting through their materials in the garden of a rural inn, the typically German 'Oberwaldhaus' (Upper Forest Lodge). Where the camera pans across the inn's outdoor restaurant tables as a natural part of showing the people interacting with one another, the conversations reflect on the particularities of how Wohmann drinks her coffee, or what she expects on seeing napkins placed on the table, as part of a natural banter between friends. Together, however, the film shots and the throwaway remarks create a recognizably German cultural environment that is part of Wohmann's wider authorship. Food, in other words, invokes a web of social conventions and broader cultural connections, and these demonstrably influence not just the conversations the author has while researching her next novel, but also how these conversations themselves become part of the biographical

---

[18] On the normative function of the Gruppe 47, see Braun, '1967-2007: The Gruppe 47 as a Cultural Heimat', 212–29.

trace left by her so-called 'electronic diary': Wohmann is (also) the author who only ever drinks half a cup of coffee, just as Barthes, the inventor of the 'biographème' is (also) the man who lights his cigarettes with his left hand.[19] This electronic diary, acting in turn as a Latourian mediator that shapes the message it is relaying, equally has a part to play in conditioning what Wohmann's authorship is in the world. Her authorship presents as minor, even though it is not, and is at the same time more of a clear product of post-war West German society than Wohmann probably even realized then or is helpful for her career later on as an ageing woman writer in the reunified Federal Republic. She is cast within the celebratory mode of authorship, but with a particularly regional inflection that will work against her in the long run.

The significance of this point can be understood if we follow Wohmann's playfully deleterious image construction and go back in time to Goethe (1749–1832). While Wohmann suggests a genealogical, and therefore human, link to Goethe, the more compelling one for my argument is in the diary-as-mediator. By the early twenty-first century, Goethe routinely lives on in courses of comparative / world literature thanks not least to his proclamation, almost two hundred years ago, of the 'new epoch of world literature': 'National-Literatur will jetzt nicht viel sagen, die Epoche der Welt-Literatur ist an der Zeit und jeder muß dazu wirken, diese Epoche zu beschleunigen' (National literature is now rather an unmeaning term; the epoch of World-literature is at hand, and everyone must strive to hasten its approach'), he declares on 31 January 1827.[20] Yet, as has been amply recorded, Goethe did remarkably little to sketch out what was really meant by the term 'Welt-Literatur'. In fact, the most significant aspect of the definition offered here points less to 'world' at all as a concept, and more to a determination that literature and literary activity should not be confined by the relatively arbitrary political boundaries of the nation state. Nor was the puzzling neologism even his invention: Christoph Martin Wieland (1733–1813), fellow intellectual at the Weimar court under the Duchess Anna Amalia, had invoked it significantly earlier than him as part of a broader earlier nineteenth-century set of vocabulary that was trying to grasp a change in how Europeans related to one another and the wider world.[21] Yet the term, endowed with a sense of global grandeur, has

---

[19] Benoît Peeters discusses how Roland Barthes uses photography to recast what is significant about his authorial biography in 'Death: On Barthes' Images of Authorship without Authority', in Tobias Boes, Rebecca Braun & Emily Spiers, eds, *World Authorship* (Oxford: Oxford U. P., 2020), pp. 102–16, p. 114.
[20] Eckermann, *Gespräche*, p. 225; Goethe, *Conversations*, p. 165.
[21] See Dieter Lamping, *Die Idee der Weltlitertur: Ein Konzept Goethes und seine Karriere* (Stuttgart: Kröner, 2010).

become Goethe's through the biographical trace created by a diary – not his, but that of his aide and frequent partner in after-dinner conversation, Johann Peter Eckermann.

Like Wohmann's documentary film, Eckermann's three-volume *Gespräche mit Goethe in den letzten Jahren seines Lebens* (1836–48, Conversations with Goethe in the Last Years of his Life) is built around the conceit of the casual exploratory conversation, albeit one that is seemingly less directed by any underlying literary project. Eckermann's text records the astonishing array of literary, scientific and socio-cultural topics on which Goethe easily discoursed with his aide from 1823, the year of Eckermann's arrival in Weimar, to Goethe's death in 1832. Distinct recurrent areas of interest, notably around ideas of renewal and the interconnectedness of all things, emerge over the course of the regular diary entries, a great many of which begin with the observation 'dined with Goethe'. The incremental picture of Goethe as an all-round intellectual that the diary thereby paints is so convincing that, for a considerable part of their publishing history, the *Conversations* were routinely attributed to Goethe as the author, re-titled *Gespräche mit Eckermann* (Conversations with Eckermann), and included directly in Goethe's oeuvre as one of the key points of reference for accessing his thought and daily practices.

Eckermann's authorial disenfranchisement from his own text is ironic, given that in the eight years (at least) it took him to craft the first two volumes, one of the main motivations that sustained him was the desire to launch his own literary career on the back of Goethe's celebrity: Eckermann would become known as the author who gave the world Goethe in his most unmediated form.[22] In this example, the celebratory mode is doubly present, consciously invoked by Eckermann for both Goethe and himself and also the main publishing motivation behind a clutch of European publishers who would solicit his work. Although Eckermann may exaggerate somewhat when writing to his fiancée in his excitement for his literary project, his description of how publishers in Berlin, Paris and London have all contacted him for further information underscores the extent to which the celebratory mode of authorship manifests in multiple ways, from multiple perspectives and to multiple ends across his project. 'Ich sehe daran die Theilnahme der Welt und daß man etwas von mir erwartet, und daran sehe ich daß ich öffentlich nicht unglücklich wirken werde',[23] he writes in 1825 (In this I

---

[22] Eckermann refers to working on the *Conversations* for eight years in a letter to Heinrich Laube in 1844. There is evidence that he began to conceptualize its publication as early as 1824. See the 'Kommentar' in Goethe, *Gespräche*, pp. 917–65 (the letter is partially reproduced pp. 917–20).

[23] Quoted in the notes to Goethe, *Gespräche*, p. 927.

see that the world is interested and that people expect something from me, and in this I see that I won't look at all bad in public).

Precisely for this reason, the *Conversations* also function as a mediator in Latour's terms. As he prepares the ground for his own arrival in literary society, Eckermann creates the 'world author' Goethe, a figure in whom not only 'the world' will be interested and who grandly gives us the term 'Welt-Literatur' that later scholarship will seize upon, but who is also a direct product of the literary world captured and mediated in Eckermann's text. This world is itself created by a series of parameters that exceed direct human control by either Goethe or Eckermann. The pair are so frequently captured dining together, for example, because Eckermann's main pay took the form of food in Goethe's company, a rather bald and exploitative financial fact when one considers the amount of work Eckermann undertook for Goethe and learns that he would die in penury, but it is an arrangement that also points to a world in which material comforts carried a high price.[24]

Following food as an actor within this network takes us further away from direct human control and self-fashioning of the kind Bourdieu has driving his literary field and that Meizoz has put at the heart of his expanded understanding of authorship.[25] Eckermann would arrive a little early for an evening's socializing on one occasion (3 November 1823), at 5.00 pm, only to find that Goethe and his assembled party were 'still eating' – their lunch, one must presume. Such leisurely progress through the day on the one hand fits into the expansive intellectual gesture that Goethe would cultivate at court, where sharing ideas in polite society was part of the whole court's *raison d'être*. On the other hand, however, it also points to a rather different understanding of time and conviviality to that predominant in urbanized twenty-first-century Germany, and this reappears across the diary. Thus, for example, the same diary entry that records Goethe's grandiloquent announcement of the dawn of a new epoch of world literature is marked out by breaks in the conversation as Goethe and Eckermann rush to the window, on the lookout for the return of a carriage that had passed by on its way to Belvedere Palace that morning. Such moments impress upon the

---

[24] Birgit Tautz sets out in intriguing detail the intense pressure on all forms of living space in Weimar of the time, weaving this into a detailed account of how the physical proportions of the city of Weimar shaped the notion of world literary culture with which it would become associated : *Translating the World: Toward a New History of German Literature around 1800* (University Park, PA: Penn State U. P., 2018).

[25] Most recently in Jérôme Meizoz, *La littérature "en personne" : Scène médiatique et formes d'incarnation* (Geneva: Slatkine, 2016).

twenty-first-century reader that this is a world in which time moves more slowly and where people-watching can provide the focal point for an otherwise perhaps rather empty day. These considerations in turn condition the very kinds of exchanges people can have, literary or otherwise, such that time itself is an actor within the literature network mediated by Eckermann's diary. The boldly pioneering Johann Wolfgang von Goethe who announces the arrival of world literature on 31 January 1827 is therefore just as much the product of a demonstrable network driven by both human and non-human actors as the minority literary 'Vielschreiberin' Gabriele Wohmann created in her film. Both resultant models of authorship, the Enlightenment man and the marginalized woman, are the tangible result of the different ways in which the celebratory mode plays out with different actors in different contexts.

These points are important because they underscore the extent to which any concept of literature, world or otherwise, is inevitably accompanied by a set of practices that are made tangible by and through the people involved, even as some of these practices also extend well beyond direct human control. While Eckermann records only a one-line definition of what Goethe might actually mean by an 'epoch of world literature' focused on openness and exchange of books, the three volumes of his *Conversations* testify to the wealth of practices and circumstances that lie behind that utterance. Eckermann's Goethe is repeatedly concerned with establishing connections across all areas of knowledge and personally keeps multiple conversations alive in parallel, facilitated by the favourable conditions (time, buildings, social prestige, central geographical location) at the Weimar court. While we might understand 'Welt-Literatur' as an overarching concept that emerges from this particular network, the phenomenon that we can tangibly observe and trace is the practice of 'world authorship'.[26] As John Noyes has pointed out, Goethe's belief in the transformative potential of literary exchange is rooted in an understanding of literature as a highly interpersonal affair, reliant on people meeting one another in the flesh.[27] Where physical encounter was not possible, his actual practice of authorship also manifested in other ways – notably, as Manfred Koch details, in the whole project of editing the journal *Über Kunst und Altertum*, which generated its own network for mediating

---

[26] For extensive discussion of how the term 'world authorship' relates to 'world literature', see Boes, Braun & Spiers, eds, *World Authorship*.
[27] John K. Noyes, 'Writing the Dialectical Structure of the Modern Subject: Goethe on World Literature and World Citizenship', *Seminar* 51.2 (2015), 100–14.

European Enlightenment ideas and encourages us to think of 'Weltliteratur als publizistische[s] Programm'[28] (world literature as a publishing programme). Alternatively, in his rich exchanges with his Scottish translator and promoter, Thomas Carlyle, Goethe substituted meeting in the flesh with learning about Carlyle's material circumstances through drawings of his remote homestead. This travel-by-proxy would allow Goethe to present to a German readership Carlyle's own writing, along with the wider Scottish tradition from which he came, as those of a kindred spirit who had similar points of entry into the imaginative and intellectual worlds opened up by literature.[29]

Wohmann's career through short stories, novels, radio plays and TV films that have now been largely forgotten may seem a rather modest echo of her co-opted literary forefather's stellar self-insertion into foundational discourses on German letters, still tangible in public spaces and values today. Yet Wohmann is representative of a certain kind of writer who makes her literary activity as informed by and as open as possible to a wider world. If Goethe encourages his world to believe that writing poetry is open to everyone, Wohmann champions the belief that such acts of authorship actually matter to the author's contemporaries.[30] Taken together, this unlikely pairing helps us grasp authorship as the iterative product of an expanded network of people, processes and material things that both relativize the autonomy of individual authors within the literature network and ensure they continue to matter to their wider worlds, precisely because so many actors are involved, and for so long.

Authors and the World: Continuity and Change across German-speaking Europe

Wohmann here has been made to stand in for a large swathe of authors from the early post-war period to the present who have consciously engaged with German-language literary traditions whilst also redrawing

---

[28] Manfred Koch, *Weimaraner Weltbewohner: Zur Genese von Goethes Begriff "Weltliteratur"* (Tübingen: Niemeyer, 2002), p. 19.

[29] For more on the material and intellectual networks developed between Goethe and Carlyle, see Rosemary Ashton, 'Carlyle's Apprenticeship: His Early German Criticism and His Relationship with Goethe (1822-1832)', *The Modern Language Review*, 71:1 (1976), 1–18.

[30] Alongside the 1982 volume by Häntzschel already referenced and the 1986 'life and works' overview in Hans Wagener, *Gabriele Wohmann* (Berlin: Colloquium, 1986), see the thorough approach to and appreciation of her wide range of activity in Gerhard Knapp & Mona Knapp, *Gabriele Wohmann* (Königstein: Athenäum, 1981).

Introduction 17

the parameters of their own context for writing.[31] The chapters that follow will go on to explore how a representative cross-section of them have positioned themselves within the cultural landscape of German-speaking Europe in ways that have sought to have an effect on that environment, even though the outcomes, including the degree of celebrity and/or canonization of the individual authors achieved, have at times been very different. My focus, therefore, is squarely on the practice of authorship as it can be traced all the way back to Goethe's 'world literature' as a form of genuine interpersonal exchange that happens within a specific worldly context, but which also looks beyond it, often in ways that the author cannot ultimately control. This diverges from common understandings of world literature that are ultimately beholden to the theoretical elaboration of a concept rather than the study of a lived practice.[32]

My key starting premise, then, is that all authors partake in authorship as a set of practices and associations around their work and person that draws in multiple people, objects, specific circumstances and intangible concepts to varying degrees. All of these are just as much part of the literary text as the author herself, and they all matter because they directly affect the cultural fabric of the multiple worlds that literature naturally unites (from national identity narratives to political reform to global trade routes). The latent affect inherent in this understanding of literature and society is captured in the historically determined modes of authorship that my study traces in detail. Furthermore, the real and imaginary worlds that accompany such an expanded delineation of authorship in turn shape how readers and future authors alike are able to see themselves and act on their impressions: the models of authorship they consciously cultivate. These may superficially appear to replace one another, as a broad-brush history of authorship from the early nineteenth to the early twenty-first century might encourage us to see the Romantic genius given over to the work of art wholly replaced by the savvy neoliberal operator

---

[31] Wohmann was ascribed such a representative function by scholars before sinking into comparative obscurity from the mid 1990s onwards, as is evidenced by the central position given to her in the overview works on the German short story and German women's writing by Durzak and Jurgensen: Manfred Durzak, *Die deutsche Kurzgeschichte der Gegenwart: Autorenporträts, Werkstattgespräche, Interpretationen* (Stuttgart: Reclam, 1980) [a third updated and expanded edition was printed in 2002]; Manfred Jurgensen, *Deutsche Frauen der Gegenwart: Bachmann, Reinig, Wolf, Wohmann, Struck, Leutenegger und Schwaiger* (Bern: Francke, 1983).

[32] For just two high profile examples of this approach, see David Damrosch, *What is World Literature?* (Princeton: Princeton U. P., 2003), and Emily Apter, *Against World Literature: On the Politics of Untranslatability* (London: Verso, 2013).

pursuing her career on the global market. We only need to scratch a little deeper, however, to see how these quite divergent models of authorship share the same set of modes, and these modes are shifting and reconfiguring themselves all the time as more and different people, things and places interact with the literature they carry. Studying authorship begins with studying people and their writing but quickly branches out into a form of cultural history, as that history and the various actors that have informed it become manifest in the web of creative texts, objects and associations left for both their peers and posterity to piece back together. In showing how to do this for twentieth- and twenty-first-century Germany, this book asks us to think again about what those particular 'world-literary' interactions have enabled, and what similar interactions might have the potential to facilitate for the future.

As the scope of such a study is potentially without bounds, it has been necessary to insert some parameters around how I set about capturing 'literary authorship' in 'modern Germany'. With regard to the former, the literary texts on which I draw are generally novels (in a wide variety of forms), but with some reference to poetry where relevant. 'Following the actors themselves', however, also took me to film and documentary televisual material, as well as journalistic pieces, political speeches, and occasionally material objects that help tell a fuller picture of the place these authors have occupied in the cultural landscape. At times the best mode of analysis for these texts was a form of close reading that also casts them as a form of literature, considering their linguistic structure and/or affective qualities and symbolic world-making significance. While this fluidity of material seemed not only unavoidable but also highly fruitful for an approach that wants to expand our understanding of authorship, I did exclude other literary genres that were less directly associated with the notion of an individual author. Properly accounting for the way authorship unfolds in theatre or film production goes beyond the scope of this study.[33] I have also, regretfully, decided against systematically including photography, as to do justice to the way in which authorship has developed through this entirely visual medium transcends the space available.[34] With regard to my latter, chronological and geographical parameter, the arc traced

---

[33] For recent interesting work broadly in these areas, see Michael Wood, *Heiner Müller's Democratic Theatre: The Politics of Making the Audience Work* (Rochester, NY: Camden House, 2017), Cecilia Sayad, *Performing Authorship: Self-Inscription and Corporeality in the Cinema* (London: Tauris, 2013).

[34] A good starting point for this is Sandra Oster, *Das Autorenfoto in Buch und Buchwerbung: Autorinszenierung und Kanonisierung mit Bildern* (Berlin: de Gruyter, 2014).

above from Wohmann to Goethe is significant, as it coincides with my study's principal focus on the parts of Europe that have gone on to become contemporary Germany while my chronological trajectory is towards understanding the present day through the recent past. This is a focus with deliberately fuzzy edges, however, given the rather different profile that those German lands had in Goethe's time and the ongoing relevance particularly of Austrian writers for the literary sector in the Federal Republic today. Furthermore, in a contemporary Europe more and more defined by migration it seems imperative to include the experiences of ethnic Germans and other migrants, who are generally based in Germany but sometimes use German as a second or third language and are not infrequently supported by the Austrian Ingeborg Bachmann Prize, in building their own, often highly compelling, expressions of authorship. In order to do justice to the cultural and political links that determine such networks, it is necessary on occasion to take a wide-angle lens on German-speaking Europe, just as West German ideologies cannot be fully understood without reference to the competing ideologies immediately over the border in East Germany, or indeed to their historical antecedents that evolved in a set of German states with different borders again.

Nevertheless, the overarching aim of the book remains to understand key aspects of literary authorship as it has developed primarily in the cultural context of the post-war Federal Republic of Germany [FRG]. In purely practical terms, of the four main post-war German-speaking countries (West Germany, East Germany, Austria, Switzerland), the FRG has provided the single largest market and media-led cultural sector for authors writing in German, regardless of their underpinning nationality. In fruitful tension with the German Democratic Republic [GDR] for all the time that state existed and invigorated by the work of individual Austrian and Swiss writers, the Federal Republic has also been the most consistently alive to the need for literature to occupy a fundamentally different place in the world in response to the destruction of much of the country's physical, moral and cultural fabric under National Socialism. The incremental changes in how this happens that can be traced across the different decades and geopolitical German locations of the late twentieth century and into the twenty-first tell a fascinating story that resonates across German-speaking Europe. To this end, while my overarching argument focuses on the FRG, it does not shy away from investigating points of contrast and comparison in both the GDR and, particularly with regard to the contemporary literary scene, Austria. I cannot hope to come anywhere close to exhausting this topic, but I do hope that the chapters that follow will go some way to reconceptualizing how we place authors, and with them literature, in the world.

A word, too, is needed on my choice of authors. My practical focus on authorship as a process that entails positioning oneself in the world by no means requires the usual roll call of post-war, white, male authors: Max Frisch, Heinrich Böll, Günter Grass, Hans Magnus Enzensberger, Martin Walser, Wolf Biermann, Uwe Johnson, Peter Handke, followed by Ingo Schulze, Thomas Brussig, Christian Kracht and Daniel Kehlmann, to detail just one way of hopping neatly through various literary styles and German-language geographies from 1945 to the present. At the same time, my study is underpinned by a version of this well-known narrative of important authors and their works precisely because these authors have routinely been ascribed this representative role. I want to examine why this happened, and what it might mean for German-language literature and culture that these authors so routinely float to the top. Writing about Böll, Enzensberger and Grass in West Germany replicates a canon, but only partially, because the gestus underpinning my analysis throughout is one of critical comprehension. I seek to understand why these authors and not others have become such giants of the German-language cultural landscape, and what the experiences accessed through their authorship tell us about this landscape more broadly. Following lines outwards from their nodes of success also allows me to make space for alternative experiences: that of Gisela Elsner, which could be described as the inverse of Grass, for example, or the unexpected return to Eckermann found in the work of Felicitas Hoppe. On the one hand, then, I am following a fundamentally different understanding of why these authors matter for my purposes – making apparent the literature network that sustains them, rather than focusing solely on their work as an individual achievement. On the other hand, however, I also sought a way of exploring other viewpoints and experiences that have not been wholly fostered from within these normative structures and therefore, by definition, are harder to find. To this end, archival reconstruction became as much about what I did not find as what I did, while my three extended conversations with contemporary women writers, who have quite different experiences of 'Germanness' to both the network norm and one another, give direct voice to a growing divergence from historically dominant models. The way in which these women reflect upon their own positioning within the contemporary literature network and the modes and models of authorship it makes available to them becomes emblematic for new ways of linking literary activity to the wider world. Indeed, it was particularly important to me that my own authorship was subject to the moderating influences of those I write about, and the ideas that I have developed across this book are challenged and extended by the perspectives of those who, historically, have not been given the last word in academic criticism.

While my set of authors does not outwardly overturn the canon, it does therefore repeatedly draw attention to itself as a deliberately chosen list of case studies in thinking about authorship that also tells us something about authorship as a practice in accessing and defending one's place in the world of literature. The result is a radically different reading of the canon, revealing how key texts both create their own foundational terms and look different to us now when we see them in this light. While chapter one provides a sweeping overview of core currents and ways of thinking about authorship across the twentieth century, chapters two to six are ordered roughly chronologically, starting in the post-war era. Chapters two and three examine the different ways in which German authorship has been affected by the attitudes to place that tended to predominate at different historical and political junctures. From this I extrapolate the foundational models of authorship with broader social relevance that were developed in the FRG (the model of the exemplary creator in chapter two, with reference to Heinrich Böll, Hans Magnus Enzensberger and Günter Grass) and in the GDR (the model of the exemplary pedagogue in chapter three, drawing on the work of Johannes R. Becher, Anna Seghers and Christa Wolf). I then look in detail in chapter four at the broader contexts of publishing that cohered around influential individuals who were well connected to specific literary institutions throughout the Cold War period. Here, the actions in Berlin of Walter Höllerer at the Technische Universität (Technical University) and the Literarisches Colloquium (Literary Colloquium), and of Siegfried Unseld at the helm of the Suhrkamp publishing house for almost fifty years in Frankfurt, are first critically reconstructed through archival material, literary texts, and documentary TV footage, and then further questioned by the perspective of those who did not find themselves so well supported by the post-war publishing scene: one-time star author Gisela Elsner and one-time influential publisher-journalist Fritz J. Raddatz.

The case studies explored across chapters two, three, and four reflect the obvious male dominance of the German literature network throughout the post-war and Cold War periods, but in a way that points well beyond any narrow understanding of gender politics to draw out the complex web of interrelations that conditions how and why some authors rose to prominence where others failed to gain any lasting traction. The political caesura of reunification at the beginning of the 1990s coincides with a tentative opening up of the network to new and different practices. Without wishing to suggest that the political circumstances of reunification led to a direct shift in modes and models of authorship, my study does mark a change that begins to set in across the 1990s, as new forms of interaction, drawing both on the availability of new media and different audiences within the context of reunified

Germany, became available. Ulrike Draesner reflects explicitly on this in my conversation with her at the end of this book, when she remembers how, at the start of her career, the only model of authorship that appeared to be available to her was that of (a very dated) Ingeborg Bachmann:

> After the readings people asked me how I wrote my poems, and when I said I that I typed them on my computer they would look aghast. Obviously, this was not what a young, blonde, female poet should be doing in 1995. I should have been writing in ink, at least! Ideally with a quill. My volume of poems was widely reviewed, very enthusiastically, but almost everybody concentrated on the love poems. My poems about the Middle Ages, science and organ transplants were hardly ever mentioned, because obviously there was a strong gender bias. I am glad to say that expectations and contexts have been considerably transformed since then. We, the generation of poets born in the 1960s, were lucky in a way. We were just about to publish our first books when 1989 happened. It took some time, but, slowly, in the nineties, things accelerated and changed. Partly because everybody expected change. And partly because we emphasized performance and the oral aspects of poetry and really worked on them, moving from a rather static understanding of meaning to more performative formats.

An attempt to understand this move away from a 'static understanding' of both individual literary texts and the wider literature network in which they exist and towards 'more performative formats' drives the final two chapters of my study and the three appended conversations. Chapters five (exploring work by Christoph Ransmayr, Herta Müller and Felicitas Hoppe) and six (reading the work of Maja Haderlap, Olga Martynova and Katja Petrowskaja through the contemporary Ingeborg Bachmann Prize) take us from the late 1980s into the second decade of the twenty-first century. The three conversations held in the summer of 2019 with Ulrike Draesner, Olga Martynova and Ulrike Almut Sandig introduce the voice of contemporary German authors directly into my analysis and represent a significant performative shift within my methodology. The conversational turn is a deliberate enactment of my own conceptual premise around authorship as an inherently co-creative practice and also represents a 'proof of concept' for this book as a whole. Taking our inspiration from the different physical surroundings in which we found ourselves each time, we reflected together on how authorship as a shared and living literary practice affected by the widest variety of things can change what we see in literature, and therefore how we place ourselves in the world.

A more devolved model of authorship emerges over the course of these chapters and conversations. It is one that draws in a more democratic base and consciously aims at a broader ethnic and geographic understanding of Germanness than in previous decades. In this sense, it aligns well with broader scholarly debate on the transnational. A deliberate turn towards a self-consciously transnational model of authorship can be seen as a subtle and measured response to the foundational models outlined earlier. It both works with the same core modes that underpinned these earlier conceptions and shows ways of positioning German literature within the blind spots that these models entailed. The result is a conscious move across the sector to bring into the literature network those voices and things that have not tended to be seen or heard and in so doing find new ways of reaching more diverse audiences, both in Germany and beyond, that better reflect the country's own changing place in the world. There is of course also a conscious decision on my part to shift focus from mainly male, straightforwardly German authors to mainly female authors of mixed provenance, but it is a shift that is made possible by the fact that the underpinning changes within the literature network itself mean there is more significant material by women and cultural minorities to choose from than was the case in earlier decades.

Together, then, the two final chapters and the three conversations show how a series of authors have explicitly experimented with ideas of literary authorship in fiction as part of a larger programme to conceptualize new forms of authorship, moving out from the literary world of the text and into the realities inhabited by their readers. The cultural continuities that the variously configured mix of modes invites us to draw across both political and linguistic borders relativize the political caesura of unification, even as the broad chronologies of political and aesthetic developments do align. They also relativize the centrality of Germanness to the German literature network, helping the latter out of the very place-bound understanding of cultural affiliation that defined the post-war period. As my study moves into the very contemporary moment, it includes authors who have multiple different national and/or linguistic backgrounds and operate in multiple different literature networks but are also clearly making their way within the established German cultural scene and adapting its modes and models accordingly. In particular, the Austrian literature network becomes an important player in terms of consecrating authors from non-traditional backgrounds through the annual Ingeborg Bachmann Prize competition. The prize and associated literature festival have been instrumental in launching the careers of a great number of authors in the much larger market of the FRG even as they also underscore the separateness of the Austrian literature network, which maintains its own cultural drivers and local politics as well. In making the relationship between the circumstances of this Austrian prize, which is itself looking ever more outward, and the emerging model of transnational authorship in Germany into one of the guiding threads of my final chapter, I acknowledge the intertwined but also distinct histories of the literature networks of a number of close cultural neighbours with that of the Federal Republic.

One Four Modes of Authorship across the German Twentieth Century

The twentieth century was the century of celebrating authors in Germany. At the end of the First World War there were 36 literary prizes awarded across the country; by the beginning of the twenty-first century, 182 serious literary prizes and 80 scholarships were awarded per year, while popular estimates run to 300.[1] Writing on this phenomenon in 2005, Marion Steinicke casts the growth in prizes across the twentieth century as an attempt at 'reintegrating the author as a person into society' after writers had increasingly rejected an explicitly political or socially representative role and turned to a more wholly artistically defined sense of their purpose over the course of the nineteenth century.[2] Although some prize foundations were certainly established with this lofty aim in mind, more mundane reasons also exist. The key actors behind the exponential growth witnessed towards the end of the twentieth century were local governments, who found a cost-effective way of honouring their commitment to culture by rewarding authors with honorific ceremonies while slashing budgets for libraries, and private commercial enterprises, who were able to use the promotional effects of a prize as a form of cheap advertising.[3]

Whatever their underlying motivations, however, the actions of these political, economic and pedagogical mediators across the

---

[1] Figures for up to 1949 are taken from the systematic lists in Dambacher, *Literatur und Kulturpreise 1859-1949*, pp. 251–7. Sonja Vandenrath, *Private Förderung zeitgenössischer Literatur: Eine Bestandsaufnahme* (Bielefeld: transcript, 2006). 300 is the figure quoted in the television feature by Thomas Palzer, *Wie wird man Bestseller?*, SWR 2009.

[2] Burckhard Dücker, Dietrich Harth, Marion Steinicke & Judith Ulmer, special issue, 'Literaturpreisverleihungen: ritualisierte Konsekrationspraktiken im kulturellen Feld', *Forum Ritualdynamik*, 11 (2005), 19.

[3] For more information on these trends, see Braun, 'Prize Germans?'

twentieth century counter the trend to autonomy that cultural theorist Pierre Bourdieu discerned in the development of a distinct 'field of cultural production' in European arts and letters over the same time period. In his influential work, Bourdieu sets out how the various human actors negotiate their place within a nationally delineated cultural field that is explicitly defined by its differing normative economic and symbolic values compared to those that pertain in the other dominant fields of politics, economics and institutionalized education. As a result, attempts to apply his conceptualization of the cultural field to what mid-twentieth-century German commentators call the 'Literaturbetrieb', or 'literary industry', automatically tend to view these negotiations and their associated practices in isolation from the many other human, material and conceptual drivers in related fields.[4] Yet the rise in available symbolic capital triggered by the growth of literary prizes provides a natural link between Bourdieu's traditions of artistic autonomy and much broader attempts to shape the nation state by appropriating narratives of achievement from multiple fields of human activity.

The way individual symbolic acts like the conferral of a prize are routinely appropriated for the purposes of building a community has more traditionally been discussed by social theorists interested in community values and rituals in the broadest sense than by literary historians, but the overlap between the two is evident. Sociologist Émile Durckheim, for example, argues that society as a whole is formed out of its core rituals from across a wide range of domains, whereby the very performative nature of these rituals is what both produces and reinforces a community's discrete sense of self.[5] Accordingly, the rituals around not just awarding a literary prize, but also a considerable number of related practices within the literature network, such as the media's reporting of the announcement, the co-optation of public spaces for the ceremonial conferral, the publisher's subsequent material choices in marketing their prize-winning author, and the author's ongoing reflections on her public persona across her oeuvre, make visible a network of relations for literary practice that both expands

---

[4] For examples of solid research in this area focusing on human factors, see Heribert Tommek and Klaus-Michael Bogdal, eds, *Transformationen des literarischen Feldes in der Gegenwart: Sozialstruktur – Medien-Ökonomien – Autorpositionen* (Heidelberg: Synchron, 2012); David-Christopher Assmann, *Poetologien des Literaturbetriebs: Szenen bei Kirchhoff, Maier, Gstrein und Händler*. (Berlin: de Gruyter, 2014).

[5] Barry Stephenson usefully glosses his work in this area in *Ritual: A Very Short Introduction* (Oxford: Oxford U. P., 2015).

what authorship is and, at the same time, concentrates attention on the individual laureate. The author, in other words, becomes both a focal point and a vanishing spot for much larger narratives about the shape and nature of the society with which she is associated. The rituals around celebrating an author perform both what that society holds literature to be and, in microcosmic form, society itself.

The rapid growth in literary prizes is a traceable phenomenon that marks out a distinctly twentieth-century context of authorship both born of and generating a certain twentieth-century conception of culture. However, it is also only the tip of the iceberg when it comes to thinking about the changing ways in which people have been linked to literature and broader attitudes towards the very concept of society have been channelled through specific literary practices. Alongside the rituals specifically foregrounded across the twentieth century for celebrating the work of contemporary authors, a culture of marking literary anniversaries also blossomed, for example. This mixes celebration of the individual with a broader commemorative gesture for society as a whole that performatively reifies at scale the presumed value of literary practice. This in turn expands the range of attitudes that can be displayed towards authors in any one particular physical place, from naïve celebration of a Romantic genius to conflicted remembrance of a persecuted poet. It also expands the range of authors who can be put to use for contemporary political, economic and pedagogical purposes. By focusing in detail on repeated acts of celebration and commemoration, this chapter explores how literary authorship is intimately bound up with a prevailing set of attitudes that are adopted within a particular society, leading to what I will go on to call 'modes of authorship'.

The methodology of archival reconstruction and close-textual analysis underpinning this approach is inductive. The case studies that follow, both in this chapter and in the book as a whole, detail my incremental approach to establishing patterns. Ultimately, my interest lies in devising a dynamic system of classification that is informed by observable practice and allows historical continuities to be drawn in both the worldly and textual practices of literary authorship alongside charting broader literary and societal change. To avoid the singularity of working either wholly at the level of the literary text or wholly at the level of society, I have opted for an approach that builds outwards from what can be read in the literary work when it is itself seen as part of a larger literature network. This represents a deliberate mixing of literary sociology, literary theory and literary analysis, as I work to express how authorship is the combined result of narrative and sociological practices and to allow for the fact that it shifts over time, as different practices are brought to bear on any one author's work as well as on the literature network more broadly. To speak with Olga Martynova, who reflects in our conversation at the end of this book on how one might set about linking authorship and the world:

> On the one hand, you have impressions of life and communicate them through a piece of art, on the other, we know that an artwork only seems to reflect life, that it actually shapes how people perceive life as well. There is a boundary between life and the work of art that portrays life. What happens when this boundary is crossed is crucial. That is actually very technical, that's part of your job as an artist to be always on the hunt for the opportunity to capture what's there, in this boundary.

I have therefore proceeded with a particular alertness to the prevailing historical discourse on German culture across the modern period, where identity narratives have been so shaped by efforts on the one hand to assert nineteenth-century German culture's place in the world and, on the other, to atone for the historical disaster with which this same culture has been directly connected in the twentieth century. The attempts made over this period by a wide variety of actors to articulate cultural value, pay heed to what has been lost or destroyed, and also retain some kind of position of critique or alterity, yields the basic set of modes within this broader cultural discourse: the celebratory, commemorative, satirical and utopian attitudes that are routinely espoused by cultural actors. Working outwards from the established notions of the author as a Romantic genius on the one hand and as an implicated cultural producer struggling to articulate anything in a culture deemed barbaric on the other, I inductively tease out how these modes condition authorship as both authors themselves and a much wider range of actors within the literature network repeatedly return to the central question of how to place oneself in respect of this difficult culture. In all of this, while the principle of linking authorship, identity and attitude in multiple mutually enforcing ways is developed through the example of Germany, my broader aim is to help us think again about how to study and articulate the place of any authors in the world.

Celebrating and Commemorating Authorship in Theory and Practice

In 1932, Germany commemorated the 100th anniversary of Goethe's death. Over the course of the spring and summer, the recent Nobel laureate Thomas Mann (1875–1955) contributed a number of speeches and public appearances to the festivities, including two pieces designed particularly to mark the anniversary: 'Goethe als Repräsentant des bürgerlichen Zeitalters' (Goethe as a representative of the bourgeois age), held at the Prussian Academy of Arts, Berlin, on the 18 March 1932, and 'Goethes Laufbahn als Schriftsteller' (Goethe's career as a writer), held in the Weimar town hall on the eve of the anniversary, the 21 March 1932.[6] Both the time and place were crucial: Mann spoke up, in a Nazi stronghold, for the importance of commemorating Goethe on the liberal-left precisely at a time when the fascist right was likely to start appropriating the nation's most celebrated writer for its own ends.[7] The exemplary use to which Mann puts Goethe thus instantly politicizes both of them, turning the figure of the renowned literary author into one of national, and indeed transnational, political importance for a community urgently seeking to position itself in relation to its own intellectual tradition.

In a Foucauldian sense, this is the equivalent of using an institutional setting to produce an image of Goethe that would then police the contemporary meaning of both his and Mann's work – that of the 'free' celebrated author whose aesthetic-intellectual achievements grant him socio-political legitimacy on a par with that of party political leaders.[8] However, while Mann unfolds his interpretation of Goethe's nineteenth-century significance within the very specific political context of contested public spaces and social classes during the first half of the twentieth century, some of the logic underpinning his assumption of generic authorial legitimacy also shows striking similarities with celebrity-making, or 'celebrificatory', structures from much later decades. These latent conceptualizations of authorship take us beyond Foucault's expressly political paradigms, and into Howard Becker's expanded 'art worlds' of the late twentieth century, Jérôme Meizoz' associated notion of the self-aware 'literary posture', and my own work on literary celebrity, a phenomenon that continues to grow well into the early twenty-first century.[9] Thomas Mann functions as a test case, then,

---

[6] Thomas Mann, 'Goethe als Repräsentant des bürgerlichen Zeitalters', *Gesammelte Werke*, 13 vols (Frankfurt a.M.: Fischer, 1960-1974), IX (Frankfurt a.M.: Fischer, 1960), pp. 297–332; 'Goethes Laufbahn als Schriftsteller', *Gesammelte Werke*, IX, pp. 333–62.
[7] Thomas Mann, [Antwort auf die Umfage] 'Wie soll das Goethe-Jahr 1932 gefeiert werden?', *Die literarische Welt: unabhängiges Organ für das deutsche Schrifttum*, 7 (1931), Issue 38, 2. For consideration of how such political appropriation of writers already happened in the nineteenth century, see Braun, 'Prize Germans?'
[8] This is the spirit of the paragraphs at the end of Michel Foucault's 'What is an Author?', pp. 221–2.
[9] Howard Becker, *Art Worlds* (Berkeley: U. of California P., 2008); Meizoz, *Postures littéraires*; Rebecca Braun, 'Fetishizing Intellectual Achievement: The Nobel Prize and European Literary Celebrity', *Celebrity Studies*, 2.3 (2011), 320–34; Rebecca Braun, 'The World Author in Us All: Conceptualising Fame and Agency in the Global Literary Market', *Celebrity Studies*, 7.4 (2016), 457–75.

for articulating not only particularly twentieth-century appropriations of authorship for larger narratives around German culture and society, but also post-structural theory's failure adequately to engage with the nuances of authorship precisely as a phenomenon of much broader social import.

Mann begins the first of his two speeches by describing Goethe's bourgeois upbringing as particularly 'German' – 'dies Schicksal von Herkunft und kühnstem Wachstum ist nirgends zu Hause wie bei uns'[10] (this fate / trajectory underpinned by origins and astounding growth is nowhere as at home as with us). This must be seen as part of his attempt to challenge National Socialist appropriations of the author with his own understanding of 'Germanness'.[11] Indeed, in invoking such rhetoric, he draws national boundaries around authorship that are never going to be far from charges of chauvinism, from a twenty-first-century perspective.[12] His rhetoric also assumes, in a way that Howard Becker will later question, that the author is at the centre of the literary world that grows around him. Common early twentieth-century assumptions about the 'great' author as a man of unparalleled genius are evident in Mann's affirmative reference to accounts from the nineteenth century of the living Goethe as a 'göttlicher Mensch' with 'mythusbildende Kräfte'[13] (divine person with powers of myth-making). Mann is clearly inclined to support the Scottish translator and Germanophile Thomas Carlyle (1795–1881), who suggested that the full extent of this author's genius would not be recognized until at least two hundred and possibly as many as two thousand years after his passing.[14]

---

[10] Mann, *Gesammelte Werke*, vol. IX, p. 298.
[11] For a detailed overview of the political context surrounding the celebration of Goethe in both 1932 and 1949, see Rainer Nägele, 'Die Goethefeiern von 1932 und 1949', in *Deutsche Feiern*, ed. Reinhold Grimm and Jost Hermand (Wiesbaden: Athenaion, 1977), pp. 97–122.
[12] Sigrid Weigel charts how an appreciation of the interconnections between an author's 'life and letters', as formulated by Wilhelm Dilthey (1833–1911), was the founding impetus of literary studies as an academic discipline in the nineteenth century. Such an approach placed the human subject at the centre of all academic enquiry, and it was bound to elevate the author into a grand spokesperson for his generation as well as re-enforce national boundaries around the resulting canon produced. Sigrid Weigel, *Genea-Logik: Generation, Tradition and Evolution zwischen Kultur- und Naturwissenschaften* (Munich: Fink, 2006), esp. pp. 165–69.
[13] Mann, *Gesammelte Werke*, vol. IX, p. 299.
[14] Carlyle expresses this in, 'Death of Goethe', in Carlyle, *The Cornerstone of a New Social Edifice / Der Grundstein eines neuen geselligen Gebäudes*, ed. Horst Pöthe & Norbert Miller (Berlin: de Gruyter, 1981/82), pp. 4–29, p. 16. For an excellent broader discussion of how Carlyle built a personality cult around Goethe, see Gregory Maertz, 'Carlyle's Critique of Goethe: Literature and the Cult of Personality', *Studies in Scottish Literature*, 29.1 (1996), 205–26.

Furthermore, in a clear nod to his own situation and person, Mann singles Goethe out as a very particular genius that trumps all others in his singular exemplarity for the emergent German 'Bildungsbürgertum' (educated middle classes):

> Sehen wir seine äußere Lebenshaltung an, die Sorgfalt der Kleidung, den Sinn für das Elegante [...]. Sein Benehmen zeichnete sich, wie sich ein Zeitgenosse ausdrückt, 'keineswegs durch exzentrisches Wesen aus, das sich bei Männern von Genius so häufig findet, sein Wesen war höflich und einfach'.[15]

> [Let's look at his external attitude to life, the care inherent in his clothes, the sense of elegance ... His manner was characterized, as one of his contemporaries puts it, 'by no means by the kind of eccentricity that one so often finds in men of genius; his behaviour was polite and simple'.]

A genius ahead of his times – which were themselves the times that invented the very idea of the Romantic author as genius –, Goethe is credited in both speeches not only with having written works of unparalleled psychological depth and aesthetic beauty, but also with anchoring the entire subsequent German intellectual tradition. Drawing a direct line from Goethe to Schopenhauer to Wagner to Nietzsche, Mann is able to conclude, 'Es ist die große Heimatwelt, deren Zöglinge wir sind, die bürgerliche Geisteswelt, die eben als Geisteswelt zugleich eine überbürgerliche ist'[16] (This is the great world of our Heimat [physical and cultural homeland – but see below], and we are its offspring, the educated bourgeois realm of the spirit / intellect, which, precisely as a world of the spirit, also looks beyond its specific bourgeois provenance [literally: is über-bourgeois]).[17]

It is worth pausing over this statement of quasi-universal belonging in the world. For a sociologist like Becker, the worlds that form around the literature of both Goethe and Thomas Mann are rather prosaically defined. They comprise the many individuals who are involved in mediating and remediating the work of literature and in so doing determining what that literary text actually is for that particular world

---

[15] Mann, *Gesammelte Werke*, vol. IX, pp. 302–3.
[16] Mann, *Gesammelte Werke*, vol. IX, p. 329.
[17] For a brief overview of how notions of authorship as an elevated intellectual activity developed alongside increasing general investment in a bourgeois work-ethic, see Rolf Parr, *Autorschaft: Eine kurze Sozialgeschichte der literarischen Intelligenz in Deutschland zwischen 1860 und 1930* (Heidelberg: Synchron, 2008).

at least as much through their practical actions as through any common ideological or intellectual lineage: 'The forms of cooperation may be ephemeral, but often become more or less routine, producing patterns of collective activity we can call an art world'.[18] Bruno Latour, as I already indicated in my introductory chapter, would also include the contribution of non-human actors to all this. In either model, the role of the author in this wider, practice-focused world is therefore considerably relativized, and I shall go on to develop this approach in depth when I look at the practicalities of German authorship in chapter four. Mann's concern with a specifically German sense of belonging, by contrast, is still formulated in complete deference to the grand intellectual figures who have metaphorically left their mark on the German cultural landscape. A 'Heimat realm' conditions present and future literary constellations, but it is itself the product of a series of key individuals, and it is first and foremost their celebrated achievements that allow it to function as a shared intellectual world across his speech.

The world in which Mann invites his listeners to locate themselves is therefore both a physical and a mental one – the Germans with whom he is sharing his speeches are 'at home' in the 'great world of our Heimat [homeland]' and in 'the educated bourgeois realm of the spirit'. Significantly, as Durckheim observes at a meta-level for all ritual performances, this latter mental realm is both generated by its local circumstances and radiates out beyond them. The educated middle-class German who perceives his place in the world through the intellectual tradition inaugurated by Goethe is also ritually taking on a place in a broader intellectual world that is shared either by other educated middle-class people, or by a set of people who are united by something greater than class opportunities alone (depending on how 'über-bourgeois' is interpreted). In either reading, the real human connections are evident, whether this is through a shared dress sense or philosophy, and they are sustained by a particular relationship to a real place, material circumstances, and access to a set of intellectual traditions. Mann's Goethe speeches, delivered in person in particular places, are part of this ritual enactment of the very Heimat being asserted, celebrated and commemorated all in one. Their performative nature further underscores the centrality of the (right sort of) author able to unite all these mediators of belonging: one who is almost certainly going to have some of Max Weber's 'charisma' about him.[19]

---

[18] Becker, *Art Worlds*, p. 1.
[19] Max Weber, 'The Nature of Charismatic Domination', reproduced in excerpts in Sean Redmond & Su Holmes, eds, *Stardom and Celebrity: A Reader* (London: Sage, 2007), pp. 17–24: this source usefully locates Weber within the celebrity discourse I am also engaging with.

This is an approach to authorship that, in line with Goethe's world literature, prioritizes the way an individual can embody a particular model of authorship that carries foundational or other normative value for society. The way belief in this model shapes and is shaped by society is the focus of chapters two and three of this study.

Mann's practical performance of Heimat as both the start and end point of German culture thus takes us into pre-existing theoretical discussions of authorship, which share the inherent problematics of trying to capture notions of origins and causality in a way that is not wholly circular. The slippery nature of the untranslatable term Heimat itself provides the bridge. As Johannes von Moltke explains, even by the beginning of the twentieth century 'the term Heimat [had] acquired multiple meanings, ranging from conservationist to utopian, from regionalist to nationalist, and from populist to elitist. [. . .] The multiple rebirths of Heimat over the twentieth century have only added to this polysemy'. Yet what von Moltke describes as the term's 'semantic flexibility [. . .] its adaptability to different contexts' by no means disqualifies it as a useful conceptual tool.[20] Quite on the contrary, when it is specifically applied to questions concerning the place of culture within a given society and the attitudes that coalesce around it, the contested nature of Heimat can help expose and conceptualize the ambiguities underlying public constructions of value in the cultural field with which authors subsequently grapple and are themselves directly equated.

An interlinked set of tangible criteria with intangible values (being educated, middle class, preferably male, probably Gentile, and living in German-speaking Europe) demonstrably drives how well-read German-language readers and writers connect up in the first place. In effect, Mann's speeches stake out a specific 'cultural Heimat' of their own. His practical twist on this set of normative characteristics derives from an attitude to being in the world that resonates with the way Goethe's 'world author' persona was the practical manifestation of an intangible commitment to his concept of world literature, and it cuts across the pre- and post-war periods. It underpins the sort of practical network of affinity that Becker discerns when he sets out how art is both the tangible and intangible result of joint activity between a large number of people. But where Becker is primarily concerned with exposing the full extent of any art world in question in relatively value-neutral terms – in my terms, showing just how expanded the literature network really is –, more recent theorists have been exercised by

---

[20] Johannes von Moltke, *No Place Like Home: Locations of Heimat in German Cinema* (Berkeley: U. of California P., 2005), p. 7, p. 8.

accounting for the way individual human agency continues to unfold within it with value-laden effects that are of significance in the first instance for that individual's broader social construction. Jérôme Meizoz in particular observes how authors adopt a specific 'literary posture' in both their personal appearances in public and in their literary writing that encapsulates an individual take on broader pre-existing literary traditions. This individual contribution to collective phenomena extends a certain 'ethos' from within the rhetorical structure of the text (Meizoz picks up on some of Barthes' early writing around myth here) to an overarching conscious positioning of the author's persona within society. This in turn amounts to an author developing and expressing a certain attitude to his or her authorship across an entire oeuvre.[21] Mann's reconstruction of Goethe in the 1932 speeches already demonstrates this overarching attitude in part, as he stresses a conscious embodiment of authorship that can be literally and metaphorically seen in specific places as well as intuited from his writing, and which is clearly motivated by a set of values that are emotively tied to a notion of Heimat. As I shall go on to discuss further below, by invoking Goethe and the cultural Heimat he calls into being, he also deliberately seeks to have an impact on the most urgent, complex issues of his own life and times. The way he presents himself in his writing and in respect of a discernible literary tradition is therefore directly linked to the appropriation of his authorial persona that he suggests to the wider world. However, this will also go on to inform aspects of his authorship that far exceed his direct control.

The value-laden criteria within Mann's re-mediation of Goethe for his own purposes, themselves carried by a powerful network of actors of which Foucault, Becker and Meizoz are all in their own way aware, emerge time and again at ritual celebrations of authorship, as the rest of this chapter will show. These commemorative celebrations are intricately bound up with the deeply entrenched racial, class and gender norms of German memory culture as well as of the wide swathe of cultural institutions touched by literature. Although Foucault, Becker and Meizoz are aware of these wider forces of authorship, they do not rigorously factor them in to what they say about authorship in their own French and Anglo-Saxon contexts. Unpicking these criteria in order better to understand how authorship is both an individual and a collective expression of attitude towards 'being in the world' in the most specific as well as the broadest of senses is therefore my major concern. In order to factor in the more practice-focused elements of

---

[21] Jérôme Meizoz, *La Fabrique des Singularités: Postures Littéraires II* (Geneva: Slatkine, 2011).

authorship, we also need to extend the theoretical way we think about authorship, from a vocabulary that foregrounds individual actions and perceptions in and around the literary text (from Booth's 'implied author', through the post-structuralist panoply of functional classifications within literary discourse, to Meizoz' more socially focused 'posture') to one that allows for broader input and significance from things well beyond Bourdieu's conventional literary field. These entail intangible phenomena like the emotional affect of place, the rather more tangible and institutionally traceable geopolitics of regional capitals, as well as the individual significance of material conditions, such as food, drink, chairs, tables and houses.

The key conceptual invention that allows me to move between the theory and practice of authorship throughout the rest of this chapter – and indeed book – is the notion of discrete 'modes of authorship'. The term 'mode of authorship' is deliberately broader than Meizoz' 'literary posture', or indeed Bourdieu's notion of 'habitus' within the literary field. While Meizoz' discussion of 'posture' helpfully draws attention to the question of how to link a deliberately adopted rhetorical ethos discerned within an individual text to a broader, non-verbal strategy of self-presentation pursued by an author over the course of a career, it is limited by its absolute focus on the conscious decisions of the individual writer as they can be intuited from her writings and actions. As I have already indicated in my introductory chapter, there are many other non-human actors involved in the construction of authorship, including broad senses of time and space as well as individual material objects and intangible concepts, many of which coalesce in the German context in the untranslatable and slippery notion of Heimat. The term 'mode' in its dictionary definition refers to style (a particular form or variety of something, or of expressing something, e.g. a mode of transport, a mode of living) and manifestation (a particular form or manifestation of an underlying substance, e.g. 'hate in all its manifestations' = modes of hate).[22] These aspects of authorship – the discernible styles, different manifestations – can be deliberately shaped by authors seeking to position themselves in a certain way in Bourdieu's literary field and in line with his notion of habitus, but they can equally result from the non-conscious affect that emanates in various ways from the kinds of non-human actors described by Latour and touched upon above.

Four main 'modes of authorship' suggest themselves from the particularly German historical and institutional contexts of literature, but, like Mann's notion of the 'über-bourgeois' and Durckheim's

---

[22] See 'mode' in the online Merriam Webster dictionary: https://www.merriam-webster.com/dictionary/mode (last accessed 29 October 2018).

discussion of rituals, they also point beyond this setting: the celebratory, commemorative, satirical and utopian modes of authorship. I discuss each in turn below, but first provide some overarching observations. Of the four, the celebratory mode, as has already been sketched above in the more general terms of celebratory practices, is both the most established within theories of authorship and the easiest to trace in practical terms, as it links directly to the nineteenth-century notion of the Romantic genius. Indeed, it still predominates across the period and into the present, as the underlying gestus of all engagement with literary writing is to presume its inherent worth. However, the celebratory mode has also been subject to significant change over the course of the twentieth century, and this needs to be factored in to what we might now mean by the term. The other three modes all also have roots in earlier centuries: satirical traditions, commemorative practices and utopian thinking are by no means confined to responding to the particular flavours of nationalist, socialist or capitalist sentiment that developed in and around the Second World War. However, as the rest of this chapter will show, they do come together in a particular way in the German post-war context of authorship – and this is a context that is itself inflected by the cognate but distinct context of Austria. They also inflect the predominant celebratory mode in distinct ways, as all four are harnessed to notions of broader social change when they are programmed into the context-specific models of authorship that will be the focus of later chapters.

My modes of authorship are therefore devised to understand how real people front up both the intangible idea and the actual practice of literature in a post-war cultural landscape that was outwardly stripped of all moral certainties and is itself the product of a whole series of tangible and intangible phenomena. They are designed to link human, structural, material and conceptual factors, all of which contribute to the way literary activity is valued within the multiple overlapping worlds of literature and society. Together, the four modes capture the different ways the attitude that ultimately underpins any sense of literary value is expressed and mediated, both by authors and by the many other actors within a literature network. They act, therefore, as a series of lenses through which to view the core practices and products of Goethe's world literature as it has evolved over the latter half of the twentieth century and into the twenty-first: literature that is very much both in and of the multiply-connected worlds in which it exists.

The Celebratory Mode: From Romantic Genius to Literary Celebrity

Subject to increasing extension and appropriation as the twentieth century progresses, the celebratory mode of authorship articulates both how authors themselves and the many other participants in a literature network value literary endeavour. As a consequence, it is structurally endemic to many of the mediators within the literature network: the very act of publishing a book displaying an author's name is itself an act of inherent celebration, for example. At this basic level, all engagement with the work of an author happens within the celebratory mode of authorship, regardless of whether that engagement is positive or negative. In his speeches Mann variously draws on nineteenth-century conceptions of the author as a pre-formed genius around whom an evolving sense of cultural achievement can coalesce for a certain community of readers and writers. However, he also moves beyond the Romantic model as a simple focus for adulation to consider the difficulties public acts of celebration cause for individual authors.

In the first of the two speeches discussed above, Mann touches on the extent to which the biographical person who is crowned 'Nationalschriftsteller'[23] (writer laureate) must bend to the expectations of others by growing into the role over time, while in the second he speaks of Goethe's awareness of the power of his personality as both a positive and a negative attribute: 'Goethe fühlte sich als ein Vorkommnis jener Größe, die die Erde ebensosehr bedrückt, wie sie beglückt. Er verkörperte sie in der mildesten, friedlichsten Gestalt, die sie annehmen kann: in der des großen Dichters'[24] (Goethe felt himself to represent an instance of this greatness that weighs as heavily on the earth as it blesses it. He embodied it in the mildest, most peaceful form possible: that of the great poet). Although he is invoking the Romantic trope of the 'genius author' in both instances, subtle linguistic turns shift the emphasis away from nineteenth-century constructions of authorship as conditioned by singular exemplarity and a sense of transcendental significance. Instead, the focus falls on the actual person behind the authorial persona. Mann shows Goethe the man reacting, as a man, to the symbolic constructions of his authorship by both himself and others (Goethe *fühlte sich als* ein Vorkommnis jener Größe; Goethe *felt himself to represent* an instance of this greatness) and actively choosing to place his body at the service of a higher ideal – er *verkörperte* sie (he *embodied* it). Goethe is quoted as being acutely aware of the effects he can achieve through the judicious application of his personality when Mann interpolates the dead author's words into his analysis: 'Der Mensch wirkt alles, was er vermag, auf den Menschen durch seine

---

[23] Mann, *Gesammelte Werke*, vol. IX, p. 326.
[24] Mann, *Gesammelte Werke*, vol. IX, p. 361.

Persönlichkeit'[25] (Man affects others entirely through the power of his personality).[26]

The will charismatically to embody or otherwise perform authorship is not only highly relevant to the position of Thomas Mann himself, speaking as a writer laureate in his own right one hundred years after Goethe's death and at a time when the country was increasingly obviously in need of strong public figures of the kind Max Weber describes. It also shows the beginnings of a more instrumentally performative approach to authorship than the purely celebratory purpose of the nineteenth-century eulogy that otherwise dominates these speeches and points back to art as an autonomous sphere rather than out to broader society.[27] In these speeches, as elsewhere, Mann deliberately chose the more functional term 'Schriftsteller' (writer) over the more consciously literary 'Dichter' (poet) when referring to Goethe, a choice for which he was attacked by the conservative forces of his time.[28] Acknowledging the author's own personal investment in embodying the role of author-as-genius, as well as a level of conscious performance to an audience that such investment will entail, Mann's thoughts about the actual lived experience of authorship can thus be read as an early awareness of the issues that will go on to form the focus of celebrity studies some thirty years later – the idea that an individual is celebrated for what he or she represents (rather than what has been achieved) and that this individual's ability to perform, something that is inherently repeatable, will become key to his or her sustained success amongst a large public.[29] There is something both self-sustaining in this (valuing the literary through its own system of value) and tantalizingly reproducible (the career of a writer, when set out as such, may appear within reach of many).

Mann's increasing awareness of the power of both his own authorial persona and his actual body and voice, together with his ability to

---

[25] Mann, *Gesammelte Werke*, vol. IX, p. 336.
[26] That they are Goethe's words is directly flagged by Mann in the speech. An example of Goethe purportedly reflecting on the power of personality can be found in Ekermann's diary entry on 13 February 1831: Eckermann, *Gespräche mit Goethe*, p. 436.
[27] For an interesting perspective on traditions in remembering 'great men', see Jessica Goodman, 'Between Celebrity and Glory: Textual After-Image in Late Eighteeenth-Century France', *Celebrity Studies* (2016), 7.4, special issue on 'Literary Celebrity', ed. R. Braun and E. Spiers, 545–60.
[28] See Tobias Boes, *Thomas Mann's War: Literature, Politics, and the World Republic of Letters* (Ithaca, NY: Cornell U. P., 2019), esp. pp. 22–5.
[29] First explored in depth in Daniel J. Boorstin, *The Image, or What Happened to the American Dream?* (New York: Athenaeum, 1962).

manipulate multiple media and public contexts for his appearances, ties in with a nascent move towards systematic appropriation of the physical person of the author that would become dominant in the period after the Second World War, first for political and then for commercial purposes.[30] With this notion of systemic reproducibility, Mann's shift in emphasis becomes symptomatic of a development within the generic celebratory mode of authorship which had hitherto underpinned nineteenth-century ideas of genius on the part of authors and their publics alike, to contain more specifically 'celebrificatory' activity, the manifestation of which becomes pronounced in the latter part of the twentieth century. Literary celebrification – I borrow the notion of 'celebrification' from Chris Rojek – builds on the inherently self-affirming gesture of all celebration of the literary, but in a way that is increasingly slanted towards reproducibility and public entertainment rather than awe and instruction.[31] As I have shown elsewhere, the mechanism by which this is achieved is a systematic attempt, across the broader cultural sector, to fuse public appreciation of literary achievement with celebrity processes. This in turn allows multiple distinct audiences to feel in some way familiar with the author and/or her work.[32]

Although the media in post-war Germany would not provide a platform for the systematic construction of literary celebrity until much later in the century, ongoing elite institutional belief in the cultural value of literary authorship meant that certain authors were propelled to the fore of public consciousness in the founding years of both emergent German states and subject to a first approximation at deliberate institutional and political appropriation.[33] The protracted attempts on the part of both East and West German authorities, for example, to secure famous living authors' physical presence in their part of the country inherently confirms the predominance of the celebratory mode of authorship in broader political narratives, as do

---

[30] On Mann's manipulation of various media, see the essays in Michael Ansel, Hans-Edwin Friedrich, Gerhard Lauer, eds, *Die Erfindung des Schriftstellers Thomas Mann* (Berlin: de Gruyter, 2009). On the various ways that other people appropriated Mann and helped him fashion his authorship, see Tobias Boes, 'Thomas Mann, World Author: Representation and Autonomy in the World Republic of Letters', in 'World Authorship', ed. Rebecca Braun & Andrew Piper, special issue of *Seminar*, 51.2 (2015), 132–47.

[31] Chris Rojek, *Celebrity* (London: Reaktion, 2001).

[32] Braun, 'Fetishizing Intellectual Achievement'; Braun, 'The World Author in Us All'.

[33] See Dietz Bering, *Die Intellektuellen. Geschichte eines Schimpfwortes* (Stuttgart: Klett-Cotta, 1978).

the related attempts to appropriate the cultural legacy of famous dead authors. The public acrimony that surrounded Thomas Mann's refusal to return to the German homeland after the war needs to be seen in this context, but so too does the enthusiasm with which his speeches were received in both East and West Germany on the occasions of the 200th anniversary of Goethe's birth (1949) and the 150th anniversary of Schiller's death (1955).

Mann was in fact able personally to present – and physically represent – appropriate narratives for both Germanys that were largely well received in each context, underscoring the adaptability of the basic celebratory mode.[34] He did this by explicitly elaborating on the ideal of art and the artist as global and transcendental in character that he had begun to point towards in 1932. Such logic still worked amidst the sites of physical and moral devastation in which he spoke, not least because both sides still bought into a fundamentally celebratory approach to valuing the 'great' German author and the literary tradition he represented.[35] Indeed, the West German journalist Erich Pfeiffer-Belli is not unrepresentative when he writes in the *Tagesspiegel* daily newspaper that, listening to Mann speaking in Frankfurt led to the 'sudden' realization,

> daß durch diese Rückkehr in die geistigen Bezirke Deutschlands etwas wieder in Ordnung gekommen sei, das einfach durch das dauernde Fehlen dieser Gestalt und ihres Bekennertums ein peinliches Vakuum hätte entstehen lassen können, das nun plötzlich ausgefüllt war und ausgefüllt bleiben wird.[36]

---

[34] For a useful overview of these debates and the historico-political context that shaped them, see Jost Hermand & Wigand Lange, *"Wollt ihr Thomas Mann wiederhaben?": Deutschland und die Emigranten* (Hamburg: Europäische Verlagsanstalt, 1999). Although Mann's 1949 visit to East Germany resulted in negative press for the author in the Western zone on this point, the reports in each zone on his visit to their zone were both largely positive, out of a mixture of political desire to be seen officially to be accepted by the author and to accept him (particularly in East Germany), and genuine appreciation for what he said. His visits in 1955 were considerably less contentious all round. For a detailed documentation of the responses in both zones, see Thomas Goll, *Die Deutschen und Thomas Mann: Die Rezeption des Dichters in Abhängigkeit von der Politischen Kultur Deutschlands 1898-1955* (Baden-Baden: Nomos, 2000).

[35] See Lutz Hagestedt, 'Sinn für Überholtes: Aspekte der Repräsentationssemantik in Thomas Manns "Deutschlandreden"', in Ansel, Friedrich & Lauer, eds, *Die Erfindung des Schriftstellers Thomas Mann*, pp. 351–70.

[36] Erich Pfeiffer-Belli, 'Festliche Tage in München', *Der Tagesspiegel*, 30.07.1949, quoted in Goll, *Die Deutschen und Thomas Mann*, p. 327.

[that with this repatriation to Germany's intellectual / cultural realm, something has returned to normal which, purely through the long-term absence of this figure and his ability to take a stance, threatened to result in a terrible vacuum; this vacuum has now been suddenly filled and will remain filled.]

Such a public belief in both the importance of the author's physical presence in Germany and in the transcendental position of authorship vis-à-vis the morally ruined and physically divided state of the country was something Mann was happy to encourage, as his comments in his 1949 Goethe speech in both East and West Germany make clear: 'Wer sollte die Einheit Deutschlands gewährleisten und darstellen, wenn nicht ein unabhängiger Schriftsteller, dessen wahre Heimat die freie, von Besatzungen unberührte Sprache ist'[37] (Who should guarantee and represent the unity of Germany if not an independent writer whose true home [Heimat] is language, which is free and untouched by the occupying forces). In turning the German Heimat, that emotive notion of both a physical and a cultural home, into the realm of the German language itself, Mann is on the one hand making his authorial persona into the self-defined pinnacle of linguistic excellence, whilst at the same time indicating that any writer – indeed anyone who can write – could attain this politically laudable, free and inherently reproducible German position.

The Commemorative Mode: Authorship and the Memory of Places

The obvious political instrumentalization of authorship and Heimat evident both in the invitations and Mann's responses to them underscores the importance of place as both a real physical attribute of everyday life and an idealized location that can provide a backdrop to mental (self-) projections. In a slightly different context, Aleida Assmann writes about the 'memory of places', using the term to indicate both the individual human subject's memory of a specific place, and the ability of a specific place to hold memories for numerous individuals and/or collectives for posterity. Further expanding on the term's polyvalency, she explores the different nature of 'places of generational memory' and 'places of commemoration'.[38] While the former is characterized by the

---

[37] Thomas Mann, 'Ansprache in Weimar', *Gesammelte Werke*, XIII (Frankfurt a.M.: Fischer, 1974), pp. 791–4, p. 793. The full text 'Ansprache im Goethejahr', from which he drew his individual addresses to Weimar and Frankfurt audiences, is reproduced in *Gesammelte Werke*, XI, pp. 481–97.

[38] Aleida Assmann, *Cultural Memory and Western Civilization: Functions, Media, Archives* (Cambridge: Cambridge U. P., 2011), p. 292.

continuity of an unbroken lineage of human subjects engaging with their environment, the latter is defined by an abyss between the past and present that poses a challenge to stable narrative constructions. In both cases, however, the memory narrative generated at any one point in time results from an interaction between a historically located interpreting subject and the 'aura' of the place.[39]

The way in which Mann was eventually convinced to set foot back on German soil makes both conceptions of place and memory evident: he was invited back to receive prizes, honorary citizenships and honorary doctorates under the auspices of a putative link to Goethe and Schiller that was ceremoniously asserted in culturally significant places. He appeared as a speaker who was happy to cast himself within their tradition – a tradition that was, according to his own exposition, specifically German in character even as it also facilitated the conscious move to 'Weltbürgertum' (cosmopolitanism; literally, a 'world' educated middle class and/or associated sense of world citizenship).[40] Given the widespread popularity of Goethe and Schiller as the reading public's authors of choice in the late 1940s and early 1950s, it is fully in line with Mann's own self-conception as a writer coming from a proud German educated bourgeois tradition to associate himself with them.[41] Going one step further, it seems legitimate to suggest that the actions of both Mann and the awarding committees focused on deliberately invoking the geographically rooted culture of a previous era in order to smooth over the enormous cultural and geopolitical caesurae that were the legacy of the Second World War. Not only did these conciliatory gestures allow each zone to assert their claim to an ongoing cultural tradition, they also permitted an alternative interpretation of Mann's exile. For although Goethe and Schiller's work has travelled many times around the world, neither classical author themselves undertook any major period of absence from the homeland that might have destabilized their

---

[39] Assmann, *Cultural Memory*, p. 322.
[40] See Hagestedt, 'Sinn für Überholtes', 2009, p. 359. For more on the historical moment that underpins this fusion of legal and literary concepts into a representative world author function, see Boes, 'Thomas Mann, World Author'; Lamping, *Die Idee der Weltliteratur*.
[41] See his 1932 essay, 'Goethe als Repräsentant des bürgerlichen Zeitalters' for a sense of the extent to which Mann identified with the material lifestyle and specifically German location of these authors. Nägele notes that no fewer than thirty different editions of Faust were published between 1945 and 1950, 'Die Goethefeiern von 1932 und 1949', p. 120. On the significance of the German Goethe reception in the immediate post-war years, see Boes, *Thomas Mann's War*, pp. 226–30.

sense of belonging.⁴² On the contrary, they are very strongly identified with specific areas of Germany, which quickly became 'places of generational memory' in the popular public consciousness. In emphasizing his intellectual link to these authors and physically now speaking in their stead, Mann was able ultimately to ensure his position within a grand cultural tradition that largely dispenses with the troublesome decades of the twentieth century.

Through its association with place, authorship thus takes on another kind of symbolic role for wider society: against the immediate evidence of rupture and the sense of physical and cultural uprootedness that was felt on a mass scale in post-war Germany, individual authors were able to function as signs of continuity, even when they were also politically controversial figures and their return was couched in a rhetoric of 'Neuanfang' or 'new beginnings'. Their physical presence in specific German places, coupled with the celebratory narratives of past untainted cultural achievements that they were able, through their role as continuing producers of literature, to extend into the present, encouraged a symbolic link to be made between living German authors and the country's cultural heritage as it could be publicly experienced in physical places.

In this sense, individual authors were able both to cement a certain memory of Germanness and to contribute to an unfolding public consciousness of what it meant to be German in the post-war German locality specifically through where and how they presented their physical bodies. Projected onto physical places they could collectively represent a rooted culture that stretched back over generations. At the same time, in their ability to roam more widely they could also invoke a symbolic openness inherent in the post-war individual that would allow them to redefine this culture as their representative lives in the media spotlight unfolded and the political places in which they were operating changed around them. Assmann again is helpful when trying to understand the mechanism behind this kind of process: 'Whereas the memory of places is firmly fixed to one particular location from which it cannot be separated, places of memory are distinguished by the very fact that they are transferrable'.⁴³ Assmann downplays the role of individual human agency in her work, preferring to leave open exactly how the symbolic and/or affective power of places is realized. My

---

⁴² One might point to Goethe's Italian journey 1786–1788, but given how common it was for such a 'grand tour' to figure as part of a young man's education, it is in a rather different category to the kind of expatriation Thomas Mann and other twentieth-century writers experienced.

⁴³ Assmann, *Cultural Memory*, p. 296.

interest, by contrast, lies in precisely this area, and thus I am adapting her conceptual frame to my purposes when I add in the biological body of the author to her thoughts about place and memory.

In my adaptation, then, the way Weimar appears to its many visitors to evoke Goethe and Schiller is an example of the 'memory of places', whereas a contemporary author like Thomas Mann visibly plays a role in creating a 'place of memory' when he visits each of the various locations around Germany and allows successive symbolic constructions of his authorship to be projected onto him through the link suggested by each locality. His appearance as the living incarnation of Goethe's world author, who allows people to celebrate the Germanness of Weimar and at the same time look beyond it, brings cultural legitimacy to the places where he speaks. Through his performative association with multiple politically opposed locations, however, his authorial persona also becomes a contested site of memory in itself that is made to function differently in different locations, and sometimes actually suppresses commemoration. As a representative literary intellectual, Mann functions as a gateway for past cultural traditions to be projected onto divergent ideological narratives about the present and near future by the different audiences with whom he interacts in politically specific times and places. The further differentiation Assmann offers between 'places of generational memory', which are primarily marked out by a positive sense of sharing an ongoing history, and 'places of commemoration', which are characterized by traumatic rupture and loss, alerts us to the high stakes around exclusivity and inclusivity within any memory-driven mode. The commemorative mode thereby shares some of the representational issues that are associated with the celebratory mode, but it is rendered distinct by the central role played by different attitudes to the past prevalent in any one setting and the way in which they will determine how this representation is connoted and for whom. Without being inherently more or less ethical or directed than the celebratory mode, there is a markedly greater likelihood that this mode of authorship will be invoked to frame ethical considerations within a culture's sense of self and be oriented towards specific publics.

The Utopian Mode: Multiple Persons in Multiple Places

A determination on the part of authors, both individually and collectively, to shape the future and/or represent different political alternatives, begins to set in in a more systematic way across the German public sphere from the late 1950s onwards with the rise of the Gruppe 47 (Group 47). The group was formed in 1947 by Alfred Andersch and Hans Werner Richter and started out meeting in informal locations to share new writing. Under Richter's idiosyncratic stewardship, it rapidly grew in cultural importance, with the annual meetings becoming the event to which new writers aspired to be invited. Although literary merit was nominally the only requirement, core participants shared a broadly left-wing political agenda. Over the twenty years of its active existence, practically all writers seeking to make their way in the German literary scene had some encounter with this group. Stalwarts of post-war writing – Heinrich Böll, Hans Magnus Enzensberger, Max Frisch, Günter Grass, Martin Walser – along with the powerful critics Walter Jens and Marcel Reich-Ranicki – were regular attendees.

Outwardly, this group of authors, which defined itself as the young generation and purported to make a clean break with the past, represents the opposite kind of authorship to that embodied by either Thomas Mann or Goethe. In terms of their performative methods and relationship to real and virtual places of memory, however, there is a marked similarity. Unlike the self-contained internationalist network of socialist writers from the first decades of the twentieth century on which one might expect a consciously left-wing literary grouping to build, the Gruppe 47 aimed from the start to have an influential media presence across the bourgeois institutions of literature that could in turn suggest new homes for it within the normative cultural landscape.[44] Throughout the latter part of the 1950s and 1960s their annual meetings to discuss work in progress were covered ever more intensely in the mainstream print media and on radio. Hans Werner Richter's decision to meet in predominantly rural, provincial locations across the Federal Republic was not just financially motivated. It also took on a symbolic significance, as the changing physical locations, themselves often remnants of a previous era, implied a kind of 'free-floating' literary spirit that the participants were quick to embrace and upon which they explicitly reflected in contributions to Richter's celebratory *Almanach* (Almanac) in 1962 whilst all the time also anchoring their own symbolic and economic capital in the German literary field.

In this almanac the very lack of a physical capital for literary endeavour along the lines of Paris or London meant that the 'place' of German-language writing was mobile – a 'fahrende literarische Hauptstadt', or travelling literary capital, in the words of Hans Magnus Enzensberger – and thus potentially accessible to the whole of

---

[44] On practices of world literature and international horizons in socialist literary networks of the first part of the twentieth century, see Christoph Schaub, 'Internationalist Montages: World-Making in Interwar Germany's Labor Movement Literature', in Chunjie Zhang, ed, *Composing Modernist Connections in China and Europe* (New York: Routledge, 2019), pp. 50–69; Christoph Schaub, *Proletarische Welten: Internationalistische Weltliteratur in der Weimarer Republik* (Berlin: de Gruyter, 2019).

German-speaking Europe.⁴⁵ Even though there was a good precedent in Germany for deliberately provincial capitals, the emphasis on organized transience was new, and it is something Richter would stress again and again in his later work for TV and radio. Indeed, the group's enforced mobility was merged in Richter's eyes with its orientation towards an expression of democracy still to come. Writing about the intellectual location of the Gruppe 47, Richter directly invokes its rootlessness in contemporary Germany, projecting the group's ideal political surroundings into the future and hoping that, for now, his group might act as a kind of 'school' in which a 'democratic elite' could be formed with a view to future public influence. His description of the group as simultaneously a 'Zentralpunkt, Kaffeehaus, Metropole und Diskussionsbühne' (central point, coffee house, metropolis, and discussion podium) casts the group as a deliberately discursive, potentially provocative space that both emanates from a certain culture and reflects critically on it.⁴⁶

Such a positioning has a distinctly utopian edge to it, both in the sense of seeking to imagine a better society and in drawing attention to the impossibility of its current existence in any kind of permanent way. This is the original pun in Thomas More's 1516 *Utopia*, which simultaneously evokes 'the good place' and 'no place' in its derivation from the Greek. More's utopia takes the form of a largely inaccessible island that is conjured up through the reports of a returning adventurer – a better vision of society made possible not through travelling either backwards or forwards in time, but laterally in space. Framed by multiple rhetorical tropes within the fictional narrative as well as a series of fictional letters between More and his collaborators, the whole text is a decidedly literary form of political polemic ultimately designed to make its readers reflect critically on contemporary English social and political conventions. Its gestus, therefore, is towards bringing about change for the future, and its principal method for achieving this is to challenge the existing spaces of normative social and political debate with the very notion of a parallel, markedly different realm that is made possible by the literary imaginary.

Richter's basic programme for both literary and political change by virtue of inhabiting a transitional space that opens up alternative ways of being in society also maps on to Michel Foucault's concept of the 'heterotopia'. Originally conceived at the same time as his 1969 essay on authorship, this term is set out and differentiated from utopia in the

---

⁴⁵ Hans Werner Richter, 'Fünfzehn Jahre', in Richter, ed., *Almanach der Gruppe 47: 1947-1962* (Reinbek: Rowohlt, 1962), pp. 8–14
⁴⁶ Richter, 'Fünfzehn Jahre', p. 10 and p. 12.

1984 essay, 'Des Espaces Autres' / 'Of Other Spaces'.[47] Foucault explains that while utopias present an image of society in perfect terms or upside down, they by definition do not exist. Heterotopias, by contrast, really do exist and are often 'formed in the very founding of society'; they 'are something like counter-sites, a kind of effectively enacted utopia in which the real sites, all the other real sites that can be found within the culture, are simultaneously represented, contested, and inverted. Places of this kind are outside of all places, even though it may be possible to indicate their location in reality.'[48] Although Richter, in his many promotional retrospectives on the group did not go so far as to formulate it exactly in either utopian or heterotopian terms, the unstable flash appearances of the Gruppe 47 in the German provincial landscape over a twenty-year period (their final regular meeting took place in 1967) had a similar inspirational / polemicizing function for their contemporaries.

Such provocation around valuing the place of German literary activity within an evolving cultural Heimat has important echoes with the German philosophical tradition's own invocation of different forms of utopia, which itself accords a particular place to literature and literary language in its conceptual apparatus of belonging. As a result, a number of these philosophers in turn become a point of reference for authors consciously developing their attitude to their craft. The stakes for both philosophy and literature can be briefly elucidated with reference to two twentieth-century German philosophers in particular, who placed their own idiosyncratic, and deeply divergent, understanding of Heimat at the heart of their (differently construed) utopian intellectual apparatus: the Marxist Jew, Ernst Bloch, and the one-time Nazi-supporter, Martin Heidegger. Bloch explicitly links the sort of political and intellectual search for grounding described in relation to the Gruppe 47 above to the concept of Heimat, ending his magnum opus *Das Prinzip Hoffnung* (1959) in a vision of how the utopia of Heimat can be achieved:

> Die Wurzel der Geschichte aber ist der arbeitende, schaffende, die Gegebenheiten umbildende und überholende Mensch. Hat er sich erfaßt und das Seine ohne Entäußerung und Entfremdung in realer Demokratie begründet, so entsteht in der Welt etwas, das allen in die Kindheit scheint und worin noch niemand war: Heimat.[49]

---

47   The essay is based on lecture notes dating from 1967: Michel Foucault, 'Of Other Spaces', trans. Jay Mickowiec, *Diacritics*, 16.1 (1986), pp. 22–27.
48   Foucault, 'Of Other Spaces', p. 24.
49   Ernst Bloch, *Werkausgabe*. Vol.5. (Frankfurt am Main: Suhrkamp, 1993), p. 1628.

[But the root of history is the working, creating human being who reshapes and overhauls the given facts. Once he has grasped himself and established what is his, without expropriation and alienation, in real democracy, there arises in the world something which shines into the childhood of all and in which no one has yet been: homeland.][50]

These closing sentences present Heimat as a mixture of ultimate inclusivity and self-realization, the comforting feeling of which is sensed in childhood but whose conscious realization still remains to be achieved by the deliberate political and philosophical labours of man. There is an ethereal quality to Bloch's Heimat, as it shines like the sun and mysteriously 'comes into being in the world', yet the underlying attachment to a real, physical place, the geographical homeland inherent in this particularly German word, invests Bloch's term with credibility as a utopian prospect that could be seized and converted into a reality by ordinary mortals with real emotional needs. With its emphasis on the successive ages of man and a linked teleological drive to human history, his concept has similarities with Assmann's 'places of generational memory'. Bloch's Heimat could be conceived as the ideal future-oriented memory narrative that emerges with, and is passed on by, generations of likeminded individuals who consciously share and contribute to the evolution of a certain political system that will become a reality in a specific physical place. Within this narrative, he prioritizes the actions of individuals over the aura of places, but clearly an enhanced relationship to one's physical location in the world is the collective reward.

A similar sense underpins the statements made by regular attendees of the Gruppe 47 concerning their contribution to German politics and culture. In their descriptions, the group is an only very briefly tangible model of a utopian democratic community, and yet it hovers as an inspiring and inclusive ideal over the contemporary physical and intellectual landscape of Germany. It incorporates both a utopian ideal and the very real hope that authors, by turning themselves into an exemplary reference point, might be able to anchor a certain concept of culture in the German-speaking world in such a manner that its geopolitically-bounded people could come to a conscious and politically responsible realization of themselves and their cultural heritage.

Martin Heidegger, by contrast, formulates a rather different understanding of Heimat and its socio-cultural importance. In his 1960 essay 'Sprache und Heimat' (Language and Heimat), he asserts that the

---

[50] Ernst Bloch, *The Principle of Hope*, trans. Neville Plaice, Stephen Plaice & Paul Knight, 3 vols (Oxford: Blackwell, 1986), pp. 1375–6.

value of literary language resides in its ability to make a pre-existing physical Heimat visible for its inhabitants in a manner that creates a heartfelt sense of belonging:

> Das dichterische Sagen läßt erst die Sterblichen auf der Erde unter dem Himmel vor den Göttlichen wohnen. Ihr dichterisches Sagen bringt erst anfänglich die Hut und Hege, den Hort und die Huld für eine bodenständige Ortschaft hervor, die Aufenthalt im irdischen Unterwegs der wohnenden Menschen sein kann. Die Sprache ist kraft ihres dichtenden Wesens, als verborgenste und darum am weitesten auslangende, das inständig schenkende Hervorbringen der Heimat.[51]

[Poetical saying is what lets mortals live at all on the earth under the sky and in full view of immortals. Their poetical saying only begins to bring into being the care and the nurture, the nursing and the guarding needed for a down-to-earth placeness, which has the potential to be a resting point in people's earthly journeying through the midst of their dwelling. Language, due to its poetic nature as the most concealed and therefore most far-reaching form, is the ardent generative revealing of Heimat.]

Heidegger's concern for origins, hidden truths and guiding life principles is part of his wider philosophical project, which seeks to locate man and the complexities of human experience in the world.[52] This concern with roots and disclosure deeply colours Heidegger's approach to literature and language, with the result that in this essay and elsewhere, as Kai Hammermeister and Michael Inwood have both shown, he prioritizes literature that strives to recreate the lost purity of a community's physical and linguistic roots.[53] For Heidegger, the truly literary act is one of melancholy remembrance and prophetic pronouncement at the same time, and literary endeavour is valued in terms of its ability to recreate and suggest the longed-for return of a lost and highly idealized physical and Ur-linguistic community. With this, his concept of Heimat maps onto Assmann's 'places of commemoration': the emphasis in this memory narrative is on the abyss to be bridged by literary language that places

---

[51] Martin Heidegger, 'Sprache und Heimat', in Martin Heidegger, *Gesamtausgabe*, vol. 13 (Klostermann: Frankfurt a.M., 1983), pp. 155–80, p. 180.
[52] For more on this, see Ben Morgan, *On Becoming God: Late Medieval Mysticism and the Modern Western Self* (New York: Fordham U. P., 2013).
[53] Kai Hammermeister, 'Heimat in Heidegger and Gadamer', *Philosophy and Literature* (2000), 24.2, 312–26; Michael Inwood, *Heidegger: A Very Short Introduction* (Oxford: Oxford U. P., 1997).

whoever engages with it impossibly at the root of what has been lost. The aura of places directly drives the creative individual in his or her extended effort to provide access to humanity's presence through the past.

While Bloch's conception of Heimat as a guiding personal and socio-philosophical ideal is tied to an optimistic orientation towards a consciously self-determined future, Heidegger's notion of cultural value rests on the rootedness of art and language in a necessarily elusive place of past perfection. Located at either end of the political spectrum, the philosophers overlap, however, in their conception of Heimat as a utopian construct that is infused with intellectual, emotional and earthly elements, but which is above all a projection, arising from a basic human desire for belonging, that is first and foremost sustained in a parallel literary world. Constructing or otherwise facilitating the emergence of a Heimat for its people amounts to creating a place of memory that will rely on a specific style of narrative that is comfortable with instability and multiple interpretations. Fashioning the world of the literary text to open up these alternatives, however briefly, within our own time therefore requires a mode of authorship that is as open to uncovering dystopias as it might seek to produce a utopia or inhabit a heterotopia, and which is unfazed by temporal and spatial clashes with the lived socio-political world around us. Unlike the commemorative or the celebratory modes, the utopian mode is invoked not primarily to emulate or return to past models or events, but rather to uncover new, parallel paths through human history that allow us to think and act differently in the now. The divergent and contradictory nature of these paths in turn renders the single location of an originating author in one historical context an impossibility. The utopian mode is only possible as a form of equally weighted dialogue that by necessity disperses authority across the text and relativizes any one authorial stance.

The Satirical Mode: Against Celebration

In 1982, it was the Austrian writer Thomas Bernhard's turn ritually to engage with narratives of German cultural achievement. He did so by, once again, invoking the popular public reception of Goethe coupled with humorous speculation around Goethe's own deliberate self-celebrification – this time on the 150th anniversary of his death. As a sign of the times, the national celebrations now focused to a much lesser extent on ceremonial speeches, with organizers preferring themed events, exhibitions, and other forms of public education that stressed democratic participation and interaction.[54] Thus the Suhrkamp

---

[54] An overview and some analysis of the events organised can be found in *Jahrbuch für internationale Germanistik*, XV/2 (1983).

publishing house joined forces with the Frankfurt Goethe University to run a national competition to find Germany's five favourite Goethe poems. In so doing, the university also conducted anthropological research on the 25,000 individual entries. The extent of the Goethe industry that was by now a fixed part of the German cultural landscape is evident not just in the overwhelming number of entries from sectors of the population that, as one newspaper report put it, ranged from 'Putzfrau zum Professor' (cleaner to professor), but also in the Goethe-themed prizes: an Italian journey (mimicking Goethe's Grand Tour), as well as trips to Weimar and New York, with the latter entailing meeting Andy Warhol to have a copy of his Goethe portrait signed in person. Remaining within Germany, the announcement of the winning poems as well as the lucky winners took place in the Frankfurt Playhouse, attended by multiple Suhrkamp literati. Thomas Bernhard dutifully also attended, and photographs of the author appeared in newspaper reports documenting the occasion.[55]

Bernhard's personal appearance as part of a 'celebrity' clique of authors operating within a canonical tradition, however, was surely overshadowed by his written authorial contribution to the occasion, which took the form of a short prose text, 'Goethe schtirbt' (Goethe corks it). It had appeared in *Die Zeit* two days before, on 19 March 1982. Here, Bernhard took a radically different approach to both Thomas Mann in 1932 and 1949 and his Suhrkamp colleagues in the Frankfurt theatre – instead of celebrating the author's immortal literary corpus, he focused on the author's dying body, and instead of offering an explanation of how the insights provided by his works that would become the root of all subsequent German literature arose from Goethe's balanced personality (a retrospective definition of his value through his works), he depicted a wilful, unreasonable and self-obsessed old man who took pleasure in the problems he would cause his successors and whose starting point is therefore his own assumed greatness that must be projected out into the world. Goethe's overstated 'genius' authorship remains future-focused right to the end, with the personal interactions it facilitates beyond his death the final yardstick by which the poet measures his achievements whilst still alive. Thus, Goethe speaks triumphantly to his chief librarian, Riemer, who in turn reports Goethe's words to the story's anonymous narrator:

> Das Nationaltheater habe er, Goethe, ruiniert, so Riemer, soll Goethe gesagt haben, überhaupt habe er, Goethe, das deutsche

---

[55] As can be found in, for example, the media cuttings collection in Marbach library.

Theater zugrunde gerichtet, aber darauf kommen die Leute erst in frühestens zweihundert Jahren. *Was ich dichtete, ist das Größte gewesen, zweifellos, aber auch das, mit welchem ich die deutsche Literatur für ein paar Jahrhunderte gelähmt habe. Ich war, mein Lieber,* soll Goethe zu Riemer gesagt haben, *ein Lähmer der deutschen Literatur.* Meinem *Faust* sind sie alle auf den Leim gegangen. Am Ende ist alles, so groß es ist, nur *eine Auslassung* meiner innersten Gefühle gewesen, von allem ein Teil, so Riemer berichtend, aber in keinem war ich das Allerhöchste. [. . .] *so habe ich die Deutschen, die dafür wie keine andern geeignet sind, hinters Licht geführt. Aber auf was für einem Niveau!* soll er ausgerufen haben, der Genius.[56]

[He, Goethe, had ruined the national theatre, said Goethe, according to Riemer; he, Goethe, had absolutely destroyed German theatre, but people wouldn't realise that for at least another two hundred years. *What I wrote is the greatest, without a doubt, but it's also what I've used to paralyze German literature for a few centuries. I was, my dear,* Goethe is supposed to have said to Riemer, *a paralyzer of German literature.* My *Faust* has fooled them all. In the end everything, however great it is, is just *an outpouring* of my innermost feelings, mastering everything in part, so Riemer reports, but the absolute master of nothing . . . *this is how I tricked the Germans, who lend themselves to this like no other people, but at what a level!* he is said to have exclaimed, the genius.]

Goethe's supreme confidence in the value of his literary work is presented here as a spoof on Carlyle's awestruck description of the great poet. It is also a comical reflection on the situation of the authors currently gathered under Unseld's leadership to celebrate Goethe's legacy in the Frankfurt Playhouse. Following the fictional Goethe's prediction, they have at least another fifty years to go before they will start to realize they owe 'the genius' not a debt of gratitude but a series of profound grievances. In actual fact, throughout the 1960s and 1970s a series of Goethe-'Verrisse', or spoofs, had begun to appear that showed authors increasingly distancing themselves from his legacy. Nor indeed was a disrespectful attitude to Goethe confined to the post-war period: in 1939 Thomas Mann had already depicted Goethe as a tyrant who has a paralyzing effect on the intellectual and emotional development of the people around him in his novel, *Lotte in Weimar*, while as early as 1908 Egon Friedell and Alfred Polgar's *Goethe: Groteske*

---

[56] Thomas Bernhard, 'Goethe schtirbt', in *Goethe schtirbt: Erzählungen* (Berlin: Suhrkamp, 2010), pp. 7–29, pp. 19–20.

in zwei Bildern, a satire on the positivist cult of the author propagated by teachers at schools, had enjoyed almost cult status and played 202 times in the Fledermaus Cabaret in Vienna.[57] Whilst poking fun at the immediate celebratory context of the Suhrkamp gathering, Bernhard's piece continues this satirical tradition. For although there is no doubt that the real-life Goethe did work hard on ensuring his fame during his lifetime and his legacy after his death, Bernhard's presentation of the poet takes such self-confidence to the extreme.[58] Goethe not only seems to know some things for sure that he could only have supposed during his lifetime – how German literature and theatre will stagnate in the later nineteenth century, for example – but also actively starts engaging with the later traditions that will, retrospectively, be traced back to him. In the spirit of Goethe's actual practice of world authorship discussed in the previous chapter, he sets about orchestrating the personal meetings that are needed for his writing to carry the kind of literary exchange and worldly relevance that he has set as his own yardstick.

Much of the story therefore revolves around his petulant wish to see Ludwig Wittgenstein on 22 March 1832, whom he describes as 'mein philosophischer Sohn sozusagen'[59] (my philosophical son, as it were) and whose work he admires at length, to the point of reconsidering the legacy of his own. His dearest wish is to sit together with Wittgenstein and discuss 'Das Zweifelnde und das Nichtzweifelnde': '*Wir werden das Thema organisieren*, so Goethe immer, *und es angehen und zerstören*'[60] (Doubting and Not-doubting: *We will set out the theme*, so Goethe continued, *take it on and destroy it*). Kräuter, Goethe's secretary, is sent off to fetch Wittgenstein from Cambridge, but unfortunately the great philosopher passes away the day before Kräuter arrives and eight days before Goethe himself will expire. Yet in fact Wittgenstein was not even born until 1889. Similarly, Goethe wishes for two other German

---

[57] Martin Walser's *In Goethe's Hand: Szenen aus dem 19. Jahrhundert* can be read in this satirical vein. On the phenomenon in both the GDR and the FRG, see Hans-Dietrich Dahnke, 'Humanität und Geschichtsperspektive: Zu den Goethe-Ehrungen 1932, 1949, 1982', in *Weimarer Beiträge*, 28/10 (1982), 66–89. See also Adalbert Wichert, *Goethefeiern: Ein Rückblick auf 150 Jahre Dichterverehrung* (Augsburg: Katholische Akademie Augsburg, 1983). On Friedell and Polgar's satire, see Roland Innerhofer, 'Die Polfried AG: Satirisches Kabarett von Egon Friedell und Alfred Polgar', in Wendelin Schmidt-Dengler, Johann Sonnleitner & Klaus Zeyringer, eds, *Komik in der österreichischen Literatur* (Berlin: Erich Schmidt, 1996), pp. 179–88.
[58] On Goethe's deliberate management of his own legacy, see Piper, *Dreaming in Books: The Making of the Bibliographic Imagination in the Romantic Age* (Chicago: U. of Chicago P., 2009).
[59] Bernhard, *Goethe schtirbt*, p. 15.
[60] Bernhard, *Goethe schtirbt*, p. 21.

intellectuals to join their meeting, Adalbert Stifter and Arthur Schopenhauer. These too are listed as already dead, when in fact they died in 1868 and 1860 respectively. When ruminating on how he first became familiar with Wittgenstein's work, Goethe's account of events takes an even more unlikely turn: '*Er wisse nicht mehr, was oder wer ihn auf oder zu Wittgenstein gebracht habe. Ein kleines Büchlein mit rotem Umschlag, aus der Bibliothek Suhrkamp*, sagte Goethe zu Riemer einmal, *vielleicht, ich kann es nicht mehr sagen. Aber es war meine Rettung*'[61] (*He no longer knew what or whom had brought him to Wittgenstein. A slim book with a red cover, from the Suhrkamp library*, Goethe once said to Riemer, *maybe, I don't know any more. But it was my salvation*). The Suhrkamp Verlag was not founded until 1950, but it was certainly well known for its rainbow-coloured paperback series; Bernhard's *Wittgensteins Neffe* (Wittgensteins Nephew) was published with Suhrkamp in 1982 with a blue cover, while 'Goethe schtirbt' also eventually found its way into a slim red volume published by that prominent post-war address in 2010.[62]

Explicitly turned by Bernhard into an author who is impossibly aware of his posthumous intellectual importance, the power of Goethe's personality is such that the three acolytes who are present at his deathbed, Riemer, Kräuter and Bernhard's anonymous narrator, feel obliged to falsify the great author's final words when he begins to waver in his self-belief. After a melancholic invocation of Wittgenstein's 'das Zweifelnde und das Nichtzweifelnde', Goethe sighs 'Mehr nicht!' (nothing more) – a late recognition, it would appear, that the Austrian philosopher's work has not just continued but surpassed his own and leaves nothing more to be said. The narrative concludes: 'Wir, Riemer, Kräuter und ich einigten uns darauf, der Welt mitzuteilen, Goethe habe *Mehr Licht* gesagt als Letztes und nicht *Mehr nicht!* An dieser Lüge als Verfälschung leide ich, nachdem Riemer und Kräuter längst daran gestorben sind, noch heute'[63] (We, Riemer, Kräuter and I agreed to tell the world, Goethe's last words were 'More light!' and not 'Nothing more!' This lie still haunts me today, long after Riemer and Kräuter's died of it).[64]

---

[61] Bernhard, *Goethe schtirbt*, p. 21.
[62] Bernhard, *Goethe schtirbt*. It was also published in book form in volume 14 of Bernhard's (dark red) collected works: *Erzählungen / Kurzprosa*, ed. Hans Hoeller, Martin Huber and Martin Mittermayer (Frankfurt a.M.: Suhrkamp, 2003).
[63] Bernhard, *Goethe schtirbt*, p. 29.
[64] This joke also goes back to the beginning of the twentieth century, where there are various versions in circulation about how he actually wanted more milk in his coffee. See Innerhofer, 'Die Polfried AG', pp. 180–1.

The story's preposterous end completes the circle back to Thomas Bernhard and the other authors and members of the public sitting in the Frankfurt Playhouse 150 years later. The fictional Goethe's anachronistic dying reference to the text that has 'saved him' from his overblown sense of cultural importance points not only to Wittgenstein as the real 'great' philosopher, but also to Thomas Bernhard, whose narrative is (or at least, will be, once the 1982 festivities are over) enclosed in the red Suhrkamp binding and is now 'telling the truth' about Goethe for posterity. Forced to think critically about hagiographic literary traditions, Bernhard's readers are given at least two ways and two different contexts in which to consider authors' literary and social value.

Firstly, the text brings to a point the extent to which the extreme celebration of Goethe by the subsequent literary industry has turned the author into a quasi-demonic genius, the ridiculous dimensions of which even the self-confident Goethe would not have seen fit to invoke, and which, in Bernhard's account of events, he explicitly rejects on his deathbed. As readers of Bernhard's posthumous collection of essays *Meine Preise* will know (2009, My Prizes), Bernhard repeatedly presents the disjuncture between the ostentatious public celebrations of culture and the way authors are actually valued as particularly symptomatic of wider failings in Austrian cultural politics. This lends his whole intervention in Frankfurt a particularly Austrian flavour, as well as underscoring the sense that broader late twentieth-century public discourse on culture is self-serving and contemptible.[65] Yet both he and Goethe somehow stand above all this, even as they directly profit from it.

Secondly, however, for close fans of Bernhard's writing, the story's end also points back to the very short passage, 'Behauptung' (assertion) in his 1978 *Der Stimmenimitator* (*The Ventriloquist*). This fictional *fait divers* also deals with Goethe's death. Revealing the extent to which the literary industry actively ensures its own survival in Bourdieu's sense, as well as a normative understanding of culture à la Foucault, the text recounts how an anonymous man from Augsburg is not only delivered to a lunatic asylum on account of his repeated claims that Goethe died saying 'mehr nicht!' rather than 'mehr Licht!' The fictional doctor who supported this decision is awarded the 'Goetheplakette der Stadt Frankfurt' (the Frankfurt Goethe plaque), a fact we are told the narrator

---

[65] Thomas Bernhard, *Meine Preise* (Frankfurt a.M: Suhrkamp, 2009). See also Rebecca Braun, 'Embodying Achievement: Thomas Bernhard, Elfriede Jelinek, and Authorship as a Competitive Sport', in *Austrian Studies* (2014), 22, special issue on 'Elfriede Jelinek in the Arena', ed. A. Fiddler & K. Jürs-Munby, 121–38.

has reliably gleaned from another major player in the literary field, the *Frankfurter Allgemeine Zeitung* broadsheet.⁶⁶ Here, then, Bernhard's satire is aimed at multiple, specifically German institutions, and champions the cause of real engagement with actual writers against that of the various self-serving institutions seeking to patrol and limit their effects.

Taken together, the two pieces pitch the independently-minded Bernhard against a self-affirming literary industry that the author is determined to reveal as deliberately, indeed grotesquely, de-humanizing in its attempts first to construct immortal literary greatness and then to maintain this myth through ritualized celebrations that demean rather than help contemporary writers. Bernhard's Austrian provenance surely shapes the sharpness of his criticism.⁶⁷ Setting it in a broader context and looking back to the beginning of this chapter, however, we can also see how the celebratory mode of authorship is both profoundly questioned within the space of the literary text and perpetuated by it. Individual acts of socio-political engagement draw their justification from the sense that the writer must actively embody his or her literary tradition and set it in dialogue with other orders and experiences. Thomas Mann found himself routinely asked to perform representative German authorship, and his experience of partaking in an influential cultural elite that facilitated exchange across nations must underpin his wholesale appropriation of the Romantic tradition of genius. Thomas Bernhard writes his authorial profile on the other side of the metaphorical coin. Deeply suspicious of social processes and media-driven acts of public celebration, he repeatedly calls the whole literary industry into question. Like both Mann and Goethe, however, he is also acutely aware of his own reputation and how this unfolds alongside the way he literally and metaphorically embodies authorship. By linking a satire on Goethe's legacy to both his own textual and actual performance of authorship in the context of the 1982 ritual celebrations, Bernhard exemplifies the key tension at the heart of the satirical mode of authorship. He refocuses attention on – and, in this sense, celebrates – himself as a socially critical and intellectually original literary author, even as he ridicules the cultural landscape that produces an over-determined Goethe in the first place. Indeed, the satire published in *Die Zeit* provoked heated readers' letters to the paper, and this of course

---

⁶⁶ Thomas Bernhard, 'Behauptung', in *Der Stimmenimitator* (Frankfurt a.M: Suhrkamp, 1978), p. 58.
⁶⁷ For extensive discussion of this broader context, see Manfred Mittermeyer, *Thomas Bernhard: Eine Biografie* (Vienna: Residenz, 2015).

further enhanced Bernhard's image for posterity as a 'great' polemical author.[68]

The satirical mode of authorship that Bernhard so clearly employs in this text can thus be seen as a direct response to the celebratory mode that remains normative across the late twentieth-century literary industry. Where the celebratory mode seeks to model an attitude of respect and shared heritage across diverse publics by focusing primarily on exemplary achievement and facilitating the attendant processes of celebrating the successful person, the satirical mode questions these very values and processes by exaggerating their reach. In this sense, in a simplifying matrix of all four modes, the satirical pairs as a corrective of sorts to the celebratory mode, just as we saw the utopian mode qualifying the purview of the commemorative mode, to move from a retrospective, re-creative focus to that of a parallel present or alternative futures. As the rest of this study will go on to show, however, the modes of authorship are not designed to be neat, mutually-exclusive categories, and all four are moderated by each other, often in apparently contradictory or counter-intuitive ways. Capturing different flavours of attitude that can accompany the basic underlying act of authoring a text on the part of both individuals and the material and physical circumstances in which this act is embedded, they are destined to have distinctly fuzzy boundaries and to interact with one another in different ways at different times.

The Four Modes in Flux: Filmic Relocations of the Gruppe 47 in the Provincial German Landscape

When the Gruppe 47 stopped meeting after 1967, the comparative consensus around the normative cultural Heimat it had managed to establish over a twenty-year period led to a series of written and visual reconstructions of the group's cultural importance. It was, in effect, repeatedly cast as a foundational model of socially critical authorship of its own, a central reference point for everything that would come next in the German literary landscape, determining what attitudes should be taken in respect of the German cultural Heimat and strongly indicating how individual authors should seek to locate themselves within it. This basic model – effectively a sort of collective public intellectual – was one whereby peers collectively supported one another in the face of a difficult past with a view to effecting both literary and social change for the

---

[68] The letters sent in to the newspaper are held in the Thomas Bernhard archive in Gmunden and are referred to in the editorial commentary in vol 14 of Bernhard's collected works: *Erzählungen / Kurzprosa*, ed. Hans Höller, Martin Huber & Manfred Mittermayer (Frankfurt am Main: Suhrkamp, 2003), pp. 571–2.

future through the exemplary power of their own hard work. Analysing how some of these reconstructions change over the latter part of the twentieth century and into the twenty-first allows us to see the different modes of authorship in action, providing a far more differentiated picture of the ongoing reception of this collective public intellectual model of authorship than a straightforward thematic or stylistic approach to the literary and political work of these authors would provide alone.

The reconstructions took the form of anniversary TV documentaries, touring library and museum exhibitions, retrospective journalistic analysis and surveys of public opinion, and well-advertised scholarly volumes, all of which continued throughout the twentieth century and into the twenty-first. In September 1987, for example, the Literary Toucan Circle, a long-standing venue for literary encounters in Munich, organized a commemorative event for the Gruppe 47 showing some of the old TV documentaries discussed below.[69] Newspaper reports reveal that the event was completely sold out. Bad Münstereifel staged a retrospective exhibition and public talk in August 1987. In Berlin, the acquisition of Richter's Gruppe 47 archive by the West Berlin Academy of Arts in 1985/86 caused extensive press reporting, while the high-profile exhibition on the group that resulted from this acquisition and ran for six weeks across October–December 1988 was granted lengthy review articles across the print media. An earlier, different exhibition had also been assembled in Nürnberg.[70] Both of these exhibitions were mounted in various locations across Germany, with the one from the Berlin Academy of Arts forming one of the main attractions at the 1997 programme of events organized by the villages of Füssen & Schwangau. Along with Füssen & Schwangau, the Berlin Literary Colloquium organized a series of well-publicized events in 1997 to commemorate the group's fiftieth anniversary.[71]

The primarily commemorative TV documentaries created between 1964 and 2007, however, provide a particularly rich seam for analysing authors' collective cultural significance in the late twentieth century through the lens of the changing mix of modes of authorship evident within their own compositional structures. At least eight programmes

---

[69] See www.tukan-kreis.de (last accessed 25 November 2016).
[70] As captured in the pamphlet by Skott Grunau, 'Gruppe 47. Nachkriegsliteratur zwischen Poesie und Politik', (Amt für kulturelle Freizeitgestaltung der Stadt Nürnberg, 'Kooperation Freizeit und Schule', July 1987).
[71] Information on all the events detailed in this paragraph was found in the extensive holdings of the Hans Werner Richter archive in the Berlin Akadamie der Küste, notably HWR-A 345 (all sub-folders) and HWR-A 1333.

have been made about the group during this time period.⁷² The tendency, common also to all of the other media outlined above, to intermingle state-sponsored cultural representations of the specifically post-war German Heimat with celebratory documentary representation of the Gruppe 47 lends itself to conservative, hagiographic programming in the vein of the 1950s Heimat films.⁷³ The resulting representations certainly seem a far cry from the group's founding spirit of openness and ascribe it a normative cultural value far different to the initial utopian intentions of Hans Werner Richter. In the TV documentaries, this can be observed in both of the programmes shot in the 1970s and 1980s: Gisela Reich and Barbara Bronnen's *Dichter und Richter: Die Gruppe 47, vorläufiges Schlußbild nach 30 Jahren* (1978, Richter and his Writers: The Group 47, Preliminary Reckoning after 30 Years), and Susanne Müller-Hanpft and Martin Bosboom's self-fulfillingly entitled documentary from 1987 *Wie sie wurden, was sie sind. Gruppe 47: eine Schriftstellergeneration schreibt Geschichte* (How they Became what they Are. The Group 47: A Generation of Authors Write History). Mixing commemorative and celebratory modes, both documentaries show a prime concern with recreating the physical and socio-political surroundings in which the group existed and show the group as both a historical product of and a continuing element within these landscapes. Both particularly relish in physically locating the historic group within contemporary rural Germany. They effectively make of the group a heterotopia. This heterotopia is conveyed through a mixture of the celebratory and commemorative modes. In their combined hagiographic determination to remember what was, these modes are diametrically opposed to the utopian mode in which key players actually considered themselves to be acting, as per Richter's almanac quoted above.

The opening scenes of the 1978 documentary give a good sense of this. The camera pans over idyllic autumnal scenes and focuses on a boyish Clemens Eich walking through a wooded setting, reading his father's famous poem 'Inventur' (Inventory), and explaining his emotional attachment to this widely known piece of post-war literature. Following an interview with Hans Werner Richter who remembers the fate of the returning soldier immediately after the war – 'dann war er

---

[72] I analyse these at length in '1967-2007: The Gruppe 47 as a Cultural Heimat', *German Quarterly* (2010), 83.2, 212–29. What follows in this section summarises some of the material in that article and links it to my current concerns.

[73] On filmic conventions in the 1950s Heimat films, see Ben Morgan, 'Understanding the Cultural Impact of Popular Film', in Rebecca Braun & Lyn Marven, eds, *Cultural Impact in the German Context: Studies in Transmission, Reception, and Influence* (Rochester, NY: Camden House, 2010), pp. 58–77.

eigentlich heimatlos' (then he actually had no Heimat) – the film returns to an atmospheric reading of Wolfdietrich Schnurre's equally influential poem, 'Das Begräbnis Gottes' (God's Funeral). Here the camera pans through a tranquil lakeshore landscape in the Allgäu and intermittently settles on Schnurre symbolically pacing through an autumnal graveyard and discussing the Gruppe 47 with one of the producers. Not only does the film visually assert a clear physical Heimat for the Gruppe 47 in these idyllic scenes, as literature by famous Gruppe 47 writers is projected onto the contemporary rural landscape. The two poems that are read out are also presented as an important intellectual root for later generations, whether this is manifested through family connections (a son is shown emotionally identifying with his father) or implied by Schnurre's attempt to explain the legacy of his own poem thirty years on in a graveyard. In both cases, the literature is celebrated, and the 'obskure Orte', the group's 'Lieblingsorte, irgendwo in der Provinz' (obscure places, favourite places somewhere out in the sticks), are directly invoked by both the voice-over and the directors' atmospheric shots as really-existing, quiet, reflective places where this literary heritage can best be brought back to life for contemporary viewers.

In fact, the film orientates itself entirely towards a telling quotation taken from Heinrich Böll's 1963/64 Frankfurt lecture series and repeated mid-way through the documentary: 'Unsere Literatur hat keine Orte. Die ungeheure, oft mühselige Anstrengung der Nachkriegsliteratur hat ja darin bestanden, Orte und Nachbarschaften wieder zu finden'[74] (Our literature has no places. The incredible, often wearisome task of postwar literature has been precisely about trying to bring back places and neighbourhoods). Where Böll's original quotation may well have been made in the utopian mode, pointing to the power of literature to carry alternative worlds with real force for the existing one, in this film the emphasis is very much on the final words of the quotation – finding those real places where literature happened, and celebrating / commemorating them accordingly. In both the 1978 and the 1988 documentaries, these places of and for literature are not so much found as entirely invented as a heterotopia through a mix of careful scene-setting and amalgamation of archival and contemporary material. The Gruppe 47 is repackaged by its later analysts in terms of a shared physical and cultural heritage that meaningfully persists into the present. As many critical reviewers commented in 1978, negative views of the group were omitted, and the programme ends on a note of high

---

[74] Heinrich Böll, *Frankfurter Vorlesungen* (Cologne: Kiepenheuer & Witsch, 1966), p. 49.

Four Modes of Authorship   61

pathos as an elderly Richter walks to the end of a wooden pier and is left looking out over the lake and its seeming infinity of gently lapping water. Despite its obvious hagiographic bias, this reductionist packaging of the group – as the utopian ideal of one visionary man that emerged from and merges back into the German provinces – has persisted into the twenty-first century, as demonstrated by the fact that the final 1978 clip of Richter was reproduced, uncommented, as a large photo in leading newspaper review articles on the occasion of the group's sixtieth anniversary in 2007.[75]

Elements of the original utopian mode are thus retained, but they are significantly overlaid by the celebratory and commemorative gestures with which this heterotopia is conveyed. Publicly remembering the group has become bound up with a creative process of artfully locating it in the physical, political and cultural landscape and visually idealizing it in a manner not dissimilar to filmic constructions of the German Heimat in the restoration period of the 1950s. This approach continues in the films shot in the 1980s and 1990s. Given the collective identification of core group members with the historically inflicted uprootedness of the 'Heimkehrer' (returning soldier), the devastation of all physical centres and the widely perceived utter discontinuity of the German cultural tradition after Auschwitz, such unreconstructed grounding of the group as itself a heterotopian site of commemoration that comes to stand for the continuity of German culture in both restoration Germany and the later West German provinces may well seem inappropriate. Indeed, later reactions to it bring to the fore a fundamental shift in retrospective reconstructions that trace the group's impact on the German cultural landscape. For the idea that the group is one of the clearest manifestations of West Germany's stolid and un-self-critical provincialism gains ever greater expression in the post-unification era. Following on from the highly public arguments about authors' respective accommodation with the West and East German states in the early 1990s and the many sensationalist media airings of left-wing intellectuals' past misdeeds that dominated much of the early 2000s, Andreas Ammer's 2007 documentary, *Vom Glanz und Vergehen der Gruppe 47* (On the Glory and the Passing of the Group 47), sweeps away all outwardly hagiographic filmic techniques and aims to destabilize the foundations of received wisdom about the group. With this, their normative status as a foundational model of authorship for the FRG is also called severely into question.

Breaking with tradition, all contemporary footage is shot indoors, implying an anonymous, metropolitan environment, and Ammer's

---

[75] For example, in Jörg Magenau, 'Freunde fürs Lesen', *die tageszeitung*, 13 Oct 2007, p. 19.

interviewees, ranging from the old guard of Grass, Walser and Jens, through the slightly younger selection of authors and critics like Jürgen Becker, Michael Krüger, Joachim Kaiser and Gabriele Wohmann, to contemporary commentators such as Heinz Ludwig Arnold and Maxim Biller, are self-consciously filmed on a dizzying array of chairs that shift location as often as the director interrupts the interviewees' memories with his cuts and self-reflexive filming. This is clearly intended as a form of demythologization of Richter's famous 'hot seat', the chair from which author hopefuls read from their work to their assembled peers at the group's meetings, but where they sat without the right to reply to any of the criticisms that might then be made. In presenting the physical act of sitting down and speaking to an audience about literature as a highly mediated act, the film draws critical attention to the celebrificatory processes that underpinned Richter's original model of shaping a so-called democratic literary sector. The way people sat on chairs could determine literary careers in post-war Germany, and this mechanism for promoting new writing clearly favoured some types of authors over others, with a significant number of authors literally silenced while others went on to become media stars.

This physical debunking of the standard group trope of the hot seat is mirrored in the soundtrack, which accompanies archival footage of the post-war devastation with easy finger-picking guitar music. Images representing Germany's terrible destruction of its own physical and cultural landscape are presented as familiar, part of the accepted German heritage, whereas discussion of the group's origins in and significance for the German Heimat is invested with a looming sense of sinister secrets to be unveiled, as slower beats and electronic sounds take over. Likewise, counter-voices are prominently placed against the group's representatives. Thus Gabriele Wohmann is both interviewed at length in 2007 and portrayed in 1960s archive material that follows the attractive young author as she poses moodily in an urban environment accompanied by mournful ballads. Discussion of the particularly male nature of the group's criticism and the way in which her readings were torn apart leads into a stylized framing of the next, alleged victim of the group, the Jewish poet Paul Celan. A soundtrack of Celan reading 'Todesfuge' (Death Fugue), the poem that was famously ridiculed at the 1952 Gruppe 47 meeting, is accompanied by the camera panning through empty inns and further embellished by tinged green footage of Celan reading the poem 'Fadensonnen' (Threadsuns) set to a slow, bass-heavy but tuneful soundtrack. It is as if the poet re-emerges from his watery bed to speak out in turn against the Gruppe 47. This then blends into a theory of latent anti-Semitism within the very origins of the group, which is developed at length by the academic Klaus Briegleb.[76] Heavily influenced by Briegleb, the film casts in a sinister light the entire story of *Der Ruf*, Richter and Andersch's literary political journal that was hitherto narrated in almost every post-1967 account of the group as a key aspect of its laudable political beginnings. Here, its genesis is set against a soundtrack of eerie electronic tones and threatening beats that indicates there are secrets being covered up. With this, we have moved from the group as a heterotopia, to something approaching a dystopia.

The attack on earlier narratives about the group is clear. Where previously the commemorative and celebratory modes were overlaid on one another and the original utopian mode in an uncritical manner that aimed only to further cement the group's foundational cultural status, now this status as a place of memory is entirely flipped around. The group becomes the traumatic rupture that stopped the development of an alternative, more ethically secure dominant model of authorship within the fledgling post-war cultural Heimat. Not just the fate of how a few authors are valued is at stake here, but the wider public re-appraisal of the post-war cultural Heimat in which contemporary culture is rooted. The same sense of ethical revision also informed media reporting on Andersch's, Jens' and Grass's troublesome pasts in the late 1990s and early 2000s. But while much of this reassessment of individual writers relied on sensational allegation and speculation, the television documentary picks up on the subtle discourse of place which, as I have been arguing, informs all management of the Gruppe 47's public image, and inverts it. Maintaining the apparently symbiotic link between the group and the 'obscure places' (in the words of the 1978 documentary) where it convened, the film moves from a critical view of the group to a critical view of its physical surroundings. Accordingly, the land itself falls under suspicion in the best anti-Heimat, dystopian film vein. Footage from the 1972 documentary evoking the eerily abandoned salon in Altenbeuern and various other empty country inns is replayed alongside a voice-over that specifically questions the group's seemingly easy existence within the German provinces. Allegations about the group's unpleasant, hidden past lead to it effectively being relocated in a by now markedly 'unheimliche' Heimat in which 'obscure places' have become threatening bolt holes for history's criminals:

> Für das Unterfangen, Literatur in einem Land zu machen, das gerade die Welt mit einem Vernichtungskrieg überzogen hatte, wählte Richter gern obskure Orte, Landgasthöfe, die wie aus der

---

[76] Klaus Briegleb, *Mißachtung und Tabu: Eine Streitschrift zur Frage "Wie antisemitisch war die Gruppe 47?"* (Berlin: Philo, 2003).

64   Authors and the World

Welt gefallen schienen; gutbürgerliche Kulisse für unerhörte Ereignisse.

[For his project of making literature in a country that had just subjected the world to a war of total destruction, Richter liked to choose obscure places, country inns that seemed to hail from another time and place entirely; hearty bourgeois backdrops for unheard-of events.]

Above all, this film shows a reaction to the group that is formulated entirely within the shifting terms of the Heimat discourse and enacts, within the commemorative mode, the kind of 'memory contest' in respect of place that Anne Fuchs has explored in relation to, amongst other things, the post-war reconstruction of the house of Goethe's birth in Frankfurt.[77] To parallel the cinematic Heimat genre, after the restorative, celebratory mode comes the critical, investigative one with its charge of unreconstructed chauvinism. This was witnessed in the anti-Heimat films of the 1970s and 1980s and it occurs here through the different manipulations of footage used to convey and discredit the group's physical and cultural surroundings. The 2007 inversion of an underlying Heimat discourse that linked the group to an evolving narrative about German national identity confirms the group's conversion into a Heideggerian Heimat for post-war Germany, meant now in its most controversial sense. Not only has the group become the lost terrain, whether positively or negatively connoted, that can only be fully glimpsed after its passing and within the re-creative process of (filmic) poetry, it has, like Heidegger himself, also become hopelessly entangled with troublesome past right-wing sympathies.[78] For many cultural commentators today, the Gruppe 47 shows clear parallels to a chauvinist philosophy of cultural value that builds on elitist obfuscation and gendered, racial exclusion, or, as the Jewish author, Maxim Biller, polemically declares:

Die Gruppe 47 war ein Kleinbürger-Stammtisch, eine Art entnazifizierte Reichsschrifttumskammer, eine Vereinigung ehemaliger Nazi-Soldaten und Hjler, von denen kein einziger die

---

[77] Anne Fuchs, *After the Dresden Bombing: Pathways of Memory, 1945 to the Present* (Basingstoke: Palgrave MacMillan, 2012), pp. 77–9. See also Anne Fuchs, Mary Cosgrove, Georg Grote, eds, *German Memory Contests: The Search for Identity of Literature, Film, and Discourse since 1990* (Rochester, NY: Camden House, 2006).

[78] For a sense of the extent to which Heidegger's philosophy is compromised by his support of National Socialism, see Andrew Bowie, *Introduction to German Philosophy: From Kant to Habermas* (Cambridge: Polity, 2003).

Kraft gehabt hätte, zuzugeben, daß er für Hitler getötet und oder zumindest gehaßt hat. Diese Söhne waren genauso verlogen, apodiktisch und kleinbürgerlich-ängstlich wie ihre Väter, und sie sprachen über Literatur wie jene über das Wirtschaftswunder: stolz, ironielos und ohne Selbstzweifel.[79]

[The Group 47 was a petit-bourgeois gathering in the pub, a kind of de-Nazified Reich Writers' Bureau, an alliance between former Nazi soldiers and Hitler Youth, of whom not one would have had the strength to admit that he killed, or at the very least hated, for Hitler. These sons were just as mendacious, apodictic, and riddled with petty-minded fears as their fathers, and they spoke about literature just like their fathers did about the economic miracle: proudly, without irony and never calling themselves into question.]

If the earlier films intermingle celebratory and commemorative modes in both the forms of authorship they present as their subject matter and in the uncritical style of their own art that is designed to stress continuity, the later one deliberately seeks to destabilize the dominant narrative about the group as the founder of a positive contemporary German cultural Heimat. Ammer's filming, combined with Biller's polemical comments and Wohmann's dismissal of the self-importance of writers like Grass who profited the most from Richter's 'hot seat', serve to recreate the intangible public space occupied by the group as a form of historic dystopia that really did exist. This harsh – and in many ways quite unfair – judgement from the future on the attempt of writers to find a place for literature that would both emanate from recent political experiences and reflect critically on them could be understood as the abject failure of their utopian mode as it rubbed up against the practicalities of the chief political and economic mediators within the post-war literature network: the compromised nature of the late twentieth-century media and publishing industries, to be explored in depth in chapter four. Despite Richter's and Andersch's attempts to create a genuine place of literary and political work-in-progress that could offer an alternative to the allure of the simple celebration of high art for its own sake, a problematic form of authorial celebrification and a selective approach to commemoration have become what the group is increasingly most remembered for. Accordingly, the film's main

---

[79] Survey response by Biller, reproduced in Joachim Leser and Georg Guntermann, eds, *Brauchen wir eine neue Gruppe 47? 55 Fragebogen zur deutschen Literatur* (Bonn: Nenzel, 1995), p. 58.

concerns appear to be demythologization of the post-war literary celebrity by revealing the loaded system from which he sprang, coupled with an ethical imperative towards greater inclusivity in the commemorative mode. The film partially invokes this latter mode by making space for those who have been silenced. However, its concern with the polemics of Heimat is also indebted to the kinds of utopian thought outlined above and underpinned where appropriate by subtle shades of the satirical mode in its choices of how to cut and splice its material. By opening up multiple takes on a past cultural phenomenon in this manner, it offers a polyvocal, multi-actor perspective on what German authorship has been, and what it could and should be. Such an ability to create and critically negotiate between multiple possible realities is, as my study will go on to show, one of the key facets of the utopian mode of authorship.

From Modes to Models of Authorship

The preceding section explored how the four different modes of authorship mutually inflect one another in the way authors have both consciously engaged with pre-existing traditions of authorship and themselves been the subject of broader mediations around literary culture and society across the post-war period. The Gruppe 47 is a unique phenomenon that dominated the cultural Heimat of the latter half of the twentieth century but has not been emulated in either the FRG or anywhere else in any meaningful way since its official demise in 1967. Indeed, as my next chapter will show in detail, the Gruppe 47 was part of a distinct model of authorship that cast authors as exemplary creators operating within the West German socio-political context and it would take on foundational status for how German authors conceived their broader relationship to the world. Yet, if Hans Werner Richter imagined he was setting up the group in line with a certain overall repeatable model of authors banding together in support of literary and democratic renewal, the different modes of authorship that underpinned how this model could appear at any one time (celebrating literary modernity or commemorating the trauma of the Second World War, for example) resulted in it being quite differently connoted and incorporated into quite radically conflicting broader social narratives over the decades.

The case study offered here by the Gruppe 47 thus allows me to articulate concisely the key conceptual and methodological differences between modes and models of authorship as they inform the rest of this study. A mode of authorship describes a certain attitude towards being an author in the world, whether on the part of that author or of the wider world that yields and validates her authorship. It can be inferred from close analysis of literary practices, whether these practices reside in the tangible structure of a literary text, are reconstructed through archival traces of relations across the literature network or are intangibly subject to philosophical concepts or social conventions. It is not necessarily directly perceived by either an author or any other actor as significant in its own right. A model of authorship, meanwhile, is the result of a collection of attitudes performed through literary practice and variously perceived across the literature network. It will necessarily have some driver behind it and is far more likely to be directly perceived as a deliberate enactment of their authorship by those directly involved in it, although the shading of interpretations around this enactment is likely to vary considerably.

Studying how the different modes of authorship inflect one another within a model allows us to differentiate how authorship is performed, whether consciously or not, and indeed whether or not people are the main drivers behind this performance. In as much as literature inherently presumes its own symbolic significance, all models of authorship draw on the celebratory mode, even when they might be seeking to disrupt or overturn normative forms of literary value (as indeed they often do). The three other modes that I have discerned – the satirical, commemorative and utopian – have emerged as particularly important in the context of post-war German-speaking Europe. They are themselves part of the ritual enactments, on the part of multiple disharmonious actors, of trying to deal with the legacy of the Second World War by relocating German culture in different discourses of progress and contrition at different times.

The chapters that follow chart a broadly chronological approach to understanding the historical trajectory of the different models of authorship sustained by different mixtures of the modes. Chapters two and three consider different balances of the celebratory, commemorative, satirical and utopian modes to explain the two different models that rose to prominence in each part of Germany in the first thirty years or so after the war. Chapter two considers in detail how the work of Heinrich Böll, Hans Magnus Enzensberger and Günter Grass is part of a broader emerging commitment to prioritizing the exemplary creative individual that, while seeking to atone for the past and inspire for the future, also blocks out models of authorship that do not conform, as witnessed in the careers of Gisela Elsner and Fritz J. Raddatz. Chapter three turns to questions of authorship in East Germany and traces a line from the conflicted positioning of Johannes R. Becher, through the seemingly straightforward espousal of a broader participatory pedagogical model in the work and person of Anna Seghers, and into the work of Christa Wolf, which partly critiques Seghers' commitment to a pedagogical model of authorship by looking back to Becher, but also leads the way for authors on both sides of the border to open up their narrative structures and attendant models of authorship to active participation from their readers. Analysing the foundational models of authorship that develop side-by-side in West and East Germany underscores my wider message of how the same modes of authorship, when mixed even only slightly differently, can lead to quite different models becoming dominant in different contexts.

Chapters four, five, and six then explore how these foundational models are both sustained and challenged in the successive chronological and geographical contexts that lead into the present moment of German literary history. Chapter four looks at the broader literature network circumstances sustained by influential West German actors such as the arch literature networker, Walter Höllerer, and elite publisher, Siegfried Unseld. The actions of these individuals, through the multiple institutions, networks and broader cultural discourse that cohered around them in the 1960s, 1970s and 1980s, created an increasingly ossified model of exemplary authorship in West Germany which seemed locked in the grand celebratory and commemorative gestures of those respective modes and which has only really begun to lose ground since the turn of the millennium. Chapters five and six detail how and why alternatives have since become available. In so doing, my case studies shift to authors with backgrounds that transcend any simplistic national frame, and I acknowledge the particularly interlinked – but yet different – contexts of Austrian authorship that both feed into the larger Federal German market context but also provide a space to the side of it. It is no accident that in this second half of the book the voices and experiences of female authors predominate as the earlier normative models are challenged. In the case studies offered by Christoph Ransmayr, Herta Müller, Felicitas Hoppe, Maja Haderlap, Olga Martynova and Katja Petrowskaja, the utopian mode plays a key moderating role. Collectively, these authors offer profoundly different ways of thinking about the writer's place in both the world and the text, one that is inherently more dispersed and open-ended than the previous models allowed. The institutional and broader discursive structures that have helped them rise to prominence can similarly be aligned with a much more open-ended transnational impetus than the hitherto dominant national models. Just as Ransmayr builds his story of rediscovering literary authorship on a model that was already in existence in previous millennia, however, my discussion of an emergent transnational model of authorship looks backwards as much as forwards: to Goethe's implicit model of world authorship that underpins the bold declaration of world literature with which this study began.

Grasping all parts of my matrix as movable and constantly open to moderation, I do not therefore present what follows as an exposition of authorship culminating in any one model or finalized state of play. Instead, as the three conversations with contemporary authors Ulrike Draesner, Olga Martynova and Ulrike Almut Sandig each enact in their own way, this book shows literary authorship to be a constant site of co-creation, with different models of authorship co-existing alongside one another as well as newer trends eclipsing older ones. While the models that come into view at any one point in time may therefore be the ostensible subject of literary and sociological analysis, the modes of their creation are what actually ensure ongoing practical human investment in the art of literary authorship.

Two The Exemplary Creator: Modelling Authorship in Post-War West Germany

The standard public narratives that were reproduced in the TV documentaries of the Gruppe 47 discussed in the previous chapter cast German authors at the end of the Second World War collectively in the role of the young and impressionable 'Heimkehrer'. The comparative 'youth' of this generation, and indeed the very idea of a 'clean break' or 'zero hour' in 1945, have since been subject to significant revision by scholars, both in terms of generic historical periodization and in the specific analysis of individuals' biographies.[1] Nevertheless, many of the names we now associate with West German writing did indeed cover many miles under duress at the end of the war, whether as soldiers or civilians, and had to spend the early post-war years in temporary accommodation in partially destroyed cities, either re-settled from lost German territories (Günter Grass, Uwe Johnson, Siegfried Lenz), or making their way back from Prisoner of War camps following a period of re-education (Alfred Andersch, Heinrich Böll, Hans Werner Richter). As Richter commented in the 1978 documentary on the group, the returning German solider 'war eigentlich heimatlos' (actually had no Heimat). By the end of the war, most young men from the age of seventeen onwards fell into this category. The shared physical experience of loss of place undoubtedly marked a personal caesura for vast swathes of the population, not just across Germany, but across the rest of Europe too. The situation in Germany was particularly critical, however: along with losing up to

---

[1] See Matthew Philpotts and Stephen Parker, *The Modern Restoration: Rethinking German Literary History, 1930-1960* (Berlin: de Gruyter, 2004); Stephen Brockmann, *German Literary Culture at the Zero Hour* (Rochester, NY: Camden House, 2004).

70 per cent of its physical fabric, a great deal of its moral fabric was also in tatters.[2]

At both a literal and a metaphorical level, then, the German Heimat had to be reconstructed. New foundational models were needed. The scale of this task was recognized not just by the politicians around Adenauer who would bring about the West's economic recovery in the 1950s, but also by the founders of the many literary and political journals that sprang up in the closing years of the 1940s and sought, in their own way, to contribute to broader socio-political debate.[3] Sensitized to their country's moral bankruptcy, the growing numbers of left-wing writers who gathered around Hans Werner Richter in his Gruppe 47 recognized in particular that they had to rebuild not just their physical surroundings, but also the language through which they could explore their relationship to it and, with this, the example that they as individuals set. In the many accounts Richter subsequently provided to public television, radio and general-interest publications about the experiences of this group, Germany of the immediate post-war years is shown in ruins, and the encounter with 'Trümmerlandschaften', or landscapes of ruins, is mapped onto the creation of 'Trümmerliteratur', a literature of ruins.[4] If authors were to learn and move on from this grim stocktaking, so the narrative repeatedly went, they would also need to find new ways of writing.[5] The self-consciously post-war author's place in society, in other words, had to be laboriously, but rapidly, constructed in both word and deed.

From the vantage point of the 1960s, the path to this would seem clear: profoundly disorientated by the negative cultural experience of National Socialism and still seeking permanent physical shelter for his person, the (West) German author aimed to become part of a literary collective. This collective has been retrospectively defined by a common purpose: for example, Hans Werner Richter's almanac from 1962 discussed in the previous chapter presents a narrative according to

---

[2] The percentage refers to common levels of destruction in major cities. See chapter three of Anne Fuchs, *After the Dresden Bombing: Pathways of Memory, 1945 to the Present* (Basingstoke: Palgrave MacMillan, 2012) for a detailed description of the extent of the destruction around the country, as well as how this impinged on mentalities in the immediate post-war period.

[3] See Stuart Parkes's discussion of these short-lived periodicals, *Writers and Politics in Germany, 1945-2008* (Rochester, NY: Camden House, 2009).

[4] Recordings and transcripts of e.g. radio programmes can be accessed in the Gruppe 47 archive held in the Berlin Akademie der Künste. A more accessible source that picks up on these dominant narratives is Heinz Ludwig Arnold's *Die Gruppe 47* (Reinbek: Rowohlt, 2004).

[5] Arnold, *Die Gruppe 47*; Brockmann, *German Literary Culture at the Zero Hour.*

which growing numbers of left-wing writers sought to take on an important position in society by pioneering and otherwise campaigning for democratic structures in both their literary work and broader sociopolitical environment. That few consciously formulated such a clear programme of action in the late 1940s and early 1950s, however, goes without saying. A sense of being uprooted and disorientated was essential to perceiving the 'zero hour' in the first place and precludes such explicit organized behaviour. Germany of the late 1940s in fact represents an extreme manifestation of the 'throwntogetherness' that characterizes social geographer Doreen Massey's concept of place. For Massey, who is interested precisely in how foundational structures come about in both physical and anthropological terms, places are not geographically fixed but dynamically unfold in time. Accordingly, the negotiations that will happen between people who co-inhabit a particular place in a particular time determine both how that place is experienced and its orientation towards the future. In Massey's refusal to put a universal, abstract idea of space against a local, specific manifestation of place (the standard distinction made by the majority of thinkers she surveys, from Heidegger to Derrida), her work lends itself to incorporation into the Goethean practice of world literature that was outlined in my introductory chapter. Like Goethe, she stresses the importance of exemplary performative action within real places that may then carry further significance. She is resistant, however, to retrospective constructions of a place's significance, emphasizing instead the importance of conceptually opening up space as a lived experience. Rather less like Goethe, who was famously conservative, this understanding of place is organized around the potential for social change that resides in the actors operating within it, and it has a profoundly political aspect, as she observes: 'Conceptualising space as open, multiple and relational, unfinished and always becoming, is a prerequisite for history to be open and thus a prerequisite, too, for the possibility of politics.'[6]

For Massey, then, all actors are operating in outwardly fluid conditions, creating the space that they seek to circumscribe through their shifting interactions in time. The way this might apply to the German context can be seen in the fluidity of a number of immediately post-war attempts to inhabit a shared cultural space. For example, Johannes R. Becher's pan-German initiative, 'Kulturbund zur demokratischen Erneuerung Deutschlands' (Cultural League for the

---

[6] Doreen Massey, *For Space* (London: Sage, 2005), p. 59. On Goethe's conservatism, see Ritchie Robertson, *Goethe: A Very Short Introduction* (Oxford: Oxford U. P., 2016), pp. 66–74.

Democratic Renewal of Germany – discussed in greater detail in chapter three) provided some of the first opportunities for writers from across Germany to meet and express a shared sense of purpose, but at the time it was not clear to what extent, if at all, literary networks were going to exist within or somehow above the controlled borders of the Allied territories. The result of this is that neither discrete spatial nor temporal boundaries could provide much orientation to the people acting within them. Nor do they provide us with a fixed point now from which to write an analytical historical narrative that can accurately recreate these actors' lived experience. The geopolitical boundaries of the space known as Germany shifted considerably over just a few short years and were not finally resolved until well into the 1970s, when Chancellor Willy Brandt formally recognized the Oder-Neisse border with Poland. Additionally, the cultural understanding of what Germany historically had been was thrown seriously into question by Allied re-education programmes, as well as by the physical reminders of total collapse across all major towns and cities. While people may be able to live under the illusion of comparative stasis in times of peace and draw up their identity accordingly, during and immediately after war there is no escaping the mutual contingency of time and space. Rather, as Fuchs has argued, people are caught within the traumatic excess of both, as all fixed points seem to disappear.[7] But within this traumatic mix of shifting time-space, there is, *qua* Massey, also a heightened need for all social actors to negotiate. This is fundamentally utopian, because it opens up the space, as experienced by the actors within it, to alternative ways of being. This is the opportunity that was immediately seized upon by people like Richter, and it entails consciously cultivating attitudes, both towards one's co-habitants and the place itself, through dynamic exchange – however confrontational and entrenched these attitudes may subsequently become.

The work of an earlier social geographer, Edward Relph, can help us grasp what exactly is at stake in this notion of a particular interaction between place and attitude, especially during times of social upheaval. Relph has reflected in detail on the role place can play in our phenomenological relationship to the world, which in turn conditions our social and political radar. In his influential 1976 work, *Place and Placelessness*, he writes about our relationship to our environment thus:

---

[7] Fuchs, *After the Dresden Bombing*. For an interesting reading of how this affected subsequent generations of writers, see her discussion of W.G. Sebald in 'A Heimat in Ruins and the Ruins as Heimat: W.G. Sebald's Luftkrieg und Literatur', in Cosgrove, Fuchs, Grote, eds, *German Memory Contests*, pp. 287–302.

There is for virtually everyone a deep association with and consciousness of the places where we were born and grew up, where we live now, or where we have had particularly moving experiences. This association seems to constitute a vital source of both individual and cultural identity and security, a point of departure from which we orient ourselves in the world.[8]

Writing significantly before Massey, Relph's consideration of place makes of it a fixed quantity defined through local meaningfulness. This is in line with much of the philosophical tradition of thinking in oppositional terms about place and space, as well as place and time, both of which Massey explicitly argues against. Alongside this, however, he develops the notion of an attitude that is both conditioned by our relationship to place and can in turn condition what place looks like. His discussion of place as a positive phenomenological construction linked to our sense of orientation, or rootedness, in a fixed and knowable world, is accompanied by reflection on the negative condition of 'placelessness'. This is not so much the opposing construction as an attitude taken to place as a bounded site of individualized identity formation. Relph defines this negative neologism as a conscious attitude of inauthenticity that emphasizes 'the common and average characteristics of man and place'.[9]

In his rather over-polarized account, the attitude of placelessness leads to many of the negative traits of globalization: mass-produced goods and architecture that adds little to the landscapes into which it is inserted and which deliberately work against regional diversities and traditions. Related just to the core definition quoted above, however, the term can be used without such negative value judgements attached. The idea that placelessness is an attitude born of and reacting to the notion of locally-bounded place not only helps to throw fixed conceptions of place into some relief, but also offers a conceptual framework for considering how individual identities are constructed through a series of negotiated interactions with the physical and social environment in which human beings exist. This is an anthropologically led understanding of place. If placelessness means consciously *not* coming from or being specific to a certain geographical and historical location and expressing this in ways that can be readily emulated, then placeness is its opposite: a deliberately cultivated attitude of communion with one's physical and temporal surroundings that takes on a locally specific expression. I have already noted how Aleida Assmann's work

---

[8] Edward Relph, *Place and Placelessness* (London: Pion, 1976), p. 43.
[9] Relph, *Place and Placelessness*, p. 79.

on the memory of places does not account for the specific ways people consciously engage with place. The question also receives surprisingly little explicit attention in Massey's championing of the dynamic and the relational. This is probably because both theoretical models are developed primarily in the abstract, as part of a general philosophy of space and time, rather than argued through the particular. Here, though, the work of Theodor Adorno can help out.

Adorno's observations on the culture industry were born of his very specific location as an intellectual of Jewish heritage working first in exile and then back in the country of his persecution. Throughout his writings on culture in general and in the 1949/51 essay in particular, 'Kulturkritik und Gesellschaft' (cultural criticism and society), Adorno stresses the imbrication of the cultural critic within both the object he studies (culture) and the industry that facilitates this study (what Bourdieu would call 'the field of cultural production'). For Adorno, there is no way out of this: the post-war poet is barbaric because he writes in a culture that has proven itself to be barbaric and adding to that culture therefore necessarily entails positioning oneself within its barbarity. The essay famously culminates in his statement, 'nach Auschwitz ein Gedicht zu schreiben, ist barbarisch' (writing a poem after Auschwitz is barbaric), which has been taken by many to enunciate a serious moral objection to all subsequent German literature.[10] But his negative dialectics are partially resolved through embracing the power of knowledge and adopting a suitably self-aware attitude: knowing your compromised position, you can seek explicitly to work with it. Throughout the piece, Adorno moves back and forth between transcendental and immanent positions for both the cultural critic and culture itself, challenging the reader to think through to what extent any form of 'Erkenntnis' (knowledge achieved through a process of transformative insight) is possible that will not be subsequently co-opted by the ruling system. Working through multiple dialectical formulations, the essay repeatedly circles around this fundamental paradox surrounding the collapse of any ideologically discrete place for culture and its consequences for critical engagement: 'Der dialektische Kritiker an der Kultur muß an dieser teilhaben und nicht teilhaben'[11] (the dialectical critic of culture must take part and not take part in it). Surprisingly though – for a piece that is otherwise built on extreme cultural pessimism underpinned by historical example – the final

---

[10] Theodor Adorno, 'Kulturkritik und Gesellschaft', in *Schreiben nach Auschwitz? Adorno und die Dichter*, ed. Petra Kiedaisch (Stuttgart: Reclam, 1995), pp. 27–49, p. 49.
[11] Adorno, 'Kulturkritik und Gesellschaft', p. 47.

sentence amounts to a call to arms for the 'critical mind' to resist her 'absolute materialization' and engage with the world:

> Der absoluten Verdinglichung, die den Fortschritt des Geistes als eines ihrer Elemente voraussetzte und die ihn heute gänzlich aufzusaugen sich anschickt, ist der kritische Geist nicht gewachsen, solange er bei sich bleibt in selbstgenügsamer Kontemplation.[12]

[The absolute materialization, which presumed intellectual progress as one of its elements and which nowadays is trying to swallow it wholesale, is something that the critical mind cannot measure up to all the time it is content to confine itself to contemplation in splendid isolation.]

Even as he pulls the moral ground away from under German intellectuals' feet, Adorno thus urges them to get out and interact with their imperfect world if they do not want to be devoured by it. The ending of his famous essay can thus be rephrased through the lens of Relph, Massey and Assmann: a fundamental attitude of placelessness must underpin all conscious actions to belong publicly undertaken by intellectuals in post-war Germany. Drawing as it does on the ability to hold multiple realities in dialogue with one another and conceive of time and space as fluid and relational, this sets an inherently utopian mode of authorship at the heart of post-war Germany's emergent public sphere, but one that has come through the context of traumatic rupture and loss. These ideas will bed down over the subsequent decades with all the power of a foundational narrative, one, that is to say, that is both normative and repeatedly subject to challenge.

Adapted to our literary historical context, the idea of placelessness, which I am taking from Relph, stripping of the evaluative element developed in the context of global capitalism, and grafting instead onto Adorno's moral imperative, offers us a way of conceiving how West German authors might set about performing Goethe's practical world author function in an age where the ethical stakes for both literature in general and individual authorial action in particular have been significantly raised. Their task is almost impossible. They are knowingly bringing the spaces of literature and politics into dialogue with one another, but, as we shall go on to see, they are also particularly aware of their own paradoxical location both inside and outside the German

---

[12] Adorno, 'Kulturkritik und Gesellschaft', p. 49.

cultural Heimat that makes them unable to look beyond themselves. The belief that, as authors, they can do something exemplary that will matter to society is an inherently celebratory approach to authorship, while their desire to open up different spaces through literature that can be brought into dialogue with contemporary circumstances is utopian. Within these dominant modes, however, the way these authors subsequently adopt and explore attitudes to their place, as authors, in the emerging post-war German society by mingling aspects of the utopian, commemorative and satirical modes of authorship also fundamentally questions their suitability to function as exemplary creator figures. The cultural Heimat that these authors help to forge is both driven by a deep ethical urge to create new and open structures of belonging and inherently exclusive and exclusionary.

Rebuilding the Linguistic Foundations for Creative 'Erkenntnis': How to Live in the German Language

All writers commonly associated with the Gruppe 47 cultivated a fundamental distrust of both linguistic and institutional markers of belonging – hence Richter's insistence that there were no 'members' and no 'constitution' for the group in the early days, and the polarization around these issues towards its end.[13] However, Heinrich Böll and Hans Magnus Enzensberger stand out for their attempts, from comparatively early dates, to articulate the specific problematics of language and place from the perspective of those deeply involved in literature.

Born in 1929 in Kaufbeuren in Swabia, southern Bavaria, Hans Magnus Enzensberger's career as a poet, novelist, essayist and political commentator stretches back into the early 1950s. A routine contributor to the Gruppe 47, he also worked in the cultural programming department of the public broadcaster, SWR, before later editing the influential left-wing magazine *Kursbuch*, working as a reader and editor for Suhrkamp, and managing his own publishing label, Die andere Bibliothek (The Other Library).[14] Too young to have experienced active service in the war, Enzensberger was neither a 'Heimkehrer' figure of the type consciously embodied by Heinrich Böll, Alfred Andersch or Hans Werner Richter, nor had he 'lost' an extra-territorial homeland in

---

[13] Richter maintains this line right from the start and repeats it many years after the group's demise. See, for example, his afterword to Hans Werner Richter, *Im Etablissement der Schmetterlinge: 21 Portraits aus der Gruppe 47* (Munich: Hanser, 1986).

[14] For extensive analysis of these different roles, particularly (but not only) in relation to Suhrkamp, see Tobias Amslinger, *Verlagsautorschaft: Enzensberger und Suhrkamp* (Göttingen: Wallstein, 2018).

the manner of Günter Grass, nor indeed been forced to flee like Bloch, Mann or Adorno. Nevertheless, the question of cultural roots and how he, as a writer, fits into the German physical and cultural landscape, runs through all his early work. On the one hand, this basic question conditions his initial poetic trilogy of sorts, the volumes *Verteidigung der Wölfe* (1957), *Landessprache* (1960), and *Blindenschrift* (1964), that would earn him the epithet of 'angry young man' but would also trace his cautious location within the German language and attendant cultural traditions.[15] On the other, he has also repeatedly looked critically at the way different kinds of discourse affect the creation of identities and public consensus in his essayistic work.

In the late 1950s and early 1960s, this latter took the form of analysing the nature and function of the West German media – an aspect of the public sphere, which, as Christina von Hodenberg has discussed in depth, underwent major ideological and structural change in the first fifteen years of the Federal Republic.[16] Enzensberger wrote two major pieces that place problems of political and geographical orientation, as played out in linguistic structures, at the heart of contemporary public debate: 'Die Sprache des Spiegel' (1956/7, The language of the *Spiegel*) and 'Journalismus als Eiertanz: Beschreibung einer Allgemeinen Zeitung für Deutschland' (1962, Journalism as Dancing on Eggshells: What a Broadsheet Newspaper for Germany might look like). The later piece exposes dubious journalistic techniques at the *Frankfurter Allgemeine Zeitung* (*FAZ*), one of the most influential conservative national broadsheets, which, in Enzensberger's view, represent a calculated attempt on the part of the press to disorientate the reader through misinformation. In so doing, he claims that the *FAZ* develops 'eine Sprache der Herrschaft' (a language of control) that deliberately supports an ultra-conservative authoritarian position and prevents the spread of any sort of democratic 'Erkenntnis' (realization through knowledge), either of the kind on which Adorno based his dialectical critique or that Böll, as described in detail below, suggested authors and their readers should be seeking precisely in order to root themselves

---

[15] The reviews by Alfred Andersch, '(In Worten: ein) zorniger junger Mann' (1958), and Martin Walser, 'Einer der auszog, das Fürchten zu verlernen' (1961), both reproduced in Reinhold Grimm, ed., *Hans Magnus Enzensberger* (Frankfurt a.M.: Suhrkamp, 1984), pp. 59–63 and pp. 63–67, give a flavour of this. Reinhold Grimm gives a useful overview of Enzensberger's early media work and contacts in 'Bildnis Hans Magnus Enzensberger: Struktur, Ideologie und Vorgeschichte eines Gesellschaftskritikers', in, Grimm, ed., *Hans Magnus Enzensberger*, pp. 139–88.

[16] Christina von Hodenberg, *Konsens und Krise: Eine Geschichte der westdeutschen Medienöffentlichkeit, 1945-1973* (Göttingen: Wallstein, 2006).

better in the world. This is directly linked to post-war Germany's provincial, inward-focused geopolitics. Because the *FAZ*'s 'language of control' conditions how knowledge is known, it deliberately works against Adorno's dictate of being self-aware.

In the earlier piece, by contrast, it is the *Spiegel*'s inability consistently to endorse any political position that attracts the author's criticism. Despite its overt desire to appeal to an educated, discerning and democratically-minded reader, Enzensberger maintains that the *Spiegel* turns contemporary history into a series of human-interest stories. These encourage an elitist personality cult that is not only ultimately disenfranchizing for the average citizen, but also beholden to a degenerate version of the rules of fiction, which prioritize a lack of narrative presence and, by extension, accountability. It is also profoundly un-self-aware:

> Das Blatt hat keine Position. Die Stellung, die es von Fall zu Fall zu beziehen scheint, richtet sich eher nach den Erfordernissen der Story, aus der sie zu erraten ist: als deren Pointe. [. . .] Die Ideologie des Spiegel ist nichts weiter als eine skeptische Allwissenheit, die an allem zweifelt, außer an sich selbst.[17]

[The paper has no position. The position that it appears to take on a case-by-case basis is much more determined by the demands of the story from which it is to be inferred: as its punchline. [. . .] The *Spiegel*'s ideology is nothing more than a sceptical omniscience that casts everything except itself into doubt.]

Where the *FAZ* misleads because it wants to create an image of a successful conservative society, the *Spiegel* misleads out of its desire to spin a good story, whatever kind of society this story may imply. Both, in their own way, are seeking to flatter their readers into a sense of intellectual belonging to the self-contained world they create. As a result, both appear to provide orientation in the world, to facilitate a sense of 'placeness' that can be rolled out for their readers across West Germany. In actual fact, however, their engagement with the German cultural and geopolitical landscape relies on linguistic trickery and misinformation, which ultimately disorientates the reader who wants to establish any reliable set of factual coordinates: 'Nicht Orientierung, sondern ihr Verlust ist die Folge',[18] he concludes (The result is not to provide orientation, but rather to dispense with it altogether).

---

[17] Hans Magnus Enzensberger, 'Die Sprache des Spiegel', in Hans Magnus Enzensberger, *Einzelheiten I: Bewußtseins-Industrie* (Frankfurt a.M.: Suhrkamp, 1964), pp. 74–105, pp. 89–90.
[18] Enzensberger, 'Die Sprache des Spiegel', p. 94.

Journalism, as carried out by two of the major post-war news organs, is thus dismissed by one of the foremost upcoming public intellectual figures as ideologically suspect and artistically self-serving. What Enzensberger misses is a sense of genuine engagement with the country's actual physical and cultural fabric as it is developing, as both newspapers are driven, ultimately, by a desire not to engage with the specifics of Germany as a post-war place at all. Their reports are the result of a carefully honed, widely reproducible rhetorical model of belonging that appears to encapsulate the essence of relationships within a certain cultural community, but in actual fact contributes to a loss of depth and breadth in the reporting of events within that community. What Enzensberger is therefore in fact diagnosing is the total absence of any commemorative or utopian mode of authorship in these publications, when in fact the ethical imperative of the country's post-war condition requires both if society is to stand a chance of learning from the past. The influential media organs are designed only to repeat their own political and aesthetic form amongst a public oriented towards the status quo.

Meanwhile, the older Heinrich Böll (1917–1985) may be taken as a representative for the 'Heimkehrer' author figure, who was old enough to have grown up within a seemingly stable linguistic and literary tradition, only to have the certainties of time and space whipped away from under his feet. Speaking in a series of Frankfurt lectures that he gave in 1963/64, he presents the experiences of his generation of authors in just such terms. Significantly, he rejects a title along the lines of 'literature and society' for the series, opting instead to emphasize 'das Humane' and 'das Soziale', the human / humane and the social / socially-minded. These are fundamental relational qualities that he believes have been lost to society in the wake of the war, but which are imminent in the notion of Heimat, especially when understood as the kind of anthropological place discussed previously.[19] The term 'Heimat' gives rise to a significant structural motif in the lecture series through which Böll explores just how 'bewohnbar', or inhabitable, Germany is for both the author figure and the population more generally. One particular passage, the end of which has been much quoted in isolation, is worth citing here in full, as in it he sets out the specific conditions that determine how authors relate to society:

> Ein Autor, ein Urheber, ein Poet also – er würde nicht nur gern wohnen (wohnen ist ein Verb, ein Tätigkeitswort), sondern auch

---

[19] Heinrich Böll, 'Frankfurter Vorlesungen', in Heinrich Böll, *Werke*, ed. Bernd Balzer, vol 2: Essayistische Schriften und Reden, 1964-1972, pp. 34–92, p. 45.

die Sprache, in der er schreibt, bewohnbar machen, es ist ja nicht gut, daß der Mensch allein sei, und er kann sich nicht selbst Heimat and Nachbarschaft, Freundschaft und Vertrauen aus den Rippen bilden, die ihm geblieben sind. Er kann auch nicht wie Abraham sein eigenes Volk zeugen; er muß auf es zu, es muß ihm zuwachsen. Er braucht nicht nur Freunde, Leser, Publikum, er braucht Verbündete, öffentliche Verbündete, die sich nicht nur ärgern oder nicht nur triumphieren, die *erkennen*. Eitelkeit, Eifersucht, Gekränktheit, Triumph, Ärger sollten Privatsache sein. *Erkannt* werden sollte, was wichtiger ist: die Suche nach einer bewohnbaren Sprache in einem bewohnbaren Land.[20]

[An author, an originator, and thus a poet – he wouldn't just like to live (to live is a verb, an action word), but also to make the language he which he writes liveable. It's not a good thing that man should be alone and he is not able to serve as his own *Heimat* [homeland], neighbourhood, friendship and circle of trust from the ribs that are left him. Nor can he raise his own people like Abraham; he must go towards them, they must grow towards him. He doesn't just need friends, readers, an audience, he needs allies, public allies who don't merely revel in outrage or triumph, but who *know insightfully*. Vanity, jealousy, vexation, triumph, irritation should be private matters. We must *use our insight to discern* what is more important: the search for a liveable language in a liveable country.]

The passage not only emphasizes that authorship must unfold in the right social context, but also that it must meet with the right attitude. Authors should write, and people should engage with what they write, not out of pure emotional need, but out of a rational drive to recognize and to learn: 'Erkenntnis' (the term appears in the German in the verbal infinitive 'erkennen' and related participle 'erkannt'). The drive to 'Erkenntnis' represents a shared public investment in progress not dissimilar to that espoused by Bloch at the end of his *Prinzip Hoffnung*. The image of belonging in which the passage culminates, however, also resounds with Heidegger's 'wohnender Mensch': actively dwelling in one's surroundings and recreating that sense of dwelling through language is cast as just as important as creating future-oriented knowledge about these surroundings. Biblical imagery and analogy are used throughout the passage in a way that strengthens the Heideggerian sense of disclosing and restoring the ideal state of being-in-the-world

---

[20] Böll, 'Frankfurter Vorlesungen', pp. 52–3.

through art. While neither Adam nor Abraham provides the contemporary author with a viable method for creating a 'liveable' physical and social environment, the Old Testament type of Heimat they represent is nevertheless the implicit ideal that the poet-author would like to recreate for his own place and time by modern methods. These methods, significantly, revolve around paring language down to its 'liveable', i.e. politically untainted, core, while the dialogue set up between the preferred and current models of Heimat invokes a form of utopian thinking. Meanwhile, the whole is encased in the celebratory mode, as the extended biblical language throughout the passage places the exemplary author who is at the heart of a receptive community on a par with a religious creator figure.

The rest of Böll's lecture series, however, shows that this ideal attitude of placeness on the part of both exemplary authors and the West German society that actively welcomes them has not yet been achieved. On the contrary, post-war Germany is repeatedly characterized as suffering from a loss of place, which has led to a loss of anthropologically determined roots both within the built environment and in wider social attitudes. People no longer spend their lives living in places but travel on long-distance trains between them; on these journeys they no longer engage with literature as a means of recreating a sense of belonging but prefer instead to flick through the sensationalist headlines disseminated by the mass media. This large-scale loss of place, which implicitly includes the loss of the ability either to lay down or even to recognize roots in any place, is held directly responsible for the negative portrayals of society that characterize contemporary writing. It also leads Böll to the comment that was used to structure the 1978 film on the Gruppe 47 discussed previously: 'Unsere Literatur hat keine Orte. Die ungeheure, oft mühselige Anstrengung der Nachkriegsliteratur hat ja darin bestanden, Orte und Nachbarschaften wieder zu finden'[21] (Our literature has no places. The incredible, often wearisome task of post-war literature has been precisely about trying to find places and neighbourhoods again).

In a paradoxical move, however, Böll also broadens his argument about literature and place to argue that, 'Dieses Nicht-wohnen-Können ist freilich keineswegs ein neues Thema – es wäre einer umfassenden Studie wert: Goethe, der wohnen und wandern, auch lieben konnte, Kleist, der nicht wohnen, wandern und lieben konnte, Stifter, seine verzweifelte Stille, er, der die großartigste Wohnung der deutschen Literatur, den *Nachsommer* schrieb – einen Traum'[22] (This

---

[21] Böll, 'Frankfurter Vorlesungen', pp. 56–7.
[22] Böll, 'Frankfurter Vorlesungen', p. 58.

not-being-able-to-live is of course nothing new – it would be worthy of extensive study: Goethe, who was able to live, wander and also love, Kleist, who was not able to live, wander and love, Stifter and his desperate silence that created the greatest living of all in German literature, *The Indian Summer* – a dream). The author's desire to belong, his attitude of seeking placeness for both himself and society, is thereby turned into a wish that has gone largely unfulfilled since Goethe, such that it is Goethe, and not the Second World War, who marks the end of a seemingly ideal, rooted authorship that can lead to a confident position of self-knowledge and sense of belonging in the world. Stifter, in my previous chapter artificially pushed back fully into Goethe's era in Bernhard's humorous account of how Goethe paralyzed all modern German literature, now heads up a venerable tradition of authorship conditioned by an existential sense of not-belonging to a society that is in any case largely inhospitable. This tradition stretches from Kleist and the Romantics through to Kafka. The physically displaced exile writers and 'Heimkehrer' are merely the most recent manifestation of German-speaking Europe's much longer-standing inability to provide positive cultural roots and facilitate feelings of placeness.

Such a description of the modern condition of German authorship is double-edged. On the one hand, Böll repeatedly implies, in a utopian manner similar to Ernst Bloch, that the challenge for the current young generation of authors is to make 'dieses Land auch in der Literatur bewohnbar' (make this country also liveable in literature) as a direct response to the physical and moral devastation wreaked by the war and as part of a broader commitment to building a cultural as well as a physical and spiritual Heimat. On the other, he makes it clear that writing born of not belonging and faithfully conveying society as inherently uninhabitable has led to a well-established canon of literature from which much can be learned. In this sense of literature as an alternative, exemplary space for responding to social ills, we find ourselves back at More's *Utopia*. A contemporary feeling of politically induced placelessness, then, is both foregrounded by Böll as the single-most significant pre-condition of post-war writing and relativized by his reference to a much longer literary tradition born of authorial non-belonging, which in turn mirrors wider societal conditions. Such a description of authors' position in society encompasses much more than simply the question of how power and influence are shared amongst political and intellectual elites. It considers how man perceives his relationship to his surroundings on both an existential and a physical level and how literary writing can express this perception by attaching it to a particular model of authorship endowed with a sense of foundational importance.

The Exemplary Creator 85

As a logical conclusion to such a conceptualization of place and his own relationship to it as an author, much of Böll's work has been concerned with improving Germany as a physical and socio-political environment, often through rather unsubtle use of the commemorative and satirical modes. Where his literature tends to foreground either uprooted figures ('Wanderer, kommst du nach Spa. . .'. [1950, Stranger, Bear Word to the Spartans We. . .], *Billiard um halb zehn*, [1959, Billiards at Half Nine]) or a society dangerously lacking any moral foundations (the West German society represented in *Die verlorene Ehre der Katharina Blum* [1974, The Lost Honour of Katharina Blum] is led by the same sensationalist gutter press headlines as he identified as problematic in his 1963/64 lecture series), his more directly political interventions have repeatedly called for the fledgling West German democracy collectively to reflect on its values and practices in the hope of making it a more humane and hospitable place – including active engagement for the Green party towards the end of his life. Placeness has been his ideal, spelled out through the examples of placelessness that he has found around him. Accordingly, underpinning all of Böll's work is precisely the trauma of rupture and loss that Assmann identifies with places of commemoration and that feeds into the ethically aware commemorative mode of authorship that Enzensberger found absent from early West German journalism but would attempt to cultivate instead in his poetry. At the same time, a deep commitment to reimagining German society as a place where a positive, but hitherto unrealized, form of belonging could be achieved equally impels Böll to write: the utopian mode. This appears in unexpected places, like the open-ended conclusion to his late work, *Frauen vor Flußlandschaft* (1985, Women in a River Landscape), where characters look both backwards and forwards to the different lives, and deaths, they might pursue in different places.[23]

Underlying all his work, however, is a pronounced scepticism regarding his own ability to belong in either German political or literary circles, as well as a certain self-pity regarding the particular historical situation in which he has found himself. This is an attitude far from untypical of the generation of Hans Werner Richter, Alfred Andersch and Günter Eich. As Böll comments in his Frankfurt lectures, 'Meine Altersklasse wird diesen Grund unter den Füßen nie finden. Es fehlt die Tradition, zum Studium die Geduld, zum Sammeln das Vertrauen auf die Dauer [. . .] Meine Altersklasse ist nicht weise, wird es nie sein, sie ist nicht einmal klug geworden und aus vielem bis heute nicht schlau'[24]

---

[23] Heinrich Böll, *Frauen vor Flußlandschaft* (Cologne: Kiepenheuer & Witsch, 1985).
[24] Böll, *Frankfurter Vorlesungen*, pp. 52–3.

(My cohort will never find this ground under our feet. We lack the sense of tradition, we do not have the money for study, nor enough trust in permanence to begin collecting things. [...] My cohort is not wise, never will be, it hasn't even become clever nor managed to draw any smart lessons from anything much, right up to this day). By the later 1960s and 1970s, Böll, who repeatedly rejected the epithet of being an exemplary 'Gewissen der Nation' (conscience of the nation) and was reticent about putting his fame to use, cut more of a self-styled melancholy outsider figure in public political debates than one who was actively contributing to the growth of new democratic structures.[25]

Böll's ultimate cultivation of distance to the notion of creative 'Erkenntnis' he helped establish within the emergent models of authorial involvement in society is in marked opposition to a number of other major West German writers whose work came to prominence in the 1950s and 1960s and who were too young to have played any significant part in the war. Günter Grass, Siegfried Lenz and Martin Walser, to name some of the best known, have built their entire literary careers around a conception of authorship that insists on the author being physically present and accessible to wide swathes of the population, as well as committed on a more metaphorical level to representing society through literature. These authors sought to achieve not just 'Erkenntnis', but also active social change, and they were prepared to channel the attendant debates through both their physical person and their art to do so. In this, they became natural acolytes of the work of their contemporary, the political philosopher Jürgen Habermas. Where Adorno stressed the unresolved dialectics of trying to obtain and act on 'Erkenntnis' of the totality of a system in which you are already a part, Habermas moved towards stressing the value of argument and interpersonal communication within that system, begun in his 1962 *Strukturwandel der Öffentlichkeit* (Structural Transformation of the Public Sphere) and subsequently developed into the landmark *Theorie des kommunikativen Handelns* (1981, Theory of Communicative Action). While not denying the imbrication of individual critic and ideological system, he adopts a more fundamentally positive belief in the power of people to negotiate with one another as real, historically and culturally located individuals, and learn from the attendant 'structures of experience and action' they mutually create.[26] In setting

---

[25] See Wilfried van der Will, 'The embattled intellectual' for discussion of Böll's reluctance to be seen as physically embodying a certain moral direction for society.

[26] See Andrew Bowie, *Introduction to German Philosophy* (Cambridge: Polity, 2003), pp. 255–64.

out his own historically informed account of the genesis of the public sphere in modern Europe that drew on actual, traceable interactions, Habermas displayed a differentiated awareness of practical and local cultural specificity that would become ever more important to the way writers perceived their particular contribution to the wider world. In so doing, he welds to the utopian mode of much of the contemporary philosophy of his day a commemorative mode, but in such a dialogic fashion as to indicate how it could be harnessed to an ethically-driven programme of social change, rather than grinding to a halt within its own imperfect system.

A similar kind of historical analysis coupled with future-forming pathways for action is evident in both the literary work and the broader socio-political positioning of the younger guard of authors who came on the scene in the mid to late 1950s. Where Böll reflected on the need for society to embrace an exemplary creator figure, Grass and Enzensberger would stridently assume this position as part of their development of the foundational 'public intellectual' model of authorship. At the same time, however, they also based their efforts at taking on a significant position within society on the profound and frequently expressed sense of the author's placelessness that Böll traces as a powerful, if not to say canonical, literary tradition of its own. Within the model of enacting exemplary creativity that emerges, then, there is a consciously post-war ethical drive both to foster a sense of belonging and not to belong, to be both an exemplary citizen and an exemplary outcast. This in turn indicates that developing one's authorial persona in line with a contradictory mix of the utopian and commemorative modes of authorship (pointing to alternative ways of belonging whilst also returning to what is lost and questioning one's own current location), all under the broader umbrella of an inherently celebratory mode that champions the creative act, is characteristic of the German authorial experience. The full paradox that this mix entails for later evaluations of what their authorship actually achieved would only become evident with the passage of time.

Establishing Foundational Cycles of Creation and Commemoration in Literature: Günter Grass's 'Danzig Trilogy'

Of the various authors mentioned above, both Günter Grass (1927–2015) and Siegfried Lenz (1926–2014) had first-hand biographical experience of being physically uprooted, and their careers were marked in similar ways by their attempts to grapple with this loss of place. The similarities range from their use of the novel as a popular and capacious form through to their political campaigning and openness to interacting directly with their readers to both political and literary ends. In what follows, I focus on Grass's early work, but I read it as characteristic of the first attempts made by writers across the Gruppe 47's twenty-year existence to link the importance of place, as both an experience and an attitude, with literary activity. Along with Lenz, the work of the Austrian Jew Ilse Aichinger (1921–2016), the West German co-founder of the Gruppe 47 Alfred Andersch (1914–1980), the one-time East German Uwe Johnson (1934–1984) and the émigré Peter Weiss (1916–1982) could all be read through this lens. What unites these writers from diverse backgrounds is the way in which their texts are born of a mixture of authorial attitude: critique towards the present and elegy towards the recent past. The centrality of the Holocaust within the cultural landscape they consciously inhabit necessitates a commemorative mode of authorship common to all of these writers, regardless of their very different biographical experiences and stylistic affinities.

Having spent his childhood and teenage years in Danzig (now Polish Gdańsk) until the final months of the war, Grass lost his Polish-German Heimat completely in the Allies' subsequent division of Germany. In the fifteen years that followed German defeat he lived first as a refugee in the Ruhr area, then Paris, and then Berlin, eking out a living as an apprentice stonemason and musician. When he first came to the attention of the Gruppe 47 through his lyric poetry in 1955, he was deemed an interesting new voice. It was not until he read out his prose from *Die Blechtrommel* (*The Tin Drum*) at their 1958 meeting, however, that this voice was celebrated across the re-established West German literary scene as stunningly different to the rather limited perspective and often drab scope that had increasingly come to characterize literary writing of the 1950s. This difference was cast in a number of ways, as Jürgen Manthey's later analysis of Grass's entry onto the German literary scene shows:

> Die Kritik der ersten Stunde hat gespürt, mehr gespürt als erkannt, daß von hier eine 'Epoche' in der Nachkriegsliteratur ausging, wenn sie dies auch mit einem schiefen Vokabular beschrieben, mit falschen Akzenten versehen und widersprüchlichen Aussagen belegt hat. Den meisten war Grass der Barbar im Garten, ein 'Kraftlatz', ein 'Berserker', ein 'literarischer Holzfäller' und 'poetischer Naturbursche', jedenfalls 'ein naiver Künstler'. All dies war der Autor gerade nicht, sondern ein unglaublich disziplinierter, belesener, textbewußter [. . .] Schriftsteller [. . .]. Die Hinweise auf Vorgänger, Grimmelshausen voran, vertrugen sich jedoch mit Vorstellungen von 'kaschubischer Naturkraft', mit der ein 'literarischer Löwe' auf einmal 'in die

Gefilde der Literatur einbrach, Hecken, Zäune und Gräben übersprang'.²⁷

[The early criticism sensed – sensed rather than fully recognized – that this marked the beginning of a new 'epoch' in post-war writing, even if it used an inappropriate vocabulary to describe this beginning, placed distorting emphases on it and supported it with contradictory statements. For most people, Grass was a barbarian in the garden, a 'prize fighter', a 'berserker', a 'literary lumberjack' and a 'poetic innocent', at any rate 'a naïve artist'. Precisely none of these epithets applied to the author, who was in fact an incredibly disciplined, well-read, textually-aware writer. But the references to precedents, Grimmelshausen in particular, chimed with notions of the 'Cassubian force of nature', that impelled this 'literary lion' to 'break into the realm of literature, leaping over hedges, fences, and ditches'.]

The significance of place for the way Grass was received in the post-German literary landscape, however, goes beyond these initial paradoxical constructions of him as an insider-outsider figure. Particularly prized in all three of the prose works that would go on to form the so-called 'Danzig Trilogy' – *Die Blechtrommel* (1959, *The Tin Drum* 1961), *Katz und Maus* (1961, *Cat and Mouse* 1963) and *Hundejahre* (1963, *Dog Years* 1965) – was his ability to recreate Danzig as an authentic place that was brought to life by a striking cross-section of characters whose petty lives unfolded against the events of recent history. Böll's Frankfurt lectures, in fact, explicitly refer to the positive sense of place that makes of Grass's work an anomaly in contemporary German writing.²⁸ We can go further than this. What holds the 'Danzig Trilogy' together is neither Grass's idiosyncratic aesthetic practices, nor his shared characters with their cameo appearances from book to book, both of which have been the focus of literary critical analysis so far, nor even the location common to all three, but an increasingly complex and explicit reflection on the nature and function of place as a deeply

---

27 Jürgen Manthey, '*Die Blechtrommel* wiedergelesen', in Heinz Ludwig Arnold, ed, *Günter Grass*, 1 (Munich: Text + Kritik, 1988), pp. 24–36, p. 24.
28 Heinrich Böll, Frankfurter Vorlesungen, p. 47. The positive reference is qualified by the fact that Danzig is a 'lost' place for the Germany in which Böll is speaking.

historically-rooted quantity that can explain people's lives.[29] The way Grass develops this reflection across his early works affords him considerable insight into his own literary and political position in post-war Germany and, as a result, it lays the ground for much of what is to come in his later writing and public appearances. The fact that, of the three, *Hundejahre* offers by far the most differentiated engagement with place also perhaps explains why Grass considered it to be his finest work, even though the other two have dominated both the popular reception and literary critical analysis ever since.[30]

Where *Katz und Maus* and the first two parts of *Die Blechtrommel* focus almost exclusively on contemporary twentieth-century life within the city and suburbs of Danzig itself, *Hundejahre* extends the chronological and geographical scope of its narrative to include life and practices in the outlying villages. These in turn gesture to the medieval history, myths and sagas that have shaped the entire surrounding Pomeranian region. As Michael Minden observes, the narrative begins by invoking the primeval force of the Vistula River and the way humans have successively interacted with the area in their attempts to cultivate it.[31] Brauxel, the novel's first of three narrators, further draws attention to the relationship between man and his environment when he explains how he variously models the spelling of his pen-name on Castrop-Rauxel, a former mining town in West Germany indicative of his post-war fate as the owner of a disused mine, and two further terms which derive from his earlier life as Eddi Amsel growing up in the Vistula

---

[29] Particularly insightful studies that focus on aesthetic techniques are Ann Mason, *The Skeptical Muse: A Study of Günter Grass's Conception of the Artist* (Bern: Lang, 1974) and Marc Silbermann, 'Schreiben als öffentliche Angelegenheit: Lesestrategien des Romans Hundejahre', in Manfred Durzak, ed., *Zu Günter Grass: Geschichte auf dem poetischen Prüfstand* (Stuttgart: Klett, 1985), pp. 80–95. The idea of place is examined in Gertrude Cepl-Kaufmann, 'Verlust oder poetische Rettung? Zum Begriff Heimat in Günter Grass' Danziger Trilogie', in Hans-Georg Pott, ed, *Literatur und Provinz: Das Konzept 'Heimat' in der neueren Literatur* (Paderborn: Schöningh, 1986), pp. 61–83, and in Nicole Thesz, 'Illusions of Return: City and Memory in Günter Grass's Danzig Novels', *Seminar*, 45/1 (2009), 64–81. Both see the texts' invocation of place as a deliberately retrospective projection from the protagonists and their author in their final, post-war context, as opposed to a discrete motivating factor in the characters' lives as they unfold during the narrative.

[30] Günter Grass, 'Schreiben nach Auschwitz: Frankfurter Poetik-Vorlesung', in Günter Grass, *Werkausgabe*, 19 vols, ed. Volker Neuhaus & Daniela Hermes (Göttingen: Steidl, 1997–2015), vol. 16, ed. Daniela Hermes (Göttingen: Steidl, 1997), pp. 235–56, p. 250. See also Julian Preece, *Günter Grass* (London: Reaktion, 2018), p. 65.

[31] Michael Minden, '"Grass auseinandergeschrieben": Günter Grass's *Hundejahre* and Mimesis', *German Quarterly*, 86.1 (2013), 25–42.

delta: Häksel, an agrarian term for cut straw, and Weichsel, or the River Vistula itself.[32] As the novel progresses, the deep historical relationship between man and his environment repeatedly simmers under the surface. Thus over the course of Brauxel/Brauksel/Brauchsel's 148-page opening section Tulla Pokriefke, the twentieth-century addressee and one of the key characters in the book's second section, is attributed a long list of possible precursors: Duke Svantopolk's thirteenth-century daughter who, characterized by her sharp incisors, was reputed to search barefoot along the River Vistula for mice; the fourteenth-century daughter of the Lithuanian Duke Kynstute who went on to become a nun; Ursula, one of the headless nuns in the mythical saga; and the Polish water spirit, Thula, associated with the lake in her parents' village. Not only later in the book, but also throughout Grass's later work, the twentieth-century Tulla Pokriefke displays characteristics that derive from all these regionally conditioned precursors. Most notably, she has a marked association with water. Early on in the second part of the book, her cousin, Harry Liebenau, narrates how her beloved younger brother, Konrad, drowns, while much later on, in *Im Krebsgang* (2002, *Crabwalk* 2003), she gives birth on the *Wilhelm Gustloff*, the sinking ship of war evacuees, to Paul.[33] Remaining within *Hundejahre*, the further associations suggested by Brauxel's passing references to Tulla-precursors strongly imply that the character's childhood viciousness, often obliquely referred to through her teeth in Liebenau's narrative, her tomboy nature (also emphasized in *Katz und Maus*), her curious communion with nature (she notably commands the crows in the central scenes detailing the transformations of the artist-figures Eddi Amsel and Jenny Brunies) and her excessive sexual energy are also pre-programmed by her place of birth. For Brauxel, the watery Vistula landscape both stores and evokes a certain, evil 'Tulla-ness'.[34] This, it should be noted, is an obviously misogynistic twist on the trope of merging women with the natural landscape. The same trope also

---

[32] Grass, *Werkausgabe*, vol. 5, ed. Volker Neuhaus (Göttingen: Steidl, 1997), p. 7. Subsequent references to this volume appear as page numbers in parenthesis in the text.
[33] Paul in turn fathers Tulla's grandson, Konny, whose obsession at the end of the twentieth century with the ship's Nazi namesake leads him to commit an ideologically-inspired murder. Tulla's repeated urging to tell the ship's story plays a significant part in this.
[34] For a very detailed analysis of Tulla's precursors and their significance for her 'evil' character, see Michael Harscheidt, *Günter Grass: Wort-Zahl-Gott: Der 'phantastische Realismus' in den Hundejahren* (Bonn: Bouvier, 1976), esp. pp. 458–69.

characterizes Böll's later *Frauen vor Flußlandschaft* as well as a great deal of Martin Walser's early work.

However, men too are shown to be profoundly influenced by their place of birth. Writing the first section, Brauxel endows Walter Matern, the novel's third narrator and a key protagonist throughout, with a regionally conditioned genealogy that sees him re-enacting the barely sublimated violence of his teeth-grinding grandmother in his younger years. What could be cast off as a personal Freudian psychosis in Oskar Matzerath's relationship to his grandmother's skirts in *Die Blechtrommel* takes on a much broader social and historical sweep in *Hundejahre*. Here, genealogy and familial relations determine both place as a collective experience over the ages and the individual's actions within it. After the war, Matern self-consciously styles himself on the sixteenth-century robber-avengers Simon and Gregor Materna, who besieged sixteenth-century Danzig and also appear in Brauxel's opening narrative. Tellingly, he invokes Heidegger as he does so. Furthermore, Brauxel sets up a particular biblical incantatory style of reference to the family tree of the locally bred Alsatians, the eponymous dogs of the book's title, which percolates through all three narratives and strengthens the text's overarching insistence on the importance of genealogies rooted in specific landscapes. The dogs' genealogy leads from a Lithuanian wolf, through the protagonists' Pomeranian and Danzig dogs, to Hitler's favoured hound, Prinz, who derives from this Danzig stock. Matern hooks up with this last dog in the confusion at the end of the war and re-names him Pluto when he spots the name on a railway sign. This is an apparently unwitting return to the dog's Pomeranian grandfather of the same name, and it thereby serves to close the circle of historico-regional significances. Attaching himself to the discharged POW, Prinz/Pluto accompanies Matern on his vengeful wanderings across post-war Germany. With Brauxel again pulling the strings by the end of the novel, the dog effectively escorts Matern back to the memory of his betrayal of his childhood friend Eddi Amsel on the dyke of the Vistula River. This was the point, some 700 pages previously, with which the narrative began, and it shows that, for all the geographical space and historical events covered over the course of the narrative, memory links between people and places determine the text's underlying structural logic. All creative acts that happen within this text – including the creative act of the text itself – are therefore undertaken in the commemorative mode, and this mode is wholly determined by the different places it is designed to relate, both to the reader and to one another.

The cycles of historical repetition that are thereby conjured up by the overall organizing narrator have strong counterparts in Grass's earlier works from the trilogy, in terms of both characterization and the

The Exemplary Creator 93

underpinning narrative logic. John Reddick, in particular, has written in great detail about the cyclical symbols in *Die Blechtrommel* and *Katz und Maus*, linking these to existential pronouncements on the part of the author that point as much to eternal cycles of return as to any specific social or political explanation of events. However, Reddick also draws a distinction between *Hundejahre* and the first two works of the trilogy, when he deems that, compared to *Die Blechtrommel*, this text 'depicts life much more in terms of a *social, cultural* process that is determined by specific factors in specific situations'.[35] In light of the theoretical framework from social geography outlined above, this observation points directly to the way the third text in Grass's trilogy engages with the 'throwntogetherness' of place. For Massey, this neologism carries particular meaning because it underscores not just the dynamic element of contingency in the way places are constituted, but also the relational. People live within a plurality of relationships that extend across both time and space, and the way they live together directly determines the future forms that place can take on. In this sense, there is a potential orientation towards a different future within the generational memory narrative, even though its strong retrospective focus means that the potential for uncovering alternative ways of relating to one another seems slim.

This is where the importance of the other narrators in Brauxel's 'documentary' text becomes evident. Although Brauxel's own opening narrative links characters to place in a way that invokes memory as a quasi-mythological force that can blur the specifics of time and place, the narrators in the second and third parts of the book show themselves to be distinctly aware of the specific cultural and political processes unfolding around them. The fact that, as numerous commentators have observed, they attempt to dissimulate their own involvement in certain events, does not detract from this awareness.[36] Quite on the contrary, Liebenau's conflicting reports of his role in Tulla's taunting of Amsel and Felsner-Imbs, and Matern's lacuna when recalling the number of SA men who attacked Amsel, show the extent of these characters' sensitivity to the particular political processes in which they became ingloriously enmeshed.[37] Furthermore, however 'timeless' an image of place Brauxel may suggest in his opening section, in his role as overall

---

[35] John Reddick, *The Danzig Triology of Günter Grass: A Study of The Tin Drum, Cat and Mouse, and Dog Years* (London: Secker & Warburg, 1975), p. 203.
[36] On dissimulation, see Katharina Hall, *Günter Grass's 'Danzig Quintet': Explorations in the Memory and History of the Nazi Era from 'Die Blechtrommel' to 'Im Krebsgang'* (Bern: Lang, 2007) in particular.
[37] On the topic of the narrators' compromising guilt more generally, see Mason, *The Skeptical Muse*.

manuscript coordinator of the commemorative 'Festschrift' (35) he goes to considerable lengths to ensure that his subsequent narrator, the Danzig-based Harry Liebenau, is well equipped with specific knowledge about the city and its cultural and political developments in the modern period. It is not enough simply to hail from the time and place of action to be described in the narrative; the narrator must be saturated in site-specific cultural and political knowledge, to the point where Danzig is the root, or 'cultural Heimat' of his very being. With site-specific love written into his very name – Liebe for 'love' and 'Au(e)' for meadow – Liebenau easily passes the citizenship test Brauxel sets him.

Where Liebenau creates his narrative by mentally retracing his childhood steps through Danzig in the form of an open-ended monologue to Tulla, Walter Matern, the narrator-focalizer in the third section of the novel, is a figure on the run from his past. In fact, just like Oskar and Pilenz before them, both Matern and Liebenau represent guilty, unreliable narrators, who have an existential as well as material investment in recasting certain aspects of their identity. They are both unhappy and uneasy figures at the time of writing, and they are both also materially reliant on the paid employment the writing task affords them. In different ways, a problematic relationship to place conditions how they set about this task, with the result that the place in which they grew up, the anthropological centre of the novel, becomes ever more fragmented and therefore unsustainable as an overarching interpretive category. The Jäschkental Woods, for example, seem to evaporate before our eyes like a bad fairy-tale as Tulla's persecution of her friend there is both recounted and glossed over by the love-struck Liebenau. Similarly, the third-person fairy-tale framing of the end of the war as an elaborate search for Hitler's favourite dog substitutes the satirical mode for the commemorative mode and in so doing ostentatiously casts the factual reliability of any of the first-person narrators' memories into doubt. Ironically enough, then, the novel, as a place-led memory narrative, throws both place and memory into question as it progresses.

The novel's increasing destabilization of 'memory of place' as an all-too-human subjective interaction between man and his environment does not, however, mean that anthropological place itself becomes a meaninglessly subjective category and we are left, as is often argued in the case of *Die Blechtrommel* and *Katz und Maus*, to contemplate the wider significance of an individual psychosis and its attendant failed relationships largely irrespective of the particular physical place in which these unfolded. Despite his own attempt to move away from anthropological place as the analytical site of twenty-first-century human interactions, the social anthropologist Marc Augé has had to admit to the concept's ongoing relevance for immediate identity issues:

Of course, the intellectual status of anthropological place is ambiguous. It is only the idea, partially materialized, that the inhabitants have of their relations with the territory, with their families and with others. This idea may be partial or mythologized. It varies with the individual's point of view and position in society. Nevertheless, it offers and imposes a set of references which may not be quite those of natural harmony or some 'paradise lost', but whose absence, when they disappear, is not easily filled.[38]

Individual place-led memory narratives, in other words, continue to resonate on a number of levels for both their authors and subsequent interpreters, even after the upheavals of the twentieth century have put paid to any ideas of a unified, rooted community. Reading someone's 'partial or mythologized' retrospective account of a place will not allow definitive access either to that place at a certain time, or to the human relationships that unfolded within it. It will, however, provide access to a specific, necessarily limited, worldview that is crucial for that person's sense of self. When this worldview is multiplied by several individual accounts that intersect as well as diverge in their reconstructions of people and places, the reader can gain an overall sense of how a place has been used and endowed with significance by its inhabitants and their later interpreters. By employing three different narrators in the construction of a commemorative text that is variously referred to as a 'Festschrift' (35), a 'Handbuch' (42; handbook), a 'Manuskript' (61; manuscript), and a 'Chronik' (555; chronicle), Grass allows precisely this 'set of references' to emerge as an operation of the collective 'memory of place', against which the continuities and ruptures in the lives of his protagonists are to be understood.

At a collective level, then, Grass's text filters Assmann's memory of place through the subjective experiences of a place's individual inhabitants. While none of these individuals come anywhere near the kind of 'Erkenntnis' that either Adorno or Böll place at the heart of cultural activity, the text as a whole works with a sufficient plurality of voices that their inability to look beyond their circumstances itself provides a form of 'Erkenntnis' – not for the characters, but for the organizing author and his readers. In this, the question of attitude becomes key. For in forcing the different voices to relate to one another to at least some degree in the overarching structure of Brauxel's memory

---

[38] Marc Augé, *Non-Places: Introduction to an Anthropology of Supermodernity*, trans. John Howe (London: Verso, 1995), p. 56.

narrative, Grass begins to imagine a fledgling public sphere that could be constituted by Habermas's 'structures of lived experience' and oriented towards not the historical cycles of repetition that have held out so far, but the power of the better argument. A range of different attitudes to place is imperative if its relational nature is to be linked to any form of potential social change. Accordingly, whereas for Matern and Liebenau the specifics of the Danzig region lead to a problematic attitude of placeness within the place-led memory narratives described above that result in endless repetition of traumatic misdeeds, for the artist-writer Amsel / Brauxel the opposite is the case. He is characterized early on by a distinct sense of placelessness.

Amsel builds an identity based around reflecting his place of birth, constructing scarecrows that represent first local village characters, then Prussian gods and generals. In so doing, however, he champions the inauthentic. His increasingly factory-line productions are not designed to be folksy re-imaginings of the past. Rather, their crudely constructed nature is intended to unsettle the viewer, as the figures appear like threatening distortions of their real-life counterparts. Through his activity, he interrupts the birds' natural cycles of nesting and feeding and introduces an element of self-awareness into the local community; this unsettling function quickly comes to characterize his being and makes him function in a similar way to Adorno's cultural critic, located both inside and outside the tradition, both subject and object of his own satire. In his later, mechanized Steffensweg productions, Amsel develops this into a conscious art-form, to the point where consciously living his Jewishness – acting as a mirror to the violent attitudes taking root in German society – results in his metaphorical annihilation and expulsion following the bloody SA attack.

Moving from his childhood existence as foil to a region's cultural traditions and emergent identity politics, through a seemingly weightless and intangible existence as Haseloff the exiled *Balletmeister*, to his post-war existence as the largely untraceable but increasingly omnipotent Goldmäulchen, Amsel's placelessness grows in proportion to his invisible influence over German society. This becomes ever more obviously the target of the satirical mode within Brauxel's overarching narrative. As Goldmäulchen, he pulls the strings behind much of Adenauer Germany's economy through extensive manipulation of people's beliefs, while as Brauxel he creates a subterranean factory that mass produces a distorted reflection of Germanness that is being sold around the world even as the 'real' German people are rebuilding their country and themselves above ground. Amsel as a character thereby becomes an increasingly thinly disguised attitude of critical reflection that can itself be put to rather sinister, empire-building use. Unlike either Liebenau or Matern, he is associated, through his own manipulation of the satirical mode, with an excess of Böll's 'Erkenntnis'. Given the mercantile nature of all his post-war activities, this 'Erkenntnis' seems ill-suited to helping him take on a socio-culturally significant place in society of the type Böll associated with the writer figure. Rather, he appears as some kind of threatening near-Adornian ethical avenger, dialectally serving back to the Germans what they had served to the rest of Europe and himself taking on 'barbaric' proportions in the process. However, although he reflects their behaviour back to others, he ultimately lacks Adorno's ability to reflect on his own imbrication within the systems he critiques. His adoption of placelessness loses its link to place.

Ultimately, the characters of Amsel / Brauxel and Matern represent extremes, neither of whom offer positive models of behaviour either for society or for individuals trying to position themselves in respect of their past lives. This very explicit problematics of place, however, turns the text as a whole into an authentic place of memory existing against the odds in an impossible space and created out of a series of individual narratives crafted in a mixture of the commemorative and satirical modes. Each individual narrative viewpoint can only ever hope to lay bare its own memories of a place and its relationship to that place. Brought to an uneasy ablutional truce at the very end of the text, Amsel / Brauxel and Matern, whose very identities become fluid as the first- and third-person pronouns become interchangeable, seem to share this final realization. Matern reports from their separate baths: 'Eddi pfeift etwas Unbestimmtes. Ich versuche ähnliches zu pfeifen. Doch das ist schwer. Beide sind wir nackt. Jeder badet für sich' (744; Eddi whistles something vague. I try to whistle it too. But that's hard. Both of us are naked. Each is bathing for himself.). There is a faint echo here, perhaps, of Bloch's Heimat, as both narrators are cast back to a naked, child-like state, cocooned in their baths and arguably with a greater degree of self-awareness and self-determination than at any other point in their narratives. However, full accession to this utopian place still seems some way off for each narrator as they are left acting alone. Accordingly, what Grass shows in his epic tale, through his consistent use for the individual narrators of the retrospectively focused and place-bound commemorative and satirical modes, is the difficulty of taking on a position of absolute authority and control in respect of Germany's necessary memory narrative. Instead, the story can only cohere on a meta-textual level, in a structure that kaleidoscopes alternative spaces and times in a manner aligned with the utopian mode. On this level, *Hundejahre* displays a much more dispersed, dialogic conception of authorship than any of the individual narrators are able to perceive on their own.

With this, Grass works out, in a highly engrossing and instructive literary form, what Adorno had decreed philosophically: the post-war German author of Grass's compromised generation, regardless of his or her religion or wartime experiences, has no place from which to write. Finding a credible place in society from which to express and act on that very placelessness must nevertheless become the object of his endeavours. The mixture of commemorative, satirical and utopian modes that underlies Grass's authorship of this text repeatedly draws attention to the accompanying question of where the remembering subject is located and how the relations that defined past places map on to those of the present. In its meta-textual structure, Grass's work thus foregrounds the foundational model of the author as an exemplary creator, as the work authored in his name invites itself to be seen as a distinct creative space that carries an important reflective impetus for contemporary society. It is both woven out of commemorative narratives and points beyond them, and it multiplies and disperses individual acts of authorship across its structure in equal measure as it does so. As such, and in the spirit of More's *Utopia*, it invites a creative dialogic response rather than slavish epigonal emulation, even as it also asserts Grass's own monumentality in fashioning the whole piece in the first place.

In the 1960s, however, as Hans Joachim Hahn has explored in a recent article on the subject, the novel was received much more as a flat monumental statement of Grass's literary prowess than as a differentiated creative invitation.[39] This underscores the ongoing dominance of the celebratory mode in the German literary field that necessarily subsumes all attempts by authors to create literary works that comment upon society within an intellectually fetishizing gesture, whether these are subsequently lauded or derided. Grass was declared (by Enzensberger) to have reached the 'pinnacle of the German Parnassus' with his third work in the trilogy, only for other critics to deem the same work too aesthetically unwieldy, perhaps as a direct result of the author's inflated ambition. Indeed, readings that underscored the author's epic literary scope, both for himself and his work, in remodelling the past as part of a grand exemplary model of authorship began to grate more and more with alternative models of citizen engagement in society that took hold as the 1960s progressed and the student movement began to gain ground. Their incumbents directly positioned themselves against the model of the exemplary

---

[39] Hans-Joachim Hahn, 'Günter Grass's Hundejahre: Ein Beitrag zur Erinnerungskultur in der Bundesrepublik der Sechziger Jahre', *German Life & Letters*, 72.2 (2019), 187–203.

creator that Grass and his sector-defining cohort from the Gruppe 47 had established. If Grass's authorship was to avoid being cast off by the supporters of these counter models as too much the celebrated product of his own literary world, he needed to locate himself more squarely within the greater structure of Habermas's public sphere, taking some of his literary techniques of self-presentation to a broader audience. This is exactly what Grass would go on to do in his political campaigning of 1965 and 1969. Here, he very consciously applied the foundational model of creative exemplarity to a sense of civic duty and encouraged a broad swathe of colleagues from across the Gruppe 47 to do the same.[40]

Against Foundations: Gisela Elsner's Dystopian Divergence and Fritz J. Raddatz' Concentric Entrapment

Günter Grass would go on to become the lead face of post-war West German literature, often quite literally, as his high media profile and own propensity towards self-portraits meant he was visually present across multiple media for many decades. His and fellow Gruppe 47 authors' proximity to leading politicians, notably in the SPD party under Willy Brandt's leadership (1965–1974), was itself emblematic of an unexpected rapprochement between liberal and left-wing writers and the German state that was unimaginable in the 1950s. Accordingly, writers like Böll, Enzensberger and Grass, who had been outspoken in their critique of the recent past at the end of that decade, found themselves in just a few short years part of the cultural establishment. The foundational model they helped shape of the author as an exemplary creator who facilitates new dialogic structures in both his writing and society would underpin both further work undertaken directly in this vein and work that positioned itself against it. The latter would follow in the wake of Enzensberger's famous 1968 issue of the cultural journal *Kursbuch* that declared the 'death of literature', and with it a certain kind of self-consciously literary author. Karin Struck, Nicolas Born, Günter Wallraff and F.C. Delius, for example, all sought to take this foundational model of authorship off its pedestal by using more open-ended, reporting-style texts in the late 1960s and 1970s. While such attempts outwardly reacted against the kind of epic sweep and grand creative gesture found in the earlier fictional texts of Böll,

---

[40] For more on this and his later career, see Rebecca Braun, *Constructing Authorship in the Work of Günter Grass* (Oxford: Oxford U. P., 2008). On his political activity in particular, see Timm Niklas Pietsch, *"Wer hört noch zu?" Günter Grass als politischer Redner und Essayist* (Essen: Klartext, 2006). Also on both points: Nicole Thesz, *The Communicative Event in the Works of Günter Grass: Stages of Speech, 1959-2015* (Rochester, NY: Camden House, 2018).

Grass, Johnson, Lenz and Walser, they also partook in a more dialogic understanding of authorship that had in fact first gained expression in these very works through the related notion of ethically-induced authorial placelessness. This had by now become innate to the distinctly post-war model of authorship that, following Adorno, cannot but question its own relation to place as both a textual and historical concern.

If simultaneously doubting and asserting one's place as an author in both the text and the world therefore became the basic attitudinal trope of post-war West German authorship, there were nevertheless ways of seeking some genuine distance, however partial, to the foundational model of the exemplary creator. This is the case both for authors and for the wider array of individuals (e.g. publishers, magazine editors, journalists) who form part of the extended authorship process. However, for reasons that will become apparent, surviving positive examples of such distance are rare. In these closing pages, I offer some insights as to why this might be the case from the examples of the author Gisela Elsner (1937–1992) and the publisher, editor, journalist and author Fritz J. Raddatz (1931–2015). Both figures were wholly embraced by the West German literary sector in the 1960s – Raddatz was indeed recruited in from the GDR – precisely for their ability to bring a fresh perspective to literary debates. To varying degrees and for different reasons, they also fell right out of it within their own lifetimes. In the first half of the 1960s, Elsner was the celebrated female equivalent of Günter Grass, while Raddatz had made himself indispensable to the Rowohlt publishing house as deputy to the charismatic managing director, Heinrich Maria Ledig-Rowohlt. By the end of the 1980s, Elsner was an isolated figure, abandoned by her publishers and addicted to drugs, and Raddatz, having lost his job first at Rowohlt and then as editor-in-chief of the literary pages of the weekly newspaper, *Die Zeit*, had begun his long self-stylization (and accompanying clinical depression) as a rejected freelance journalist. With the benefit of hindsight, this trajectory was already evident by the closing years of the 1960s.

Eerily, in fact, Elsner foretells much of this, albeit inversely, in an obituary she contributed to the playful volume *Vorletzte Worte: Schriftsteller schreiben ihren eigenen Nachruf* (1970, Penultimate Words: Authors Write Their Own Obituary). The daughter of a well-to-do industrialist, Elsner was born in Nürnberg, took part in a number of meetings of the Gruppe 47 and shot to broader media attention when she won the Prix Formentor in 1964 for her debut novel, *Die Riesenzwerge* (*The Giant Dwarves*). 'Die Auferstehung der Gisela Elsner' (The Resurrection of Gisela Elsner) is written by an anonymous reporter for a small magazine, purporting to tell the truth about a funeral that has been hushed up in the regional and national press and, in so doing,

The Exemplary Creator 101

imagining a celebrity legacy to a long and glittering career that the real Elsner would never experience.[41] The 97-year-old Elsner, so we are to believe, orchestrated her own death and funeral proceedings, including a route through the town that would cause maximum inconvenience on a day that would be sure to make people sweat in lieu of shedding tears. Other unlikely things follow. En route to the author's final resting place, the Gisela Elsner literary society reveals an oversized Gisela Elsner statue complete with a walk-in library, distributes free branded pens, and recruits further members to their ranks with promises of free passes to the newly established pop-up Gisela Elsner University. The procession culminates in the unveiling of an automated mechanism in the glass coffin that uses the decaying author's body as a kind of peep-show puppet that can apparently spring into life and is accompanied by a recorded voice. The reporter retrospectively confirms that local yobs and international literary tourists routinely gather to cause further trouble and/or witness the grotesque event of her repeatable resurrection in large numbers, both draining the council of resource and providing further money-spinning, conflict-ridden schemes for it to administer.

Like the rest of Elsner's early fiction, this auto-obituary is effective because it shows how society really is by showing how it really isn't, and it manages to do so by the author being present and not present at the same time. Many of the elements of the story are individually credible and point to the very real value attached to writing and writers – the celebratory mode that surrounds them in society at large, with universities named after authors, literary societies and public monuments supporting their afterlives, sites of literary tourism harnessed to multiple contemporary uses. However, the basic black humour of the piece resides in the fact that it is quite inconceivable that Gisela Elsner would ever form the object of such public celebration. Elsner already knows this by 1970 – in fact, she probably knows it as soon as she starts writing in earnest in the 1950s: her first book, *Triboll: Lebenslauf eines erstaunlichen Mannes* (Triboll: The Life Story of an Amazing Man), was published in 1956 as a co-authored volume of short stories with her husband-to-be, the writer Klaus Roehler, even though he made it clear to interested publishers that he had not written them.[42] But if there is an obvious, and very significant, point to be made about

---

[41] In K. H. Kramberg, ed., *Vorletzte Worte: Schriftsteller schreiben ihren eigenen Nachruf* (Berlin: Goldman, 1985), pp. 54–60.
[42] As reported in the editorial comments to Gisela Elsner, *Versuche, die Wirklichkeit zu bewältigen*, ed. Christine Künzel, 2 vols, vol. 1, pp. 255–56.

gender in the German literature network here, it is one that is amplified by Elsner's specific choice of predominant authorial mode: she uses the satirical mode to send up the inherent self-celebration on which the literary sector relies. While women are generally at a disadvantage when it comes to positioning themselves within the established canon, Elsner makes it clear that she in particular is not the right kind of author to form the focus of a sustained public expression of the celebratory mode. The dynamic that unfolds around her imagined afterlife is deliberately grotesque, and this points to the inherently grotesque nature of the whole celebratory mode of authorship that determines the West German model of authorial exemplarity more broadly. In fact, mastering the satirical mode, Elsner responds to the trope of placelessness that, as we have already seen, is a constituent part of this model, with hollow other-worldly laughter that seems to well up from within the text itself, as she shows herself to be both omnipresent and absolutely absent in this text's alternative image of literary lives in West Germany. This tactical inversion of the trope of placelessness into death-by-satire, through a satirical mix of the celebratory and utopian modes, is both an accurate critique of what is wrong with the practical forms the West German cultural sector has taken, as chapter four will elaborate in more detail, and a very significant problem when it comes to managing her actual ongoing career and any afterlife that may remain in this sector.

The practical failings within the sector that Elsner would encounter as a woman operating in the satirical mode were in fact already evident when she was awarded the glamorous international publishing prize, the Prix Formentor, for *Die Riesenzwerge*. The prize had been called into life at the start of the decade at least in part to ensure the commercial success of a work across Europe – its translation into the major European languages and dissemination across fourteen countries was ensured. However, the seemingly large cash prize and obvious commercial intent made some doubt its literary merits.[43] When it launched the career of a glamorous woman who routinely wore a Cleopatra-style wig and had a penchant for luxury clothing, the suspicion that the literary decision had been further compromised by PR input was tangible in comments across the German literary world. It must be

---

[43] The cash sum was rumoured to be the equivalent of a family home, although in actual fact it was tied to rights advances. See Michael Töteberg, '"Das wärs, lieber Herr Verleger, für diesmal": Eine Hausautorin wird verramscht: Gisela Elsner und der Rowohlt-Verlag', in Künzel & Schönert, eds, *Ikonisierung, Kritik, Wiederentdeckung: Gisela Elsner und die Literatur der Bundesrepublik* (Munich: text + kritik, 2014), pp. 54–71.

stressed that the work itself by no means supports such aspersions. The vignettes provided by the eleven interlinked stories it comprises are strongly reminiscent of the best of Grass's early writing, providing an off-centre view that identifies all of the metaphorical skeletons in the fledgling Federal Republic's closet, but assembled in such a way as to create a fantastical satire, both in the individual stories and across the work as a whole. The way in which this satire was initially described as the result of the author's 'böser Blick', or evil view on the world, however, would set the tone for Elsner's reception for decades to come. Her subsequent seven novels and various radio plays and short story collections were constantly reduced to the phrase that marries an implicit value judgement on her authorial attitude with one about her relationship to appearances, including her own.[44]

Indeed, even when the term 'böser Blick' is taken, as it was probably initially intended, merely as another term for 'satire' when discussing the achievements of *Die Riesenzwerge*, the term falls short, for the metaphor employed implies a singular reporting view on the world where in fact none is directly present. The whole point of Elsner's text is that neither the mode in which it is written, nor the overall meaning, can be directly attributed to any one standpoint, not least because the principal focalizer from within the fiction is a young boy who can neither read nor count beyond ten. Instead, situations unfold, producing an all-encompassing, inescapable satire in the attempts they record on the part of West German characters to celebrate (the shared Sunday roast that turns into mass cannibalism in 'Die Mahlzeit' / 'The Meal'), commemorate (the coffee circle that turns into a mixture of double blasphemy and morbid resurrection of fallen soldiers in 'Der Herr' / 'The Lord') and educate (the Nazi-inspired doctrine of self-reliance to be followed into absurdity that is meted out by the teacher to his pupils in the imaginary sewing lesson of 'Der Knopf' / 'The Button').

Indeed, where Fuchs has spoken about narrative excess as a literary reaction to trauma, Elsner's stories unleash a specific version of this in the form of satiric excess around easily recognizable blind spots in society: the characters are locked into impossible situations where it becomes self-evident that the grotesquely satirical outcome is the only available option, and this will repeat across the collection, as society is collectively unable to perceive, let alone address, its own failings. The mother's failure to produce a perfect Sunday roast in the opening story,

---

[44] See Christine Künzel, 'Eine "schreibende Kleopatra": Autorschaft und Maskerade bei Gisela Elsner', in Christine Künzel & Jörg Schönert, eds, *Autorinszenierungen: Autorschaft und literarisches Werk im Kontext der Medien* (Würzburg: Königshausen & Neumann, 2007), pp. 177–90.

'Die Mahlzeit', will result in her husband being eaten by a hungry mob, in a story that grows out of observations about how social power dynamics are played out through food, but without any of the characters consciously realizing this. The mother, father, child and head teacher are defined by the ways they sit at the table, the movements of their bodies compellingly conditioned by the ritual of the various meals in a manner that brings to mind Bruno Latour's insistence that agency inheres in things as much as people. The final story in the collection, 'Die Hochzeit' (The Wedding) brings to an aesthetically logical conclusion how this kind of social observation emanates from a group's own blind enactment of relations through food. The story is spun out through mirrored repeated reports on events, as participants and onlookers tell one another what they have just been telling one another while the wedding feast is slowly consumed in a room characterized by *trompe l'oeil* effects created by the positioning of open windows, mirrors and paintings. What is actually communicated is the lack of substance in people's lives, coupled with the shared desire to relate to one another through constant evaluation of each other's actions, all of which is captured in meaningless stock phrases. Perspective, as mediated by language itself, is turned into a seemingly autonomous author operating in the satirical mode, as the evaluative truisms that make up the story simultaneously undercut it: the words reflect themselves in a way that makes them look both uncomfortably appropriate and quite out of place in a literary text that, in the broadest of senses, aims to relate something of substance.

Such dispersal of agency across both characters and objects is what makes *Die Riesenzwerge* so distinctive. With this in mind, the composition of the work as a whole can be understood as the result of a radical invocation of the satirical mode of authorship. Unnervingly, the satire appears to come from nowhere in particular. Unlike in the early texts of Elfriede Jelinek, for example – an author who has repeatedly identified the older Elsner as an important inspiration for her work – there is not even a residual sense of an authorial voice offering a judgement.[45] Rather, the reader is compelled to witness the texts' own satirical unfolding. The only consolation is that Lothar Leinlein, the child focalizer who spends much of the collection being eaten up from the inside by a parasitic worm while food, corpulence and hedonism abound around him, appears to escape. He finally learns to count to eleven and leaves the final frame as the eleventh departing guest from

---

[45] Elfriede Jelinek, '"Ist die schwarze Köchin da? Ja, ja, ja!": Zu Gisela Elsner', in Christine Künzel, ed., *Die letzte Kommunistin: Texte zu Gisela Elsner* (Hamburg: konkret, 2009), pp. 23–28.

the wedding – an indication, perhaps, that he has found a way out that may stem from his will to learn from what he can see. At the same time, the question of where he might possibly go is left wholly unanswered. This systemic inability to leave the satire behind for a better (or at least different) place is a problem shared by Gisela Elsner. Even though her authorial perspective is markedly absent throughout the text's own unfolding of its satirical mode, she will end up wholly responsible for the satirical visions imparted by the stories. This is because she cannot place herself anywhere else (as Böll manages in his melancholy invocations of alternative homes for the writer, for example) and does not create fictional mediators of the satire (in the manner of Grass's army of fictional narrators who are tripped up by their own narratives).

The result is that even though she does quite deliberately embrace the broader contexts of West German publishing, in both her texts and her person – including taking them on directly in her own counter appropriation of a distinct Cleopatra image that she intends to make work for her on her own terms – she is also readily cast as inherently extreme, and thus not the kind of exemplary creator figure West German literature wants or needs. Accordingly, despite her initial apparent suitability for modelling a new kind of literature in the Federal Republic, after just a few short years she will be increasingly sidelined. When, in later decades, her politics and lifestyle do not readily square with those of the literary mainstream (her feminist, Marxist leanings coupled with her propensity for haute-couture and bourgeois background prove unpalatable to many), she loses first her publisher and then her entire back catalogue, which Rowohlt remaindered in 1991. Hermann Kinder notes that Elsner was largely unknown to students of German literature just three years after her death in 1992, and this despite her having been one of Rowohlt's more lucrative authors throughout the 1960s.[46] By using the satirical mode to highlight really-existing dystopias unfolding both in contemporary society and in the contemporary literature network, it would thus appear that Elsner also metaphorically wrote her actual obituary. By insisting on the actual placelessness of the author in the work through her radical use of a satirical mode that seemed to unfold itself, her own writing made her oddly incidental to her work. This, coupled with Elsner's satirical presentation of her own person, foreclosed the kind of coy celebration of her considerable achievements in questioning the kind of place that the Federal Republic had become that similar work by her male counterparts – not least Grass – routinely

---

[46] Hermann Kinder, 'Gisela Elsner – der entsorgte Stachel', in Gisela Elsner, *Die Riesenzwerge* (Berlin: Aufbau, 2001), pp. 283–94. Sales figures are taken from Töteberg, 'Eine Hausautorin wird verramscht'.

built right into the centre of its literary structures and used to ensure ongoing attention across the literature network.

Finally, although Raddatz' positioning in respect of the foundational model of authorship is quite different to Elsner's, it shares a broad trajectory in the way it turns from wholesale affiliation with the normative power structures in publishing to distance and bitterness. Born in 1931, he occupied multiple roles within the literature network, from journalist to editor to publisher to author. His extended exertion of authorship from within these roles in the 1960s and 1970s, when he was at the height of his own identification with the European canon and new German writing, adds a useful insider perspective on the celebratory mode of authorship that Elsner undercuts with both her text and her person. His activities in this decade both help us better understand some of the practical challenges facing individuals trying to turn the foundational tropes of creative 'Erkenntnis' and placelessness into viable literary projects (both commercially and intellectually). They allow a fresh perspective on how supporting the model of authorship that coheres around these tropes might play out in practical terms for individual careers where one's own literary oeuvre will not take centre stage.[47]

Raddatz has provided multiple retrospective accounts of his life in publishing, beginning with his 2005 memoirs, *Unruhestifter* (*The Troublemaker*), and then in expanded form in his two-volume set of diaries (2010, 2014) that run to some 1,650 pages and cover the years 1982–2012. *Jahre mit Ledig* (*The Years with Ledig*), his 2015 account of working for the Rowohlt publishing house in the 1960s partially reproduces sections from his 2005 memoirs, but supplements them with photographs and facsimiles of documents that visually recreate the glamour, power and intense activity that underscored the pioneering spirit of West German publishing in the 1960s. The very fact that these retrospective publications, over 2,000 pages in total, could appear in such proliferation in the first fifteen years of the twenty-first century testifies to the ongoing significance attributed to the post-war West German foundational model of authorship.

Rather like Grass's *Amsel / Brauxel*, Raddatz has occupied multiple positions under different regimes within this period, and like all of the authors discussed in this chapter, he staked the broader significance of his public persona on the way his exemplary literary activities would be interpreted in the wider public sphere – his diaries alone make this clear. These activities ranged from being the editor-in-chief at the Volk and Welt publishing house in the GDR of the 1950s, through to the same

---

[47] Raddatz did try to write literature himself, but with little real success.

powerful position at Rowohlt in the Federal Republic of the 1960s, before going on to edit the literary review section of *Die Zeit* from the mid 1970s to the mid 1980s. At all times, including during his later years working freelance, this also involved liaising with writers, journalists, academics, editors and publishers at literary events, ceremonies and parties within and beyond West Germany: key mediators for the dominant celebratory mode of authorship across the literature network. If during his time in the East he was known primarily for representing modernist or otherwise innovative writing that pushed at the boundaries of what was considered acceptable under the tenets of socialist realism, at Rowohlt he mediated in the other direction. Here, he sought to make space for alternative, left-wing views, and introduced, amongst other things, the highly successful left-wing political paperback series, 'Ro-Ro-Ro Aktuell', whose first book was the bestselling collection of essays by left-wing writers advocating a vote for the Social Democratic Party in the 1961 general election, *Die Alternative oder Brauchen wir eine neue Regierung?* (The Alternative, or Do We Need a New Government?). Thus, Raddatz records that, although Heinrich Böll was initially supposed to appear as editor of this venture and, due to his ill health, it was subsequently published in Martin Walser's name, the person who actually did all the editing and organizing was Raddatz himself.[48]

This sort of basic fact check is useful for our purposes, as it both frames and relativizes authors' individual actions, and the narratives that they – and their academic interpreters – like to spin about their socio-political actions and importance. Collectively, Raddatz' memoirs paint a picture of the everyday business of being an author in post-war Germany that involves multiple actors, all the time. They also help understand why someone like Raddatz, for all the power he may have appeared to wield in deciding whether or not authors should be published, was himself in a vulnerable position. There is not space for detailed analysis of these interactions themselves here, but some salient features should be recorded and will be discussed in greater depth in chapter four. First, the working practices Raddatz outlines during his years with Heinrich Maria Ledig-Rowohlt are stunningly male: business deals with writers and other publishers alike are routinely clinched in Hamburg's red-light district, while the photographs illustrating Raddatz and Ledig's working life together mark achievement out as exclusively masculine – at times grotesquely so, as evident in the 'Verlagscollage' (publisher's collage) of the five key Rowohlt directors

---

[48] Raddatz, *Unruhestifter: Erinnerungen* (Munich: Propyläen, 2003), p. 233.

108 Authors and the World

posing in an acrobatic pyramid in front of the publishing house wearing nothing but their swimming trunks (figure 2.1).[49] If this is obviously exclusionary for women – and Elsner's reputational problems have been directly attributed to this environment –,[50] it is not without

Figure 2.1 The 'Verlagscollage', undated. Reproduced courtesy of Rowohlt Verlag.

---

[49] Raddatz, *Jahre mit Ledig: Eine Erinnerung* (Hamburg: Rowohlt, 2015), p. 93. For in-depth discussion of this image, see Rebecca Braun, 'World Author: On Exploding Canons and Writing Towards More Equitable Literary Futures', in Joel Evans, ed., *Cambridge Critical Concepts: Globalization and Literary Studies* (Cambridge: Cambridge U. P., forthcoming 2022), pp. 226–43.

[50] See e.g. Michael Peter Hehl, 'Vom "Spießbürger" zum "flexiblen Menschen": Überlegungen zum Verschwinden und Wiederauftauchen Gisela Elsners, in Michael Peter Hehl & Christine Künzel, eds, *Ikonisierung, Kritik, Wiederentdeckung: Gisela Elsner und die Literatur der Bundesrepublik* (Munich: text + kritik, 2014) pp. 112–28.

difficulties for someone who leads an intense homosexual sex-life and comes from a background of childhood abuse, as Raddatz outlines in detail in his memoirs.

Second, if publishing in the East in the 1950s is marked out by wearisome interpersonal negotiations and revisions to avoid censorship, as my next chapter will go on to explore, publishing in the West in the 1960s is characterized by apparently spontaneous sensational deals and a considerable amount of spare cash. Raddatz describes Ledig as routinely promising large monthly stipends to young authors who have yet to prove their worth, while the deals he negotiates for a media tie-in with a new publication by better known writers (such as, on his first day of work at Rowohlt in 1959, 50,000 DM from *Stern* to prepublish parts of Ernst von Salomon's *Schöne Wilhelmine*) belie the notion that literature was always the poor relative of TV and radio.[51] They also underscore the challenge that such a world will pose for people with an addictive tendency, as was the case for both Elsner and Raddatz.

Third, as Raddatz' description of the way Walter Kempowski's literary career was launched with his first work, *Im Block* (1969), makes evident, authors routinely also worked as readers and editors, such that the notion of individual publishers and/or editors as all-powerful gatekeepers also needs to be relativized.[52] Hans Magnus Enzensberger, Joachim Kaiser, Peter Rühmkorf and Jürgen Becker all wrote detailed reports and gave writerly advice to Raddatz, who in turn worked intensively with Kempowski, to turn his initial manuscript into its finished form over the course of some six years.[53] At the same time, publishing in the West also remained subject to intense wrangling and at times rested precariously on key players, and this would prove the first traumatic downfall suffered by Raddatz, whose ability to draw in authors through his collaborative work practices had otherwise significantly enhanced Rowohlt's literary reputation. He lost his job and broke for many years with Ledig when it was revealed in 1969 that the FRG Ministry of Defence had been balloon-dropping into the GDR an anti-Stalinist biography published by Rowohlt, with advice about how to become an FRG informant printed on the back of it. While neither Ledig nor Raddatz had known the full extent of the Ministry of Defence's Cold War plans for the special print-run, internal company

---

[51] Raddatz, *Unruhestifter*, pp. 196–97, and pp. 205–6.
[52] See also the Rowohlt documentation around the publication of Kempowski's *Im Block* gathered in Fritz J. Raddatz, *Zur deutschen Literatur der Zeit 2: Die Nachgeborenen. Leseerfahrungen mit zeitgenössischer Literatur* (Reinbek bei Hamburg: Rowohlt, 1987), pp. 450–65.
[53] Raddatz, *Unruhestifter*, pp. 211–13.

politics meant that the company director Hintermeier, who was fully in the know throughout, was happy to have Raddatz effectively framed as a kind of double agent.[54] Having risen to a position of near omnipresence in German publishing very quickly, Raddatz was effectively too present – too readily placed in any of the multiple mutually opposing camps – to avoid the perils of personal and political intrigue.

Collectively, these economic, political and sociological observations help recreate a sense of the multi-faceted, multi-media world in which West German writers of the late 1950 and 1960s were operating, as the wider infrastructure began to take on the Cold War influenced form that it would retain until the fall of the Wall in 1989. For enterprising and extrovert characters, like Raddatz, Grass and Enzensberger, there were more opportunities to build both a literary and a political profile across diverse media and as part of diverse groupings than they could humanly realize. But there were also various political pitfalls that they could not fully control nor reckon with in advance, as well as significant blind spots that they, as Gentile white men, were programmed not to be able to see. Raddatz' desire to be at the very heart of the West German publishing sector, the intense relationships he cultivated with authors, journalists and academics to facilitate new writing and associated literary activities as part of his attempt to belong, also fed into his blindness on a more pragmatic level, his failure to see things coming as he tended to be caught up in his immediate dealings in individual areas and with individual actors which did not always harmonize well with each other. This would repeat itself in the 1980s, when Raddatz was dismissed from his editorial position at *Die Zeit*, supposedly because he embarrassingly slipped up in his knowledge of Goethe and did not show sufficient contrition, but more likely because a complex web of cultural politics was militating against him once more.[55]

The way in which Elsner's career failed to take off and Raddatz' ran severely aground on several occasions is instructive on several levels. Their public failures are testament to the normative nature of the FRG's foundational model of authorship of exemplary creativity, which mixes ambiguous literary positioning with clear physical and attitudinal position-taking on the part of the author and has ultimately coloured so much of West German writing with a strong moral imperative. Writers and other literary professionals overlooked or kicked against this at their peril. The ways in which Elsner and Raddatz did not fully comply with this model also allow us to consider the ethical problems of West Germany's foundational models of authorship from a different

---

[54] Raddatz, *Unruhestifter*, pp. 295–303.
[55] Raddatz, *Unruhestifter*, pp. 355–408.

perspective, just as conceptually significant but more pragmatically grounded than the historically contextualized literary readings of place offered earlier. For reading Elsner's work as the work of someone who will never succeed in the Federal Republic, regardless of how well executed it is, and following Raddatz' activities at Rowohlt as those of someone destined to be hoist by his own petard precisely because his path to success required him to face in multiple different directions within a complex network of conflicting interests, allows us to follow the blind spots, the things that cannot exist and therefore definitely did exist – the heterotopian elements – in West German publishing. The next two chapters will expand this approach, first by looking at an alternative foundational model of authorship that is underpinned by a different notion of place developed in the GDR, and then by looking in greater detail at the question of agency in the West German literature network.

Three The Exemplary Pedagogue: Alternative Foundations for Belonging in the German Democratic Republic

When the Berlin Wall was erected in August 1961, Wolfdietrich Schnurre and Günter Grass initiated a series of open letters between West and East German authors. Drawing attention to the protest activities that West German authors had engaged in over the course of the 1950s – notably against nuclear armament – , Grass and Schnurre decreed that their Eastern colleagues must be equally bold in respect of the GDR authorities: they should clearly state their position on what the letter presented as an effective incarceration of the East German population. The logic that Schnurre and Grass initially offered for such an unambiguous public declaration from GDR authors drew directly on the pan-German collective failure of writers and intellectuals who remained in Germany in the 1930s and 1940s to provide any effective moral leadership against Hitler. As the first letter declared, 'Wer schweigt, wird schuldig' (keeping quiet makes you guilty). Behind the historically founded sense of moral imperative, however, was a growing irritation with what was seen by the letter's West German writers to be a particularly German inability to embrace authors' potential to take on a leading role in society. In a subsequent article published in *Die Welt* in September 1961, Schnurre put his grievances quite explicitly, 'In Polen, in Ungarn, in Frankreich, in Italien, in fast jedem europäischen Land sind die Schriftsteller das Gewissen ihrer Nation. In Deutschland, will man, sollen sie schweigen'[1] (In Poland, Hungary, France, Italy, in almost every European country, writers are the conscience of their nation. In Germany, the expectation is that they should keep quiet).

---

[1] The exchange is reproduced in part in *Vaterland, Muttersprache: Deutsche Schriftsteller und ihr Staat von 1945 bis heute*, ed. Klaus Wagenbach, Winfried Stephan & Michael Krüger (Berlin: Wagenbach, 1979), pp. 184–88, and more fully in *Das Mauerbuch: Texte und Bilder aus Deutschland von 1945 bis heute*, ed. Manfried Hammer, Edelgard Abenstein, Daniel Danisch et al. (Berlin: Oberbaum, 1986), pp. 135–41.

The anxiety that German authors were failing to be 'good' European intellectuals because of a wider socio-political context that held them back is first and foremost a reflection on 1950s West German society, and it is expressed from the standpoint of the dominant critical, left-wing, male, post-Holocaust, Gentile inflection of authorship that had developed within it. This is a point that the GDR author Stephan Hermlin did not neglect to make in his public response to Grass and Schnurre's letter. Yet Schnurre remained obstinate in his invocation of an ideal moral posture to which all authors should aspire, regardless of the context in which they are operating: 'Seit wann hat sich die ethische Verpflichtung eines Berufs nach der Bequemlichkeit oder der Unbequemlichkeit des jeweiligen Wohnsitzes zu richten? Schriftsteller ist Schriftsteller' (Since when should the ethical imperative of a job be determined by the comfort or discomfort of the respective surroundings in which it is carried out? Writers are writers.) His response shows how the particular mix of celebratory, commemorative and utopian modes of authorship developed by writers of his generation leads into a socio-politically inflected exemplary model of authorship, which he then casts in absolute terms.

Such a projection of West German assumptions onto East German groups and individuals is by no means confined to the heated exchange of views on Cold War politics that took place in the late summer of 1961. Nor does it merely reflect Western authorial blindness to cultural and political difference.[2] Discussing developments across the 1960s, David Bathrick suggests that the very writing of GDR literary history that has taken place on multiple levels over subsequent decades has been significantly affected by the unacknowledged imposition of Western value judgements, right from the initial reception of GDR authors and their works in the West:

> [Das Entstehen eines DDR-Dissidententums] war auch das Produkt einer im Westen entstehenden DDR-Industrie. Kulturpolitik und Kulturindustrie arbeiteten manchmal Hand in Hand, waren oft zwei Seiten eines komplizierten Systems, in dem man Schriftstellern internationale Anerkennung gewährte oder sie im Mülleimer der Geschichte zurückließ.[3]

---

[2] That this blindness existed not only in West German authors but also in the West German literary industry more broadly is well set out in Katharina von Ankum, *Die Rezeption von Christa Wolf in Ost und West: Von Moskauer Novelle bis "Selbstversuch"* (Amsterdam / Atlanta: Rodopi, 1992), pp. 32–45.

[3] David Bathrick, 'Die Intellektuellen und die Macht. Die Repräsentanz des Schriftstellers in der DDR', in Sven Hanuschek, Therese Hörnigk and Christine Malende, eds, *Schriftsteller als Intellektuelle: Politik und Literatur im kalten Krieg* (Tübingen: Niemayer, 2000), pp. 235–48, p. 242.

[GDR dissident culture was also the product of a GDR industry developed in the West. Sometimes cultural policy and the creative industry worked hand in hand, were two sides of a complicated system in which writers were granted international recognition or confined to the dustbin of history.]

My focus on the GDR in the following pages aims to explore the models of authorship that were facilitated by the GDR regime but have subsequently been discussed within a primarily Western-led debate about intellectuals and politics that often repeats the pseudo-universalist value judgements underpinning Grass and Schnurre's letters in 1961. These arise from a series of assumptions around how modes of authorship should attach to a particular model of exemplary creativity in order for writers to become agents of socio-political change. Following my previous discussion of the way individual West German authors worked with ideas of 'placelessness' both in their literature and in their personal interventions in their immediate cultural and socio-political contexts in the 1950s and 1960s, my interest here is in tracing how a certain dominant understanding of the East German author's place in society evolved in the GDR over the same period, using often very similar concepts and literary techniques, but resulting in an ideologically very different understanding of the author's social and literary position. In the foundational models that emerged in the GDR, the dominant modes of authorship and attitudes towards place are mixed differently to the West and often in seemingly counter-intuitive ways.

Living Literary Examples: Comparing the Careers of Johannes R. Becher and Anna Seghers

Returning to 1961, it is understandable that Schnurre and Grass viewed writers such as Stephan Hermlin, Johannes R. Becher and Anna Seghers as like-minded compatriots who shared a common literary-cultural heritage and basic left-wing intellectual investment in society. All three of the elective 'East German' writers cultivated literary networks across German-speaking Europe throughout their careers.[4] In the immediate post-war period, Becher in particular subscribed to the value of a pan-German cultural tradition at both an intellectual and an

---

[4] Of the three, only Hermlin was actually born in the east of Germany. Becher and Seghers, born in Munich and Mainz respectively, both took up residency in the Soviet zone on their return from exile in Russia and Mexico.

institutional level. His own poetic work throughout the 1940s and 1950s repeatedly referenced Hölderlin and long-standing notions of Heimat,[5] while the kinds of authorial links and literary style that he supported in his work for fledgling GDR institutions also led many to associate him with an elitist understanding of authorship that aimed to promote what remained of high literary culture across German-speaking Europe.

The reasons for such association, as well as the ambiguities in which it resulted, are abundantly evident in two high-profile speeches Becher gave in the emerging GDR on the occasion of the Goethe celebrations in 1949. On 1 August 1949 he delivered the official address to celebrate the award of the National Goethe Prize to Thomas Mann, while on the 28 August he gave a lengthy speech to commemorate the 200th anniversary of Goethe's birth.[6] Becher's celebration of both Mann's and Goethe's authorship in the context of the official socialist cause, on both occasions in the highly symbolic city of Weimar, involves some paradoxical manoeuvrings within the underlying respective genres of the eulogy and the commemorative address. In the first of these two speeches, he praises the bourgeois author Thomas Mann in the highest terms, but not without also re-casting him as a supporter of the Russian Revolution who has actively incorporated the fruits of Russian literary culture into his own work. Furthermore, not only is Mann described in arch celebratory mode as proof of Goethe's immortality – Goethe lives on through Mann, and in both cases the authors' inspirational personality is gratefully embraced by the 'Volk' (people) of East Germany – but the German Heimat itself is rooted in the living author in a way that manages to largely overlook the traumas of the war. Mann is described as having maintained a bridge, or 'hochgewalt'gen Bogen' (a mighty / celestial arch), to the nation's cultural roots throughout the National Socialist period. Becher pens a sonnet that explicitly states how the German Heimat 'hat sich [. . .] in Dir heimgefunden'[7] (found its home in you / its way back home through you), following Mann into exile and living on in his literary language. This highly conservative, quasi-Heideggerian understanding of the poet's relationship to his linguistic

---

[5] See Jens-Fietje Dwars, *Abgrund des Widerspruchs: Das Leben des Johannes R. Becher* (Berlin: Aufbau, 1998), esp. pp. 166–70. On how Becher's attempts to work Hölderlin into a specifically GDR literature sit within a wider context of GDR engagement with the poet, see John Pizer, *Imagining the Age of Goethe in German Literature, 1970-2010* (Rochester, NY: Camden House, 2011).

[6] Johannes R. Becher, 'Rede zur Verleihung des Goethe-Nationalpreises an Thomas Mann' and 'Der Befreier', in *Gesammelte Werke*, ed. Johannes-R.-Becher-Archiv, vol. 17 (Berlin: Aufbau, 1981), pp. 218–22 and pp. 223–63.

[7] Becher, *Gesammelte Werke*, vol. 17, p. 222.

community maps almost word for word onto the way Mann describes himself as guarantor of Germany's cultural unity in the speech that he delivered both here, in accepting the prize, and in West Germany, where he also received a Goethe medal, as discussed in chapter one. In both cases, a strong claim is made for the author who facilitates a kind of generational memory that is publicly expressed through the celebration of cultural achievements. Within the celebratory mode of Becher's eulogy, a commemorative gesture (respecting cultural inheritance across generations in spite of the traumatic rupture of the war) is appropriated to found a positive contemporary East German identity.

The problematic nature of this becomes particularly evident in Becher's obvious concern with owning and managing culture as a kind of foundational national inheritance. His thinking draws heavily on the legal rhetoric of the educated bourgeois middle classes. Commenting on this unreflecting tendency within the GDR more broadly, Wolfgang Emmerich notes how the notion of cultural inheritance can be traced back to the nineteenth-century leaders of the German workers' movement, August Bebel and Wilhelm Liebknecht, and has little to do with Karl Marx – a paradox that was never addressed within the GDR structures that repeatedly supported such 'appropriation' of cultural 'goods'.[8] In buying into both the content and the celebratory rhetoric of this bourgeois German cultural canon, Becher was thus replicating a larger blind spot in the state's official management of its cultural roots. However, he was also aligning himself with future West German understandings of the author's role in society. August Bebel in particular is referenced many times by Günter Grass, who also used Herder's underlying concept of a 'Kulturnation' (a nation united by its culture – as opposed to political unity) as one of the key reasons for justifying his own political campaigning throughout West Germany in the 1960s. However, where Grass used the term primarily to encourage fellow Western writers consciously to take on a position in society in the wake of the rupture caused by German fascism, for Becher the classical cultural inheritance represents an idealized place of unity, a place where language and morals are untainted by recent political developments. The extent to which Becher, by mixing the celebratory mode with commemorative gestures, develops a rhetoric of place and belonging that is premised on the lionizing of individual authors is significant for the kind of authorship he is proposing for GDR society. Ironically, it prioritizes the individual over the collective and the past over the present in a way that Grass's later West German politicking deliberately

---

[8] Wolfgang Emmerich, *Kleine Literaturgeschichte der DDR*, rev. edn (Berlin: Aufbau, 2005), pp. 84–5.

does not promote, even when he too is explicitly writing a eulogy or seeking to lead others in an exemplary fashion.[9]

These unexpected contradictions continue in the second speech, which is outwardly a commemorative piece. Here, Becher explicitly distances himself from the kind of monumentalizing approach to great authors that results in plastic busts in stuffy drawing rooms. He categorizes this as a specifically bourgeois phenomenon and links it to the historical decline of German culture and its nadir in the nihilism of Nietzsche. Against this, he argues that authors need to be reborn in each era and their spirit actively embraced by successive generations if their cultural legacy is to thrive – the emphasis, therefore, is as much on context-specific emulation as on universal adoration. Where the former eulogy's collision with ideologies of inheritance could perhaps still pass under the political radar on account of the specifics of its genre, this speech is very obviously part of the East–West polemics over the 'rightful' ownership of the 'right' national culture. Becher's portrayal of how Goethe's qualities and intentions can be embraced by the GDR people was thus always going to be understood in the context of the protracted 'Erbediskussion', a state-led call critically to appropriate the legacy of Weimar Classicism.[10] Here then, Becher chooses to address matters of fetishization directly, arguing that the specifically bourgeois adoration of Goethe in previous decades has turned the author into 'ein Sternbild, fernher blinkend, unnahbar'[11] (the image of a star, shining from afar, unapproachable) – a description that would not sit too uncomfortably with his own eulogy on Thomas Mann delivered just a few weeks earlier. This shift is primarily one of mode, as Becher here appeals to ideas of generational memory (Goethe is kept alive through successive generations' engagement with him) that this time around are more clearly attached to an ethically driven commemorative mode. While the celebratory mode is still much in evidence, as the lionizing language in the examples below illustrates, a powerful mixture of the commemorative and the utopian modes is carried through the inherent

---

[9] See for example his 1965 election campaign speech, which doubled as a eulogy of Willy Brandt written in the face of CDU defamations of the politician, 'Loblied auf Willy', in Günter Grass, *Werkausgabe*, ed. Volker Neuhaus & Daniela Hermes (Steidl: Göttingen, 1997), vol. 14, ed. Daniela Hermes, pp. 99–109.

[10] Set out, for example, in Katharina von Ankum, *Die Rezeption von Christa Wolf in Ost und West*, pp. 22–32. The question of 'suitable' literary antecedents is also addressed head-on in a 1965 interview between Christa Wolf and Anna Seghers, 'Ein Gespräch mit Anna Seghers', in Wolf / Seghers, *Das dicht besetzte Leben*, pp. 85–98, esp. pp. 87–90.

[11] Becher, *Gesammelte Werke*, vol. 17, p. 240.

recognition in this speech that times have significantly changed. There is an implicit sense of rupture, if not trauma, behind the positive exhortation to relate differently to Goethe, and the whole is welded on to the idea of a new ethical orientation for GDR citizens and the way they relate to one another.

Accordingly, in his exhortation to engage with Goethe from the bottom up by reading him through these 'new eyes' of socialism, Becher describes the author in contemporary geo-political language that is appropriate to the place-bound commemorative and utopian modes, whilst still also playing on the register of the celebratory mode: 'das Reich, das Goethe heißt'[12] (the empire called Goethe) has, in Becher's geo-cultural history of Germany, been left 'verwahrlost im Innern Deutschlands'[13] (destitute in inner Germany / at Germany's heart), and it is up to the inhabitants of the GDR to reclaim his cultural legacy as their own as a quasi-ethical service both to the dead author and to the resurgent 'better' Germany. Although, according to Becher, Goethe showed the way by stressing in his lifetime that intellectual achievement needs not only political recognition, but also an anchor within the common people, his realization has hitherto gone unheeded. 'Beides bedarf also der Geist, damit er sich vollende: Volksverbundenheit und Machtwerdung'[14] (The intellect needs both in order to fulfil its potential: proximity to the people and political influence). Becher's message is clear: Goethe the great author must become the GDR, through the dialogic efforts of everyone to engage with him in their own time and place; the man must be reborn as a place that is marked out by a better use of the kinds of insight that literature can provide. If this trajectory is indeed followed, then engaging with Goethe could amount to enacting the utopian mode within the very heart of East German society: people become able to imagine a different, better social order. This would, in fact, also be an ideal re-enactment of Goethe's world literature as a dynamic, interpersonal process of authorship, played out in the GDR context.

In formulating this message, however, Becher's rhetoric is subject to significant slippage. Goethe is both an inspirational, real-life figure, embodying ideals of personal freedom and cultural and political unity (best grasped through the celebratory mode), and a mal-appropriated genius who needs to be freed from the shackles of bourgeois scholarship and competitive, destructive art (the ethics of commemorating correctly

---

[12] Becher, *Gesammelte Werke*, vol. 17, p. 226.
[13] Becher, *Gesammelte Werke*, vol. 17, p. 241.
[14] Becher, *Gesammelte Werke*, vol. 17, p. 239.

and appropriately, which Becher is implicitly aligning with a socialist approach to cultural heritage). Even as the great author is repeatedly characterized as a lost empire that must arise anew in the form of the GDR, his work also becomes a 'leuchtender Gipfel'[15] (shining peak) that already stands out across the cultural landscape, indicating the ready availability, even before anyone has engaged with it in any form of co-creative gesture, of a utopian mode that merely needs to be accessed. These paradoxical characterizations of Goethe's past achievements and present positioning lead to him being placed at both the hands-on collective bottom and the far-removed solitary top of Becher's cultural landscape:

> Wer so bescheiden von seiner Leistung spricht wie Goethe, der hat es verdient, daß er von Geschlecht zu Geschlecht erhöht werde und daß er in dem Kollektivwesen, das nach ihm jeder von uns darstellt, nicht nur einen Ehrenplatz, sondern den Platz eines besonders tätigen Mitarbeiters an unserem eigenen Lebenswerk einnehme.[16]

> [Whoever speaks of his achievement in such modest terms as Goethe deserves to be singled out / raised up from generation to generation and take on not just a place of honour but that of a particularly active co-worker helping each of us shape our own lives within the collective body that, according to him, we all form.]

The slippery nature of these spatial metaphors and the mutual interference of multiple modes that drives this slipperiness point to a fundamental insecurity within the speech: what is the future of German culture in a divided Germany whose greatest cultural achievements appear to lie in the past? In fact, as the speech reaches its conclusion and its East German listeners are directly encouraged to move 'vorwärts zu Goethe und mit Goethe vorwärts!'[17] (onwards to Goethe and with Goethe onwards), the author and his actual achievements fade away to a mythical ideal: 'Goethe – ein schönes ungetrenntes Ganzes'[18] (Goethe – a beautiful undivided whole). The spatial metaphors, with their roots in the German Romantic Heimat and obvious resonance in the current

---

[15] Becher, *Gesammelte Werke*, vol. 17, p. 229.
[16] Becher, *Gesammelte Werke*, vol. 17, p. 249.
[17] Becher, *Gesammelte Werke*, vol. 17, p. 260.
[18] Becher, *Gesammelte Werke*, vol. 17, p. 262.

geo-political context, take over, but their coordinates, like those of More's *Utopia*, are markedly vague. Arguing for an unbroken ideological and cultural link between GDR socialism and Goethe, Becher tries to suggest that, collectively, the people of the GDR will free the celebrated author from repeated mal-appropriation. As he does so, however, his projected resurrection of the Goethean Reich slips into an idealized future, and he offers no practical steps for how the restoration of the Reich might begin. Significantly, his speech ends with the Goethean verb 'hoffen'[19] (to hope). Apart from a few references to 'freie Menschlichkeit' (emancipated humanity), 'Volk' (the people), and Heimat, we learn nothing about the current cultural context of the GDR, nor how Goethe can really be anchored within it. All we have is the expression of an attitude: the desire to belong in a cultural landscape that both pre-exists the new socialist order and provides the writer with the motivation (but not the actual tools) she needs to play a key role in bringing about a better future.

For all of Becher's dismissal of bourgeois appropriation of great author figures, both the eulogy and the commemorative speech thus draw on a mixture of modes of authorship, where each mode sits awkwardly alongside the others. The result is a confused pedagogical model that undermines itself. Where the utopian mode is invoked as part of a grander ethical frame, it appears as a kind of vanishing point, caught between the pull of the other two modes and thus incompatible with actual contemporary action on cultural identity issues. While Becher seeks to develop a cultural politics based on the Marxist ideal of collective ownership of intellectual endeavour, he ends up presenting the celebrated author figure primarily as an inherited cultural good, a place of memory that is owned in a fetishizing rather than emancipatory kind of way. Accordingly, both Goethe and Mann hover over the real challenges facing East German society in an obfuscatory manner. Becher wants to argue that Thomas Mann and Goethe are inspirational models for the hands-on development of the Marxist state, but he ends up pointing backwards, to a previous place of linguistic purity and cultural unity that sits uncomfortably with the need to innovate and develop new social structures. Perhaps above all what these speeches show, then, is Becher's intense desire for a sense of cultural belonging – a desire that hovers unfortunately between the opposingly politicized rhetorical structures of East and West, as well as being ever more difficult to place within the tension that was also developing between

---

[19] Becher, *Gesammelte Werke*, vol. 17, p. 263.

elite and popular forms of culture.[20] As chapter one already set out, in the immediate post-war years cultural representatives in East and West Germany were keen to believe that individual authors who appeared in culturally significant places had the authority personally to facilitate a sense of generational memory in respect of German cultural achievement that could be claimed by each state and made tangible for its citizens. That such an appropriation might use living authors to paper over the enormous rupture of the Holocaust and look away from the urgent need for fully-fledged commemorative narratives in these places should be clear.[21]

The paradoxical nature of Becher's ideological positioning and the increasing frustration this caused him was also evident in his ill-fated attempts to navigate emergent GDR institutional politics. His personal intellectual affinities with a wide range of authors who shared a certain understanding of the roots of German culture are evident in his work in initiating first the 'Kulturbund zur demokratischen Erneuerung Deutschlands' (Cultural League for the Democratic Renewal of Germany) and then the East German 'Akademie der Künste' (Academy of Arts). Both of these initiatives aimed to make a shared cultural heritage into the cornerstone of future German reunification.[22] However, such personal and intellectual affinities could not bear long-lasting fruit. Initially the Kulturbund was granted a reach that transcended military zones. As Günther Rüther comments, it recruited strong interest across Germany (45,000 members after the first year, rising to 120,000 after the second) not least because it offered 'den Orientierung suchenden deutschen Intellektuellen eine geistige Heimat' (a spiritual home to German intellectuals seeking direction) that managed to

---

[20] On the growth of a sense of belonging through popular culture and its representation across various institutions, including the Kulturbund which Becher himself initiated, see Jan Palmowski, *Inventing a Socialist Nation: Heimat and the Politics of Everyday Life in the GDR, 1945-1990* (Cambridge: Cambridge U. P., 2009).

[21] On the general cultural politics in the GDR of not owning the Holocaust and emphasising instead the state's rightful inheritance of classical German culture, see Peter Davies, *Divided Loyalties: East German Writers and the Politics of German Division 1945-1953* (Leeds: Maney, 2000) (discussion of cultural institutions) and Laura Bradley, *Cooperation and Conflict: GDR Theatre Censorship, 1961-1989* (Oxford: Oxford U. P., 2010) (discussion of theatre practice). On the way anti-fascism becomes part of a socialist narrative about place, see Palmowski, *Inventing a Socialist Nation*.

[22] On the hopes for reunification across intellectual and political spheres in the early years of the GDR, see Stephen Parker, 'Brecht and *Sinn und Form*: The Creation of Cold War Legends', *German Life and Letters* (2007), 60.4, 518–33, and Davies, *Divided Loyalties*.

transcend the impending sense of political divide across the zones.[23] In line with the founding anti-fascist myth of the GDR, Becher's Kulturbund set out to combat all traces of National Socialist ideology within society. This is an ideal that was closely mirrored in the declared intentions of the slightly later, looser authorial grouping in the West, Hans Werner Richter's Gruppe 47. However, although the organization started out pursing an 'all-German' cultural policy defined by its key author members and relatively independent of direct SED (Sozialistische Einheitspartei Deutschlands [Socialist Union Party of East Germany]) or Soviet control, its proximity to Soviet political interests quickly rendered it suspect in Allied eyes. Following a failure to renew its licence on time in 1947, it ceased to exist in the three Western zones – an abrupt end to interzonal institutional cultural cooperation that was widely reported in communist circles to be a deliberate ban of the Kulturbund on the part of the West. By 1949 the Kulturbund had become a solely East German phenomenon that was increasingly openly incorporated into official socialist cultural politics. Furthermore, it dropped its stated intention of combatting ongoing traces of National Socialism, with SED-led rhetoric emphasizing instead the importance of supporting the political growth of the GDR.[24]

These developments not only undermined Becher's attempts to turn the pan-German classical tradition and its attendant celebrated great author figures into the roots for current and future socialist models of literature. They also put a fundamental question mark over his *attitude* of cultural belonging: his 'placeness' as an author in East German society who could educate and instruct in an appropriate manner.[25] Becher's elitist approach to literary value was difficult to reconcile with the ideal of a broad-based 'Volksverbundenheit' (close attachment to the people) that SED cultural policy decreed should define both the scope and purpose of literature, even if he did repeatedly reference the term in his public speeches. As German division became more certain, the only way he could counter a nascent negative evaluation of his positioning within society as too culturally regressive was to prove his bureaucratic loyalty to the emerging state-led cultural institutions of the GDR. For unlike his grand but empty rhetoric that placed elite authors at the heart of socialist society in the text of his speeches, his

---

[23] Günther Rüther, *"Greif zur Feder, Kumpel": Schriftsteller, Literatur und Politik in der DDR 1949-1990* (Düsseldorf: Droste, 1991), pp. 23–4. Emmerich, *Kleine Literaturgeschichte der DDR*, p. 77.
[24] Davies, *Divided Loyalties*, pp. 148–9.
[25] For an in-depth biographically led discussion of Becher's place within German society, see Dwars, *Abgrund des Widerspruchs*.

support of the Free German Youth with both anthems and personal engagement and his willingness personally to embody the official face of literary achievement in the GDR entailed documentable expressions of belonging that he ritually re-enacted for all to see. Becher's public attempts to reconcile a personal sense of cultural Heimat that was nourished by the intellectual inheritance of Hölderlin and Goethe with a state-led rhetoric of collective cultural belonging conditioned by Soviet dictates therefore began to appear increasingly ambivalent to both broad ideological groupings. As a result, both his work as the Minister for Culture from 1954–1958 and his literary legacy have attracted significant and sustained criticism in both East and West ever since.[26] His assertion of strong literary foundations for his own proposed foundational model of instruction that would build a positive sense of belonging in the GDR was shaky from the start.

Anna Seghers, by contrast, represents both a literary tradition and an authorial attitude of belonging that, superficially at least, mapped much more neatly onto the institutional organization of authors and their literary work in the East German zone. When Seghers returned to Germany from exile in Mexico in 1947 and took up residence in Berlin, she was courted by both private individuals and cultural institutions across Germany as the famous author of *Das siebte Kreuz* (1942, *The Seventh Cross*) – to the point where she commented to a friend that her own celebrity was perhaps more of a hindrance to her travel around Germany than the bureaucracy associated with the multiple interzonal borders.[27] Her novel, set in the surrounding area of her hometown of Mainz, tells the exciting story of the socialist Georg Heisler's escape from a labour camp in the late 1930s. It combines the pace and focus of a thriller with the underlying ideological trajectory of socialist literature: Gregor escapes Hitler's Germany with the aid of left-wing comrades whose commitment to both the cause and each other is given renewed vigour by the example he sets. The international popular success of the novel, combined with Seghers' roots in the interwar German socialist artistic community and the wide-ranging international literary contacts she forged while in exile, made her an ideal representative for a progressive foundational model of authorship within GDR structures that had the potential to make a substantial intellectual contribution to

---

[26] See Dwars, *Abgrund des Widerspruchs* for the complex reception of Becher's life and person, both within his lifetime and in the context of the demise of the GDR and the literary debates of the 1990s.

[27] Anna Seghers, *Hier im Volk der kalten Herzen: Briefwechsel 1947*, ed. Christel Berger (Berlin: Aufbau, 2000), p. 136 (but for a sense of her privileged position particularly in respect of travel, see p. 134).

society. This was certainly how the Allied authorities saw it, as the deputy mayor of the Berlin city council, Ferdinand Friedensburg, issued her in 1947 with official documentation that stressed her international success as a writer and decreed 'Im öffentlichen Interesse ist ihr jede Förderung zu gewähren'[28] (In the public interest she must be granted every possible support).

Despite her initial reluctance to lay down roots in any part of Germany (she spent the first year of her return housed in a hotel in Berlin-Wannsee, travelling to engagements across the country and repeatedly questioning how long she would remain on German soil), Seghers went on to be closely associated with the GDR establishment. This is shown not least by her twenty-six-year stint at the head of the 'Schriftstellerverband der DDR' (1952–1978, Writers' Union of the GDR). The Schriftstellerverband was the only fully politically aligned institutional representation of authors' professional interests in the GDR, and it was at all times openly led by SED cultural policy. It was therefore endowed with a firmer position within East German cultural politics than the more ambivalently delineated Kulturbund and East German Academy of Arts.

For many cultural commentators, Seghers' politically compliant position at the helm of this organization represented an opportunistic, if understandable, betrayal of authors' duty as public figures to speak out against the authorities when necessary for the wider good of society. The Western critic Christiane Zehl Romero, for example, posits that Seghers became complicit with the regime's questionable cultural politics not least because she feared losing her hard-won sense of belonging, which included (but was by no means confined to) the material comforts she enjoyed in the physical space of the GDR.[29] Nor was criticism confined to the West. Walter Janka, head of the main GDR literary publishing house Aufbau until 1956, makes Seghers into one of his prime targets when he writes of East German writers' collective and systemic 'difficulties with the truth' and failure to speak up against injustice at key moments for fear of how this may materially affect them.[30] For him, the cowardice of both Seghers and Becher in the face of party political intrigue resulted, amongst other things, in the complete

---

[28] Seghers, *Hier im Volk der kalten Herzen*, p. 79.
[29] Christiane Zehl Romero, *Anna Seghers: Eine Biographie, 1947-1983* (Berlin: Aufbau, 2003). For a nuanced discussion of the wider subject of individual complicity with the regime on the part of state-sanctioned writers, see Sara Jones, *Complicity, Censorship and Criticism: Negotiating Space in the GDR Literary Sphere* (Berlin: de Gruyter, 2011).
[30] Walter Janka, *Schwierigkeiten mit der Wahrheit* (Reinbek bei Hamburg: Rowohlt, 1989).

lack of public support he received from any of his authors in a show trial. He was sentenced to five years isolated internment in Bautzen in 1957 on the basis of fabricated evidence against him that they could have overturned.

The historical background to both Seghers' and Becher's desire for the material benefits of 'placeness' in their wider socio-political context should certainly not be overlooked. Indeed, they share this with other key figures like Bertolt Brecht and Peter Huchel. Both their desire physically to belong and their genuine ideological investment in the greater project of socialism meant these early GDR authors were prepared to look away or otherwise collude with the SED authorities when injustices were perpetrated that they could downplay as necessary for the greater good.[31] Of more enduring interest for my discussion of the different models of authorship to emerge in East and West Germany, however, is the way Seghers' various biographical experiences of physical exile and ideological belonging inflect the modes of authorship that are employed within her literary work and subsequently taken up by later writers. For while Seghers' actions and non-actions on the public stage of GDR cultural politics have repeatedly fed into negative evaluations of committed East German authors' achievements as public intellectuals, her literary work very unambiguously represents a coherent aesthetics of placeness in respect of socialist society that can be understood as her exploration of how authors can contribute to the wider social good. As such, it represents an important alternative foundational model of authorship to the dominant oppositional Western models discussed in the previous chapters. It also contrasts with Becher's increasingly regressive and politically unsustainable attempt to educate through emulation of past bourgeois models, and with the path of notable self-censorship followed, for example, by Bertolt Brecht and Stefan Heym.[32]

---

[31] On the complexities of this position and the institutional manoeuvring of cultural and political capital around Brecht and Huchel, see Parker, 'Brecht and *Sinn und Form*'.

[32] I am thinking in particular of the posthumous publication of the bulk of Brecht's *Buckower Elegien* and Heym's long-running difficulties getting published at all, particularly for the text *Fünf Tage im Juni*, which was rejected in 1956 and not finally published in the GDR until 1989 (it appeared in the West in 1974). See Parker, 'Brecht and *Sinn und Form*' for discussion of the ways in which Brecht collaborated with censorship out of a mixture of ideological conviction and political expediency. For broader thoughts on the spectrum of relations between artists and the authorities that ranged from cooperation to conflict in the GDR from the 1960s onwards, discussed through the case of theatre, see Bradley, *Cooperation and Conflict*. On the ubiquity of some level of self-censorship as endemic to writing at all in the GDR, see Jones, *Complicity, Censorship and Criticism*.

Both of the novels that Seghers wrote in the GDR, *Die Entscheidung* (1959, The Decision) and its sequel, *Das Vertrauen* (1968, Trust), hinge on the adoption of fundamental attitudes in respect of one's geo-political and social environs. Over some 1,100 pages, Seghers pursues the lives of two communities: the East German inhabitants of the imaginary Kossin, whose lives are focused on the expropriated Bentheim factory and the party politics that unfold within it, and the West German owners and associates of the original parent plant in the Frankfurt area. While the first book covers the immediate post-war years and shows people putting their lives back together from amidst the physical and moral ruins that characterize both sides of Germany equally, the second focuses on the workers' uprising in the GDR in 1953 and documents the undeniable material differences between the two territories. In the first work, a whole series of individuals find themselves faced with life-changing decisions: the embittered Anton seeks revenge for the brutal murder of his Jewish wife by the former SS-officer and incoming director of the Western factory, Otto Bentheim; the engineer Heinz Büttner is recruited by Western agents to bring the lead scientists from the East German factory into the West; Ernst and Katharina Riedl repeatedly try to resolve their family difficulties as one of them has to relinquish what they believe is the better life and move to their spouse in the other half of the country; Lene Nohl decides not to flee Kossin with her long-awaited husband to the West; Robert Lohse, who broods over his unrequited love for Lene and his inability to love the younger Lisa, finally decides to channel his interpersonal energies into teaching and gains a place on a teacher training course for factory interns. In all of this, the cultural and political rupture caused by the Second World War is omnipresent, such that Fuchs's narrative excess in response to trauma (see my second chapter) tangibly spreads across Seghers' creation of a fictional world. In creating this world, the author clearly seeks both to commemorate the real events that have led to these kinds of constellations in the real East and West Germany, and to work through how engaging with them – taking on an attitude in respect of them – may be literature's contribution to bringing about a better social order for the future. The commemorative mode, in other words, gestures both backwards and forwards, including to heterotopian alternative spaces that can be brought about by literature and may not only exist in parallel to the GDR's own place and time, but be actively fostered within it.

Although the different geographical locations in East and West Germany are thus crucial to the story, they are conveyed through markedly little description of the physical settings in which the characters act. Structurally also, the text shows considerable fluidity as sections move between East and West Germany, America, and occasionally Mexico and France. With geographical difference downplayed, the places are marked out instead by the ideological stances they inspire in their inhabitants as they set about rebuilding their lives after the traumatic rupture of the war. People make their way in the West by placing emphasis on material goods, turning a blind eye to the past and, in the case of ex-Nazi officers, quietly assimilating themselves back into a society that is prepared not to ask too many questions. Anton's act of revenge stands out in stark contrast to this, and he is quietly incarcerated as a result. In the East, by contrast, people live in more impoverished circumstances, but they do not shy away from difficult conversations and confrontations, both about the past and the present. Where personal gain motivates the actions of those living in the West, in the East the individuals are repeatedly (and not always successfully) shown assessing their personal needs in the context of the collective. When the heavily pregnant Katharina Riedl finally crosses the border from West to East, there are no physical markers to indicate where she is; it is the kindness of the stranger who immediately comes to her aid, rather humorously coupled with his co-worker's concern to meet their daily target, that indicate that she is in the GDR. Over the course of the narrative, the characters naturally gravitate towards their ideological homeland, and, in this sense, 'make' the culturally and politically specific 'places', West and East.

Here we see Massey's political understanding of place as a dynamic and thus changeable quantity coming to the fore: from an initial post-war situation of 'throwntogetherness', people negotiate their relations and actively shape the delineations of 'East' and 'West' through their political decisions and physical movements. The text highlights how different attitudes of belonging stem from different places, but also help further shape those places as physical manifestations of alternative kinds of social order. In organizing her storyline, characters and narrative description to portray this, Seghers intermingles the commemorative and utopian modes of authorship across the text. Where Grass's utopian mode was tangible only at a meta-textual level and served to underscore the placelessness of the author trying to hold up any sort of authoritative mirror to society, Seghers' utopian mode is linked to demonstratively rewarding characters who make 'good', ethically informed decisions and thereby gain access to the heterotopia of an idealized socialist society. This is clearly part of a broader pedagogical model of authorship being deliberately developed on Seghers' part.

Placeness, then, as a mutually grounded sense of belonging between the individual and his or her political, cultural and physical environment, is the ultimate reward meted out by the author to the characters who make the right basic decisions to bring them into line with the prevailing ideology and who manage the emotional challenges of sticking to a certain set of beliefs in testing circumstances. This becomes particularly apparent in the second novel, *Das Vertrauen*. The characters' basic decisions about where and how to live have by now been made, so the emphasis falls instead on their emotional adaptation to their chosen environment. The attitude of believing in the potential of a better future and being prepared to overlook temporary setbacks in favour of this goal is staunchly foregrounded for those who identify with the GDR. However, although the narrative's morally-inflected portrayal of East and West Germany clearly polemicizes against Western capitalism, which is portrayed as engendering markedly rootless characters and patterns of behaviour, a basic conception of placeness as a mutually enforcing pact between man and his environment underpins both territories: each side gets the kind of loyal subjects it deserves. Such rigid division of the known world into two camps defined by two opposing notions of belonging clearly maps onto Seghers' own biographical experiences and reflects her unwavering support of the party line within the GDR cultural context. Her Western counterparts, meanwhile, want to re-shape contemporary society to map it better onto the needs of the individual, and pursue much more openly combative themes and structures in their writing as a result.

Arrived at now through Seghers' lens on placeness, Böll's diagnosis of contemporary West German literature's suffering from an almost total lack of affective place seems not only broadly appropriate to the differently calibrated models of authorship each German state conditions, but also the logical consequence of a divergent mixture of authorial modes. In Seghers' textual world, characters can be clearly rewarded with access to a better alternative society, once they have acquired the right attitude to be able to perceive this nested heterotopia within the sometimes-challenging circumstances around them. This in turn derives from their own ethical management of the excesses unleashed by the traumatic rupture of the recent past, as they school themselves to seize the positives from within their 'throwntogetherness' in the East. Where foundational models in the West prioritize the attitude and creative actions of the individual author seeking to create the possibilities for political challenge and social change, Seghers' inherently pedagogical foundational model proudly reflects the official party line of collective growth achieved through a shared vision in the East. It seeks to fold the individual into a broader cultural movement that grows, apparently organically, out of the ground in which it is rooted, transforming it as it does so.

Perhaps it should come as no surprise, then, that, taken together, Seghers' two GDR novels offer a model of authorship that looks well beyond their own author's personal political experiences. In spite of the seemingly vast array of characters and their intricate relationships spanning a number of countries, at a meta-level the narrative's driving message does not concern the particular fates of the individuals documented within it at all. In a recurrent self-reflexive gesture, the texts also document the fate of the fictional Herbert Melzer, an aspiring author who promised his friends Richard and Robert (two of the key protagonists attached to the GDR factory) when they all lay wounded in the Spanish Civil War that he would write a book about their experiences if he ever got out alive. While Seghers' narrative ostensibly follows the post-war fates of Richard and Robert, it also documents the emergence of Melzer's novel, which is composed in ignorance of Richard and Robert's actual subsequent lives. This imaginary text has at its heart the early lives of Robert and Richard up to their involvement in the Spanish Civil War and some speculation about what happened to them subsequently. Itself a commemorative gesture, the writing of this speculative-documentary text within the fiction of Seghers' own two novels opens up the space within them to explore the power of literature to emerge from and talk back to the socialist collective. In creating a dialogue across multiple locations, both real and imagined (within the fiction), she is also extending her exemplary exploration of the utopian mode of authorship, as well as creating a socialist inflection of Goethe's dynamic, interactive world literature.

First drafted in American exile, Melzer's text undergoes substantial revision when he returns to Europe and meets up with old communist acquaintances. Here he decides to turn Celia, the key female protagonist and muse-like figure of desire for the wounded men, into a character unwaveringly committed to the ideal of social renewal. His redrafted narrative shows how her commitment to the cause results in a martyr's death that inspires subsequent generations. The novel opens with her words 'Ich bleibe bei meinen Leuten' p. 410 (*Das Vertrauen*; I'm staying with my people) – a significant conscious expression of placeness – and is constructed so as to celebrate the protagonists' trust in each other and ongoing commitment to the cause. As such, it exemplifies how the commemorative mode of authorship (in this instance: Melzer's commemoration of Celia's commitment to her people) can be directly harnessed to a broader ethical programme of activity in society. Predictably, the revised socialist trajectory renders the novel unpublishable within the capitalist setting. Melzer, following the (imagined) Celia's steadfastness, refuses to alter his ending. Not only does his text, like Celia's body, disappear from public view as it languishes at an American publisher's, but he himself dies a similar death. For while his fictional Celia dies trying to avoid interception by the fascist authorities as she runs errands in the mountain for the underground communists, Melzer himself gets caught up in West

German protests over fair pay and is hit on the head by riot police. His actual death is one of the concluding scenes of *Die Entscheidung*, and it could be read symbolically as the death of the socialist author in the FRG. In *Das Vertrauen*, however, the vanished Herbert becomes a figure of ideological inspiration for others, just as Celia does in his (still unpublished) text.

The deaths of these fictional characters are thus doubly commemorated by Seghers, first as a traumatic rupture within their interpreters' / followers' preferred social order (the rise of socialism) and second as key defining moments on which later socialist identities are built. Not only does the unhappily married Helen Wilcox spend much of the narrative tracking down the lost manuscript and in so doing become estranged from her industrialist husband. When the text is finally unearthed it also becomes an instant hit throughout the East German community. While individual workers who know Robert and/or Richard are inspired by the celebratory tale of their past bravery and commitment, the protagonists themselves find that Melzer's text allows them to see their actions and difficult emotional decisions within a wider context that makes sense of their own lives and reaffirms their plans for the future. The mix of celebration and commemoration evident in Melzer's authoring of his text is thus directed by his readers in a utopian gesture of their own into helping the text serve as a foil to their present and aspirational future lives. Furthermore, beyond shoring up everyone's individual sense of placeness in the socialist setting, the novel takes on a greater importance as a pedagogical tool for society, as underlined in the closing paragraph of *Das Vertrauen*. Robert and Richard's old teacher, Karl Waldstein takes solace from the thought that his boarding school, in reality about to be closed, will always be open in Melzer's book. The narrative, welded together partly out of celebration of the pair's deeds and partly out of commemoration of their lost object of desire, Celia, thus takes on the allure of a co-created parallel literary heterotopia in Seghers' fictionalized GDR. The fictional pedagogue Waldstein's remark on Melzer's novel is clearly also meant to apply for the real-life Seghers' novels too. *Die Entscheidung* and *Das Vertrauen* are both constructed from a mixture of celebratory and commemorative storylines, woven together and presented with deliberately pedagogical intent that comes from an underlying belief that the literary text can show society how to be a better place.

This concluding overlap between writer and pedagogue is a double expression of the author's position right at the heart of socialist society. Clearly Seghers' novels themselves aim to provide orientation for the reading public by inspiring reflection on the GDR as an ideological homeland where one can belong, provided the correct decisions are made and the correct emotional responses developed in challenging circumstances. Her decision to insert a socialist author figure and explicitly trace both his fortunes and those of his text throughout her narratives allows her novels also to reflect quite explicitly upon the role of the author in this emerging society, as well as contrast it with his fate in the capitalist West. However, given her own position at the heart of party-led cultural institutions and her own celebrity as a socialist institution of her own, the exact positioning of this role is not quite as clear-cut as one might expect. On the one hand, her novels do work with a Soviet-led image of the author falling into line with his people, giving intellectual expression to a shared ideology that is in turn at the centre of the land in which they all live. His writing is accessible, inspirational and directly orientated towards the real-life socialist struggles from which it emerges. On the other hand, however, there is something rather intangible about Melzer. Although he travels from America to France to West Germany, he never actually makes it into the East. Over the course of the narrative, the Western publishing and industry barons become increasingly hostile to him, and the circle of communist friends or sympathizers he can draw on shrinks, culminating in his death at the hands of the Western authorities. His actual impact on the East is therefore posthumous. This could be read as a symbolic appropriation by the East of precisely those kinds of cultural figures who were disenfranchised by capitalism's focus on the speedy construction of economic value: Melzer finally makes it 'home' to 'his people'. Yet the narrative's rather schematic description of the widespread celebration of an author who is no longer alive makes it hard to conclude that Seghers' novels provide us with an actual image of the author at the heart of socialist society. Rather, it seems more like a hazy utopian dream in the manner of Ernst Bloch's Heimat discussed in chapter one, or Becher's longed-for Goethean Reich. The socialist author himself has become part of the projections into an idealized alternative social reality provided by foundational literary texts that eerily take on an afterlife of their own.

Given the repeated difficult decisions that Seghers had to make as a result of her own position at the heart of state-led GDR cultural politics, this slight distancing from the image of the socialist author who blossoms at the centre of the country's moral and intellectual life is significant. While the idealized image of the author as pedagogue is at the heart of official GDR cultural rhetoric, both in Seghers' text and in her own life the author's biographical person is marginalized to the point of serious ill health, if not death, in the service of this ideal. Increasingly overwhelmed with work and illness in her later years, her comment to her friend and colleague Maria Werner, captures Seghers' growing sense of the sacrifices that the position of the socialist author demands:

Ich befinde mich fast immer in einem Zwiespalt, daß ich entweder persönlich oder schriftlich ausgiebig mit den Menschen zusammen sein kann, an denen mir etwas liegt, oder hinter meiner eigenen schriftstellerischen Arbeit her bleiben. In der letzten Zeit bin ich viel mehr kaputt, als Du mich kennst, und manchmal muß ich, durch Kraft und Zeit gezwungen, einfach die Wahl treffen.[33]

[I find myself almost constantly torn between spending time, whether in writing or in person, with the people I care about, and carrying out my own literary work. Recently I have been much more exhausted than you would expect from me, and sometimes, forced by the lack of time and energy, I have simply had to make a choice.]

While Seghers aspires towards the ideal of collective fulfilment in both her life and her writing, the kind of authorship she comes to embody is also increasingly tinged with the real-life experience of the difficulties posed by being a living institution or – borrowing Becher's delineation of Goethe – a Reich of one's own. In taking up such a position of 'placeness' within society, both authors also experienced first-hand the challenge to personal happiness that such an overwhelmingly public pedagogical position can entail. Becher not infrequently contemplates suicide in his 1950 diary, describes a profound sense of loneliness, and clearly draws very heavily on his wife for emotional support.[34] Perhaps Seghers' novels themselves are the best expression of her recognition that living and working within the socialist context requires decisions and compromises that do not always come easily, and will certainly not be understood by those of a different ideological persuasion. It is certainly no surprise that both her work and person met with substantial criticism in the West. In the East too, however, Seghers always had to be careful to ensure that her public interventions (including her literary writing) hit the right tone, and, although her work enjoyed official support, she could never be sure it had found the 'right' audience. As Christa Wolf commented in 2000:

Aber hat es für sie denn zeitlebens das 'richtige' Publikum gegeben? War nicht auch in der übermäßigen Verehrung, die ihr in der DDR von ihren Lesern entgegengebracht wurde, ein gut

---

[33] Anna Seghers, *Tage wie Staubsand*, p. 248.
[34] Dwars notes how he drew on quite a few other women as well, *Abgrund des Widerspruchs*.

Teil – oder ein schlecht Teil – Verkennung, zu schweigen von der bis zur Gehässigkeit gehenden Ablehnung, die sie immer wieder von anderer Seite auf sich zog, bis heute auf sich zieht?[35]

[But did she ever have the 'right' audience, even in her own time? Wasn't the impossibly high esteem in which her GDR readers held her in good part – or in bad part – a matter of misrecognition, not to mention the rejection, bordering on the vindictive, with which she met from the other side and still experiences today?]

The constant self-monitoring that such uncertainty entailed was surely draining. Certainly, the sense of exhausting isolation expressed above is not just felt by Seghers and Becher, but by numerous other notable GDR writers who were incorporated within structures that officially celebrated their foundational instructive position within society – Bertolt Brecht at the helm of the Berliner Ensemble, Stephan Hermlin as Secretary of Poetry at the East German Academy of Arts, and Peter Huchel as chief editor of the literary journal *Sinn und Form*, for example. Albeit in different ways, these different institutional contexts also worked politically to silence and exhaust the famous names most closely associated with them.[36] This aspect of GDR writers' 'placeness' stands in ironic contrast to the collective sense of purpose and active collaboration that increasingly drew together left-leaning, 'placeless' West German authors in the 1950s and earlier part of the 1960s.

Refining the Model: How Christa Wolf Thinks Through and After Seghers and Becher

The models of authorship proposed by Becher and Seghers in the early years of the GDR share a clear pedagogical understanding of how and for whom they are writing, but the two authors proceed very differently in their execution of this self-imposed task. Anchoring himself in the past, even against his own better judgement, Becher uses a celebratory-tinged commemorative mode to summon inspirational literary forebears and in so doing undermines his own attempts to function as an exemplary pedagogue for the GDR people. This is not least because the bourgeois models these forebears provided largely precluded any engagement with a kind of utopian thinking that could connect to the

---

[35] Christa Wolf, 'Im Widerspruch: Zum hundertsten Geburtstag von Anna Seghers', in Christa Wolf / Anna Seghers, *Das dicht besetzte Leben: Briefe Gespräche und Essays* (Berlin: Aufbau, 2003), pp. 174–92, pp. 174–5.

[36] For further detailed discussion of how individuals fared in these ambiguous contexts, see Jones, *Complicity, Censorship and Criticism*.

lived experience of socialism. Seghers, by contrast, dedicated her life and work to embracing the potential of this new world in an exemplary manner. She uses her authorial position both to reward her fictional characters and to instruct her real readers, leading those fit to perceive it towards an idealized heterotopia that is nested within the GDR world, waiting to be unlocked. There are clear lessons to be learned in her texts, both in the art of responsible social action and in the importance of maintaining an appropriate attitude of belonging, with both predicated upon an honest relationship to one's past. Yet although her pedagogical purpose is much more consistent in itself than Becher's, it is also very overtly schematic, and thus open to wholesale rejection on ideological grounds. When external circumstances discredit socialist structures, her entire alternative literary world is also discredited, as the attitude required to perceive it as an accessible space in the first place is swept away.

Nevertheless, Seghers' vast body of literary work and her correspondence with an astonishing array of leading authors, industry insiders and politico-cultural bodies and institutions throughout her life is in itself testament to the success with which she actively embodied the position of a committed author acting at the heart of socialist society. In so doing, she did much in particular to inspire younger writers, and, as her correspondence shows, she also did much on an inter-personal level to support them as their careers unfolded within the particular GDR context. Whatever her own reservations may have been towards the end of her life about the extent to which she was able to access her own utopia in and through literature, for the next generation of GDR writers the pedagogical model of authorship embodied by both her literary corpus and her biographical person was an important reference point for the evolving question of how exactly authors fitted into society. Christa Wolf, in particular, maintained a life-long friendship with Seghers; she also very publicly positioned herself within the legacy of Seghers' authorial person by writing numerous forewords and editing various collections of her work.[37] On a number of levels, in fact, Wolf's literary work develops the model of the prominent socialist author-pedagogue that Seghers' physical person and literary corpus represented. Specifically, her writing of the 1960s probes the fissures between a committed author's public stance of support for the socialist project and her search for a more personal sense of 'placeness' within her immediate surroundings. In so doing, she not only gives expression to certain issues that can only be inferred from Seghers' immediate literary legacy, but she also provides an unexpected link back to the

---

[37] As documented in Wolf / Seghers, *Das dicht besetzte Leben*.

work of Johannes R. Becher and the tensions that underscored his public positioning. In this sense, Wolf very directly builds on the foundational model of authorship as a public pedagogic practice – and its own particular paradoxes – that these two authors helped initiate.

Wolf's 1963 novel, *Der geteilte Himmel* (Divided Heaven), sets out issues of belonging very similar to those explored in the romantic relationships caught between East and West in Seghers' *Die Entscheidung*.[38] Manfred Herrfurth, who has broken all emotional ties to his family and is defined by his cynicism towards society and his bitterness about the past, is attracted to Rita Seidel. Ten years his junior and a trainee teacher who is temporarily gaining experience in a train factory, Rita embodies an attitude of hope towards the future and the desire to engage with the world around her. Although the narrative traces the complex emotional pulls on the protagonists as their lives unfold within the challenging economic context of the GDR in the early 1960s, the impossibility of a happy romantic ending is marked out right from the beginning by the opposing attitudes that define Rita and Manfred's characters. Where Rita seeks consciously to cultivate roots by contributing to her social surroundings, Manfred's emotional and intellectual distance from others make his defection to the West in search of a better life inevitable.[39] What holds the pair together as well as drives them apart is a mutual fascination with each other's opposing approach to life. Manfred grudgingly admires how Rita has the tenacity to stick with something that is difficult, while the whole relationship is brought about in the first place by Rita's curiosity towards Manfred's aloofness: 'Ist das schwer, so zu werden, wie Sie sind?'[40] (Is it hard to become like you?).

In as much as the painful end of the relationship is programmed into the narrative right from the outset, the real decision-making that takes place within the text occurs on a meta-level. The narrative as a whole is presented as Rita's reminiscences as she recovers from a near-fatal accident / suicide attempt that happened shortly after she decided against staying with Manfred in West Berlin and returned to her

---

[38] Wolf's first meaningful contact with Seghers took the form of an interview that she carried out with her about *Die Entscheidung*, published in *neue deutsche literatur* in 1959 as 'Fragen an Anna Seghers'; reproduced in Wolf / Seghers, *Das dicht besetzte Leben*, pp. 61–68. Seghers very clearly sets out her (straightforward) understanding of socialist realism; with reference to the novel's East–West divide, Wolf distinguishes between '"unsere" Leute' and 'die anderen' (p. 64; "our" people and 'the others').

[39] Wolf discusses the idea that he is 'predestined for the other side' in her correspondence with Seghers: Wolf / Seghers, *Das dicht besetzte Leben*, pp. 11–13.

[40] Christa Wolf, *Der geteilte Himmel* (Munich: dtv, 1981), p. 10.

summer job in the train factory. This extra narrative layer transforms Rita's position in the text from being merely a narrative object in Wolf's schematic East / West tale of romantic failure to an author-pedagogue figure in her own right. The very existence of her narrative represents her determination to confront difficult issues in her recent past, and this process of piecing together the different ideological positions and the consequences they have had on her recent life is attributed a strong healing effect. Engaging in this commemorative mode of authorship allows her to get to a different mental place by the end of the narrative. In the final paragraphs of the text, Rita's retrospective narrative has given her the strength to conceive of a positive future in the East, despite the very real personal turmoil that the end of her relationship has caused her. This final point has in fact already been foreshadowed a number of times in the text, when Rita, from the position of her hospital bed, has consciously reflected on her narrative and the moral growth of her character in which it has directly resulted: 'Dieses grüne Ding, dem jeder die Nestwärme anroch, hat sich in etwas mehr als einem Jahr in eine blasse, großäugige junge Frau verwandelt, die lernt mühsam, aber für die Dauer, dem Leben ins Gesicht zu sehen, älter und doch nicht härter zu werden'[41] (this greenhorn, fresh from the nest, has turned in the course of just over one year into a pale, wide-eyed young woman who is learning the hard way, but for good, how to look life in the eye, to grow older but not harder). The trainee teacher, using the commemorative mode to work through a personal trauma that is embedded in the wider political trauma of post-war society, writes her own exemplary socialist Bildungsroman. As such she represents an empowered and empowering image of nascent female authorship that consciously finds her place in the GDR context.

While *Der geteilte Himmel* follows the schematic presentation of placeness in general and authorial placeness in particular that depends on the kind of East / West ideological split pursued at length by Seghers, Wolf's next novel, *Nachdenken über Christa T.* (1968, The Quest for Christa T.) both develops and internalizes the concept in a purely East German context. The named protagonist is a sometime teacher and closet author who has reflected a great deal on the nature of writing and how it relates to her attempt to fit in with her surroundings and find meaning for her life. Meanwhile, the unnamed narrator from whose standpoint Christa T.'s posthumous material is presented is clearly engaged in commemorating her friend in such a way as to use the literary text to help society learn from a non-conformist pattern of behaviour that has been squeezed out of it. Where earlier texts and

---

[41] Wolf, *Der geteilte Himmel*, p. 33.

statements by Wolf and Seghers merged the role of the author-pedagogue with the progressive GDR society into which he or she fitted, this later text represents a sustained reflection on the difference that makes the author figure stand out from the generation she represents. Just as Rita is attracted to Manfred, the narrator is fascinated by Christa T., who in many ways challenges the by now established socialist attitudes and conventions of belonging. Unlike Manfred, however, Christa T. genuinely wants to belong in the GDR, and unlike Rita, the narrator is also critical of its shortcomings.

Christa T. is presented as rootless throughout the narrative. Over the course of her adult life, she changes her location within the GDR on numerous occasions, and she also tries out multiple different career paths, from primary school teacher to academic to writer to mother and housewife. Her geographical mobility combined with her inability to settle into any one type of work is repeatedly presented as the result of a fundamental character trait that marks her out as a free spirit: from her early childhood, she has stood out for her non-conformism, whether this takes the form of startling self-expression (her distinctive trumpet whistling), her mysterious absences from university, or her determination to design and build her own home even as her terminal illness is entering its final stages. Not only does such idiosyncrasy seem out of sync with the collectivizing structures of her socialist surroundings, she also seems chronologically adrift. Where her fellow literature students efficiently 'bury' the 'Dichter der Vergangenheit'[42] (authors of the past) on the grounds that they are no longer applicable to the contemporary progressive socialist context, Christa T. develops an affinity for the careful, reflective style in which their nineteenth-century novellas are written. In her academic dissertation on the work of Theodor Storm, she investigates how an author can explore himself and his potential – 'sich verwirklichen'[43] – through literature, and she celebrates the way in which Storm found his role within society, both in his own time and for posterity. In terminology reminiscent of Becher's invocation of the classical German tradition and likewise merging celebratory and utopian modes of authorship, she argues that Storm's ability to recreate places and experiences through literature creates a 'Sehnsuchtslandschaft'[44] (landscape of longing) that resonates with the like-minded reader today.

Indeed, Becher is consciously referenced in Wolf's text: the whole narrative is introduced by an epigraph that is a quotation from his

---

[42] Christa Wolf, *Nachdenken über Christa T.* (Neuwied: Luchterhand, 2002), p. 67.
[43] Wolf, *Nachdenken über Christa T.*, p. 107
[44] Wolf, *Nachdenken über Christa T.*, p. 110.

work: 'Was ist das: Dieses Zu-sich-selber-Kommen des Menschen?' (What does this mean: man's 'finding-himself'?). Becher's phrase is part of an entry taken from his published diary of 1950, *Auf andere Art so große Hoffnung*. Here, and in other related sections, he explores the philosophical potential for man actively to shape his own destiny and, in so doing, overcome any sense of 'Selbstentfremdung', or alienation, imposed upon him by economic and/or social circumstances. While this may sound outwardly Marxist, it is taken from a larger literary-philosophical project, entitled 'Der Aufstand im Menschen' (Rebellion in Man), on which Becher worked over an eight month period between 1947 and 1948 and which he abandoned, dismantled and partially re-inserted into his published diary.[45] In their new diary context, these philosophical thoughts are explicitly flagged as such (they all carry the attribution, 'Aus dem Leben eines bürgerlichen Menschen unserer Zeit'[from the life of a bourgeois in our time]), and they range alongside more mundane musings on the changing seasons, dealings with personal and professional contacts, and drafts of poems and pieces of prose. Repeatedly Becher reflects on the experiment with form that his diary represents and, in line with his own problematic pedagogical model of authorship, expresses the wish that it will take on an exemplary role in society – by encouraging a wide cross-section of the population to become reflective diary-writers like him at the same time as he devotes himself over many pages to quoting from past, decidedly bourgeois authors.[46] The exhortation towards Marxist philosophy and action, then, is just one part of Becher's very conscious self-stylization as a politically-committed author-pedagogue figure for his East German readers, but also with roots in earlier German cultural traditions.

Bearing all this in mind, Wolf's opening reference to Becher's soul-searching question directly links her text to a growing set of problems surrounding a specifically East German model of authorship. How can writers be good pedagogues when they are themselves the product of a still imperfect socio-political system and their art requires iterative relocation to the past as much as immersion in the present? And how can they both conceive themselves to be the Soviet-style cog in the

---

[45] The title prefigures Albert Camus's 'L'Homme révolté' (1951) in an uncanny manner.

[46] 'Man müßte die Menschen anhalten, Tagebücher zu führen. Mit einem Tagebuch läßt sich besser leben, das Leben übersichtlicher gestalten. Das Tagebuch ein großartiges Mittel zur Selbstverständigung' (Wolf, *Nachdenken über Christa T.*, p. 21; people should be made to keep a diary. Diaries improve your life, help you keep your life in a much better order. The diary is a great way of keeping in touch with / understanding yourself). Also p. 65.

machine and take on a representative role? By referencing Becher's diary, Wolf draws attention to the obvious parallels not just in content (Christa T.'s philosophical quest for self-fulfilment) but also in form between the two works. If her text is in some way responding to the questions thrown up by Becher's, then its explicit construction in the commemorative mode must also be seen as a response of sorts to Becher's invocation of the diary form. As the ever-present implied author within his text, Becher organizes not just the material taken from his earlier 'Der Aufstand im Menschen', but also the various aphorisms and other pieces of literary material that lay buried in his unconscious and suggest themselves to him as he is piecing together his work for posterity. The narrator of *Nachdenken* is equally retrospectively focused in her editorial role, as she repeatedly uses short quotations from Christa T.'s posthumous papers to reflect on the idea of a search or a journey that is inherent in writing and will allow access to the 'great' and emancipated individual: 'Schreiben ist groß machen'[47] (writing is to make great) and, on two occasions, 'Daß ich nur schreibend über die Dinge komme!'[48] (The way I can only get over things by writing!).

However, where Becher repeatedly (and often unconvincingly) tries to align himself with the 'common' GDR citizen, the unsettled life of Christa T. is pieced together by the narrator in a way that always emphasizes its difference to those of her East German peer group. Once she does finally lay down roots as a wife and mother in a small provincial community, her life symbolically ends in death, and its trajectory can be readily understood as part of a long-standing literary-historical narrative about authors' inability to belong in society.[49] Both Christa T.'s alignment with a Romantic tradition of placelessness – expressed through her references to Novalis, for example – and Christa Wolf's later exploration of Heinrich von Kleist and Karoline von Günderrode's suicide pact in *Kein Ort, Nirgends* (1977, No place, Nowhere) underscore this interpretation.

Furthermore, Christa T.'s symbolically unstable position in comparison to the rest of the founding GDR generation is repeatedly expressed through place metaphors that emphasize impenetrable obstacles and boundaries. Describing her university peer-group's collective investment in creating a socialist heterotopia, the narrator observes how, in their enthusiasm to be the perfect inhabitants of a

---

[47] Wolf, *Nachdenken über Christa T.*, p. 185.
[48] Wolf, *Nachdenken über Christa T.*, p. 42, p. 108.
[49] It seems to me that the text is more obviously problematizing this literary tradition than using it to express veiled dissent with the GDR, which is how Colin Smith reads it in his detailed analysis of the references to authorial and literary antecedents throughout the text: *Tradition, Art and Society: Christa Wolf's Prose* (Essen: die blaue Eule, 1987), esp. pp. 92–119.

perfect world, they misguidedly immured themselves within the cause: 'Denn die neue Welt, die wir unantastbar machen wollten, und sei es dadurch, daß wir uns wie irgendeinen Ziegelstein in ihr Fundament einmauerten – sie gab es wirklich'[50] (For the new world that we wanted to render unassailable, even if this meant that we had to immolate ourselves within its foundations like bricks – this world really existed). While Christa T. shared the utopian vision of her classmates, her sense of not-belonging, which is born out of her conscious failure to live up to the impossible standards required for the perfect heterotopian inhabitant, is recurrently expressed in terms of concrete physical exclusion:

> Mir steht alles fremd wie eine Mauer entgegen. Ich taste die Steine ab, keine Lücke. Was soll ich es mir länger verbergen: Keine Lücke für mich. An mir liegt es. Ich bin es, der die notwendige Konsequenz fehlt. Wie ist mir doch alles, als ich es zuerst in den Büchern las, so sehr leicht und natürlich vorgekommen.[51]

> [I am blocked off from everything by a wall. I feel my way along the stones: no spaces. Why should I hide it from myself any longer: there is no space for me. It's because of me. I am the one who is not acting on her principles. But how easy and how natural everything seemed to me when I first read about it in books!)]

Christa T.'s failure to fit in – which is ultimately a failure to adopt a realist conformist attitude and accept the kind of compromise that leads away from the model of collective fulfilment promised in socialist literature – is presented as the precondition for her symbolic position at the heart of the text's narrative. It is also a more accurate assessment of the consequences of pursuing a predominantly utopian mode of authorship in a really existing socialist society than either Becher's or Seghers' schematic attempts to marry celebratory, commemorative and utopian modes in their pedagogical models of authorship. Her position slightly outside her main peer group both inspires the narrator's extended written reflection on this group and makes Christa T. into a focalizing point for the group's increasingly conscious experiences of themselves as part of contemporary history. Thus where the rootlessness of her early years is presented as indicative of the position of a whole post-war generation – 'damals, übrigens, fiel sie wenig auf: Jedermann

---

[50] Wolf, *Nachdenken über Christa T.*, p. 60.
[51] Wolf, *Nachdenken über Christa T.*, pp. 81–2.

war gezwungen, den Mut zur Bewegung in sich wachzuhalten'[52] (Back then, incidentally, she hardly stood out at all: everybody had to keep themselves open to change / movement) –, the ongoing unassimilated position of her later years makes her the ideal trigger for that generation's conscious construction of collective memories. Now becoming part of a 'Sehnsuchtslandschaft' herself, Christa T. gives her socialist friends a shared past, or, using my conceptual vocabulary from chapter one, a place of generational memory. This process is, in fact, remarkably similar to the way Gruppe 47 authors would move from being, in Richter's words, 'eigentlich heimatlos' (actually without a home) in the immediate post-war years to providing the very ground for a contested cultural Heimat in the closing decades of the twentieth century that is itself characterized by a resurgence of the commemorative mode shot through with the problematics of celebrification. Commenting on the New Year's Eve party that Christa T. hosted shortly before her death, the narrator writes pointedly:

> Diesen einen Abend lang, die Silvesternacht von einundsechzig auf zweiundsechzig, ihr vorletztes Silvester, soll sie, Christa T., uns das Beispiel abgegeben haben für die unendlichen Möglichkeiten, die noch in uns lagen. [. . .] Wir arbeiteten an einer Vergangenheit, die man seinen Kindern erzählen kann, die Zeit rückte schließlich heran.[53]

[Throughout the course of this evening, New Year's Eve 1961/62, her penultimate New Year's Eve, she, Christa T., was to set an example for the endless possibilities that remained within us . . . We were working on a past that could be told to our children; time was marching on after all.]

Christa T.'s unstable location – in life, she is constantly on the move, while in death her memories and actions hover over the whole narrative – literally enacts placelessness within the text on multiple levels. Along with her own attitude of distance and difference, the commemorative process through which her character is brought back to life by the narrator accordingly entails repeated slippage in narrative time and space, as well as a tendency towards typecasting. The actual facts and feelings of her life remain a subject of speculation for the narrator, who is given to casting her instead in the literary tradition of the self-made

---

[52] Wolf, *Nachdenken über Christa T.*, p. 51.
[53] Wolf, *Nachdenken über Christa T.*, p. 183.

outcast: Sophie La Roche and her protagonist Fräulein von Sternheim, as well as Gustav Flaubert's Madame Bovary (although this latter is subsequently rejected). With this, the narrator's commemorative mode becomes tinged with the celebratory. Christa T.'s own efforts to reach out both to others and herself through writing are therefore doubly self-referential: her writing on writing is in itself self-reflexive, and it is further programmed by the narrator into a mixed mode of authorship that references past 'great' authors and their achievements in setting out a path of emancipation for capitalism's downtrodden subjects, with which Christa T. herself is suggestively aligned. Despite the very obvious traumas of the war that surround Christa T.'s figure, the narrator consequently casts her text as a celebratory memory narrative that coalesces around a powerful, exemplary personality, albeit *ex negativo*. In so doing, she uses the Romantic tradition to look away from the trauma of the Second World War, even as the failings of contemporary socialism to house its own utopian ideal are brought more sharply into focus.

When the narrator's framework is itself viewed as a literary conceit, deliberately held up to us by the text's author, Christa Wolf, – and the opening epigraph encourages us to read it like this –, the narrative spun around Christa T. represents the retrospective search for the individual's sense of self within the literary tradition. Indeed, the whole text functions like an inverse Bildungsroman, further exemplifying Wolf's iterative refinement of the emergent East German pedagogical model of authorship.[54] The narrator and her generation, the putative readers of *Christa T.*, are both deliberately framed retrospectively reconstructing the would-be author figure Christa T. in order to arrive at their own past. Not unlike Eddi Amsel in Grass's *Hundejahre*, although for different reasons, Christa T. acts as a foil for those who have become firmly anchored within society. As such, she allows the construction of their experiences within the GDR as a place of generational memory to begin. Beyond this, the character of Christa T. is primarily instructive for contemporary GDR readers and writers as a cautionary tale in attitude, as the narrator herself comments openly:

---

[54] I prefer the term 'inverse' to 'anti-Bildungsroman' used by Anna Kuhn in her discussion of the text: *Christa Wolf's Utopian Vision: From Marxism to Feminism* (Cambridge: Cambridge U. P., 1988), p. 58. The basic didactic impetus of the Bildungsroman is clearly present in this text, but, with its retrospective teleology, it is developed like a mirror-image of the conventional genre. For more on the Bildungsroman and the move from documenting individual to collective social growth, see Tobias Boes, *Formative Fictions: Nationalism, Cosmopolitanism, and the Bildungsroman* (Ithaca, NY: Cornell U. P., 2012)

Sich selbst überlassen, ging sie eben, das hat sie an sich gehabt. In letzter Minute besinnt man sich darauf, Arbeit an sie zu wenden. [...] Und bloß nicht vorgeben, wir täten es ihretwegen. Ein für allemal: Sie braucht uns nicht. Halten wir also fest, es ist unseretwegen, denn es scheint, wir brauchen sie.[55]

[Left to her own devices, she left; she had a habit of doing that. Just before it's too late, we're making the effort to engage with her.... But don't pretend we're doing it for her. For once and for all: she doesn't need us. So let's be clear, we're doing this for us, because it seems that we need her.]

Commenting on the symbolism of Christa T.'s trajectory, the West German critic Marcel Reich-Ranicki famously declared that Christa T. dies of the GDR.[56] Yet, as the earlier quotation indicated, her death is framed within the novel as the starting point for an active process of conscious, collective self-realization on the part of the narrator, her peers and the text's future readers. The idea, then, that the whole text functions as a response to the problematic pedagogical model of authorship represented by Johannes R. Becher in his diary, helps understand the extent to which this work was positioned as a piece of pedagogical instruction for both the East German reading public and other future authors. Christa T. represents a case study in not-belonging, not because she fails to identify with the socialist project, but because she identifies with it, in its idealized form, too much and reflects too hard on her personal position within it. She struggles with the pragmatic accommodation to everyday life demonstrated by the school children and the street-smart survivors they will go on to become, because she believes too much for too long in realizing a utopian vision (in the form of a heterotopia that she then cannot access), rather than using it productively as a foil. By embodying an attitude of placelessness in respect of her actual surroundings that is the direct inverse of Manfred Herrfurth's, her character shows the dead-end to which literary constructions of not-belonging lead, as well as the human cost of over-identifying with a socialist utopia. As a result, her character encourages active reflection on the part of the reader about how both to contribute to society and retain a personal sense of self. At the same time, the sympathy developed throughout for Christa T.'s thoroughly likeable character avoids the pitfalls of the kind of obviously biased,

---

[55] Wolf, *Nachdenken über Christa T.* pp. 10–11.
[56] Marcel Reich-Ranicki, 'Christa Wolfs unruhige Elegie', *Die Zeit*, 25.05.1969, quoted in Kuhn, *Christa Wolf's Utopian Vision*, p. 51.

undifferentiated pedagogical constructions favoured by Seghers and personally embodied by Becher in his work with the Free German Youth.[57]

The way in which Wolf's text thus communicates both the importance of inspirational writer-pedagogue figures and their limitations represents a reconfiguration of the East German pedagogical model of authorship. This can be understood as a clear move away from the fetishizing gesture towards male canonical writing that dogged Becher's literary output and political speeches alike, and a direct refinement of Seghers' explicitly ideological line that led to personal exhaustion. Working clearly within the commemorative mode, Wolf carves out a space that allows utopian alternatives to exist in parallel with the historical circumstances of the post-war socialist order, and she explores how author-pedagogue figures may or may not be able to hold open this space for their peers. The act of 'Nachdenken' – literally 'thinking after' – is an act of learning how to think in the aftermath of the great intellectual figures of Germany's (hitherto bourgeois) literary landscape. It happens from a position that is decidedly *within* the new socio-political context for which it is in the first instance designed, not just in terms of an emotional identification with the landscape and culture of a pre-existing Germany, but also in terms of a positive political identification with the opportunities that the current ideological system provides. In this sense, it also represents a socialist take on the thought of Adorno explored in the previous chapter. It explicitly opens up a space for the reader and for future generations to partake in the process of 'coming to oneself' whilst remaining consciously within the prevailing social order, including being constructively critical of it. This holistic sense of embedded social futurity is lacking in contemporary writing from the West.

Accordingly, although it was not explicit enough for many of her reviewers at the time, both in the East and the West, a corresponding sense of current and future placeness is discernible in the fabric of the text.[58] An implicit authorial attitude of belief in the potential of socialist society to embrace and properly engage with the individual underpins the very gesture of contemplation – 'nachdenken' – in which the narrator's editorial activity takes place. Indeed, directly referencing Johannes R. Becher's protracted thoughts about such issues on the first

---

[57] On Becher's appropriation of the *Aufbaubewegung*, a movement towards the literal and ideological reconstruction of society that was particularly driven by youth and worker cooperatives, see Dwars, *Abgrund des Widerspruchs*, p. 588.

[58] For the highly politicized reception of the text in both German states, see von Ankum, *Die Rezeption von Christa Wolf in Ost und West*.

page, it is explicitly framed as such. Equally important for literary posterity and the construction of a particularly East German mode of belonging for authors, however, is the way in which the text's actual author, Christa Wolf, embodies placeness with her own biographical person. This is an expression of physical and ideological belonging that happens in spaces beyond the literary text. In the first instance, her much-cited non-fictional self-interviews and essays were clearly designed to give her critics and readers a clear sense of how she believed that she, as an author of this challenging text, fitted in to society. In particular, her extended essay 'Lesen und Schreiben' (1968, Reading and Writing) argues that modern literature is above all inflected by an authorial attitude of placeness that decrees that the author should play an important pedagogical role within the social context that defines him or her: '[Der Autor] soll den Vorteil des geographischen und historischen Orts bis auf den Grund ausschöpfen und sich, als Person, jeder Empfindung stellen, die ein tief beteiligtes Leben mit sich bringt'[59] (The author should take full advantage of the opportunities afforded by her geographical and historical location and open herself up, as a person, to every emotion that a life lived in the midst of society entails).

Christa Wolf's 'placeness' is consequently not only qualitatively different to that of the would-be author Christa T., it is also energetically put into practice in a way that her first-person narrator can never personally enact (this latter remains stuck in the text, after all, only able to use textual rhetoric to urge her readers to act on her narrative). As is well documented, Christa Wolf, along with a small army of publisher friends, reviewers, fellow authors, and academics went to a prolonged effort between 1967 and 1972 to ensure the text would be made freely available in the GDR. These steps continue the precedent of accommodating oneself to the political regime already well established by Seghers and Becher: Wolf had to demonstrate her willingness, indeed determination, to belong within the political apparatus by making apparent concessions to the censors in including an extra chapter, as well as outwitting the party politicians who sought to exclude her from the Committee of the Schriftstellerverband in 1969.[60] In the subsequent interviews and essays that came about as a result of increased national and international interest in her work, she further builds on her text's success to develop a model of literary authenticity

---

[59] Christa Wolf, 'Lesen und Schreiben', in *Die Dimension des Autors: Essays und Aufsätze; Reden und Gespräche, 1959-1985*, 2 vols, (Berlin: Aufbau, 1986), vol. 1, pp. 7–47, p. 42.

[60] As documented in Angela Drescher, ed., *Dokumentation zu Christa Wolf "Nachdenken über Christa T."* (Hamburg: Luchterhand, 1992).

for the author who takes on an exemplary function for society. Her determination to realize her author potential within, and through direct engagement with, the existing socialist system means that her literary work and her biographical person together publicly embody an exemplary combination of an authorial attitude of 'placeness' with a differentiated pedagogical purpose. She wants her writing to help both individuals and the social order in which their lives unfold through the kinds of thinking her literary work sets free. This dual purpose would be held against her when it came to reunification and the controversies around collusion that echoed throughout the final twenty years of her life.[61]

Exemplary Differences

For all that they have since been questioned, the achievements of Wolf's generation of literary compatriots, such as Günter de Bruyn (b. 1926), Irmtraud Morgner (1933–1990), Sarah Kirsch (1935–2013), and Volker Braun (b. 1939), in building a differentiated pedagogical model of authorship beyond the Western celebratory frame of grand intellectuals modelling 'good' confrontational political behaviour are considerable. Wolf's recurrent return, in both theory and practice, to the notion that the literary text explores the writer's subjective sense of belonging forces modifications to the prevailing East German model of the socialist realist writer embodied by Seghers and her straightforward representation of the author-pedagogue. In both East and West contexts, Wolf's differentiated approach to conveying authorial attitude has directly influenced how literary texts by GDR authors are read. In each case, the implied attitude of the author becomes a crucial analytical category – not just for the relatively small number of literary critics either side of the Wall, but for a wide range of individuals working within the literary industries and cultural-political institutions who promote authors like Wolf in order to shore up their own economic and political narratives about the GDR.[62] Historically, Western analysts have looked for the text and the actions of the author who represents it to contain coded criticism of the socio-political circumstances, while their

---

[61] See for example Stuart Taberner, *Aging and Old Age Style in Günter Grass, Ruth Klüger, Christa Wolf, and Martin Walser: The Mannerism of a Late Period* (Rochester, NY: Camden House, 2013).

[62] This interpretative approach remains influential today in how Wolf's texts are marketed around the world. See Caroline Summers, *Examining Text and Authorship in Translation: What Remains of Christa Wolf?* ([n.p]: Palgrave, 2017).

Eastern counterparts find instead proof that the author is providing sympathetic guidance from within.[63]

Yet what Wolf most clearly adds to the foundational pedagogical model of authorship with which she understood herself to be operating is a degree of open-endedness that orientates all modes of authorship towards readers. Unlike both the paradoxically regressive canonical model that Becher invoked and the idealized omnipresent pedagogue position that weighed heavily on Seghers and her work, Wolf's version of pedagogical authorship relies on publicly communicating an internalized moment of self-realization within a distinct and changing geographical and historical context. Importantly, this moment of self-realization is not just readily emulated but must in fact be activated in and by her readers if her text is to work at all: the readers need to empathize with the narrator's desire to commemorate and set about inhabiting Christa T.'s lost world as part of a revelatory dialogue with their own. The increasing importance of the utopian mode in her writing, which will even determine the title of her authorship-focused *Kein Ort, Nirgends*, is a feature that clearly links Wolf to Morgner and Kirsch and can also be discerned in the work of de Bruyn and Braun. All five writers develop dialogic structures across their work that support a shifting of place and opening up of alternatives nested within the recognizable worlds they describe. They invest considerable expectation in their readers not just to follow them, but to make the texts as they go. Wolf's early work shows a new kind of pedagogical exemplarity that is a precursor to this broader trend in the way it invites the reader in to explore the real political potential of Massey's throwntogetherness within the texts' own narrative frame. If this process of negotiation is then re-enacted on a larger scale in an actual society, it has the potential to have a direct transformative effect on it: relations between people unfold in such a way as to directly shape the place that facilitates them in the first place. As a result, Wolf's placeness as an author remains adaptable to the individual circumstances of both writer and reader. This partly explains why Wolf's didactic literature was able to resonate, in sometimes quite different ways, with readers and writers in both East and West Germany throughout her subsequent career in a manner that Seghers' and Becher's did not.

Running throughout the chapter has been a concern with the extent to which underlying ideological differences in respect of place between East and West German writers might be accompanied by a different

---

[63] For extensive discussion of this phenomenon, particularly in the last twenty years of the GDR, see David Bathrick, *The Powers of Speech: The Politics of Culture in the GDR* (Lincoln: U. of Nebraska P, 1995).

ethical drive to the distinct models of authorship, even as both groups of writers also remained in touch with and mutually influenced one another. The ethical trend that has emerged across the material studied in this chapter has been towards sharing a greater collective responsibility between author and readers to perceive alternative spaces and ways of being within the existing social order. While individual authors may have paradoxically found themselves increasingly institutionally isolated in the way they took up a role at the heart of socialist society, their work nevertheless models collective belonging through the way it first stakes out a direct pedagogical claim for literature and then refines its broader methods of engagement to gain traction with its readers. In the West, by contrast, authors overtly clubbed together in order both to draw attention to their lack of an assured position from which to write and in so doing challenge the social order. The modes adopted in their writing, however, still tend towards an exemplarity born of splendid isolation, as the texts unfold complex messages of not-belonging that tend to pitch literary space against the real social space in which they are read. Somewhat counter-intuitively, the Western model of the exemplary creator arises from authors who want to 'show and tell' more than their Eastern counterparts, such that their potential for public engagement and inspiration through literature is correspondingly less differentiated. The celebratory mode of the charismatic leader, which itself increasingly attracts the hollow laughter of satire, is still much in evidence throughout both the art and politics pursued by West German writers in the 1960s, and the danger is that their literary posturing (in Meizoz' sense) remains at the level of the conceptually inspirational for an elite literary minority rather than the practically instructive for bringing about actual broad-based social change. Despite its ethical drive towards an open democracy, the result of this author-centric understanding of authorship is therefore arguably to keep readers, along with anyone else who doesn't fit the dominant West German author mould, at arm's length.

Four Mediating Authorship in Berlin and Frankfurt, 1959–1989

In this chapter, I look up from the actions of individual authors to trace the broader sociological map which both shaped and was shaped by these collective actions across the 1960s and into the following two decades. Reading this map is equally important when seeking to understand how the various modes of authorship routinely inflect one another, as the modes reside just as much in those broader places where literature unfolds as in the literary text itself and are thus traceable to multiple actors. Drawing up such a map entails a methodological shift from textual close reading to archival and other forms of historical reconstruction. It also requires sharpened tools for exploring implicit values and biases that determine how certain paths are forged and become dominant over others. Although authors carry cultural authority and attract widespread public interest because they appear to be particularly insightful, well-educated individuals, the more complex the literary support system becomes, the more cultural blind spots and ethical shortcomings become apparent within it. Precisely because literary authorship is constituted within a large network of relations, it is also vulnerable to failings in the normative cultural values that shape and sustain it. In fact, the more individuals and institutions act in concert to try to promote a certain poetics and politics of place inherent in the foundational models of authorship that they have helped to build, the fuzzier the ethical edges around Goethe's distinct space of literature headed up by responsible, exemplary individuals become. In order to unpick this, we need to move to a larger systems level. In this and subsequent chapters, the organized literary system – what I have been terming the 'German literature network' – largely takes the form of a discernible network with distinct human actors at its heart. The fact, as I shall develop below, that the concept of a network of actors can also include non-human actors, such as institutions, material buildings and intellectual ideas, however, adds an important dimension to my study of authorship, and I shall return to it in due course.

Extending Authorship across a Sociological Plane: Actor-Network-Theory

'Was bleibt nun übrig. Es gibt nur zwei Wege, einmal sich selbst zu modernisieren, das heißt eine Art Höllerer zu werden, oder die Literatur ganz aufzugeben'[1] (What can you do. There are just two ways to modernize yourself, you either have to become a kind of Höllerer or give up on literature entirely). Responding to the provocation from fellow West German writer and critic, Walter Jens, in 1961 that he was old-fashioned, Hans Werner Richter sensed a fundamental shift in the kind of networking activity that was required of the successful 'modern' mediator of German authorship at the beginning of the decade. I borrow the terms 'mediation' and 'mediator' from the sociologist Bruno Latour, whose use of ANT in defining what 'the social' is and how it can be studied maps well onto my own interest in making historical patterns of authorship and their attendant literary and social effects visible. Latour's conceptualization of mediators and the networks they sustain, which I briefly referenced in my introduction and elaborate on more fully below, is not in any way bound either to a particular historical period or even to tangible networks; for him, anything that links something to something else and, in so doing, transforms, translates or otherwise leaves its own trace on the association it facilitates, is a mediator. Mediators are interesting precisely because they leave a trace, and thus can be studied.[2]

Richter seriously doubted the suitability of his ad-hoc organization to keep pace with these rapidly expanding tendencies, as they required not just connecting with ever more people, but also with multiple forms of media and different kinds of institutions. He was right. As media historian Christina von Hodenberg has set out at length, the hallmarks of the largely re-built public sphere by the mid-1960s were increased media profiling for all sorts of political and cultural endeavour and a groundswell of educated young people who were seeking not just instruction, but genuinely interactive, critical engagement with the issues of the day.[3] Richter continued to pour considerable energy into organizing writers to stake their position within these debates, but his own floating position outside any wider supportive institutional infrastructure, coupled with his somewhat autocratic sensibilities when it came to actually collaborating, meant that this became an increasingly wearisome task. Challenges from the younger student generation to

---

[1] Hans Werner Richter, *Briefe*, ed. Sabine Cofalla (Munich: Hanser, 1997) p. 346.
[2] Latour, *Reassembling the Social*.
[3] Christina von Hodenberg, *Konsens und Krise: Eine Geschichte der westdeutschen Medienöffentlichkeit 1945–1973* (Göttingen: Wallstein, 2006).

Richter and some of his closest Gruppe 47 affiliates also meant that authors' self-organization increasingly divided along generational lines – as Peter Handke's appearance at the group's 1966 meeting in Princeton famously demonstrated.[4]

Richter's melancholy observations from the beginning of the decade, together with Hans Magnus Enzensberger's famous comments on the irrelevance of literary activity in *Kursbuch* at the end, imply a wider social context in which the undertakings of authors *as literary authors* in the Federal Republic dramatically lost purchase on society over the course of the decade.[5] Such a development is routinely linked to the crumbling of the Gruppe 47 in 1966/67 and the much-cited 'inward turn' of literature in the 1970s, as well as the rejection of literary forms entirely on the part of some of the more radical left-wing writers. However, this narrative that is popularly offered to us not least by key authors themselves tells, at best, only half the story. What is missing is any actual assessment of the extent to which authors had collectively been successful at imbricating themselves within wider institutional and media networks, from academe through publishing and broadcasting media to diverse cultural and political foundations, such that they remained securely able to alter or otherwise effect social change *however* literature was being talked about and individual authors fell in and out of public favour as the decade advanced. While the increasing irrelevance of the inherently self-reflective medium of literature in a turbulently political environment may seem a logical tale to tell, it is not supported by the growth and diversification in the literary publishing sector throughout the 1960s and 1970s. The Deutscher Taschenbuch Verlag and Suhrkamp launched highly successful paperback series following Rowohlt's pioneering move in the 1950s and an increasing number of alternative presses opened for business, as discussed below. Nor is it supported by the visibility of authors at high profile public events and in the broadcast media over the same period. Furthermore, while there was a gradual shift in literary style and subject matter from one decade to the next, this does not easily map onto forms of writing that are in any way more or less 'complex', 'political', or socially 'effective'. The story that is told about German literature in the narrow sense, in other words, needs to be complemented

---

[4] See Rebecca Braun, 'Cultural Impact and the Power of Myth in Popular Public Constructions of Authorship', in *Cultural Impact in the German Context: Studies in Transmission, Reception and Influence*, ed. by R. Braun and L. Marven (Rochester, NY: Camden House, 2010), pp. 78–96.

[5] Hans Magnus Enzensberger, 'Gemeinplätze, die Neueste Literatur betreffend', *Kursbuch*, 15 (1968), 187–96.

by the story of extended authorship that always unfolds within the German literature network in which it exists and has multiple aspects of literary practice (i.e. well beyond an individual's initial creation of a literary text) in its purview.

Both the specific literary work of the arch 'Literaturmanager' (literary manager)[6] Walter Höllerer and his wider mediating activities throughout the 1960s and 1970s support a critical revision of the dominant narratives outlined above surrounding the social relevance and aesthetic expression of German literature over the two decades. Höllerer's actions, as I describe in detail below, were the result of a fundamentally different understanding of networked relations from Richter's, and it is one that takes us much more readily into the 1970s than that of the embattled individualists that emerged from the increasingly hostile retrospective media coverage of the Gruppe 47. Indeed, there are many reasons to see in Höllerer the true collaborative, democratizing spirit of the 1960s that precedes the hardening of lines around diverse collectives and interest groups in the 1970s. He worked with many of the same authors as Richter from as early as 1961, and yet the model of socially relevant authorship he facilitated over the course of the decade and well into the next was strikingly different. Furthermore, as a literary mediator he was not an isolated phenomenon. His activities find their echo in the work of other institutionally well-connected individuals who emerged in the same period, such as Siegfried Unseld at the helm of the Suhrkamp publishing house in Frankfurt am Main, or Fritz J. Raddatz, whose career I have already touched upon in chapter two. Like the '45er' generation of journalists and broadcasters, all three rose to positions of considerable institutional influence in the early 1960s, believed in the importance of hosting democratic debate and cultural exchange within the framework of their institutional operations, and sought to make their resulting innovations as accessible as possible to a broad-based public.[7]

The kinds of authorial communities that these individuals were able to create and nurture well into the 1970s and 1980s must therefore be seen on the one hand as the direct product of well-networked actors. The powerful individual's agency as a mediator is a decisive factor in shaping the mid- to late twentieth-century German literary scene. On

---

[6] Helmut Boettiger with Lutz Dittrich, *Elefantenruden: Walter Höllerer und die Erfindung des Literaturbetriebs* (Berlin: Literaturhaus Berlin, 2005), p. 7.

[7] See in particular ch. 4 of von Hodenberg's *Konsens und Krise* for a discussion of generational groupings in the Federal Republic's media sphere, and ch. 5 for a sense of how a move towards critical contemporary reporting and investigative journalism began to take hold in the early 1960s.

the other hand, however, these actors are also a product of their circumstances, and thus a much wider network of interactions between people, concepts and things inevitably also affects their exertion of agency. The broader social manifestation of authorship traced over the following chapter is thus much more than merely the exemplary creative actions of these specific literary mediators on the immediate literary industry and its political hinterland. A set of very real considerations around both the material and the conceptual infrastructures for literature has an equally important role to play. Both aspects taken together – the actions of those individuals together with all the other relations that feed into their literature network – give us authorship in the extended sense and allow us to reflect much more fully on the actual place of literature in society.

For a sense of what this means in practice, we need to revisit Latour in greater depth. Arguing against Pierre Bourdieu and his methodological imposition of a conceptual system from above on to a field of cultural production that remains synchronic, nationally bounded, and driven exclusively by human interactions, Latour's work champions the empirical approach of 'following the actors themselves'. He does this in an attempt both to understand the activities that underpin our experience of 'the social' at any one time, and to allow for the fact that the networks thus constituted are constantly and consciously shifting. As I already briefly set out in my Introduction to this study, he uses spatial terms to pin down what is really at stake in any discussion of a theoretical phenomenon:

> [. . .] even though the question seems really odd at first – not to say in bad taste – whenever anyone speaks of a 'system', a 'global feature', a 'structure', a 'society', an 'empire', a 'world economy', an 'organization', the first ANT [Actor-Network-Theory] reflex should be to ask: 'In which building? In which Bureau? Through which corridor is it accessible? Which colleagues has it been read to? How has it been compiled?'[8]

Punning throughout on the abbreviation of ANT and the busy scurrying of ants, Latour insists on grounding all attempts to enhance our knowledge of the social structures that inhere in any given context in the affiliations that can be traced between human and non-human actors: 'Things, quasi-objects, and attachments are the real centre of the social world, not the agent, person, member, or participant – nor is it

---

[8] Bruno Latour, *Reassembling the Social: An Introduction to Actor-Network-Theory* (Oxford: Oxford U. P., 2005), p. 183.

society or its avatars'.⁹ The social becomes a dynamic experience of associations and affiliations that are habitually traced by a variety of actors and which shake down into a web of more and less well-connected nodes. These nodes in turn facilitate the profiling of events, individuals, ideas at local, national and global levels and are what allow the network both to function and to be visible to itself.

In the following pages, I shall adapt these insights to a study of the interplay between individual human actors and other powerful transformative phenomena that also function as mediators of authorship: developments in media technologies, changes to the built environment of education and publishing in West Germany, and the emergence of emotive historiographical debates across the 1960s, 1970s and 1980s that problematized notions of belonging in a variety of ways. All of these play a role in the shifting models of authorship that prevail in any one place and time. While Höllerer and Unseld were both very consciously manipulating contacts and playing vital mediating roles within an industry whose key players moved increasingly seamlessly between radio, TV, journalism and literature, their actions are also typical of a certain generation and its approach to locating itself in the world and determining literary value.¹⁰ By focusing in detail on the authorship they facilitated through both their individual actions and the ways in which they were more widely networked, my aim is to bring out their conscious enactments of authority within the literary industry, as well as to show the limits of their all-too-human, sub-conscious actions and the related institutional and processual blind spots that characterized the social fabric they were helping to weave.

Walter Höllerer's Literature Network: Authorship in Cold War Berlin

Throughout the 1960s, Walter Höllerer (1922–2003) achieved veritable cult status across a variety of overlapping literary, educational, political and cultural fields. An established poet and well-liked critic within the Gruppe 47 meetings, he began to attract students away from Theodor Adorno's lectures when he worked as an Assistant Professor in Frankfurt in the 1950s. On accepting a position at the Technical University in Berlin in 1959, he not only established a cutting-edge research institute for the study of 'literature in the technical age', but, shortly after that, managed to leverage large amounts of funding from industry

---

[9] Latour, *Reassembling the Social*, p. 238.
[10] On authors' multiple media links, see von Hodenberg, pp. 283–90, and sections 3 and 4 of Harro Segeberg, *Literatur im Medienzeitalter: Literatur, Technik und Medien seit 1914* (Darmstadt: Wissenschaftlich Buchgesellschaft, 2003).

and political sources to establish the Literarisches Colloquium Berlin (Literary Colloquium Berlin, LCB) as a physical venue for literature. Here already we can see a difference between the narratives sustained within the Gruppe 47 circle and those to which Höllerer's activities gave rise. While metaphors of absent place continued to exercise the contributors to Richter's 1962 almanac on the Gruppe 47 referenced in chapter one, Höllerer was busy gathering together funds from the American Ford Foundation and the Berlin Senate to establish an actual physical home for producing and celebrating literature in the culturally highly-charged location of Cold War Berlin. This venture comprised not only a large villa, Am Sandwerder 5 in Wannsee, with bedrooms for visiting writers and representative public rooms, but also an affiliated film production department and publishing operation, as well as a well-funded programme of academic and public literary events. A further premises, Carmerstraße 4, was rented in the centre of Berlin for public events and administrative purposes. On an active political level, Höllerer's willing alignment with American cultural policy can be seen as a direct response to the establishment of the Leipzig Institute for Literature in the GDR in 1955, which was later named the Johannes R. Becher Institute.[11] It is also a very specific manifestation of the particular situation in which West Berlin found itself. No longer Germany's capital, it existed now as an effective island of Western democracy in the East, on the one hand representing the virtues of this whole political system, but on the other hand with its inhabitants wholly reliant on supply lines from the West and unable to take part in national elections. With this, West Berlin is oddly outside of West German life, but an important microcosm that reflects back on it and very deliberately projects a certain message about it to the East – another version of Foucault's heterotopia, in fact. Early memoranda testify to Höllerer's understanding both of this general heterotopian situation, and of authors' particular political and social importance in the Cold War context. In 1962, for example, he sets out the key activities the LCB will pursue, and explains the rationale as follows:

---

[11] On the founding of the Johannes R. Becher Institute, see Marina Micke and Matthew Philpotts, 'Irreconcilable Differences: The Troubled Founding of the Leipzig Institute for Literature', in 'Post-War Literature and Institutions', ed. Seán M. Williams and W. Daniel Wilson, special issue of *Oxford German Studies* (2014), 43:1, 5–19. On the history of the LCB's links to American Cultural Policy, see Michael Peter Hehl, 'Berliner Netzwerke: Walter Höllerer, die Gruppe 47 und die Gründung des Literarischen Colloquiums Berlin', in *Poetik im technischen Zeitalter: Walter Höllerer und die Entstehung des modernen Literaturbetriebs*, ed. by Achim Geisenhanslüke and Michael Peter Hehl (Bielefeld: transcript, 2013), pp. 155–89.

Es soll dadurch erreicht werden, daß Berlin von internationalen Autoren besucht wird, daß diese Autoren über Berlin schreiben, daß Berlin für die Nachwuchskräfte, sowohl der westlichen Länder wie auch, wenn möglich, etwa aus Polen und Jugoslawien, ein Zentrum wird, daß hier in Berlin die Verbindungen zwischen den Schriftstellern und den Massenmedien hergestellt werden, daß auf diese Weise die Ideen der Schriftsteller nicht nur im kleinen Zirkel bleiben, sondern sich auf breite Bevölkerungskreise auswirken.[12]

[This will ensure that international authors visit Berlin, that these authors write about Berlin, that Berlin becomes a centre for the next generation of writers from both Western countries and, if possible, places like Poland and Yugoslavia, and that links are made here in Berlin between writers and the mass media, so that the writers' ideas do not remain confined to a small circle, but reach a broad cross-section of the population.]

This rationale figures almost word-for-word in the later grounding statutes of the LCB, and Höllerer will draw on it time and again as he gathers support from businesses and industry over the course of 1963 and 1964 (e.g. in letters to the Fritz Thyssen foundation and the Bundesverband der Deutschen Industrie [Federal Consortium of German Industry]). The success of the resulting institute also functions more passively as an early prototype for the network of regionally funded Literaturhäuser (literature centres) that would spread throughout the West German provinces in the 1980s. Their rise follows a similar broad understanding of the culturally representative role that literature can play within federal policy when turned into an experiential set of relationships publicly enacted by living authors.

Perhaps Höllerer's biggest media coup when it comes to raising the general profile of German-language authors and setting up an alternative discourse of belonging, however, was to run a series of public readings from novelists and poets as well as hosting theatre and film performances throughout the 1960s and to ensure that these were financed from 1961/62 onwards by the TV and radio channel, Sender Freies Berlin. These events were so popular that, in the early iterations of the series, the venue had to be changed from the Technical University's

---

[12] Walter Höllerer, typescript, 'Stiftung zur Förderung der neueren Literatur in Berlin', 27.11.1962, in LSR Nachlass Walter Höllerer, Materialien zum Literarischen Colloquium Berlin – Ford Foundation, uncatalogued.

largest lecture hall, complete with video link to another room, to the city's Congress Hall to accommodate the huge numbers of students, literary professionals and local Berliners who wanted to attend (the Congress Hall seats up to 1,000, and there are reports of over 1,500 people trying to get in).[13] Unlike the Gruppe 47 meetings, which kept TV cameras firmly outside the closed doors of their literary 'workshop' discussions, Höllerer's events were broadcast on both local and national TV from the early 1960s.[14] Significantly more people were literally allowed in to partake in the authorship emerging from these activities.

The public success of both Höllerer and the events he organized seems to have arisen from this very openness and accessibility. In this, he proved himself at the cutting-edge of wider democratizing developments in the media: popular TV shows, such as *Panorama*, brought a critical investigative impetus to public broadcasting that gained them a huge following in the early years of the 1960s, while the expanding left-liberal print media began to make a decisive shift away from simple reporting towards more polemical tones and formats that naturally encouraged interaction and debate.[15] Through live events with authors, poets, theatre directors and film-makers, Höllerer brought creative individuals as far removed from one another as the American beat poets and Soviet gulag writers into contact both with each other and a curious wider public audience. By association, he also placed German-language writers into a network of important global literary trend-setters: figures such as Günter Grass, Peter Rühmkorf, Max Frisch and Ingeborg Bachmann were well represented in his series and often

---

[13] Helmut Böttiger, ed., *Elefantenrunden: Walter Höllerer und die Erfindung des Literaturbetriebs* (Berlin: Literaturhaus Berlin, 2005), p. 7.

[14] It should be added that there were also pragmatic reasons for including TV – the Sender Freies Berlin helped finance the whole 1961/62 series with international writers, and later the LCB itself. Their withdrawal of financial support for the LCB in 1968 provoked a crisis and is surely the reason why Höllerer subsequently came to an agreement with Dieter Stolte, Commissioning Director at ZDF, to cover LCB events for 1969. For information on the funding of 1961/62 series, see Christoph Gahl, 'Literatur im technischen Zeitalter', in *Colloquium: eine deutsche Studentenzeitung*, (1962) 16:3, 11–13. For later funding problems, see material in LSR, Nachlass Walter Höllerer, Materialien zum Literarischen Colloquium Berlin, Ordner 1a, Mappe 1, ohne Signature [uncatalogued]. For more on the events broadcast throughout the 1960s, see Böttiger, *Elefantenrunden*. Discussion of individual readings can also be found in Achim Geisenhanslüke and Michael Peter Hehl, eds, *Poetik im technischen Zeitalter: Walter Höllerer und die Entstehung des modernen Literaturbetriebs* (Bielefeld: transcript, 2013).

[15] For in-depth discussion of the significance of Panorama and other similar TV shows for the development of democratic structures in the Federal Republic, see von Hodenberg, *Konsens und Krise*, pp. 302–22.

helped host the foreign visitors, as well as actively collaborate in ensuing publications.[16] In so doing, Höllerer gave literature in Germany an accessible, public face that built directly on the belief, fostered too within the Gruppe 47, that post-war writers should engage with their immediate wider context in what amounts to a direct re-enactment of the processes of exchange and enrichment implied by Goethe's world literature. Unlike the Gruppe 47, however, his series of public events followed a much more flexible model that translated well into multiple forms of media, placed individual authors at the heart of the public experience of literature, and drew its life blood from interaction and technical innovation. All of these helped expand the practice of authorship even further through an intricate web of underlying nodal connections between human and non-human actors.

With this in mind, his remarks on the occasion of the public presentation of his TV-film series, 'Die literarischen Profile europäischer Großstädte' (The literary profiles of European capital cities; produced by the Literary Colloquium Berlin 1969–1971), read like a riposte to Enzensberger's pronouncements on the death of literature in 1968:

Literatur ist Semiologie: der Versuch, neue Zeichen, Signalelemente zu finden für neue Möglichkeiten des Zusammenlebens; für eine neue Rolle des Individuums im Kollektiv. Dieser Versuch kann nicht so aussehen, daß Autoren fertig ausgebrütete Verständigungssysteme anbieten. Er sieht so aus, daß Autoren den Leser, Hörer, Zuschauer, den mitarbeitenden Rezipienten auffordern, mit ihnen gemeinsam diesen neuen Zeichen auf die Spur zu kommen und Folgerungen daraus zu ziehen.[17]

[Literature is semiology: the attempt to find new signs, signal elements that would help establish new ways of living together; a new role for the individual within the collective. This attempt is not a case of authors offering their fully hatched systems of understanding. It means authors encouraging the reader, listener, viewer, the reviewer who is working alongside, to help trace this new sign together and draw consequences from it.]

---

[16] For example, Günter Grass's translation and public reading of Beat Poetry, in the presence of Gregory Corso and Lawrence Fagin, at the Berlin Academy of Arts in 1960 – see Böttiger, *Elefantenrunden*, pp. 113–16. See also my discussion of the deliberately international *Ein Gedicht und sein Autor: Lyrik und Essay* (Berlin: Literarisches Colloquium Berlin, 1967), ed. Walter Höllerer, below.

[17] 'Literatur in der Konsumgesellschaft', quoted in Böttiger, ed., *Elefantenrunden*, pp. 179–80.

Bridging the collective and the individual, the serious literary text and the mass public audience, and linguistic and technological systems, Höllerer's networking and promotional activities throughout the 1960s rely in an exemplary fashion on a multi-modal opening up of literature by the author making him or herself accessible to readers and critics. We have already seen a similar trend emerging in GDR literature over the same period, although for markedly different reasons and with much less of an orientation to the public media or indeed other forms of media.[18] The kinds of encounters and interaction that Höllerer promotes are facilitated through a combination of live dialogue-style events and dissemination through multiple media that aims to build a 'buzz' around literature and see it holistically as part of the wider social world, with the interactive author providing a key way in.

Yet Höllerer did more than merely profile an expanded, interactive, media-friendly framework for authorship from his position as avant-garde academic, although in this respect he certainly pioneered new ways of being an intellectual mediator.[19] Crucially for our purposes, he also initiated a number of creative experiments that specifically set out to innovate in the way underlying models of authorship were mediated by contemporary texts, such that the sorts of encounters facilitated by both his academic institute, and the Berlin Literary Colloquium that grew from it, might go beyond democratic discussion around the text and actually change what happens within the text too. Inspired by the North American creative writing schools, Höllerer's first official undertaking in the context of the newly-founded Literary Colloquium was to pioneer a five-month residential visit to its city-centre location in Carmerstraße 4, Charlottenburg, for sixteen novice writers, who worked under the guidance of Hans Werner Richter, Peter Weiss, Günter Grass, Peter Rühmkorf and Walter Höllerer. For aspiring and established authors alike, such sustained collaboration was untested, and many were sceptical of what it would achieve. The 1964 volume

---

[18] This assessment applies to the state-sanctioned forms of literature in the GDR. Various forms of dissident writing do make use of multiple media and the power of live performance, partly precisely in order to overcome institutional limitations. For more on this, see Ann Stamp Miller, *The Cultural Politics of the German Democratic Republic: The Voices of Wolf Biermann, Christa Wolf, and Heiner Müller* (Bock Ration: Brown Walker, 2004).

[19] For an interesting take on how he managed to bridge a number of different roles within the literary industry by always placing himself on the edge of groupings and, in so doing, acting as a wider centrifugal force across the different networks, see Rolf Parr, 'Walter Höllerers Neuakzentierung der Intellektuellenrolle im Literaturbetrieb', in *Poetik im technischen Zeitalter*, ed. by Geisenhanslüke and Hehl, pp. 192–211.

Prosaschreiben documents this first attempt within the FRG collaboratively to explore the writing process as a form of tutelage and it is an illuminating record of the kinds of activities they undertook and the discussions they pursued.[20] In addition, however, Höllerer and fourteen of the sixteen participants also produced a collaboratively written novel, *Das Gästehaus* (1965), which took collaborative innovation into the specific frame of one literary text and, in so doing, directly challenged conventional notions of both the author and the text.[21]

The novel comprises fifteen individually authored chapters that each present the viewpoint of a different character who has been invited to the fictional guest house run by the mysterious Elmshäuser in Berlin. This multi-perspectival textual framework allows for significant diversity of style amongst its authors: Peter Bichsel, Walter Höllerer, Klaus Stiller, Peter Heyer, Hubert Fichte, Wolf Simeret, Elfriede Gerstl, Jan Huber, Hans Christoph Buch, Wolf D. Rogosky, Martin Doehlemann, Corinna Schnabel, Nicolas Born, Joachim Neugröschel and Hermann Peter Piwitt. According to the dust jacket, the project it represents is to be seen in a historical tradition staked out by two earlier novels, also by Berlin collectives – *Die Versuche und Hindernisse Karls*, initiated by Varnhagen van Ense and his circle of Romantics in 1808, followed by the 1908 *Der Roman der Zwölf*. This latter amounted to a kind of 'know your author' guessing game set up by a group of established authors that included Hermann Bahr and Gabriele Reuter and which promised prizes for those readers who could correctly identify who had written what. *Das Gästehaus* continues these attempts to present a collective serious literary product that is marked out by the individual style and collective vision of its collaborators, but it departs from its predecessors in choosing writers who were not particularly well known – and thus identified with any particular style of writing – at the time.[22] Accordingly, as one of the founding missions of the Berlin Literary Colloquium was to provide a real and metaphorical base from which to foster new talent, who had written what was made clear in the

---

[20] Walter Hasenclever, ed., *Prosaschreiben* (Berlin: Literarisches Colloquium Berlin, 1964).

[21] The two authors who dropped out were the Israeli Daniel Lustig and Ror Wolf – *Prosaschreiben*, ed. Hasenclever, notes in their biographical entry that each could only attend the colloquium for a short spell, but does not give reasons why.

[22] An introductory overview of other forms of collective authorship across the twentieth century in Germany can be found here: http://www.kollektiveautorschaft.uni-koeln.de/theorie.html (last accessed 15 April 2015).

paratextual materials.[23] The title page deliberately lists the authors in order of their chapter contribution, while a short interview with Höllerer at the end provides further information about how the project was collaboratively executed. Furthermore, the dust jacket design underscores Höllerer's key curatorial role, as his name hovers over the grand entrance door to the guest house sketched on the front, while the names of the aspiring authors stand at the windows (figure 4.1).

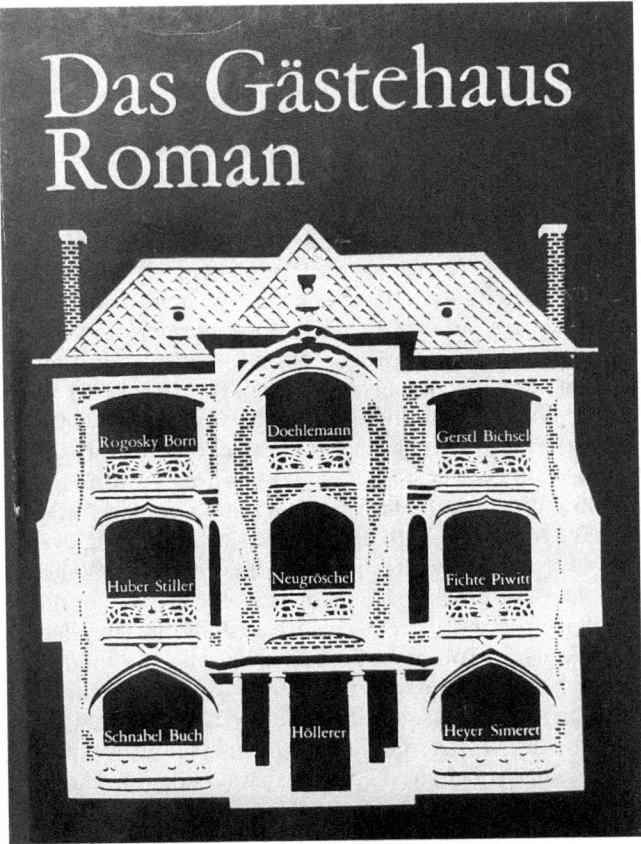

Figure 4.1 Dust jacket of the co-authored novel, *Das Gästehaus* (Berlin: LCB, 1965). Reproduced courtesy of the Literarisches Colloquium Berlin.

---

[23] The authors were also filmed for TV reading from their chapters as part of the novel's launch publicity: anon, 'Schreib-Schule: In starker Beleuchtung', *Der Spiegel*, 17.02.1965, also available online: http://www.spiegel.de/spiegel/print/d-46169515.html (last accessed 15 April 2015).

One of the questions posed by the text's conscious framing of its own project is therefore the extent to which each individual aspiring writer 'einem Einheitsstil entgegenarbeitete oder ihm vielleicht erlag'[24] (either worked towards a homogenized style or perhaps fell victim to it). This can be incorporated into a wider question about the extent to which the text provides an insight into the practicalities, on both a textual and a societal level, of authorship as an iterative, shared endeavour.

The question of how the individual relates to a broader collective is clearly also central to the story itself: each fictional guest ruminates over the reason for their invitation and their relationship to both their physical surroundings and to other guests in the hotel, as well as to Elmshäuser, who remains largely absent throughout. Over the course of these narratives, Elmshäuser is variously assigned the role of a black marketeer, a spy, a drug dealer, a collector of eccentricities, a bureaucratic construct, a conductor of socio-scientific experiments, as well as a philosophical partner in dialogue, and a man overly given to drink and sex. His age is also liable to shift, and there is some confusion over how many generations of Elmshäuser may be present – as many as three are suggested. The potential for the characters' musings to take on the form of dream sequences laden with portentous symbols in the manner of Martin Walser's early writing, or existential self-interrogations reminiscent of Max Frisch's narrative works from the 1950s, is clear, and a number of the contributions show such affinities (Stiller, Heyer and Fichte represent the former, Bichsel and Schnabel the latter). Collectively, however, the chapters interlock like nodes within a shifting network of understanding between the fifteen protagonists, as each reflects on the role they have to play in both anticipated and unfolding events, or, in the words of the Swiss waiter from the first chapter: 'Vieles geschah mehrmals. Die Gespräche schienen vorgeformt, alle ahmten etwas nach, der Pfarrer einen Pfarrer, seine Haushälterin eine liebe biedere Frau, Lebouc eine Sphinx, ein Souvenir aus Ägypten, und der Schriftsteller einen Schriftsteller'[25] (Many things happened several times. The conversations seemed pre-formed, everyone was imitating something, the priest was imitating a priest, his housekeeper a goodly, well-mannered lady, Lebouc a sphinx, a souvenir from Egypt, and the writer a writer).

Following Latour's terminology, it is clear that the individual narrators are all aware of their own agency; their narratives willingly retrace the extent to which, in responding to Elmshäuser's invitation

---

[24] Peter Bichsel et al., *Das Gästehaus: Roman* (Berlin: Literarisches Colloquium, 1965), inside back flap of dust jacket.
[25] Bichsel et al., *Das Gästehaus*, p. 14.

and taking part in his intended gathering, they have functioned as mediators, acting out his designs and changing or otherwise shaping them in the process. The gesture of multiple retellings and reflections in the absence of any central, authoritative construction of meaning thus becomes the text: its readers also act as 'ants', tracing the associative pathways set out by the characters. These pathways, it should be noted, are as liable to be influenced by material objects and abstract notions as by human interactions: a stray hamster looms large in one account, while others are dominated by their reactions to the physical fabric of the Wilhelminian villa and by psychological explorations of belonging, substitution and sexual repression that are triggered by their interaction with any number of animate and inanimate objects. Accordingly, the text opens out onto a wide swathe of cultural history and geography. The reader follows the various links that the characters themselves suggest as well as those suggested by echoes across the various narratives, and gradually pieces together a picture of the connections that place some characters in central positions and others on the periphery within the emerging web of the text. The process of constructing meaning through a series of more or less directed interactions with people, things and experiences thereby becomes the collective experience that the text offers its reader.

The search for meaning in a specific, prototypically German location on the part of a widely delineated group of individuals caught up in the act of writing brings us back to Heinrich Böll's search for 'Bewohnbarkeit', or 'liveability', and 'Erkenntnis' for the author in the German cultural landscape. Latour's ANT theory too is concerned with tracing the actual lived experience and real-world associations that bring about a sense of the social in the first place, in order to make the whole visible to the actors themselves. This is another form of 'Erkenntnis', positioned, unlike Böll's, at the collective level, but whose starting point is still to respect the activities and connections undertaken by all mediators; accordingly, the individual is not lost in the collective, and the network is built from the bottom up and in real-world locations, rather than imposed from above and constructed in the abstract realm of theory. On a meta-level, the novel's collaborative exploration of position-taking within language and within different traditions of making meaning applies also to its real-world genesis. In this sense, *Das Gästehaus* can be read as Höllerer's attempt to act out in the collective Böll's melancholy hopes that some level of individual 'Erkenntnis' can be attained in writing and rendered socially relevant for both writer and reader, as Höllerer underscores in his interview at the end of the book:

> jeder hat, so scheint es mir, aus einem Winkel seines Bewußtseins das herausgeholt, womit er noch zu tun hat, womit er sich

vielleicht befreien will, sei es nun eine Eigenschaft oder ein Problem, oder was ihn in der kritischen Beschreibung seiner selbst oder der Anderen am meisten amüsierte. So kam eine Geschichte zustande, die nicht nur äußerlich von heute ist.[26]

[everybody, or so it seems to me, extracted from somewhere in his unconscious the thing that he is dealing with, what he perhaps needs to liberate himself, whether this is a characteristic or a problem, or the thing that when critically describing himself or others most amused him. And so a story came together that is not only superficially of the now.]

    A first answer to the question I posed earlier, then, is that the authors are quite deliberately both showcased as individual writers and subsumed within an expanded framework of network relations. This framework uses the tools of literature to emplot the social, which is always experienced on an individual level as an associative space, and to make the conscious realization of this experience available to the reader. Living is all about following assumptions, experiencing uncertainties, and navigating one's way more or less well through situations that place individual, definite 'Erkenntnis' of the bigger picture beyond reach, just as neither the individual characters nor the authors who created them can single-handedly explain their text. In its emphasis on a direct mediation of conscious experience and mental processes for both characters and authors, *Das Gästehaus* points forward to the wealth of writing from the 1970s that draws on the associative actions of the inner consciousness and is particularly found in the work of Rolf Dieter Brinkmann, Peter Handke, Nicolas Born and Gabriele Wohmann, although it is, perhaps counter-intuitively, rather less optimistic about how much the individual can ultimately determine the meaning of his or her immediate wider circumstances. Drawing on the practicalities around the actual experience of authorship, then, the text makes the relative blindness of individual authors operating within the normative literature network directly accessible to readers and equates it with a fundamental characteristic of living in the world, whatever one's occupation may be. No one person can know everything – or indeed anything – for sure. This becomes an existential statement about both authorship and life.

    Indeed, the parallels between the novel's plot and internal aesthetic qualities and its practical genesis and wider literary historical significance for the authors involved in the project themselves are

---

[26] Bichsel et al., *Das Gästehaus*, pp. 233–4.

striking. As indicated above, the very dustjacket demands that the text is always also read within its own wider literary and institutional context. The fourteen invited authors share writing scholarships at the Literary Colloquium as part of Höllerer's attempt to build a literary network that can provide logistical, financial and intellectual support to contemporary German writers – these are very practical steps towards making the German literary landscape inhabitable ('bewohnbar') for its authors. Berlin is the urban setting for both Höllerer's real-world activities and Elmshäuser's fictional invitations, both of which are directed at assembling a disparate group to reflect on how they might come together to share their lived experiences. In both instances, a Wilhelminian villa provides a physical base for the networks thus brought to life and therefore plays a significant role as mediator in the proceedings. The nightly intrigues and often eccentric exchanges between self-conscious individualists that unfold within the text mirror those described by Hans Werner Richter and others in their reminiscences of Gruppe 47 meetings, which were equally marked out by the faded interiors of provincial inns that often seemed to hark back to a different age. There is every reason to assume that such episodes were either directly experienced by the younger authors too at the Literary Colloquium or at meetings of the Gruppe 47, or that they were at least familiar with the narratives that were popularly told about such occasions.[27]

Yet on a more unconscious level, the collaboratively authored text also seems to mirror authorial experiences of real life. The blatant gender imbalance within the Gruppe 47 continues in Höllerer's fellowship holders: although the writers have travelled from across Germany, Austria, Switzerland and America, geographical inclusivity is undermined by gender exclusivity: just two of the authors are female. The content of the text reflects this: the fictional guests too are predominantly male, figures who have either travelled the world (in military positions or high-class hotel service), currently occupy positions of authority in the world (as a priest), or are hoping to make their own revolutionary contribution to the world (through technological innovation, philosophical writing, journalism). By contrast, the three women within the group occupy subordinate positions (notably here: the much-disliked housekeeper of the inn), largely defined by their

---

[27] For example, Hans Werner Richter, *Im Etablissement der Schmetterlinge: 21 Portraits aus der Gruppe 47* (Berlin: Wagenbach, 2004). Carmerstrasse 4 would not have accommodated the authors, but it seems likely that the camaraderie will nevertheless have been intense, and there will have been plenty of comings and goings in their respective Berlin lodgings.

sexual relationship to Elmshäuser and one or two of the other guests. Ludmilla is convinced she has been invited to marry Elmshäuser, while the priest's housekeeper, Beate von Muskat-Bethe, believes that rekindling her relationship to Elmshäuser of thirty years ago is the sole reason not only she, but the whole entourage, are gathered together. In an objectionable move, both women are given earlier careers as actresses, which, in the eyes of their fellow characters, makes them particularly willing consenters to the various sexual intrigues that unfold.

The young male psychologist's description of the group assembled in the house, himself tellingly the product of one of the text's two female authors, is thus accurate in more ways than one: 'die meisten zwar Männer (mit Glatzen, mit Bäuchen, mit Bärten, mit Handtüchern), Männer verschiedener Altersstufen und farblose Alibidamen'[28] (most of them men (bald, with paunches, beards and towels), men of various ages and insipid alibi ladies). The comparative exclusion of women from the collective meaning-making experience of the text turns the search for 'Bewohnbarkeit' and 'Erkenntnis' within literary forms into a markedly male affair, both within the framework of the narrative and outside it. One can easily point to further exclusions: there are no characters, or authors, of Jewish origins, and politically more conservative voices are equally absent.[29] In as much as these groups are repeatedly either entirely neglected by both the contemporary accounts of authorial groupings and the literary historiographies that succeeded them, or placed at best on the periphery, the visible network mapped by the text is entirely accurate. It is confirmed by the many (self-) presentations of the Gruppe 47, as well as Höllerer's other collective projects across the decade.[30] The publication that arose from his public poetry reading series 1966/67, for example, *Ein Gedicht und sein Autor* (1967, A Poem and its Author), profiles just one female poet – Friederike Mayröcker – and twenty male poets.[31] While the male poetic tradition made available is, by the Eurocentric standards of the

---

[28] Bichsel et al., *Das Gästehaus*, p. 83.
[29] It seems significant, in this context, that there was one Israeli in the original *Prosaschreiben* volume, Daniel Lustig, but that he left the project early.
[30] For critique of the ethnically-blind nature of these groupings (esp. Gruppe 47) see Briegleb, *Mißachtung und Tabu*.
[31] The gender balance of the translators – listed with a short biography at the back – is barely better: of 13, just two are women (Maria Bosse Sporleder, Arianna Giachi). The collection includes Peter Rühmkorf, Günter Grass, Günter Kunert, Hans Carl Artmann, Friederike Mayröcker, Ernst Jandl and Helmut Heißenbüttel alongside poets from Sweden, France, Yugoslavia, Poland, USA, Italy, Czechoslovakia, and the Soviet Union.

day, international in scope (Soviet, American, Italian, French, Polish, Swedish, Yugoslavian and Czech poets figure alongside their German and Austrian counterparts) and this international dimension is further expounded upon by Höllerer in his short scholarly introduction to each poet and the traditions in which they operate, the Austrian Mayröcker has to stand in for both the German-speaking and the 'international' dimension of any form of women's writing.

In fact, for all their technological innovation and commitment to mobilizing different institutions and sections of the population, the blinkered nature of all of Höllerer's networking activities throughout the 1960s undermines his attempts to insert German authorship into a wider, truly democratic semiology of existence. The literary and political mediation he carried out at the Literary Colloquium, the academic mediation that characterized his professorship at the Technical University, and his wider media appearances all trace the same narrow pathways between literature, institutions, and an almost exclusively male, Gentile, well-educated set of individuals.[32] His obvious blindness to these shortcomings is all the more surprising in the context of his own poetry and prose. His early and highly successful volume of poems, *Der andere Gast* (1952, The Other Guest), for example, focuses specifically on questions of poetic position and vision in relation to one's lived environment. The motif of the guest, who passes through a landscape, tries to interpret it and finds himself changed in the process, runs through the collection. This not only slots in with my observations in chapter two concerning the extent to which overriding concerns of authorial placelessness dominate the early West German cultural landscape. It also emphasizes how, from an early point in his career, Höllerer was particularly concerned with both capturing phenomenological interactions with one's physical and intellectual surroundings and finding a position from which to stand outside those interactions and see them as part of a bigger picture. 'Du warst nur selten Dir zu Gast' (You were only occasionally a guest in your own house), he chides both his own lyric persona and his readers. In the later volume of poems and accompanying instructive essay, *Gedichte: Wie entsteht ein Gedicht?* (1964, Poetry: How Do Poems Come About?), he very clearly attempts to take perspectives gleaned from traumatic historical moments or from other cultural traditions in order to shine a critical light back on the normative West German experience and

---

32   For a slightly different but largely complementary analysis of his failings in this respect but that emphasizes the changing political context more, see Michael Peter Hehl, 'Poetik der Institutionen: Walter Höllerers institutionelles Engagement und die Literatur der Moderne', *kultuRRevoltion*, 63 (2012), 45–53.

encourage a change in both intellectual patterns and everyday behaviour.

Yet even as, to borrow Rolf Parr's term, he 'rotates' between the different interest groups that gather around the poet, the academic, the literary mediator and the media personality, Höllerer repeatedly attracts the same basic kind of authorial grouping and, in spite of his poetic credo, comes to express a surprisingly limited, normative view in his own literary output.[33] In addition to my observations on his collaborative novel and public poetry initiatives, the novel on which he spent a good deal of his literary career working, *Die Elefantenuhr* (*The Elephant Clock*, begun in the mid-1950s, first published 1972; shortened paperback version 1974), enacts the author's own search for a broader semiotics of authorship, but it does so in such a way as to repeat many of the shortcomings evident in his other mediating activities. The inability of any one individual to get beyond his own actions within the literature network, even as he deliberately tries to facilitate and reflect on multiple interlocking relations with other people, things and concepts, is particularly exemplified here.

The protagonist, Gustaf Lorch, is an archivist attempting to mount an all-encompassing exhibition in the small-town of Murrbach – an obvious fictionalization of Marbach, where the new buildings for the Deutsches Literaturarchiv (German literature archive) were erected between 1970 and 1972. The fictional German name entails a play on 'murren', to grumble, yielding 'Grumble-ville', a place that invites an attitude of either dismissal or solipsism. Lorch's efforts to gather material that will open up the semantic richness of the whole world as a meaningful cultural object that far transcends the purview of literary documents stem from his deep dislike of what he describes as the monumentalizing, simplifying gestures inherent in the public veneration of dead authors and other intellectual figures – the celebratory mode of authorship. He is therefore an unhappy figure within the traditional German archive system, and he points in the opening pages to the state of hypnosis that has befallen the whole town, its human relations and even the material fabric of its buildings: Murrbach is caught in the overwhelming flood of literary records that force a never-ending, retrospective cataloguing of the past; nobody has much time to keep up with the present. However, his desire to show a radically different way of conceiving of literature's contribution to the

---

[33] Rolf Parr, 'Kein universeller, kein spezifischer Intellektueller: Walter Höllerer im Literaturbetrieb der 1950er und 1960er Jahre', *kultuRRevolution*, 61/62 (2011), 76–85; Hehl also works with this concept throughout his article, 'Poetik der Institutionen'.

current social order – a utopian vision that remains always just out of reach – is constantly interrupted by his paranoid construction of the alter-ego, 'G'. This figure, with his proper academic qualifications as a professional linguist and illustrious career through international institutions, is always literally and methodologically one step ahead of him. As Lorch becomes enmeshed in trying to beat his own self-projection by finding a meaningful sign-system all around him that can rival that of the professional academic, he grows ever more divorced from the practicalities of mounting his exhibition. The wild and fanciful notes he takes on what will be included show, in particular, a lack of sensitivity to gender, as he spies on his female travel companions to catalogue their sensual responses to the world, as well as a megalomaniac tendency to be the orchestrator of a form of total meaning and interconnectedness that can be immediately and directly experienced. When the news finally comes through that, after a week of fevered preparations in which he has hardly slept, the funding for his exhibition is to be cut, Lorch blows up the Schiller memorial outside the archive as well as the new archive building itself.

While Lorch is both a satirist of the traditional German literary scene and himself a satirized figure of fun in his counter-megalomaniac tendencies, the text remains curiously devoid of any external position from which to make sense of it. In fact, it is a perfect enactment of Latour's exhortation to 'follow the actors themselves', as the reader follows every associative twist and turn that Lorch's thoughts and experiences take over the course of the week leading up to his explosive act, including within the projected life of G. This allows a perfect map of provincial West German institutions and mentalities to be drawn up, the blinkered nature of which is total. Like Bernini's elephant-and-obelisk statue referenced in the poem 'Elephant von Bernini, Piazza Minerva' from Höllerer's 1952 collection and which also underpins this title, the whole network portrayed is an entirely self-sufficient, self-stabilizing sphere that carries its own markedly male monument on its back. The semiotic significance of both the Roman statue and the German literary archive is that they exist *in spite of* everything around them; composed of a wealth of different cultural traces, they are happily oblivious to any wider social function. This refusal to yield their literal and metaphorical place to the world around them wins out.

It is tempting to read *Die Elephantenuhr* as a wryly melancholic admission on Höllerer's part of his own failure to get beyond the normative literature network he spent his career up until that point actively developing. Although there is no position from which to get beyond Lorch's perspective in the text, the urge to tell his tale must come from somewhere beyond the fictional frame, and the author must mean something by the obvious parallel he draws. However, where

Lorch failed to mount his grand semiological exhibition and in so doing turned himself into a criminal, Höllerer was spectacularly successful with his in 1972 and continued to play an active role in West German cultural networks for the decades to come.[34] The notion that there is some form of authorial self-criticism thus seems unlikely. Rather, the diverging fates of author and protagonist encourage a reading of the text as a social satire on the naïve idealist who does not have the political contacts to secure the foundations of his project. Here again, however, we run into problems, for the very similarities in the blinkered networks traced by Lorch and the obvious limitations of the pathways traced by Höllerer bring the satire uncomfortably close to home for the literary mediator himself, in spite of the divergent outcomes. When read through the lens of Höllerer's gender-blind mediation of literature across the 1960s, Lorch's continued reduction of women to the status of sexual companions for the male actors in his network (or worse: sexual objects to be displayed in his exhibition) seems too close to the actual practices in the literature network that Höllerer was himself sustaining to count as irony or satire. Lorch consequently functions as a spoof on an unsuccessful Höllerer, but one who is more revealing of the author's weaknesses than the latter probably intended. Although the text was widely received as a satire on the German literary sector, it is testament to the self-regarding nature of that sector that Höllerer was unable to gain any sort of outside purchase on the satire that would have allowed him to do something other than produce hollow versions of himself and his colleagues that would make just an elite circle laugh. Although feted by a few, neither the original nor the shortened paperback version sold particularly well, and the novel has since been largely forgotten by both the commercial literary sector and academe.

---

[34] Höllerer curated the highly successful multi-sensory exhibition on language, 'Welt als Sprache' (World as language) for the Berlin Academy of Arts in 1972, with input from poets, novelists, linguists, film-makers and visual artists, philologists, architects and musicians. Basic details are provided in Walter Höllerer, ed., *Autoren im Haus: Zwanzig Jahre Literarisches Colloquium Berlin* (Berlin: Galerie Wannsee, 1982), p. 229. See also the exhibition catalogue: *Welt als Sprache: Auseinandersetzung mit Zeichen und Zeichensystemen der Gegenwart* (Akademie der Künste: Berlin, [1972]). Moving into the later decades, LSR archive material shows that, despite suffering a burn-out at the end of the 1960s, Höllerer remained highly active with a busy LCB programme until he stood down as Managing Director in 1983. After this, he continued to be a significant face for Berlin literature (and point of reference for other, younger actors) up to and including the 750th anniversary of Berlin, focusing particularly on film and photography ventures. He also continued to edit the literary journal *Akzente* and the academic journal *Sprache im Technischen Zeitalter*.

In its full-length, 535-page version, *Die Elephantenuhr* is thus a problematic apogee to Höllerer's authorial career. It both shows the author's intimate and accurate knowledge of the literature network that he was actively constructing, and it reveals him to be a fully complicit mediator within this monolithic, self-sustaining structure that is blind to its own failings. This seems to clash with his genuinely aspirational ideas for democratizing the base of literature. In a supposedly democratic, public-facing and internationally-orientated conception of how literature can be brought to bear on society, the question I have already outlined in previous chapters thus repeats itself ever more urgently: why are there so many obvious blind spots in the authorial groupings that are increasingly systematically generated by these innovative, democratically-minded literary mediators, and with ever more political and economic support from a broad base of institutions? In order to answer this, we need to open up our investigation of mediators within the literature network to non-human, material and conceptual actors.

Non-Human Actors in the Literature Network

I already indicated above that the networks traced both in real life and in Höllerer's fiction revolve as much around institutional structures (the Literary Colloquium and the Technical University in Berlin, for example) and individual objects (the Wilhelmenian villa, the stray hamster, or the obelisk) as they do around powerful people. These non-human actors also mediate, in Latour's sense of leaving a trace on the message / phenomenon being transmitted that alters it in some way. The 'literature network' is not therefore a case of a network of people simply conveying a discrete literary text to market in line with a set of economic, cultural and political interests; rather, literature is shaped within and by the network and the network is shaped within and by the literature, and all of the interests that we might routinely consider around our study of the text itself only gain expression and wider meaning within this dynamic process. To add in my own terminology at this juncture, the modes of authorship condition this multi-directional shaping, as gestures and attitudes on the part of all actors are the dynamic element that drives the linkage between nodes and ultimately makes some nodes more significant than others.

Importantly, however, these attitudes can also be discerned in non-human actors. This is perhaps one of the most counter-intuitive, but also most significant, aspects of Latour's development of ANT. For Latour, acknowledging the agency of – say – a proton to disempower a scientist by disobeying the laws they are developing – is important as a means of breaking down the nature / culture divide which has conditioned much of modern Western thought. For my examination of authorship, it matters because it helps understand how patterns of exclusion can prevail even when human actors believe themselves to be acting in an open, democratic manner. This is not to excuse individuals and shift the blame for their failings onto objects. Rather, it is to allow for the power that is equally invested in the material circumstances and intangible 'laws of nature' and 'natural laws' that make the question of agency inherently dispersed. If individuals want to make substantive changes to the way links play out within a network, they need to reckon with the agency that also resides in the non-human aspects of it.

Sigrid Weigel's work on the notion of 'generation' can serve as a useful illustration of what is at stake here as we try to account for material structures and their relationship to the less tangible practices that unfold within institutions. Unpicking the genealogy of the concept itself, Weigel is critical of the dominant understanding of generation popularized by Karl Mannheim in the early twentieth century and still highly influential today. Mannheim's notion of 'Prägung' (literally: minting, or shaping) emphasizes the role of external coordinates in determining how individuals relate to or are otherwise assigned to collective experiences: the specific historical time and political circumstances into which one is born form entire cohorts; such collective experiences are expressed in art; this art in turn becomes normative as a level of aesthetic consensus coheres around it and, in a circular move, makes the art representative of the epoch. Against this, Weigel unfolds an alternative understanding of generation by drawing on older cognate terms, such as 'Geschlecht' (genus and gender are both inherent in this term), family, inheritance, lineage. This genealogical model of generation emphasizes the continuity of wider social structures as they are carried through individuals and their material circumstances over time, rather than the form of cyclical epochal singularity proposed by Dilthey and Mannheim and which still drives the majority of German twentieth-century literary and social historiography.[35]

The advantage of Weigel's shift (back) to a genealogical understanding of generation lies not just in the associative links it opens up across a longer-term historical continuum, but also in the ethical purchase it affords on the narratives that are popularly told about generational groupings, often by individuals with a more or less vested interest in those groupings, as we have already indicated is the case for both Hans Werner Richter and Walter Höllerer. Once these groupings are seen as part

---

[35] See Susanne Vees-Gulani & Laurel Cohen-Pfister, 'Introduction: A Generational Approach to German Culture', in *Generational Shifts in Contemporary German Culture*, ed. by Laurel Cohen-Pfister & Susanne Vees-Gulani (Rochester, NY: Camden House, 2010), pp. 1–23.

of a deliberately constructed genealogy underpinned by a traceable network of conventions and assumptions in material form – rather than the hapless result of epoch-defining history and politics – the nature of the association in the first place becomes open to challenge and debate. This can be tied into our ongoing adaptation of Assmann's 'memory of places' and used to question exactly how notions of place and agency combine to produce tangible cultural effects in respect of German experiences of authorship that inhere as much in objects and material circumstances as in people themselves. When Assmann elaborates on 'places of generational memory', she places her emphasis on understanding how certain associations become dominant, and therefore accessible to posterity, in a particular place over a given period of time. However, her discussion of agency – those traceable actors or mediators that drive all this – remains underdeveloped. Weigel's work, by contrast, specifically traces pre-twentieth-century norms concerning successive iterations of groupings, and, in so doing, indicates the extent to which markedly patriarchal legal and economic structures underpin these iterations. Latour would immediately point to the fact that these structures do not exist independently of the phenomena they transport: rather, they emerge from the relationships traced, and these relationships are traced in multiple material and conceptual ways which can be studied.

Indeed, Weigel is particularly critical of the use key players within the Gruppe 47 made of the notion of generation, understood in Mannheim's immaterial, circumstantial sense. She argues that, in focusing on the specific historical circumstances that putatively bound them together, they underplayed links to both past and present problematic longer-term forms of behaviour that inhere in material structures and thereby practiced a form of exclusion and self-exculpation. Hans Werner Richter and Alfred Andersch's programmatic self-presentation as 'young Europe', for example, determined both contemporary reactions to the founding cohort of Gruppe 47 writers in the immediate post-war period, and, on account of their influence within the subsequent academy, much of what has been written since: the authors' German nationalist roots, themselves part of a much longer tradition, were downplayed and dissolved in a vague project of European-wide renewal in the wake of the shared trauma of war.

When Weigel's critique of the way founder members of the Gruppe 47 manipulated concepts of generation is applied to our broader consideration of the post-war evolution of German authorship, similar trends that underplay the persistence over time of non-human agency can also be observed. As far as the kind of group identity forged by active involvement in everyday politics goes, German authors of the 1960s consciously came together to an unprecedented extent in response to the specific social challenges of the period. The enhanced material infrastructure around authorship that was in place by then, as elaborated above in respect of Höllerer's development of representative physical spaces for literature in Berlin, meant that their actions were quickly disseminated as those of an important socio-historical grouping. For many, this shared sense of purpose was certainly linked to a shared sense of their own historical positioning and it continued to define the core motivation underpinning the subsequent various interest groups that formed throughout the 1970s. At the same time, however, many of the more successful writers and public intellectual figureheads were equally aware of the much further reaching debates about the lasting value of literary and intellectual endeavour that they were also carrying. Thus, Grass would repeatedly emphasize both his specific historical circumstances and at the same time stress how he conceived himself to be positioned within the chronologically much larger 'Kulturnation' which gestures to a whole set of historical physical and conceptual structures that necessarily must emerge with this concept. Genealogical narratives of German-language authorship framed both their public appearances in the media and their literary self-conceptions as much as the simplistic division into historically determined age cohorts. The dual sense of operating within both a contemporary, progressive, politically-defined generation and a broader genealogy of authorship that relied on the continuity of basic structures and values (including significant blind spots) placed a paradox right at the heart of the democratic impetus that was sweeping through German intellectual life of the late 1960s and early 1970s. Discussion of the two TV documentaries, *Das literarische Profil von Berlin* (The literary profile of Berlin, directed by Wolfgang Ramsbott and scripted by Walter Höllerer in 1970/71), and *Der Verleger oder Die Lust am Buch* (The Publisher, or The Joy of Books, produced by Hilde Bechert and Klaus Dexel in 1987), will exemplify the ongoing significance of this point.

'Memory of Place' Reconsidered: TV Portrayals of Literature Networks in the 1970s and 1980s

Höllerer and Ramsbott's programme was the final instalment of the 1969–71 series *Das literarische Profil europäischer Großstädte* (The literary profile of European Cities), produced in the Berlin Literary Colloquium and encompassing Prague, Stockholm, Rome, London and Berlin in that order. Höllerer was heavily involved in overseeing the series as a whole, often travelling to the cities and always drafting the individual scripts and production instructions for each of the five films.[36] The

---

[36] See archive material on *Literarische Profile europäischer Großstädte* in LSR Nachlass Walter Höllerer, Materialien zum Literarischen Colloquium Berlin, un-catalogued.

whole project was a direct expression of his ongoing concern to encourage active public reflection on how literature, through its authors, related to the wider world, and the different cities were chosen not least because they allowed entry points into different traditions of valuing literature and its human face. In line with my argument above, they are themselves instances of non-human actors in the literature network and include multiple instances of physical infrastructures and material objects that equally carry attitudes in respect of authorship.

Indeed, the very idea of shooting a documentary of one hour and twenty-two minutes' duration in order to convey a city's 'literary profile' is in itself worthy of comment. The very term 'profile' evokes portraiture and an implicit sense of attitudinal positioning. Accordingly, we see a mixture of modes of authorship converging in an author-led mediation of a cultural Heimat for a mass audience. The auratic 'memory of places', filtered through the corresponding celebratory and commemorative modes of authorship discussed in chapter one, is thus again made tangible here. Indeed, the film opens with almost two minutes of gravestones, explicitly and rather solemnly setting out the long line of past great (male) German authors who are prominently associated with Berlin: Gottfried Benn, Bertolt Brecht, Hans Fallada, Johann Gottlieb Fichte, Theodor Fontane, Jakob Grimm, Georg Wilhelm Friedrich Hegel, Ludwig Tieck, Heinrich von Kleist, Heinrich Mann, to name just some of the better known ones. Such an opening clearly sets up a genealogy of authorship that is understood to persist in the specific 'memory of place' that Berlin facilitates into the present of the early 1970s.

The documentary continues the emphasis on place as a facilitator of ongoing cultural activity. It begins amidst a backdrop of extensive building sites in West Berlin. The ageing Berlin author Friedrich Luft (at the time also President of the LCB's Board of Trustees) bemoans the lack of a 'Romanisches Café', a famous literary meeting point in Weimar Berlin, and suggests that contemporary authors no longer feel the need for contact with one another. The rest of the documentary, however, is designed to disprove this notion. The television crew seek out popular meeting places – first the Warnecke hostelry in Zehlendorf, where Berlin-born authors discuss their plans and hopes for German literature over beer and cigarettes (figure 4.2), then Café Matala, run by the Austrian writer Oswald Wiener and a popular place for émigré Austrian and Romanian-German writers, and, later on, Günter Grass's favourite haunt in Friedenau, the Bundeseck. The physical fabric of publishing houses is also on display, as gatherings at the Wagenbach Verlagskollektiv (Wagenbach publishing collective), the Berliner Handpresse (Berlin hand-press) and an editorial meeting for Wagenbach's literary journal, *Kursbuch*, are all brought before the viewer's eyes.

Figure 4.2 Still taken from *Das literarische Profil von Berlin*. Reproduced courtesy of the Literarisches Colloquium Berlin.

The extensive smoke-filled footage testifies to Berlin's ongoing vibrancy for literary endeavours, ranging from the 'Klanggedicht' (sound poem) of Ernst Jandl, through the radical collective endeavours of the political Kreuzberger Straßentheater (street theatre) and the pirate publishing practices of the Berliner Handpresse, to the more mainstream prose writing of a wide range of Berlin-born, FRG, GDR, Austrian and Romanian-German authors. Key players and the groupings they initiated are introduced: Günter Bruno Fuchs and the Ricksdorfer Werkstatt (Ricksdorf workshop); Kurt Neuburger and the literarische Werkstatt Kreuzberg (Kreuzberg literary workshop); Klaus Wagenbach and his publishing house. In terms of basic content, then, the mode of the film is one of celebration: literature appears to have taken root in Berlin, authors from across German-speaking Europe find themselves attracted to its mixture of a certain genealogical literary aura and actual physical spaces in which their authorship can unfold. All of the groupings presented are hopeful, seeing themselves initiating real and significant changes in the future, whether this is to counter capitalist publishing practices, provide a lasting political education to the wider public, or champion the ability of fiction to provide a different perspective on reality. Collectively, these authors are surely looking to

Brecht, Kleist and Grimm's gravestones as they work towards the realization of a cultural Heimat in the manner of Ernst Bloch.

Alongside this celebratory sense of the possibilities available to authors in Berlin, however, are visuals and asides that point to a loss of place and the recent traumatic ruptures of the past. The cafés are all presented as temporary homes, with the first scene at the Warnecke Inn prefaced by a dilapidated image of the building approached through an abandoned garden, and a voice-over explicitly listing the many meeting points that have come and gone over the past twenty years. In the interviews held in Wiener's Café Matala it is evident that what binds the émigré authors together is their lack of a home in the vanished Austro-Hungarian context, and the young publishing collectives too are presented as the coming-together of wandering souls who could not find a niche for their work elsewhere in the Federal Republic. The peculiarity of Berlin as an insecure, temporary home that bares its scars for all to see is visually underlined by the closing image of the ex-GDR author Uwe Johnson, who sits in his home in front of a wallchart of the city and its environs at the end of the documentary (figure 4.3).

The chart is stitched together from a mixture of wartime and post-war maps: Berlin is a place that cannot even officially be recorded without the rifts that tore it apart in the Second World War visibly

Figure 4.3 Still taken from *Das literarische Profil von Berlin*. Reproduced courtesy of the Literarisches Colloquium Berlin.

overlaying parts of the map. With a very explicit nod to his own biography (he left East Germany in 1959), Johnson positions himself in front of this contemporary visualization of the ongoing blank spaces and historical throwbacks that define Berlin in the early 1970s. Furthermore, as he speaks, the sound of planes flying in and out of Tempelhof airport distorts the sound-recording, causing him to reflect directly on Berlin's fragile links with the outside world and the impending sense that at any point they might be cut off. Thus, even as the film's content exudes a positive sense of flux and literary creativity in the many projects and individuals it highlights, this is tempered by an implicit sense of loss, both past and impending, that brings the groupings together in the first place and is articulated in the material objects and temporary meeting places they inhabit. The obvious attempt to celebrate Berlin as a place of generational memory for German-language literary traditions is continuously undercut by a more troubled commemorative mode that underlies many of the subjects' authorial self-conception, as well as the physical fabric of their surroundings.

The documentary's insistence on tracing the various literary projects of renewal that characterize contemporary Berlin can also be read as an excessive referencing of the absence that underpins them all: the absence of any unified sense of the German-language cultural Heimat, and the corresponding placelessness of the writer, lie at the heart of all of these narratives of re-generation across the various divides. However, the gravestones at the beginning of the documentary that took the viewer back to Fichte, Hegel and Grimm, also indicate that this absence may be a far older one than merely that caused by the cataclysmic events of the mid-twentieth century. Indeed, the self-help element to the many individual, transient groupings shown ultimately reinforces the sense that, although modern German-language authors live and die within an important cultural tradition that goes back at least as far as the mid-eighteenth century, the most enduring element of that tradition is the collective struggle to belong. A secure position within that tradition was only really granted those earlier authors through their retrospective assimilation into a physical place and a literary canon upon their death. The authors alive at any one point in time are consequently continually exercised by the challenges of practically and metaphorically placing themselves within a tradition that, thanks to the placelessness that underpins it, is unlikely to provide any definitive sense of immediate wider belonging in their lifetime.

Such an insecure positioning in respect of the canonical past and the difficult present is bound to yield both critical perspectives and myopia. In the documentary, the determination to capture contemporary German-speaking Europe as it is and to reflect this back to a broad audience in challenging ways clearly drives the work of emerging and established writers such as Günther Schulz, Ernst Jandl and Ingeborg Drewitz, as well as that of the emergent publishing collectives and editorial boards who are trying to provide innovative infrastructures for such dissemination. The insularity of the groupings thus constituted, however, cannot be left uncommented. The emphasis on personal networks takes the viewer inside Latour's bureaus and buildings to reveal a world of almost exclusively male actors, united by a normative Western, Gentile experience. In the first part of the documentary, we see elderly Berlin authors gathering younger acolytes around them: the passage of local 'Berlin' literature from one generation to the next is exclusively through the male line, helped along with Schultheiss and Schwarzbrot (Berlin beer and bread) (figure 4.2). With the exception of a brief interview with Ingeborg Drewitz, the artist Natascha Ungeheuer's impassioned description of the Kreuzberg Street Theatre (which is immediately belittled by her male peers), and a reading from Friederike Mayröcker, such women as there are in the film's broader engagement with writers are silent. Marina Schnurre sits demurely next to her husband Wolfdietrich Schnurre. While he speaks at length about why he has come to Berlin and what he believes literature can achieve, she is merely glossed as the illustrator on their collaborative children's books and visually presented as his muse. We see some women in the publishing collectives, but they too remain silent, just as the woman who sits in on the editorial *Kursbuch* meeting between Wagenbach and Hans Magnus Enzensberger. She has little tangible impact on the discussion, is side-lined by the camera shots, and primarily seems to be there in a supportive, secretarial role. One cannot help thinking of the frustrations of Karoline von Günderrode and Bettina von Arnim, who found themselves assigned similar positions in the circle of the Berlin Romantics, and whose plight is in fact directly referenced in the film by Drewitz. There is also no tangible ethnic diversity, nor indeed much diversity of experience across the groups shown, as becomes all too evident in the collective incomprehension with which Günther Schulz is met when he tries to present his recent experience of the Romanian dictatorship. In a repeat of the 1961 open letter discussed at the beginning of chapter three, the assembled authors in the Friedenau bookshop chastise him for not speaking out openly and clearly enough about repressive structures, showing gross insensitivity to the different literary context in which he was working and the aesthetic opportunities and challenges it might provide.

Viewed as part of the series on European literary cities, *Das literarische Profil von Berlin* both foregrounds the particular wealth of literary activity that characterizes Berlin of the early 1970s and points to deep-rooted insecurities and blind spots within the wider physical and conceptual fabric of the German literature network. These insecurities do not militate in favour of genuinely progressive structures and politics. A preponderance of male, Gentile authors look to past models of achievement and literary genealogies as they meet in public houses and printing presses that are historically marked out as male public spaces. While women and those with different ethnic backgrounds are by no means deliberately excluded, they are so few in number in the documentary material that they are bound to appear exotic and/or on the periphery of the ongoing collective attempt to find spaces and places for literature in German-speaking Europe. The result of this is an undeniable provincialization of the literary greatness that the documentary sets out referencing. However many distinctive individuals and unusual creative initiatives Ramsbott and Höllerer's project presents, all of these efforts to create work of lasting literary value are underpinned by an astonishingly uniform, patriarchal politics of genealogical and physical place. Only a certain kind of author has the privilege of belonging to a discourse of not-belonging. The legitimate positioning from which to group together as a self-defined cohort and try to do something about this writerly inheritance is correspondingly reserved for the few.

Ramsbott and Höllerer's documentary hardly sets out to critique these problematic literary genealogies. Unlike Ammer's much later documentary on the Gruppe 47 discussed in chapter one, there is nothing in the way it is filmed that indicates distance or dissent from either the historical literary traditions and their positioning within patriarchal lines of inheritance or the contemporary literary groupings it presents. Its own assumed mode of authorship is celebratory. Nevertheless, seen from a twenty-first-century perspective it provides first-hand insight into how the underlying structures supporting the pursuit of literary authorship – both human and non-human – that it references directly affect the composition of those 'generations' that rise to the fore within a certain place and time.

If the Berlin groupings discussed above convey the superficially diverse formation of literary groupings that found willing participants in the many different spaces of Berlin, my discussion would not be complete without consideration of the inverse phenomenon that emerged several hundred kilometres further west over a similar period of time. Writing in 2000, the German journalist Bärbel Sonntag reminisces on the spectacular rise of the Suhrkamp publishing house that was to become Frankfurt's elite literary address and functioned as a tightly run ship throughout the last four decades of the twentieth century with Siegfried Unseld at its helm:

> Welcher Verlag hat sonst schon die literarische Szene so geprägt, dass er für eine spezifische Kultur steht? „Rowohlt-Kultur"? – Die

gab es vielleicht mal in den Fünfzigern nach dem Siegeszug des rororo-Taschenbuchs. „Fischer-Kultur"? – Das waren wohl eher die Goldenen Zwanziger. „Suhrkamp-Kultur" hingegen steht für die ambitionierte deutschsprachige Nachkriegsliteratur und die theoretischen und politischen Debatten der 68er.[37]

[Which publishing house has had so great an influence on the literary scene that it stands for a particular kind of culture? 'Rowohlt culture'? – that might have existed in the fifties, after the triumph of the rororo paperback. 'Fischer culture'? – that would have been more the golden twenties. 'Suhrkamp culture', by contrast, represents the ambitious German-language literature of the postwar period and the theoretical and political debates of the 1968 generation.]

Unlike the multiple actors that can be traced across the Berlin literary scene of the 1960s and 1970s, in Frankfurt all paths lead to one address, and one particularly powerful individual: Siegfried Unseld in the Klettenbergstraße (Klettenberg Street). If 1959 is widely held to have been a turning point in German literary history with the emergence of accomplished major works by Günter Grass, Heinrich Böll, Uwe Johnson, Martin Walser and Hans Magnus Enzensberger, it also marks the accession of Siegfried Unseld to the helm of the Suhrkamp publishing house. Born in 1924, the dynamic and ambitious Unseld, like Grass, Walser and Enzensberger, represented the potential of the next generation to effect sweeping changes within the culture industry. Having worked alongside Peter Suhrkamp since 1952, he witnessed first-hand the fallout from Suhrkamp's split with the S. Fischer Verlag and the resulting re-grouping of authors between the two companies. Consequently, he was well acquainted with the importance of cultivating effective group dynamics if a publishing house is to function as a good address that can command both the 'best' literary authors and the biggest possible market share. By 1973, Unseld's 'political vision and technical acumen' had been expressly singled out for praise in the *Times Literary Supplement*. Admiring Unseld's long-standing promotion of influential philosophical and aesthetic writings, George Steiner coined the phrase 'Suhrkamp culture'. While the phrase was eagerly seized upon by the publisher's marketing department and has been in use in their publicity material ever since, Steiner's admiration was not entirely unqualified. In considering the massive twenty-volume collected works of Adorno as the

---

[37] Bärbel Sonntag, 'Unser aller Unseld', *die tageszeitung*, 23.06.2000

immediate product of this culture, he was also sensitive to the dangers of the canonizing gesture that had facilitated them. He raised gentle questions about the suitability of monumentalizing a body of work whose lifeblood were dialectical notions of self-correction and progress.[38]

These mild misgivings are worth investigating further in the context of my consideration of authorship as an extended, network phenomenon. Under Unseld's leadership, the Suhrkamp publishing house undoubtedly achieved a canonical status of its own, occupying a leading position within the German literature network throughout the last four decades of the twentieth century and bringing a large and diverse group of authors to prominence on the back of his financial support. Just as we have seen in the much more fragmented example of Berlin, however, the framework he provided was not without its blind spots when it came to the composition of the elite collective it was by default creating. Given the importance that the Suhrkamp headquarters in Frankfurt's Klettenbergstraße took on for the West German literary industry, these failings and oversights have had a significant normative influence on the kind of group dynamics that have surrounded authorship in the Federal Republic ever since. Furthermore, they offer us new ways of understanding the increasing paradoxes and hypocrisies that came to characterize the careers of Unseld's first generation of contemporary authors, such as Enzensberger and Walser. Many of these first fully post-war writers spearheaded individual groupings in the Berlin context, or otherwise communicated a certain genealogy of literature to their younger colleagues. While they may have started out as distinctive lone voices that challenged society in their own highly individualized way, by the end of the twentieth century they had come under repeated attack for being particularly problematic parts of the cultural establishment.[39] The 1987 TV biopic, *Der Verleger oder Die Lust am Buch*, provides considerable insight into the dynamics that underpinned these developments in both Frankfurt and Berlin. The interest of this case study lies in the light it throws on the way in which

---

[38] George Steiner, 'Adorno: Love and Cognition', *The Times Literary Supplement*, 09 March 1973.

[39] Notably Martin Walser, first in the Walser-Bubis Debatte (see Frank Schirrmacher, ed., *Die Walser-Bubis-Debatte* [Frankfurt a.M.: Suhrkamp, 1999]), and then with the publication of *Tod eines Kritikers* (2002). Stuart Parkes shows how a number of other significant writers (Handke, Grass) got drawn in to media-led charges of anti-Semitism at the turn of the millennium: 'Martin Walser's *Tod eines Kritikers*: 'A "Crime" of Anti-Semitism?', in *German Text Crimes: Writers Accused from the 1950s to the 2000s*, ed. Tom Cheesman (Amsterdam & New York: Rodopi, 2013), pp. 153–74.

a powerful literary mediator is himself constructed within the network he seeks to convey, and this as much by the non-human actors and intangible concepts they sustain as by the human actors all around him that he believes himself to be mediating.

Shot in late 1986 and aired on the main public channel ARD in 1987, the biopic is just one of many forms in which Unseld sought to present a certain image of himself and his publishing activities to the media and wider public in Germany. Throughout his career he gave countless interviews to the media, lectured on the relationship between various authors and their publishers, published much of his own correspondence with his authors, and wrote essays on the craft of publishing, to name but a few of his interventions in the general public construction of his professional person.[40] The nature of the medium of television, however, is such that the biopic will have reached the widest and most diverse audience of all his public interventions. Viewed in its sixty-minute totality, the programme is undoubtedly Unseld's own carefully crafted expression of how he, as one of the major players within the literary industry, set about facilitating a certain place for authors within West German society. The biopic pieces together multiple scenes that show the publisher surrounded by his 'family' of Suhrkamp authors in social settings, including looking through his collection of authors photographed with him, while footage from internal board meetings further marks out his extended patriarchal role. The way in which both Unseld and the Suhrkamp authors interviewed in the feature express this authority, however, merits closer scrutiny, because the language they use tells us much about the wider relations within the by now well-established German literature network in which Steiner's 'Suhrkamp culture' was widely acknowledged to be a dominant force.

The early scenes in the biopic focus on Unseld's relationship with Martin Walser. This relationship is played out through a game of chess at a party at the Suhrkamp villa, which Unseld characteristically (so we are told) wins. Claiming victory, the arch strategist revels in the moment and loosely quotes the Bible to Walser, 'Opfer sind dem Herren wohlgefällig; Opfer sind dem Herren wohlgefällig' (sacrificial offerings please the Lord, sacrificial offerings please the Lord). Walser, reflecting on his relationship to Unseld a little later on, uses an alternative, planetary metaphor to describe his subservient relationship to the man who is bold enough publicly to describe himself as a 'glücklicher Mensch' (happy person): 'Dass jemand so zu seiner Helle sich bekennen

---

[40] Siegfried Unseld, *Der Autor und sein Verlger* (Frankfurt a.M.: Suhrkamp, 1985) and Siegfried Unseld, *Briefe an die Autoren* (Frankfurt a.M.: Suhrkamp, 2004) are two examples.

kann, das sehe ich aus meinem tiefen Schatten sehr gerne, diese Art von Sonnenexistenz' (that someone can embrace his own radiance like that, that's something I love to see from my position deep in the shadows, that kind of life in the sun).

In these metaphors alone we see the publisher filling the role of Christian God, centre of the solar system, and, with possible reference to the 'Sonnenkönig' (sun-king) Louis XIV of France, a powerful enlightened monarch.[41] Other voices lend their weight to these descriptions during the course of the biopic. Thomas Bernhard reflects at some length on the publisher's power as a god-like figure. Authors, he claims, like farmers, do their best to plough the field of literature and cultivate successful works. At the end of the growing season, the publisher delivers his potentially fatal judgement, just as the Lord may work against the farmers' efforts and send a drought or devastating storm. The literary critic Marcel Reich-Ranicki takes a more benevolent, but no less dramatic, view of the publisher's power when he pontificates: 'Wenn ein Verleger oder ein Kritiker Macht hat, muß immer die Frage gestellt werden, zu wessen Gunsten oder Ungunsten wendet er diese Macht an? Und ich glaube, dass Unseld, *summa summarum*, seine enorme Macht auf sehr gute und richtige Weise angewandt hat, nämlich zugunsten der Literatur' (If a publisher or a critic has power, then the question always has to be asked: whom is he helping or harming by using this power? And I think that, all in all, Unseld has used his tremendous power in a very good and right way, namely to serve literature).

Reich-Ranicki's description of literature as an inherently 'good' and 'right' thing into which to channel one's energies paves the way for a particularly circular display of logic when Unseld assesses the social and moral value of his activities just over halfway through the biopic. Explaining his own playful inversion of Adorno's dictum 'Es gibt kein richtiges Leben im falschen' (there is no right way to live a life that is wrong) to read 'Es gibt kein falsches Leben im richtigen' (there is no wrong way to live a life that is right), he argues with considerable conviction: 'Wenn man fühlt, denkt und handelt in Übereinstimmung mit sich selber, dann ist das Leben richtig' (If you feel, think and act according to your own principles, then your life is right). The exemplary individual, according to Unseld, is his own moral yardstick – just as 'good' literature is an inherently good cause, according to Reich-Ranicki. Throughout the biopic more generally, whether invoking a

---

[41] Lechner documents how, in the extended media coverage of the 'Suhrkamp crisis' in the 1990s, Unseld eventually accedes to the title of 'king': Lechner, 'The Making of the "Suhrkampkrise"'.

pernicious, vengeful God or an enlightened monarch, the metaphors employed by publisher, critic and authors in their attempts to characterize the nature of the publisher's role share one defining characteristic. The inherent wider social value they imply is entirely self-defined. God is great because this is how He, in the beginning, defined Himself. The king is ruler of his subjects because this is the power that the very notion of kingship has invested him with. And authorship has as much value and meaning as its key proponents within the literary sector at any one time choose to accord it and the wider material infrastructures allow. On this last point, we can think again of the show of power in terms of both infrastructural support and masculine posturing in Fritz J. Raddatz' documentation of everyday life at the rival publisher, Rowohlt-Verlag, discussed in chapter two.

The fact that Unseld, in a biopic of his influential career at the heart of the German literary scene, emerges as a successful patriarchal figure in an industry that is built on patriarchal understandings of power and value is, given my argument thus far, hardly surprising. Yet when Unseld took over from Peter Suhrkamp in 1959, he was widely perceived as a modernizing force in German letters, just as the Gruppe 47, by then reaching the height of their influence on literary trends and many of whom would become key Suhrkamp authors, had also styled themselves as breaking with past canonical traditions. From a twenty-first-century perspective, Unseld's complete blindness to the absence of both women and democracy in 'Suhrkamp culture' is at odds with this modernizing mission, and it must certainly call into question the canon of both German and European literature that his networking activities produced.[42] The circular nature of the logic underpinning his grasp of the literature network and his role within it, however, does go some way towards explaining why both he and his authors, despite a common belief in creating a new, outward-looking kind of mid-twentieth-century literature, are unable to view their industry from anything other than the hegemonic perspective of a white man. The wealth of material culture playing into this, from grand publishing houses through to carefully curated archives of photographs, completes the explanation, underscoring as it does the extent to which the celebratory mode of authorship conditions the whole literature network.

---

[42] For a straightforward celebration of the progressive nature of 'Suhrkamp culture' both in the company's heyday when Steiner coined the phrase and today, see Lutz Hagestedt, 'Das Glück ist eine Pflicht: Der Suhrkamp Verlag wurde fünfzig Jahre alt', 01.07.2000, published in *literaturkritik.de*, 7/8, July 2000 and available online at: http://www.literaturkritik.de/public/rezension.php?rez_id=1261&ausgabe=200007 (last accessed 19 July 2019).

Visually in the film the lack of women in Unseld's professional surroundings is immediately obvious, from the photographs that are almost exclusively of great male authors through to the all-male gatherings around the chess board and in the management meetings. With the exception of a balanced editorial board that has gathered to discuss the publication of an all-female anthology – three men and three women, including the long-serving Elisabeth Borchers –, the only women who visually figure as actively contributing to 'Suhrkamp culture' are Unseld's secretary, Barbel Zeeh, who dutifully types up his dictated daily 'Chronik' (chronicles), and, fleetingly, Karin Struck, whose striking white dress makes her appear almost otherworldly in the black and white photos of Suhrkamp authors perused at the beginning.[43]

This lack of influential women in 'Suhrkamp culture' does not, however, mean that the notion of femininity itself was absent. As part of the patriarchal narrative consciously spun at the villa in the Klettenbergstraße, male authors were quite prepared to cast themselves as Unseld's subservient women. Reflecting in the biopic on the unequal distribution of power between publisher and author, Walser compares the relationship to a marriage, and then goes on to qualify his comparison: 'natürlich ist sie eine Spezial-Ehe, das macht sie schwierig, weil der andere, der Verleger, *per definition* hat ja eben 100 Autoren, und der Autor hat nur einen Verleger' (of course this is a special kind of marriage, that's what makes it difficult, because the other person, the publisher, by definition has of course 100 authors, and the author only has one publisher). He describes this as 'ein bißchen morgenländisch, ein bißchen muselmanisch' (a little oriental, a little Muslim), before comparing the publishing house directly to a Harem and concluding, 'und so kriegt man eine Vorstellung, wie es den Frauen dort so zumute sein wird' (and so you get a sense of what it must be like for the women there). Such a comparison is naïve to say the least, but it is fully accepted within the circular, self-sufficient logic of the authorship related in this biopic. Indeed, not only do the successful white, male authors occupy both gender categories, they also claim wider experiences of physical and economic disadvantage for themselves. Thomas Bernhard for his part casts the publisher as a doctor and the author as his patient: 'Der Verleger ist wie ein Arzt, ein Mediziner; die Autoren sind eher Patienten. Da muß er halt rauskriegen, was er mit den Einzelnen spricht, was er

---

[43] Two volumes of Unseld's *Chronik* have been published, *Chronik 1970*, and *Chronik 1971*. Unseld officially began recording daily life at Suhrkamp in 1970, but the publication includes also documentation from 1967 onwards: Siegfried Unseld, *Chronik*, 2 vols, ed. Raimund Fellinger (Berlin: Suhrkamp, 2014).

sagen kann und was nicht' (the publisher is like a doctor, a medic; the authors are more like patients. And he has to figure out what he can discuss with each one, what he can say and what not).

Both authors have developed these metaphors at length elsewhere, to the extent that notions of gender transgression and illness underpin their respective oeuvres. The inclusion of these metaphors in the context of this biopic, however, is significant beyond Walser and Bernhard's own experiences of authorship. Unseld himself clearly embraces their all-encompassing gesture. Expounding on the publisher's craft, he is keen to show himself as a positive, life-affirming force, and he expresses this sense of motivation in a mixture of Blochean and Goethean terminology: 'Ins Gelingen verliebt sein, daran zu glauben, dass mal das, was man macht, richtig ist; *erotisch* gewissermaßen' (to be in love with succeeding, to believe that what you are doing is right, *erotic*, even). The phrase 'ins Gelingen verliebt' comes from the foreword to Bloch's *Das Prinzip Hoffnung*, where it describes a positive attitude to seeking self-knowledge, and it has been widely quoted as an aphorism since. Meanwhile, the idea of the individual's creative actions being inherently erotic is something that Goethe famously formulated in his *Römische Elegien*, to the point where both acts (of writing and sex) happen simultaneously. If Bloch is referenced at the beginning of this comparison and the virile Goethe implicit by the end, James Joyce is doubly flagged as a point of reference in Unseld's subsequent comments. He is quoted first for the comment he made, in German, on his self-conception as a male author, 'Ich bin der [sic] Fleisch, der [sic] stets bejaht' (I am the flesh that always affirms), which is itself a play on Mephistopheles' 'Ich bin der Geist, der stets verneint' from Goethe's *Faust* (I am the spirit that always denies). Unseld then immediately adds in the famous female voice of Molly Bloom that brings *Ulysses* to a close and, in Joyce's eyes, endows the whole text with meaning: 'Yes, I said, yes, I will, yes'.[44] As Unseld explains how the ability to say 'yes' is an important part of his professional identity, the film repeatedly cuts to images of pulsating machinery and books being produced and lifted out of machines in a manner that is reminiscent of the human birthing process. The implication is clear: the successful white man also incorporates the experiences of the downtrodden and/or minority woman, such that nothing is missing from his own inner moral compass.

---

[44] The significance of the concluding sentence by Molly as well as Joyce's comment re the Fleisch der sich bejaht are further explored in Unseld, *Der Autor und sein Verleger*, pp. 33–6. See also his *Briefe an die Autoren* for obvious example of different treatment of male and female authors (shared, incidentally, by that other great networker, Hans Werner Richter).

All material circumstances and physical infrastructure portrayed within the biopic is oriented towards underscoring this message.

Although the biopic *Der Verleger oder Die Lust am Buch* sets out to explain the mentality and publishing practices of one of post-war Germany's most successful publishers to a wider, non-literary audience in celebratory fashion, it in fact reveals Unseld's 'Suhrkamp culture' to be not just exclusive and hierarchical, but actively crowding out alternative voices and viewpoints in all the physical and metaphysical spaces alike available to it. The hegemonic gesture that accompanies these exclusions is almost always one of reference to the conventional Western cultural canon. The metaphors and images developed in all earnestness by the publisher and his authors to express their positioning in the literature network derive from the Bible, the Enlightenment (including Western notions of the Orient), and the established nineteenth- and twentieth-century intellectual figures of Goethe, Adorno, Bloch and Joyce. That Unseld sees himself continuing and expanding this tradition into the late twentieth century is expressed in the classic psychoanalytical terms of Sigmund Freud and Harold Bloom when he reflects on how he felt on succeeding Peter Suhrkamp: 'dieser Suhrkamp war für mich ein zu großer Übervater, als dass ich da hätte nachdenken können, was ich da machen wollte. Ich wusste nur eines: ich wollte das mindestens ebenso gut machen, wenn nicht besser, wie er' (this Suhrkamp was too much of an über-father for me to have been able to reflect consciously on what I wanted to do. I just knew one thing: I wanted to do things at least as well, if not better, than him). The 1980s biopic allows him to show exactly how he has achieved this, and in so doing firmly mark out his own place within the German-inflected Western canon. More broadly, Unseld's account shows how the celebratory mode of authorship permeates all aspects of the literature network, increasingly to the detriment of literary diversity and with an attendant closing in of audiences.

Mediating Authorship

Just as we saw with Walter Höllerer, not only Unseld's successes, then, but also his shortfalls, have significantly shaped the post-war German literature network. At the same time, the material aspects of the network have significantly shaped the authorship that both literary mediators were able to represent for themselves and others. Unseld and Höllerer act as important mediators in a network defined by significant material and conceptual blind spots, but they are themselves also acted upon by other mediators in this network, such that the network as a whole is keyed to amplify its failings. Accordingly, while individual authors used literature to explore the limits and possibilities of the literary text in its relation to the wider world, and individual publishers sought to promote the best writing as part of a well-intentioned programme of broader public education, the degree of public posturing and conscious networking that accompanies these activities is inherently reductive and exclusionary. Both the tangible and intangible heritage inherent in the physical infrastructure and wider places where these relationships unfold supports these reductions and exclusions and underscore the importance of non-human actors within the German literature network. West German authors like Walser, Höllerer, Grass and Enzensberger were genuinely trying to find new ways of engaging with their physical, cultural and political surroundings, and they intended their own activities to have exemplary effect. They interacted, across conventional generation boundaries, with younger writers and cultural dissidents, as well as across geographical boundaries in their attempts to help both contemporary and younger colleagues in the Eastern bloc. But they were also very much caught in the wider reductive celebratory framework of post-war German publishing that took on a particular material, physical form over the course of the 1960s, 1970s and 1980s that had much stronger links with past places and spaces for literature than the conventional narrative of the epochal singularity occasioned by a physical and cultural zero hour would lead us to believe. Their careers as successful authors within an industry, the power of which was literally becoming more concrete over the course of the entire post-war period, did not predispose them to questioning the more troubling aspects of this context. And the very success of these careers meant there were few others invested with the authority to do so in their stead.

Five After the Death of the Author: The Rise of the Utopian Mode, 1988–2018

This chapter looks at what happens to the established models of authorship when the utopian mode, a natural ally of textual play that entails mirroring and dispersal, becomes dominant. The previous chapter has shown the extent to which writers in the West in the late 1980s had to negotiate a closed circle of powerful cultural mediators who seemed set to reign supreme for the foreseeable future. This included Austria, where authors were often reliant on deals with West German publishers to secure their position in the much larger West German market. Meanwhile, for writers in the East, exile to the West often seemed the only option if they were to speak of the political and social issues that were most important to them. In both settings, literary authorship was more than ever routinely bound up with live political and economic issues that did not encourage innovation in the mix of modes of authorship routinely espoused.

Against this background, Austrian author Christoph Ransmayr published the seemingly obscure *Die letzte Welt* (1988, *The Last World*), a finely crafted re-working of Ovid's authorial persona and the stories of his *Metamorphoses*. Ransmayr's text earned unanimous literary acclaim, making it one of the bestselling novels of 1988 and securing his subsequent career in German-speaking Europe. Written just before the demise of the Eastern Bloc and the turn of the second millennium, the story it tells about how an exiled author relates to a dictatorial regime two thousand years earlier makes of it, in retrospect, a particularly timely text for my own consideration of late twentieth-century German-language authorship. Furthermore, in terms of its literary historical importance, the text looks both backwards and forwards to different imaginary worlds and/or alternative literary spaces in which authorship can unfold. Ransmayr's engagement with Ovid's fate sits within the emergent trend of the later 1970s and 1980s to re-discover the Classical world or explore the mythical in natural landscapes in order to make more oblique reference to contemporary issues – Christa Wolf's *Kassandra* (1983, Cassandra), Peter Handke's *Langsame Heimkehr* quartet (1979–81, Slow Homecoming), Günter Grass's *Zunge zeigen* (1988, Show Your Tongue), for example. However, it also incorporates deliberate anachronisms and a level of textual self-reflexivity that make of it a forerunner for some of the more self-consciously postmodern writing of the 1990s and 2000s, stretching even to the beginnings of what a number of critics have explicitly termed the flowering of 'late style' in twenty-first-century German-language writing.[1]

My interest in exploring Ransmayr's text as a watershed moment in German literary history is not fuelled by a desire to re-draw the set of key texts and dates on which we conventionally hang changes in literary style and content, even if this chapter's starting point just in advance of German reunification may look suggestive. Rather, what I want to do here is to grasp the opportunity that analysis of both his work and that of Romanian-German author Herta Müller offers for exploring changes within the literature network that take effect quietly in German-language writing over the course of the late 1980s and 1990s and are linked to notions of textual rebirth. My guiding aim is to understand how the ground is gradually laid for new models of authorship. These new models emerge partly in response to French post-structuralist thought but also as a result of a gradual shift in constellations of the historically conditioned modes of authorship outlined in earlier chapters. This goes on to produce a variety of examples of textually and politically self-aware authorship in German-speaking Europe that have been fully in the ascendancy since the turn of the millennium and go well beyond the neoliberal, media-focused play with the authorial persona that begins rather underwhelmingly with the posturing of writers like Florian Illies, Christian Kracht and Rainald Goetz in the mid-1990s, followed a little later and with considerably more finesse by Daniel Kehlmann.[2] This latter kind of self-promotional literary

---

[1] Stuart Taberner, *Aging and Old-Age Style in Günter Grass, Ruth Klüger, Christa Wolf, and Martin Walser: The Mannerism of a Late Period* (Rochester, NY: Camden House, 2013).

[2] For more on Kehlmann's engagement with authorial posture, see Rebecca Braun 'Daniel Kehlmann, *Die Vermessung der Welt*: Measuring Celebrity Through the Ages', in S. Taberner and L. Marven, eds, *Emerging German-Language Novelists of the Twenty-First Century* (Rochester, NY: Camden House, 2011), pp. 75–88; Ina Ulrike Paul, 'Autorfunktion, Autorfiktion: Schriftstellerfiguren bei Daniel Kehlmann', *Gegenwartsliteratur* 16 (2017), 77–99. For a sense of how Kehlmann's posture yields further posturing on the part of other authors, see Benjamin Schaper, *Poetik und Politik der Lesbarkeit in der deutschen Literatur* (Heidelberg: Winger, 2017).

activity – which has been the key focus for the majority of academic studies to date with a direct interest in contemporary German-language authorship – tends to reflect on cultural processes of commodification in such a manner as to dismiss the ability of both the author and the text to hold any kind of autonomous value within the neoliberal system. Accordingly, it points to the impending end of literature as a play of degenerative self-reference, just one of a number of cultural forms (and probably not the most convincing either) that employs such techniques in the service of a generic cultural critique of neoliberalism that is pre-programmed to fail to break out of it.[3] By contrast, the writers and writing I am interested in manage to hold open the space of literature – the aesthetics and the imaginary world of the text itself, as well as its broader place in society – so that the author figure not just of the last two hundred but of the last two thousand years can appear and disappear in a rather more productive fashion.

To a degree, Roland Barthes' 'Death of the Author' from 1967 and Michel Foucault's 1969 response to it provide a conceptual framework for grasping how the poetics of these texts map on to the various worlds, real and imagined, that have conditioned them. Ransmayr's novel is all about a reader who finds himself, quite literally, in the text after its author's politically motivated disappearance and putative death. Although the political significance of this remains largely implicit, the thrust of the work is to celebrate what engaging with the literary text on its own (aesthetic) terms can do for the embattled individual: it offers a perspective on events that yields transcendence through inner mental escape that is arguably akin to relinquishing one's biographical identity and merging instead with the never-ending flow of discourse. There is a clear political poignancy to this in the final years of Cold War Europe, where the sense of imminent disaster that had characterized the first part of the 1980s had given way to a seemingly insoluble stalemate. Müller's novel, *Reisende auf einem Bein* (1989, Travelling on One Leg), meanwhile, picks up the Foucauldian line on discourse, showing the power of words and objects to police lives in both the actual world and in the literary space of the text. With more overt political resonance than Ransmayr, her work shows how an individual might try to assemble herself out of snippets of phrases and story fragments that seem to offer some resistance to a hostile political order: living becomes a case of

---

[3] Anke Biendarra, *Germans Going Global: Contemporary Literature and Cultural Globalization* (Berlin: de Gruyter, 2012) provides a well-informed overview of these trends, both as regards the kinds of literature that were widely discussed in this period and the practical publishing circumstances within which this profiling was taking place.

assembling and disassembling the resulting identities in response to the policing of any one particular time and place. In this vein, consciously engaging with language entails questioning authorship – and the notions of authority associated with it – for any individual who is trying to make sense of their life, as well as for any reader trying to follow it.

Yet, as this chapter will go on to discuss in detail, both texts do much more than merely act out the twists and turns of either post-structuralist theory or a surveillance society. Each also draws in its own way on the German commemorative, celebratory, satirical and utopian modes of authorship that inflect such literary poetics. Felicitas Hoppe's work too continues this intertwining of post-structuralist poetics and literary authorship, with an ever more distinct literary space emerging in which the satirical and utopian modes of authorship have the potential to overturn existing foundational models of German authorship and replace them with a more humble, ethically considered one. The poet, novelist and multi-media performer Ulrike Almut Sandig is typical in this respect, when she articulates in her conversation with me at the end of this book what it means to her to position her work in the world:

> [T]he fact that it's my text doesn't trump everything else, it's just one part of the action, so to speak. It's just one part of the original creative act that I happen to have written this text. The circumstances of my life, or the fact that I am, for example, a woman, are really not that important. These details come into play, of course, but they also merge into something else, something bigger.

For Sandig, Hoppe and many other contemporary authors working across media and in deliberate collaboration with others to develop new angles on old themes, this can be read in terms of putting Foucault's concept of the heterotopia to practical use as well as living Barthes' famous 'death of the author' in a deliberately constructive way. It entails extending into new media a version of the literary heterotopia that is already implicit in Ransmayr's work from over two decades earlier. The direction of travel across the works discussed in this chapter accordingly shows a realignment of textual poetics and authorial positioning in the wider world towards conscious inclusivity of multiple people, concepts and things, all encapsulated in a variety of more and less open forms. In what follows, I examine progress towards a new model of German-language authorship at the turn of the millennium that, in its very heterogeneity, is deliberately not exemplary, but also decidedly not dead. Underpinning all this is a marked turn towards greater use of the utopian mode of authorship as both a political and a poetic practice on the part of authors themselves.

It is no coincidence that two out of the three authors discussed in detail here hail from beyond Germany: in both this chapter and the next the contours of 'Modern Germany' are deliberately approached from literary positions that sit to the side of the German literature network. In reputational and financial terms, however, the authors under consideration have reached their largest audiences in the Federal Republic. Viewed on a meta-level, these authors themselves occupy a utopian space, with their identity dispersed between different, overlapping contexts and their reception conditioned by a certain shuttling back and forth between these contexts. This positioning within multiple national Bourdieusian fields is increasingly characteristic of the contemporary 'German' literature network. It suggests that a deliberately transnational model of authorship may be the natural manifestation of an underlying increase in the prevalence of the utopian mode at the level of both textual and worldly performances of authorship. This is a two-part argument: this chapter focuses more on tracing the utopian mode as an element of structural importance within literary texts, while chapter six considers the transnational model of authorship in the broader context of how authorship inheres in the world.

The Poetics and Politics of Late Twentieth-Century Authorship: Christoph Ransmayr and Herta Müller

Die letzte Welt is a kind of literary detective story, questioning where the author is in multiple ways. It follows the fate of Cotta, a contemporary of Ovid's, who disbelieves the reports of the poet's death that have reached Rome from his place of exile on the Black Sea and hopes to find, if not the poet himself, at least the finished version of the *Metamorphoses* amongst his belongings in Tomis (Tomi in Ransmayr's German text). The unpublished text of *Metamorphoses* had already become legend in Rome during Ovid's lifetime, and Cotta functions as an enthusiastic reader figure who is prepared to go to considerable lengths to follow the celebrated author, popularly known as Naso. It is surely no accident that Cotta shares his name with a famous publishing house that was pivotal in establishing modern authorship in Germany, with Goethe, Schiller, Herder, Hegel, Kleist and Alexander von Humoboldt, amongst others, on its list. This gives the reader a clear hint right from the outset that more is at stake here in the poetics and politics of literature than one man's lone search for a text and its author. It is also about how German authorship relates to the world.

With this in mind, the bulk of Ransmayr's narrative, told by Naso's acolyte Cotta, focuses precisely on Cotta's attempt, for his own purposes, to traverse the multiple places of memory that the inspirational author Naso provides. In this sense, the mode of authorship that he both emulates (the particular value he ascribes to a literary work) and increasingly sets in train himself (the lightly ironic writing style he employs to describe his actions) is a mixture of the commemorative and the celebratory, not dissimilar to the attitudes in earlier West German writing discussed in chapter two and which were also given a sarcastic twist. Yet what starts out as a search for the finished manuscript that will bring Cotta fame if he can bring it back to Rome turns into an existential re-tracing of Naso's unknown life in exile by uncovering the uncanny links between the author and the place in which his text lives. This will ultimately profoundly alter Cotta's sense of who he is and how he relates to the literary space he (literally) traverses in a way that intersects with both the utopian mode of authorship and playfully self-referential trends in post-structuralism.

This literary space is uncanny from the start, although it does not initially unsettle Cotta, who is only partially familiar with the content of Ovid's *Metamorphoses*. On arriving at the far eastern reaches of the Roman Empire, Cotta finds the 'iron city' of Tomis peopled by modern-day namesakes of Ovid's cast of characters. It does not take him long to establish that the Naso he seeks no longer lives amongst these curious townsfolk, and that he must search out the poet's last known abode in the even more inaccessible mountain hamlet of Trachila if he is to stand any chance of finding him alive. Yet here too he arrives too late, and can meet only with the seemingly imbecilic Pythagoras, who now guards the dilapidated dwelling and garden in which Naso left a mysterious assemblage of carved stone pillars proclaiming the immortality of his work, along with tattered fragments of cloth with individual words and phrases on them. A first interpretation of these, for both Cotta and his extra-textual reader, is that the author has left clues as to his whereabouts in the different materials and textiles pressed into service to carry his text. For Cotta, however, they lead only into disturbed dreams and visions.

If the early chapters of the novel thereby underscore the impossibility of finding an author who has been officially banished from civilized society, subsequent chapters present the liminal space of literature that provides, to some degree at least, an alternative home to both the exiled writer and his devoted reader. Unable to extract meaning from the final material traces left by the poet, Cotta returns to Tomis and begins to fall in with the locals. It gradually becomes apparent that these people, despite their initial reluctance to share any knowledge of Naso with Cotta, are in fact familiar with the mythical stories and characters underpinning his tales – to the point first of acting them out during a carnival, and then, as Battus is turned to stone and Lycaon disappears with his wolf-skin, eerily re-enacting their fates with their own lives. At this point, at the very latest, Ransmayr's text veers away from the commemorative-celebratory modes of authorship. The eastern fringes of the Roman Empire turn into an alternative, heterotopian space that challenges Rome's rational, biographically led appropriation of authorship by literally being the place of story and myth conventionally assigned to it by the Greek and Roman writers. In so doing, it pushes any individual author figure into the background.

It is consistent with the utopian mode of authorship, then, that Naso cannot live in either Tomis or Trachila – he can only exist in Cotta's dialogic shuttling between Rome, Tomis and Trachila, always only a projection from one realm onto the other. The liminal space that opens up in Cotta's recorded experience of looking for Naso requires a different mode of authorship to those that routinely trace the individual author's positioning in any one society. This is a specific kind of space that is entirely brought about through individuals' active involvement with one another and their wider worlds. At the same time, in merging the utopian mode that is invoked by both Naso and Cotta's authorial dispersal with Cotta's original celebratory-commemorative impetus, Ransmayr takes this notion to an extreme: the literary text literally is the place both of memory and of the utopian projection it records, such that the whole place and all the relations within it collectively author a logically impossible text that swallows up everyone and everything that engages with it – a heterotopia as Foucault defines it: 'something like counter-sites, a kind of effectively enacted utopia in which the real sites, all the other real sites that can be found within the culture, are simultaneously represented, contested and inverted. Places of this kind are outside of all places, even though it may be possible to indicate their location in reality.'[4]

The place that Cotta initially visited in search of the author most famously exiled to it thus begins to merge into the fabric of this author's stories. Cotta can only realize this gradually, for he does not yet know the full content of Ovid's unseen manuscript. In the middle chapters of Ransmayr's novel, Cotta begins to realize that he can piece the coveted manuscript together through the stories that the locals must have absorbed through their interactions with Naso – notably Echo's oral memory of a 'Book of Stones' recounted to her by firelight, and the deaf and dumb Arachne's visual recollections of a 'Book of Birds' that she read from the poet's lips and wove into her tapestries. In the closing chapters, as he finally loses all hope of finding the poet and instead becomes ever more involved with the individual characters in Tomis, he also begins to understand that the stories he had been seeking in manuscript form are in fact happening all around him, with the

---

[4] Foucault, 'Of Other Spaces', p. 24.

community collectively curiously immune to the dramas unfolding in their midst. In fact, the whole place comes to emulate the structure of the *Metamorphoses*, as individual fates are acted out in a text that arranges them paratactically, a series of self-contained dramatic and traumatic events that happen individually. As Cotta himself successively experiences them, they are held together by a common theme of transformation, but with no intertextual comparison across the collection or empathetic involvement in one another's tales on the part of the protagonists. This inherent difference / distinctness from one another, as well as to the wider world outside, is another defining feature of Foucault's heterotopia, underscoring the curious stasis that defines such a liminal place.

In this respect, Tomis has none of Doreen Massey's 'throwntogetherness' of a real geopolitical place. Where ordinarily extreme weather events provide a talking point across a community, nobody in Tomis even seems to notice the storm that batters the town and makes Cotta fear for his life. Likewise, the rope maker Lycaon's disappearance provokes no comment. In fact, the community only visibly comes together whenever a distinctly literary framework is provided: to watch Cyparis's film projections of classical myths on the butcher Tereus's blank outdoor wall, or to re-enact these tales themselves in the town's carnival parade. Both serve as a kind of *mise-en-abyme* for the larger fact of the townsfolk's exclusively literary existence: they are only gathered in Ransmayr's text collectively to recreate the text of Ovid's *Metamorphoses*, 'the last (literary) world' that this author created at the turn of the Christian era and which accompanied him into his own exile from civilized Roman society. The anachronisms that Ransmayr weaves into his presentation of these people – their unlikely use of film projectors and guns, for example – repeatedly breaks any sense of naïve celebration of myth. Rather, the idiosyncratic portrayal of a strangely static community goes hand in hand with the text's assertion of a heterotopian literary space that, in asserting a really-existing different way of being, also reflects back differently, but mutely, on geopolitics.

Accordingly, the sorts of issues that pertained in both the geopolitical space of Rome and late twentieth-century German-speaking Europe – complex interpersonal relationships and how they underpin the potential for political change – are little more than background colour in this heterotopian literary space. They are playfully evoked and intermingled in passing through Ransmayr's deliberately jarring anachronisms: the references to crumbling heavy industry and practices of espionage including the use of cameras, for example. By contrast, what actually keeps this place alive (in contradistinction to the abandoned villages nearby) are the stories that collectively give birth to the characters and fix them around the absent author who has drawn them together in his text and determined that they must gather where he has perceived them: the world is his text, and his text is the world. Realizing this becomes Cotta's epiphanic moment, and it transports him into a state of quasi-delirium: he realizes how literally tracing authorship can free the individual from the constraints of his real place and time and allow him to retreat instead into a textual heterotopia, a place that is reassuringly removed from contemporary politics and physical hardship and where the author can thus both fully assert himself and fully disappear:

> Aus Rom verbannt, aus dem Reich der Notwendigkeit und der Vernunft, hatte der Dichter die *Metamorphoses* am Schwarzen Meer zu Ende erzählt, hatte eine kahle Steilküste, an der er Heimweh litt und fror, zu *seiner* Küste gemacht und zu *seinen* Gestalten jene Barbaren, die ihn bedrängten und in die Verlassenheit von Trachila vertrieben. Und Naso hatte schließlich seine Welt von den Menschen und ihren Ordnungen befreit, indem er *jede* Geschichte bis an ihr Ende erzählte. Dann war er wohl auch selbst eingetreten in das menschenleere Bild, kollerte als unverwundbarer Kiesel die Halden hinab, strich als Kormoran über die Schaumkronen der Brandung oder hockte als triumphierendes Purpurmoos auf dem letzten, verschwindenden Mauerrest einer Stadt.[5]

> [Banished from Rome, the empire of necessity and reason, the poet had narrated his *Metamorphoses* to the end at the Black Sea, had made the stark, steep coast where he suffered homesickness and felt the cold, into *his* coast, just as he made those barbarians who hassled him and drove him to the abandoned site of Trachila into *his* characters. And so Naso had finally freed his world of people and their regimes by telling every story to its end. And then he himself probably entered the scene that was devoid of people, tumbled down the slag heaps like a sturdy pebble, glided as a cormorant over the frothy tips of the breaking surf, or squatted as triumphant purple moss on the last disappearing walls of a town.]

The physical place of Tomis, in other words, becomes the heterotopian literary space opened up by Roman accounts of Ovid's *Metamorphoses*, because it is where Cotta, searching for the author, finds only the text in and through which the author has disappeared. This text does not take

---

[5] Christoph Ransmayr, *Die letzte Welt* (Frankfurt a.M.: Fischer, 1988), p. 254.

the expected form of a manuscript but is a mixture of shared material culture (Arachne's tapestries that adorn many of the buildings; the stones and cloth scraps Cotta collects), oral history (the stories Echo retells) and the peculiar lived experiences of individual characters. As Cotta experiences it, it therefore tells us nothing about the author Naso, but everything about the reader Cotta, who, by living through the literary space of this text, witnessing all its stories, and increasingly interacting with the locals, finally begins to hear his own name echoed back at him by the landscape. The text's closing paragraphs explicitly celebrate how the heterotopian space of literature is kept open not by the great poets who have already told their stories, but by the readers who are able to read themselves into the texts, and, in so doing, make the places where these texts happen. In a Barthesian vein, then, the reader makes the work and the author is relevant only in as much as his initial actions facilitated this repeatable experience. Accordingly and in a highly symbolic move – for the land around the real-world Constanța is decidedly flat – Cotta ascends once more to Naso's dwelling and place of writing as if to a higher plane, a kind of Romantic-inflected heterotopian world that hovers just out of sight of the stories that play out in its shadow.[6] Now he is certain that he will find not a direct reference to Naso anywhere in the surrounding landscape, but a scrap of material addressed to himself. Because he has fully begun to merge, as a diligent reader, with the literary landscape, this 'place of memory' can yield his name, echoing his own fate back at him in both the language and the material of the literary text, as the final paragraph of the text makes clear.

As he symbolically ascends beyond the plane of the narrative content (the stories experienced in and around Tomis) and embraces his own literary placeness along the way, Cotta becomes the author he was looking for and the text can enfold him in it along with everything else. In a highly ambivalent gesture, the text thereby documents how he becomes the author of his world by increasingly removing himself from the world. Through a mixture of the celebratory / commemorative and the utopian modes, Ransmayr, through Cotta, ekes out a model of authorship that is both creative and pedagogic, but in a radically introspective manner: the author is held up to his reader as an immersive exemplary lesson in how to read and write, but one that will result in a social death for reader and author alike as they disappear into the textual heterotopia.

* * *

---

[6] The notion of ascent from one realm to the other and the use of material writing culture to encode clues indicating a kind of higher order meaning calls to mind E.T.A. Hoffmann's *Der goldene Topf* (1814, The Golden Pot).

Herta Müller's 1989 text, *Reisende auf einem Bein*, represents a journey of a different kind to Ransmayr's deliberately intertextual poetics of reading and writing, but it is equally concerned with the transformative potential of liminal literary space, and brings a valuable political perspective to my discussion of late twentieth-century authorship. The third-person narrative re-creates a prolonged period of transience, as Irene, a migrant from an unnamed country reminiscent of Romania, settles in West Berlin. Although the narrative is not directly concerned with literary acts, its tight structure, coupled with Müller's trademark 'Fremder Blick' (sic; foreign / strange / alien gaze or perspective) and recurrent motifs, makes it a very self-consciously constructed piece that, like an epic poem, draws attention to itself as something that needs to be approached on its own terms. However, as Müller stresses in 'Der Fremde Blick oder Das Leben ist ein Furz in der Laterne' (The Alien Perspective or Life is a Fart in a Lantern), the 1999 essay that specifically elaborates upon how her 'alien perspective' results from a life subjected to state surveillance, all her attempts to put experiences into words are as much underpinned by a real historical background that has nothing to do with literature as by a specifically literary stylistics that may subsequently seem inherent within them.[7] In this sense, her first fictional text set in West Germany and explicitly addressing issues of not-belonging doubly points to her performance of authorship both within and outside the text. Müller herself left Romania in 1987, and there is no way of not conflating the author's own contextual background as a writer who fell foul of the state, which precedes and is different to the world of the literary text, with the particular textual positioning inherent in the act of writing that so clearly results from this lived experience.

Perhaps for this very reason, Müller's text failed as spectacularly as Ransmayr's succeeded in the first instance on the West German book market. Somewhat ironically, given the cautious sense of arrival with which the narrative concludes, it was published just before the fall of the Wall. This political event would further complicate Müller's longstanding liminal socio-political positioning between German and Romanian readers and East and West regimes, and it led to her text largely losing its contemporary readership in all areas: the perspective on geopolitics that *Reisende* offered was suddenly out of step with the times and seemed to hail from a place that no longer existed. However, this politically induced failure of her poetics of transience, identity and place does nothing to shake the literary significance of the way she

---

[7] Herta Müller, *Der Fremde Blick oder Das Leben ist ein Furz in der Laterne* (Göttingen: Wallstein, 1999).

deals with these issues in her text, and Müller returns to them repeatedly in later works.[8]

In fact, the biographical trajectory set in motion with *Reisende* and officially recognized twenty years later by the award of the Nobel Prize, is one that moves from extreme, explicitly politically motivated placelessness to some form of implicit placeness within literature. In her 1999 essay, Müller is at pains to reject the notion that her 'alien perspective' is either the simple result of being foreign in Germany, or a carefully crafted literary device for seeing the world differently. Interleaving autobiographical narrative with collage poetry, she takes a dual-pronged approach to explaining how the Romanian regime of surveillance and intimidation taught her to see agency in inanimate objects and project distrust onto the most diverse aspects of her surroundings. In so doing, she explains as a wholly non-literary, historical phenomenon on the one hand what she performs as highly stylized literature on the other. 'Der Fremde Blick ist alt, fertig mitgebracht aus dem Bekannten', she writes on a page facing a poem made out of magazine cut-outs of text and image. 'Er hat mit dem Einwandern nach Deutschland nichts zu tun. Fremd ist für mich nicht das Gegenteil von bekannt, sondern das Gegenteil von vertraut. Unbekanntes muß nicht fremd sein, aber Bekanntes kann fremd werden'[9] (The alien perspective is old, brought along readymade in what is known; it has nothing to do with immigrating to Germany. For me, alien is not the opposite of what is known, but rather the opposite of what is familiar. What is not known does not need to be alien, but what is known can become alien). This kind of unsettling alienation effect is exactly what characterizes her literary work both before and after the 1999 essay. The Nobel Prize was in fact specifically awarded to Müller in 2009 for the startling *attitude* underpinning her literature, or, in the words of the Swedish Academy president, for the way she 'with the *concentration* of poetry and the *frankness* of prose, depicts the landscape of the dispossessed' (my emphasis).[10] More than any other author in this study, Müller thereby exemplifies the extent to which the complexities of (not) belonging can coalesce in the life and writing of an author as both biographical fact and literary stylistics. Where the authorial exile explored in *Die letzte Welt* was the subject of a fictional text that culminated in the exploration of a

---

[8] Lyn Marven, 'Life and Literature: Autobiography, Referentiality, and Intertextuality in Herta Müller's Work', in in Brigid Haines & Lyn Marven, eds, *Herta Müller* (Oxford: Oxford Univeristy Press, 2013), pp. 204–23.
[9] Müller, *Der Fremde Blick*, p. 11.
[10] https://www.nobelprize.org/prizes/literature/2009/muller/facts/ (last accessed 01 November 2019).

literary heterotopia, here the author repeatedly uses fiction to reposition herself towards her own multiple experiences of exile, which range from eerie disappearances to cautious utopian visions.

As part of her life at a particularly significant political moment, *Reisende auf einem Bein*, with its explicit focus on identities in transit, can thereby also be read on a meta-level as implicitly opening up the space of literature in ways that will resonate across much of Müller's subsequent career. Although the protagonist is not set up as a writer, the perspective on place that unfolds through and around her actions is accompanied by a mode of authorship that, as many analysts have commented, represents a form of 'working through' trauma.[11] A sustained engagement with trauma fits within the commemorative mode within my framework, where ultimately the text keeps referring back to a disjuncture or something major that has been irretrievably lost, or, in Müller's terms, occasioned the 'alien perspective' that proves as unsettling as it is persistent in the new environment: 'In der neuen Umgebung, wo die meisten ihn nicht haben, flackert er im Gesicht. [...] Er läßt sich nicht von heut auf morgen abstellen, vielleicht nie mehr'[12] (In the new surroundings, where most people don't have it, it flickers across faces. It can't just be switched off overnight, perhaps ever.) Such a sense is created within the very fabric of the text through Müller's short, often acausal sentences, which point to a wealth of repressed experiences that feel constantly about to resurface.[13] At the level of content, too, Müller's spartan descriptions of situations are intriguingly over-determined. Most notably, inanimate objects are repeatedly on the move around the protagonist: bushes, curtains, paperclips, jewellery, eyebrows and mouths rustle, twitch, or wobble seemingly of their own accord, as the phrase 'bewegte sich' (moved; literally: moved itself) acts as a leitmotif across the text. The bleak external cityscape, the men who drift in and out of Irene's life, and the associative internal workings of her mind also alternately exert a mysterious and often threatening agency of their own across the narrative, as Moray McGowan notes in his detailed reading.[14] The throwback to a context where nothing can be

---

[11] The various traditions in reading Müller are excellently set out in the introduction to Haines & Marven, eds, *Herta Müller*, pp. 1–15.
[12] Müller, *Der Fremde Blick*, p. 18.
[13] For an in-depth consideration of how biographical trauma can be expressed in literature, see Lyn Marven, *Body and Narrative in Contemporary Literatures in German: Herta Müller, Libuše Moníková, and Kerstin Hensel* (Oxford: Oxford U. P., 2005).
[14] Moray McGowan, '"Stadt und Schädel", "Reisende", and "Verlorene": City, Self, and Survival in Herta Müller's Reisende auf einem Bein', in Haines & Marven, eds, *Herta Müller*, pp. 664–83.

trusted or taken at face value in one's surroundings is evident, with the result that the personal in the present is at all times pervaded by the political in the past. The commemorative mode of authorship implicit throughout the text is thereby pushed to an all-pervading focus on gaps and an unbridgeable loss of agency that the reader vicariously experiences through Irene's unsettling focalization – and, with this, pushed to its own limit too.

Yet this profound lack of ease in any place or time – what one might term 'absolute placelessness' – does not result in a capitulation of the human subject. In fact, the direct intertext, introduced when Franz compares the protagonist to the symbolic figure of Italo Calvino's Irene, the name given by Marco Polo to one or more of the manifestations of the ever-changing, adaptable and thus resilient city in Calvino's *Invisible Cities*, fixes the moment of 'Erkenntnis' within the individual who engages with change and difference, and who lives. For all of the personal trauma that is evident in Irene's character, she is a survivor who knowingly steps forward into the future and determinedly inhabits places, as the novel's closing sentence underscores: 'Irene weigerte sich, an Abschied zu denken'[15] (Irene refused to think of leaving). Much of this resilience comes in one way or another from the way she uses different forms of literary language – words, images and individual elements of creative composition, including position and colour – to exert control over her experiences at the margins of society.

Most obviously, she has singled out individual sentences from works of literature and adapted them over the years to her changing circumstances. The first of these, 'Aber ich war nicht mehr jung' (But I was no longer young) is also flagged up in the book's epigraph as a direct intertext, taken from the work of Cesare Pavese. Its later appearance in the text is worth examining in detail, for it is paradigmatic of the associative writing style that Müller employs across the text to link highly literary language with deeply personal political experiences. In the immediate context of the plot, Irene is waiting to be met at the airport when she arrives in West Germany and observes herself waiting to see whether there are any other Irenes who might walk up to the man holding her name card. As she does so, she both reflects back on previous experiences of holding out in a position of uncertainty and uses the quotation from Pavese to express her current sense of liminality, in terms of a certain belatedness in both time and place:

---

[15] Herta Müller, *Reisende auf einem Bein* (Frankfurt a.M.: Fischer, 2010), p. 176. The same sentence is singled out in a paragraph of its own in ch. 1, p. 15, when Franz returns to Germany after their initial encounter.

Irene versuchte sich zu erinnern, wann das war, daß sie zum ersten Mal etwas nicht ausgehalten hatte. Und ob sie damals geahnt hatte, daß sich das fortsetzen und immer neu ergeben würde. Und ob sie damals überlegt hatte, was sie mit sich tun sollte, wenn sie etwas nicht aushielt.

Da fiel Irene einer der Sätze aus Büchern ein. Ein Satz, den sie jahrelang mit sich herumgetragen und verwandelt hatte: Aber ich war nicht mehr jung.

Es war so oft, wie gewöhnlich, wie immer, wenn etwas vorbei war: am Gaumen stand ein Wunsch. Irene kannte ihn nicht. Wußte nur, daß er etwas vor ihr verbarg.

Ein Nachgeschmack hatte Irene eingehüllt.

Ja, es war wie gewöhnlich, wenn etwas vorbei war: zu spät schälten sich Bilder heraus, grau in grau, und wehten sich an. Und eine Spur davon war im Kehlkopf geblieben.[16]

[Irene tried to remember when it was that she had first not been able to stand something. And if she had guessed back then that this would continue and constantly reoccur. And if she had considered back then what she should do with herself when she couldn't stand something.

Then Irene remembered one of the sentences from books. A sentence that she had carried around with herself for years, altering it as she went: But I was no longer young.

It happened so often, always the same, always like this, when something was over: at the back of your palate there was a wish. Irene didn't know what it was. Just knew it was hiding something from her.

An aftertaste had enveloped Irene.

Yes, this was how it always was when something was over: too late pictures would form, grey in grey, and wave at each other. And a trace of that had stuck in her larynx.]

As she deliberately stands to one side of herself in the arrivals hall, Irene's perspective on events is developed through the dual sense of greater life experience and over-ripeness, the positive and negative interpretations inherent in Pavese's sentence. The 'Erkenntnis' that she has gained over the years of finding herself in familiar situations of difficulty comes with a bitter aftertaste of still not knowing, not feeling sure of herself, or that she can stand the situation she is in. This aftertaste

---

[16] Müller, *Reisende auf einem Bein*, p. 24.

has lodged in her palate, seeding at the very core of her sensory system a physical experience of longing for more but also not knowing what exactly it is she wants. This lack of certainty is expressed in threatening terms that anthropomorphize the longing, turning it into an oppositional force deliberately hiding something from Irene and undermining her subject position. In line with her stated technique of literary adaptation, she changes Pavese's sentence accordingly into the equally ambiguous, 'Ein Nachgeschmack hatte Irene eingehüllt' (An aftertaste had enveloped Irene). With it lexically unclear whether Irene is the subject or object of her perceptions (tasting or being tasted), she occupies a paradoxically liminal position in respect of her own narrative that is reminiscent of the fate of the exiled subject in Ransmayr's text, and meshes directly with Müller's statements elsewhere about her 'alien perspective'.

Yet while the immediately following image of 'something that is over' connotes both the dictatorship and Irene as she stands outside of herself and out of the time and place of this dictatorship, pathos is held in check. The underlying intertext with Pavese's ambiguous act of looking over one's shoulder at a former self to see oneself differently in the now structures the following two closing sequences of the chapter, and it does so with an intensity of seeing that restores Irene to an active commemorative position within the narrative. She defiantly locks eyes with the dictator in her imagination, and then she interprets Stefan's visual exchange with her as 'Blicke auf der Flucht'[17] (the kinds of look exchanged by fugitives). This observation identifies an unease in Stefan that his words did not betray, and in so doing draws him in to the migrant experience on which she can pronounce with authority. Accordingly, she diagnoses in her fellow migrants as they speak aloud in the arrivals hall 'noch eine andere Person im Kehlkopf'[18] (they still have another person in their larynx), a ghostly presence who silently undermines the normal interactions these people are trying to sustain and makes them 'fremder als Fremde'[19] (stranger than strangers), presumably to both themselves and their German hosts. Irene's failure to speak at all, by contrast, heightens her ability to observe and reflect on herself in the moment, so that she can add knowledge of herself and her environment both past and present to the unfolding life experience that, in literary terms, she represents and which was explicitly heralded by the quotation from Pavese. Even at this early point in the text, Irene is cast as both a representative traumatized subject and the means for

---

[17] Müller, *Reisende auf einem Bein*, p. 25.
[18] Müller, *Reisende auf einem Bein*, p. 25.
[19] Müller, *Reisende auf einem Bein*, p. 25.

reflecting on the subject's experiences at one remove, indicating therefore also how to overcome them on an individual level. In this sense, even though she is not a writer herself, she embodies the commemorative mode of authorship, as both its subject and its object, the focalizer and focalized of Müller's 'alien perspective' within the text.

This shifting liminal position – between being the focus of the novel (her liminal life as a migrant as its subject) and being the means of meta-level reflection on this life – is picked up in the two further direct literary quotations inserted in the text. The first is an unattributed sentence from a book that, following her propensity for collage, Irene has written on a stolen road-works sign depicting a man with a shovel: 'Graben ist immer am Rande der Legalität'[20] (digging is always on the edges of legality). It hung over her bed in the country she has just left, alongside another stolen sign depicting a man falling headfirst and carrying the warning, 'Gefahr ins Leere zu stürzen'[21] (danger of falling into the abyss). Irene applied both signs directly to her life in the dictatorship, but it is clear that they echo forward into her present situation too. Her associative memory work that determines how she experiences everything around her in West Germany – in particular, the everyday violence in interpersonal relationships – is itself a kind of digging that unearths images of each society that neither would gladly sanction, as well as constituting an activity that is always on the edge of destabilizing Irene. Yet the fact that she carries on eking out this uncomfortable perspective and precisely does not cross any definitive line that would push her and the narrative into a void is what produces the text. In fact, as it progresses, her modest life in West Berlin begins to fill up (with furniture) and settle down, as the three potential love interests (Franz, Stefan, Thomas) resolve into one more meaningful companionship (Thomas). With this, a position from which to commemorate her past becomes ever more tangible.

The final direct intertext – the longer extract from Italo Calvino's *Invisible Cities* that Franz sends to Irene – encapsulates the idea of Irene as a carefully positioned symbolic device. In Calvino's text, Irene stands for the distanced perspective on a city: 'Irene ist der Name für eine Stadt aus der Ferne, und nähert man sich ihr, so wird sie eine andere'[22] (Irene is a name for a city in the distance, and if you approach, it changes).[23] The point that Marco Polo is making to Kublai Khan in this

---

[20] Müller, *Reisende auf einem Bein*, p. 90.
[21] Müller, *Reisende auf einem Bein*, p. 90.
[22] Müller, *Reisende auf einem Bein*, p. 100.
[23] Italo Calvino, *Invisible Cities*, transl. William Weaver (London: Vintage, 1997), p. 112.

text is the multi-faceted, multi-perspectival nature of cities that makes them impervious to the total direct control of one ruler. Each time you try to pin a city down from a slightly different perspective, the nature of what that city is shifts, and differentiating definitively between these perspectives is mired in difficulties, as Polo concludes: 'vielleicht hab ich von Irene schon unter verschiedenen Namen gesprochen; vielleicht habe ich überhaupt nur von Irene gesprochen'[24] (perhaps I have already spoken of Irene under other names; perhaps I have only spoken of Irene).[25] In Müller's text, Irene is directly confronted with this notion of herself as a narrative device, a perspective on a city that will change and become something / someone else as the beholder travels. The way in which person and place are merged here is highly reminiscent of Assmann's 'place of memory' and my discussion in chapter two of how the commemorative mode of authorship adds agency to this notion. Yet as the experiencing subject in the narrative, Irene does not respond to this representative symbolic role, and indeed she rejects the original sentence Franz quoted to her from the same text as 'not hers'. For Irene, books are distilled down to individual sentences that stay with her as a reader and are useful all the time they manage to resist incorporation into her voice and perspective. Once the 'fremde Stimme'[26] (foreign voice) has merged with her own, the sentence it spoke is no longer 'waghalsig' enough to carry on enriching her own experience[27] (daring – note that the German 'Hals', for throat, is part of this word: literally 'risk-throating', underscoring the importance of voice). Effectively, then, the text both opens up a way of seeing Irene as the historically authentic, literary enactment of Müller's 'alien perspective' and allows Irene to resist reduction to the role of mere literary device. As an individual in her own terms, she insists on her right not to become a literary projection space for someone else (both Franz and Stefan each try to do this in their own way), but to make the space of literature work directly for her.

Although she does not write anything down, Irene is in fact constantly reading her environment and finding stories in it that take her tendency towards commemorative focalization in a different direction. Throughout the text, Irene recodes the world through visual cues: the colour green, remembered from the scrub vegetation of her homeland, becomes a leitmotif for her that will guide some of her decisions, for example, while her manipulation of photographs and

---

[24] Müller, *Reisende auf einem Bein*, p. 100.
[25] Calvino, *Invisible Cities*, p. 113.
[26] Müller, *Reisende auf einem Bein*, p. 100.
[27] Müller, *Reisende auf einem Bein*, p. 100.

collages is a clear exertion of control over how she is seen and how she decides to see current affairs in response to her past experiences of surveillance. Alongside this, however, she also creates her own dramas and crime scenes that allow her to fix her position as the observer while others travel through. Thus, the second half of chapter four unfolds 'das Bühnenbild für ein Verbrechen' (the stage-set for a crime) at Wilhelmsruh station, where she first plays out a highly stylized imagined sexual encounter with the transport officer and then a failed moment of tenderness between an old lady and a child. Each scene is built out of precise positional observations of the people around her and regularly punctuated by the arrival and departure of the U-Bahn (train). The 'alien perspective' that structures these scenes is therefore one that sees the city up close and personal, rather than with cool observational detachment from afar, and the short sentences in which the scenes are relayed betray this over-determined emotion: 'In den Küssen war eine Klemme'[28] (the kisses were cornered) and 'Es war eine Stille wie zwischen Hand und Messer gleich nach der Tat'[29] (there was a silence like between hand and knife just after the deed). The sense that everything means so much more is a sense oriented toward the future: to the reader who is going to interpret the latent significance of a world, the multi-layered nature of which Irene can only capture for now, filtered through her commemorative lens.

In fact, Irene's use of both covert and overt literary strategies to fix her own position in the world brings to mind a further intertext, namely with Ingeborg Bachmann's *Malina* (1971, Malina), a narrative that is famously also directly concerned with finding a position from which the traumatized female subject can authentically relay her experiences and ends with the narrator immolated within a crack in the wall. *Malina* too is framed like a radio drama around a crime scene, and the increasingly tortured phone conversations that the first-person narrator has with both Ivan and Malina, the two male presences in her life, seem to find their echo in Irene's various telephone exchanges with her three lovers, ending notably in her alienation from Stefan in terms directly reminiscent of the ending of *Malina*: 'Irene legte auf. Ihr Blick war so hart, daß er im eigenen Gesicht schmerzte, den Fußboden entlang die Telefonschnur anschaute, bis zu der Stelle, wo sie in die Wand kroch'[30] (Irene hung up. Her gaze was so hard that it hurt her face, looked along the floor to the telephone cable right up to the point where it disappeared

---

[28] Müller, *Reisende auf einem Bein*, p. 32.
[29] Müller, *Reisende auf einem Bein*, p. 35.
[30] Müller, *Reisende auf einem Bein*, p. 175.

into the wall). Although the pronoun 'sie' logically refers to the telephone cable that disappears into the wall, there is sufficient grammatical ambiguity for it also to refer to Irene herself (this cannot be sustained in the English translation). Such a reading suggests itself in the light of Irene's observation just three pages earlier, 'Irene merkte ihrem Körper an, daß er darauf eingestellt war, lange zu leben: Da wollte sich Irene in die Enge zwingen, in der das Leben nicht mehr sicher war'[31] (Irene could tell her body was planning to live for a long time: that made Irene want to squeeze herself into the narrow space where life was no longer safe). Yet unlike the first-person narrator of *Malina*, Irene does not conclude that being immured within the walls of her own textually determined perceptions is the end point to which she aspires. While the final chapter plays through her distress on learning of the death of her friend back home and the resultant destabilization this causes to her sense of creating a meaningful life in West Berlin, she ultimately rejects further flight in any direction.

In so doing, Irene is also rejecting the lifestyle of the harried traveller who seems to play a game of eternal catch-up, 'Reisende mit dem erregten Blick [. . .] Hinter den Bewohnern her. Reisende auf einem Bein und auf dem anderen Verlorene. Reisende kommen zu spät'[32] (Travellers with a harried look [. . .] Following after the residents. Travellers on one leg and on the other lost souls. Travellers come too late). The negative completion of the phrase that also provides the novel's title significantly alters the perspective on travelling that the reader is encouraged to take – a point that is curiously absent in scholarship on this text so far. For although Irene represents the migrant experience and the perspective it affords, the whole trajectory of the text is that she becomes less 'lost' and more settled, while she conversely discerns in the settled 'Bewohner' (residents) around her a distinct tendency to lose one's way. Just as Böll reflected in his 1964 Frankfurt poetics lectures on the increasingly long distances regularly travelled by people in West Germany for work purposes, Irene records the larger cityscapes around Frankfurt and Berlin as punctuated by people on the move who have grown increasingly emotionally destabilized by their peripatetic lifestyle, as captured in the plaintive graffiti message, 'kaltes Land kalte Herzen ruf doch mal an Jens'[33] (cold country cold hearts please ring Jens). While the graffiti is what first triggers her thoughts about the harried travellers, on the final page of the novel she resists the urge to flee Berlin when, in her mind's eye, such a journey would put her in the company of

---

[31] Müller, *Reisende auf einem Bein*, p. 172.
[32] Müller, *Reisende auf einem Bein*, p. 98.
[33] Müller, *Reisende auf einem Bein*, p. 97.

'Menschen, die nicht mehr wußten, ob sie nun in diesen Städten Reisende in dünnen Schuhen waren. Oder Bewohner mit Handgepäck'[34] (people who no longer knew whether in these cities they were now travellers in flimsy shoes. Or residents with hand luggage).

The 'alien perspective' that Irene enacts within the text is thus neither simply coterminous with being foreign in a place, as Müller herself will also dismiss in her later essay, nor is it exhausted in the historically conditioned experience of trauma. In fact, it resides primarily in a lingering gaze that allows things to be seen, and the past to resurface – precisely not by travelling through places, but by stopping and looking, again and again.[35] The precondition for this is a fundamentally commemorative perspective: an ability to perceive the gap or break that lies behind what can be seen in the world, and to try to use literary language to work with this – yielding the commemorative mode of authorship. Much of this is haunting and unsettling, and accounts for the difficulty in reading Müller. Yet alongside this, in the deliberately intertextual figure of Irene, runs a gently utopian impulse – to allow for a multiplicity of perspectives that can be projected into this gap, the consequences of which have still to be actualized, and which might transport the reader who can follow them to a better place. Underpinning all Irene's open-ended interactions with both people and objects is a sense that there might be other ways of being and thinking that could be made tangible if we were only inclined to act differently on what can be seen. To speak with Bloch, Irene is therefore oriented towards a positive, shared Heimat that can be grasped and actualized, even though she has never yet been there and makes only very tentative steps towards it in the text.

On a meta-level, however, the distinctly literary space her gaze opens up does allow a fundamentally different way of existing in time and place, as well as a different mode of seeing, both of which are made available to the reader. In this sense, Müller's literary form not only, in the words of the Nobel awarding committee, creates the 'landscape of the dispossessed' as a striking place of memory for past political trauma, but also actualizes it as a future-oriented belief that things could be other and should be seen and engaged with through multiple perspectives. This multiplicity of interpretation chimes with the thrust of post-structuralist constructions of authorship and the literary space of the text, but in a way that also has direct purchase on recent history, as well as meaningfully gesturing to the future in the way that Adelson

---

[34] Müller, *Reisende auf einem Bein*, p. 176.
[35] See in this context also Herta Müller, 'In jeder Sprache sitzen andere Augen', in Herta Müller, *Der König verneigt sich und tötet* (Munich: Hanser, 2003), pp. 7–39.

envisages.[36] Unlike Ransmayr's text, the utopian literary space is thereby less a realm that crowds out or otherwise relativizes contemporary politics by rewriting them on its own aesthetic terms to create a literary heterotopia. Rather, it is a place to get to after working them through, however difficult this process of perception may be. For both Irene and Müller are literary survivors: by combining the painful commemorative mode of authorship with a utopian one that provides multiple grounds for interpretation and action, they hold out for a much more open-ended, inclusive perspective on the future whilst keeping their eyes wide open to the lessons from the past. These modes sustain a model of authorship that is deliberately and demonstratively open to the world even as it also highlights the difficulties of not excluding or looking away.

'Man liest nicht, was der Autor oder der Text ist, sondern was man selbst ist': Felicitas Hoppe's Collaborations Across Time and Space

Hamelin-born Felicitas Hoppe (b. 1960) has been holding textual mirrors up to her readers since the publication of her first collection of short stories, *Picknick der Friseure* (The Hairdressers' Picnic) in 1996. The subsequent novels *Pigafetta* (1999), *Paradiese, Übersee* (2003, Paradises, Overseas), *Johanna* (2006) and *Hoppe* (2012) all use literary techniques to re-cast real and imaginary journeys through real and imaginary worlds, with the implied author reflecting on the contemporary situation of writing literature and re-telling myth through multiple extra-textual winks along the way.[37] In the 2017 biopic, *Felicitas Hoppe sagt* (Felicitas Hoppe Says, dir. Oliver Held & Thomas Henke), Hoppe reflects on this career to date, and in particular on her relationship with her readers, many of whom she claims at least initially believe that the main point of her writing is to confuse them.[38] Where her autofictional *Hoppe* from 2012 was widely hailed by critics as a masterful deconstruction of grand narratives of authorship (and ironically coincided with the award of the prestigious Georg Büchner Prize to its author in the same year), the biopic at first glance appears to offer more straightforward access to

---

[36] Adelson, 'Literary Imagination and the Future of Literary Studies'.
[37] The ubiquity of travel is captured in the title of a 2012 edited volume on her work: Thomas Homscheid & Esbjörn Nyström, eds, *Geschichten des Reisens – Reisen zur Geschichte: Studien zu Felicitas Hoppe* (Uelvesbüll: Der andere Verlag, 2012). Her reference to 'honest inventions' has also been much taken up in the literary criticism and yields the title of a further collection reviewing her work along these lines: Svenja Frank & Julia Ilgner, eds, *Ehrliche Erfindungen: Felicitas Hoppe zwischen Tradition und Transmoderne* (Bielefeld: transcript, 2017)
[38] See her comments at 33'30".

what Hoppe actually thinks about the place she tries to occupy in the world. Yet here too she quickly begins to deflect. 'Man liest nicht, was der Autor oder der Text ist, sondern was man selbst ist', she comments some fifty minutes in (You don't read what the author or the text is, rather what you are yourself). Such deflection plays on the one hand to the Barthesian paradigm of the death of the author, as well as to more recent theories that relativize the author's position within processes of literary reception, notably David Damrosch's rather autonomous system of world literature as a mode of circulation. Such conceptualizations of the dynamics of both literary space and the literature network absolve the author from any particular responsibility for the text's subsequent existence. On the other hand, however, and drawing on how Ransmayr and Müller open up author–reader relations in their textual worlds, we can also hear in Hoppe's observation the ultimate identification of the reader with the author, as they each discover a common purpose in the literary text that echoes Adelson's ideas of the literary imagination as a transformative space for all who engage with it. This is linked to an existential sense of self-discovery through the process of each engaging creatively with the opportunities afforded by the particular time and space of the text, as she expands in the biopic when talking about what happens during her public readings: 'mir scheint, dass nicht ich mich befreien muss [. . .], sondern dass sich das Publikum befreien muss. Also, das Publikum zu sich selbst befreien und ich zu meinem eigenen Werk'[39] (It strikes me that I am not the one who has to free myself, rather the audience needs to free itself. So, free the audience up to itself and me to my own work.)

Such a presentation allows us to move away from either confrontational or hierarchically pedagogical models of author–reader relations and/or engagement across the literary text. Rather than one set of experiences being somehow 'killed off' or otherwise rendered irrelevant by the other, they augment each other as the conventionally understood border between text and world becomes blurred. As Hoppe sets out at length in her 2008 Augsburg lectures, her work explores a literary space that allows wishful thinking and socio-political realities shared by both author and reader to enter into a new kind of relationship, the challenges of which are channelled through paradoxes that run right through the author position. In the context of my study, such an opening up of the authorial persona can be seen as a significant twist on the performances of position-taking enacted by dominant writers across the Cold War period in West and East Germany. Whether these happened primarily in the celebratory, satirical, commemorative or

---

[39] Oliver Held, Thomas Henke, *Felicitas Hoppe sagt*, at *c.* 55'.

utopian mode, the literary performances of Böll, Grass and Enzensberger in the West and Becher, Seghers and Wolf in the East did little to unpick the integral exemplarity of the authorial persona, even as they did much to provoke debate about the place and purpose of literature in the context of numerous broader socio-political phenomena. Accordingly, their twentieth-century aesthetic innovations and attempts at intervening in society were premised on continuing the notions of charisma and personality set out by Max Weber and Goethe before them, which are themselves constituent of modern-day, neoliberal celebrity.

The extent to which Hoppe, by contrast, uses her authorial persona to hold open the impossible and, in so doing, also negate herself and her own writing, is what both aligns her with writers such as Ulrike Draesner and Ulrike Almut Sandig from the late-1990s onwards, and allows her work to do something more than merely reproduce the commodification of all spaces and interpersonal practices as has tended to characterize the work of Kracht, Illies, Goetz and, to a degree, Kehlmann. In fact, as she elaborates upon in her Augsburg lectures and in her later biopic, she consciously writes as part of a much broader 'disappearance' of German language and cultural practices against the background of global English on the one hand and global capitalism on the other. Yet, as the overarching design of the biopic underscores, with its overt stage sets, thespian masks and filmic reflections on being in the world, Hoppe takes her inspiration from the creative challenge of facilitating 'a good death', one that, in effect, opens up multiple perspectives on what German culture is, has been and could be, when seen in dialogue with shared roots from across the late Western literary tradition.[40] In so doing, she makes plastic and spatial a temporal process of positioning. Her interaction with literary history takes the form of creating palimpsestic literary worlds, filled with curious objects, that exist within the contemporary moment and are accessed in various ways by both her characters and her readers and critics.[41] These allow alternative takes on what is important from the past and how it might be woven into a meaningful and perhaps comforting insight for the present and the future, as we all, inevitably, pass. Such marshalling of the distant and impossible with performative force for the here and

---

[40] For discussion of this broader tradition, see Ben Hutchinson, *Lateness and Modern European Literature* (Oxford: Oxford U. P., 2016).

[41] Svenja Frank is particularly insightful on this: 'Ikonisches Erzählen als Einheit von Realität und Imagination: Zum Verhältnis von ästhetischer Reflexion und narrativer Realisation im Werk von Felicitas Hoppe', in Frank & Ilgner, eds, *Ehrliche Erfindungen*, pp. 207–36.

now is the utopian mode of authorship at its most pure. The increasing foregrounding of this mode in writing from across the turn of the millennium maps on to a new model of authorship that has foundational force for the early twenty-first century.

All of Hoppe's oeuvre to date raises questions of access. These are appropriate to the paradoxical notion of utopia as both an inherently desirable, 'good' place and a hermetically sealed, 'no' place, from which we nevertheless hear narrative reports. As compelling literary accounts, these have the rhetorical power to change our world for the better, because, as with More's *Utopia*, they provoke debate around different ways of seeing things. However, where Hoppe's earlier texts mentioned above repeatedly present fluid boundaries between real and imaginary worlds in a distinctly timeless setting and within narrative frames that are often circular or otherwise self-sufficient, her more recent work reflects more explicitly on the processes of creating and inhabiting these hybrid literary worlds in the present.[42] In so doing, she focuses ever more directly on the position of the author and autofictional experimentation. The conclusions that can be drawn from this for our study of authorship shift considerably from *Hoppe*, her first major biographically led work, to *Prawda*, her second. One reason for this may reside in an increasing awareness on her part of embodying not just an example of a particular kind of literary aesthetics or positioning herself in a particular way in the literature network, but potentially invoking a whole new paradigm of authorship.

Published in 2012, *Hoppe* is arguably the culmination of her postmodern literary play – 'arguably' not least because Hoppe herself repeatedly takes her distance from the literary critical assessment of her oeuvre as guided by postmodern tricks. She prefers to stress the extent to which she is guided by folk tales, in themselves highly accessible literary forms, and casts herself as in many ways an heir to the Romantic period of Ludwig Tieck and the Brothers Grimm. Both interpretations of Hoppe as the postmodern and/or Romantic author can be found in this text, which functions as a double autofiction: the biographical facts of Hoppe's childhood in Hamelin are turned into the fiction of the fictionalized Hoppe. This fictional Hoppe is in turn the famous author of Hoppe's work, but endowed with a childhood in Canada and a direct link to the real-life ice-hockey star, Wayne Gretzky. Hoppe has never met Gretzky in real life, nor, it turns out, did she even visit Brantwood,

---

[42] On the idea of self-sufficiency and/or narrative circularity, see Frank, 'Ikonisches Erzählen', and Svenja Frank, 'Inzest und Autor-Imago im Marionettentheater: Zum Identitätskonzept in Felicitas Hoppes *Paradiese, Übersee*, in Michaela Holdenried, ed., *Felicitas Hoppe: Das Werk* (Berlin: Schmidt, 2015), pp. 49–68.

the setting for the shared Canadian childhood of their fictional alter egos, until late 2015, when she was embarked on the journey of literary re-construction that underpins *Prawda*. She has, however, been the real-life focus of critical reviews and scholarship on her work that are quoted extensively in the text – but which are inspired by popular journalism and scholarship rather than direct quotations from them.[43] These reviews are presented as often correct in essence, but, because they do not reference Hoppe's (fictional) Canadian and Australian lives, they are unable to account for the perspectives in her work that, according to this autofictional literary autobiography, stem from these (imaginary) formative years.

With reality and fiction so thickly braided together that the idea of any underlying biographical authorial truth is rendered untraceable, Hoppe draws up at least three different authorial positions for herself in the text. Characteristically for her work, all three are developed simultaneously: the fictionalized autobiographical subject of the narrative, whose early works provide some of the first-person reflection on her life; the ordering, archival, author figure stitching together the resulting text and making meaning of the fictionalized life (intervening, often unnecessarily, in parenthesis as fh); the published author Hoppe, already known to many readers through her actual works and the subject of the largely negative reviewer comments that the real-life author inserts. The published works and the reviewer comments often provide the narrative impetus for relaying events from the fictional Hoppe's childhood in the first place. In fact, where literature, and particularly that of women authors, is often read autobiographically, in this autofiction the inverse is the case: the putative autobiography is guided by Hoppe's pre-existing fiction and its accompanying critical reception, with the result that the (real) fiction writes the (fictional) life. Thus where one (fictional) critic, Reimar Strat, writes despairingly of the way Hoppe manages role-play in *Johanna* and takes particular exception to her use of clothing, fh has prepared the ground for this idiosyncrasy by setting out the fictional Hoppe's love of school uniforms, ice-hockey kit, and internalized role-play, and then linking this more abstractly to a love of pressing content into (literary) form in the preceding paragraphs.[44] More generally, the autofictional Hoppe's thoroughly incredible insistence on having an intact German family in

---

[43] Friederike Eigler provides a very helpful guide to what is real and what is not in this text: '"Könnte nicht alles auch ganz anders sein?" Hoppe zwischen Autofiktion und Metafiktion', in Holdenried, ed., *Felicitas Hoppe*, pp. 145–59.

[44] Felicitas Hoppe, *Hoppe* (Frankfurt a.M.: Fischer, 2012), pp. 166–8.

Hamelin from whom her 'inventor-father' abducted her, repeatedly discredited by fh but returned to throughout the text as the young Hoppe persists in sending unanswered letters to them, is of a piece with the picture painted by literary critical reaction to Hoppe. These voices and judgements are marshalled by fh throughout the text and collectively invoke an author who believes more in her own private invented worlds than anyone else, a writer who is accordingly frequently accused of losing her readers along the way, just as the autofictional Hoppe's letters are all returned unopened. The way in which the autofictional Hoppe's life is presented thereby appears reverse-engineered to support the later assessments that her published works will meet (the joke here being that the family in Hamelin, along with the published works, are the only parts of the text that are biographically 'correct'). Likewise, the motif of Hoppe's socially incongruous rucksack (she insists on wearing it whilst playing ice-hockey and conducting orchestras), the eerie reoccurrence of round tables throughout her travel narratives, and life-changing journeys on ships extend into the early years of her fictional autobiography some of the most obvious symbols from the author's actual published works.

The repeat assessment from the literary establishment that Hoppe's works are impenetrable because of the idiosyncratic way in which she blurs fact and fiction is thus appropriated by the author in order to extrapolate from such a discourse the correct biography, complete with imagined early works and accompanying archival material, to support it. The result is that, to no small extent, the published works and the critical response to them author the autofiction. This is both a radical relativization of the biographical author, and an unchecked celebration of her. For the real-life Hoppe, through the alter ego of the overly fastidious fh who presents herself as just sorting through the materials left by others, is of course ultimately controlling everything and appearing everywhere as the natural(ized) voice of the text, even as she is ostentatiously *not* writing her own biography. As I have charted elsewhere for the careers of both Elfriede Jelinek and Günter Grass, appropriating the voices of your critical detractors can be the ultimate display of individual authorial power within the confines of the text.[45] In the case of Felicitas Hoppe, however, she significantly also turns the implied criticism on its head – where the individual voices rail against her inaccurate use of history, her fanciful creation of characters and her

---

[45] Rebecca Braun, '"Sticks and Stones may break my Bones": The Aesthetic Enactment of Violence in the Work of Elfriede Jelinek', in H. Chambers, ed., *Violence, Culture and Identity in Germany and Austria* (Oxford: Lang, 2006), 343–58; Braun, *Constructing Authorship in the Work of Günter Grass*.

over-determined employment of symbols, the whole thrust of the narrative of *Hoppe* is to extend to the maximum the life lived in literature that total engagement with such a literary space allows. The world that received her authorship becomes the world that writes this authorship into existence in the first place. The fact that she invents her own negative criticism in order to enter all the more fully into that space is entirely consistent with this logic.

Indeed, the fictional literary criticism is in many respects both entry to and exit point from the literary space Hoppe creates, as it represents the process of engaging with her world-making and, in so doing, expressing an analytical sense of how the world exists through language, politics and place. The idea that there might be something odd or otherwise distinct about Hoppe's life in writing is nurtured throughout the text, in both positive and negative ways. This begins with the observation from the fictional Reimar Strat that her German does not appear to be 'today's German', but, as another anonymous critic subsequently suggests, represents 'die Besetzung eines verlorenen literarischen Raums, der keinerlei Schnittmengen mehr mit der Wirklichkeit bildet'[46] (the occupation of a lost literary space that no longer offers any intersections with reality). Fh, however, immediately counters these observations, pointing out 'dass Hoppes "Sonderraum" keineswegs imaginiert, sondern Realität war. [...] Selbstverständlich war Hoppes Deutsch "nicht von heut", besser gesagt, es war "nicht von hier", weil sie selbst nicht von hier, sondern von dort war'[47] (Hoppe's 'special place' was by no means imagined, it was real ... Of course Hoppe's German was 'not from today', or rather, 'not from here', because she herself wasn't from here, but from over there). This is an example not only of the autofiction being designed in such a way as both to stem from and to correct the later literary criticism, but also to assert the particular value of this odd or 'particular' literary space that the autofictional Hoppe has been deliberately designed to carry. Each chapter ends in a veritable tour de force, as the literary worlds the young Hoppe has fashioned merge with the reality (in the autofiction) of her own world, often incorporating key motifs and figures from the published fiction of the reader's real world as they do. Expertly poetically worked, these scenes celebrate the power and form of the literary space to carry a compelling perspective on the world by moulding together multiple sources that permit multiple points of entry into the larger question of what our world means anyway – and

---

[46] Hoppe, *Hoppe*, p. 33.
[47] Hoppe, *Hoppe*, p. 34.

thus chiming with Adelson's argument about the wider potential for social change inherent in literary space.

The young Hoppe's status as a wilful dreamer who seems permanently both out of time and out of place is key to carrying this off, as it makes her the authentic voice of a set of traditions and way of life that is largely inaccessible to contemporary readers: German literature of the late eighteenth and early nineteenth centuries. This point is made forcefully towards the end of the narrative and is directly allied with the celebration of literary space discussed above. In an abandoned biography of her father, Hoppe reflects on their shared German background:

> Denn in Wahrheit ist Deutsch bloß ein literarischer Trick, ein Extra für Schwärmer, für Verliebte, Verlorene, Romantiker, für die letzten Bewohner eines Zwischenraums, den es bald nicht mehr geben wird, für alle, die keinen Plan haben. Weshalb mein Erfindervater mich aus Deutschland entführt hat, um ein neues Leben mit mir zu beginnen, ein einfaches, praktisches, englisches Leben.[48]

> [For in reality German is just a literary trick, an extra for enthusiasts, for lovers, lost souls, romantics, for the last inhabitants of a space in-between that will soon no longer exist, for everyone who has no plan. Which is why my inventor-father abducted me from Germany, in order to start a new life with me, a simple, practical, English life.]

This alignment of German literary culture with an impractical space that is under threat – in Foucault's terms, possibly a heterotopia in decline, like the nineteenth-century boarding school – resonates powerfully across the text as a whole. From the contemporary North-American-led perspective of global English and global capitalism, the Central European literary tradition of knights' romances, the folk tales collected by Hans Christian Andersen and the Grimm Brothers, and tales of seafaring adventures on which her oeuvre has built seem all the more 'not from today' and 'not from here' than in the published Hoppe's German context. Yet *Hoppe* shows precisely how wedging the author into a literary space *between* the German and the Anglophone traditions of language and sport, fairy tales and jazz, culture and infrastructure, Romanticism and postmodernism, can change the way we see the world, and thus where and what we want the world to be. The 'Zwischenraum' or 'space in-between' of literature, complete with a

---

[48] Hoppe, *Hoppe*, p. 288.

certain postmodern impossibility, can still be championed as a Goethean response to the emergence of global trade some two hundred years ago. Indeed, one of her hostile fictional critics, Kai Rost, is reportedly driven to declare 'eine unverbesserlichere Romantikerin werden wir in der Postmoderne kaum finden'[49] (postmodernism will hardly yield us a more incorrigible Romantic) before wishing he could chat to Hoppe in a bar or cycle with her through provincial Germany. With this, he readily enters into the utopian literary space Hoppe has managed to hold open, even as the real biographical author has had to disappear from her text in a thoroughly postmodern gesture. For, underscoring my points on multiple levels, both the biographical author and her autofictional double have disappeared by the end of the text in order to allow the published literature, with its distinctly Romantic utopian space, to stand on its own.[50] Hoppe leaves her box of manuscripts with the tellingly named Hans Herman Haman, before walking out of the text altogether, apparently to re-join the biographical Hoppe's siblings. In the narrative, Haman is a professor of German literature in Oregon but surely also a reference to the counter-Enlightenment philosopher of language, Johann Georg Hamann (1730–1788), whose ideas would carry on to influence Goethe's age.

The idea that Hoppe finds an ally in Goethe and some of the underpinning ideas about language, truth, and literary perspective from his era gains even more explicit support in Hoppe's subsequent autofictional work, *Prawda*. 'Pravda' is the Russian for truth, in terms of true facts / a knowable truth (as opposed to 'istina', a more abstract form of veracity), and it is also the name of the main Soviet Communist newspaper that was in continuous print from 1917 to 1991. In 1935, the newspaper sponsored two satirical writers, Ilja Ilf and Jewgeni Petrow, to do a four-month round-trip across the United States along with a Russian émigré engineer, Salomon Trone, who worked for General Electric, and his American wife. On completion of their trip they wrote a book about their experiences that sits ambiguously between communist and capitalist ideologies and readily sacrifices historical truth for a good story. In 2011, Die andere Bibliothek (The Other Library), the publishing company founded by Hans Magnus Enzensberger, made the Russian text available in German as *Das eingeschossige Amerika* (literally, one-storied / bungalowed America).[51] This was accompanied by a foreword from none other than Felicitas

---

[49] Hoppe, *Hoppe*, p. 295.
[50] On Hoppe's engagement with the Romantic period throughout her work up to and including Hoppe, see Frank, 'Inzest und Autor-Imago'.
[51] The published English title from 1944 is *Little Golden America*.

Hoppe that probes questions of perspective, belief and ideology, fact and fiction, as they apply both then and now.[52] In 2015, inspired by this engagement with the text and eighty years after the original, Hoppe then repeats the journey in her own team of four, sponsored by the North American Goethe Institutes and the Villa Aurora, another German cultural institute in Los Angeles. As the project's accompanying website www.3668ilfpetrow.com records, Hoppe checks in along the way to multiple Goethe Institutes and delivers readings, interviews and updates on her group's travels that enjoy further dissemination through 'Radio Goethe', as well as her own project's website.

Referring to both the state-funded institution that takes care of the logistics of her literary journey and a multi-media form of dissemination, 'Goethe' thus readily becomes a shorthand for the distinct literature network that Hoppe both experiences as she travels in real time and subsequently further creates as a literary space in her book. To underscore the point, she refers to herself on numerous occasions as 'Frau Eckermann', writing herself into the position of Goethe's partner in conversation and subsequent famous diarist. This is to be understood as part of her broader strategy of self-fictionalization that makes the text into much more than a straightforward travel narrative or set of sociopolitical observations from a well-known author.[53] The appellation first comes as part of her own disparaging reference to herself as someone who is merely jumping on the bandwagon of the literary greatness of others, but it is subsequently taken up and thrown back out to her as something of a refrain throughout the narrative (e.g. 'vergessen Sie eins nicht, Frau Eckermann; now don't forget this, Frau Eckermann).[54] In this, Hoppe's text mimics that of Ilf and Petrow, in which Solomon Trone's fictional alter ego of Mr Adams refers to the pair of writers throughout as 'gentlemen', often in the imperative, and not infrequently when he is challenging them to note or comment on particularly American phenomena. While Hoppe's text retains that sense of challenge to what is written, and how – and repeatedly also employs the refrain, 'schreiben Sie das in Ihre Notizbücher, Gentlemen'[55] (write

---

[52] This is reproduced in a shortened and lightly revised form on the project website: "Kolumbus geht an Land', http://www.3668ilfpetrow.com/1935/das-eingeschossige-amerika (last accessed 17 July 2018).

[53] For some further reflection on what Hoppe may or may not be trying to achieve by muddying genres in this text, see Stephanie Obermeier, '"Im beweglichen Umgang mit den störrischen Fakten": Attitudes to Genre in Felicitas Hoppe's *Prawda: Eine amerikanische Reise*', *German Life & Letters*, 72.3 (2019), 378–98.

[54] Felicitas Hoppe, *Prawda: Eine amerikanische Reise* (Frankfurt a.M.: Fischer, 2018), p. 20, p. 28.

[55] Hoppe, *Prawda*, e.g. p. 11, p. 29, p. 60.

that in your notebooks, gentlemen) – this challenge is distinctly more disembodied. Not only is it impossible to trace the interpolations to 'Frau Eckermann' and 'gentlemen' back to any single speaker beyond a generic voice of the text, the whole assembly of the group is portrayed as following some higher-level orders: 'Denn jemand hat uns erkannt, jemand hat uns gerufen, irgendjemand hat uns für die nächsten sechs Wochen beurlaubt, um einen rubinroten Ford zu besteigen und zwei Russen zu folgen'[56] (for somebody recognized us, somebody called us, somebody somewhere gave us leave for the next six weeks to get into a ruby red Ford and follow two Russians), states the text simply on the question of how they all came to be together. Demoting herself to the status of a modest scribe within this constellation, Hoppe further reliably retreats to her 'Tocquevilleerker', or 'Tocqueville corner' in the Ford. Playfully named after the French diplomat and historian, Alexis de Tocqueville (1805–1859), her seat in the car where she has the least responsibility for guiding the party represents a physical space which she has been officially given leave to occupy by a higher authority for two months, just as Tocqueville was released from his ministerial duties to travel around America for nine months in 1831. This included a side-trip to Canada that Hoppe also adds in, knowingly following in both his footsteps and her own, as she finally visits the Brantford and Walter Gretzky she had evoked in *Hoppe*, and thereby mingles historical and literary journeys even further.

Nestled out of sight directly behind the driver, Hoppe thereby travels with Goethe, in Tocqueville's place, impersonating Eckermann, and following Ilf and Petrow as part of a creative design that denies any one point of origin. She manages all of these literary identities in such a way as to justify her tendency to re-make the world around her through imaginative flights of fancy in order to see more and engage with history differently than merely following the facts and sights pointed out by their guide. The implausibly named MsAnnAdams is the fourth member of the group, a stereotypically no-nonsense Austrian-born professor of German and the decidedly straitlaced alter-ego of Professor Ulrike Rainer, who is listed on the website as the third benefactor of the trip. She will find herself repeatedly outwitted by the three creative members of the group but is ultimately chiefly responsible for bringing them all safely back to their point of departure.

This ostentatiously diverse structure of authority and responsibility across the group and indeed the project as a whole is the key departure from the logic underpinning Hoppe's earlier works up to, and including, *Hoppe*. For although novels like *Johanna*, *Pigafetta* and *Paradiese, Übersee*

---

[56] Hoppe, *Prawda*, p. 26.

carry out a similar kind of re-mapping of real and imaginary motifs and journeys popularized by others, they ultimately all point to the author as both their point of origin and their ultimate signification. The satisfaction of reading *Paradiese, Übersee*, for example, rests on understanding the contents of a note that the author does not disclose to both the reader and the first-person narrator until the last line, while *Johanna* sets up an opposition between historiography and literature that is most readily decoded through Hoppe's numerous statements elsewhere on the topic. *Hoppe* is the outrageous culmination of this tendency. Here, every position in the text, and any that could be taken in response to it, is already occupied by the author, such that reading the text becomes a wholly immersive experience in being the author Hoppe – with the important qualification that of course nothing within the text is actually Hoppe at all, and this is also made clear, by Hoppe.[57] *Prawda*, by contrast, opens up authorship to the reader in a fundamentally different way, as it sets about making the phenomenon tangible. Returning to the Romantic period even as she apparently sets herself in dialogue with twentieth-century political satirists, Hoppe finds an alternative model of authorship. This is precisely not what unfolds within the literature network around an individual that exemplifies, celebrates, and/or commemorates in line with normative post-war values, but a more utopian-driven mode of collaboration that goes significantly beyond one geopolitical or chronologically bounded frame. Her principle model for this is Goethe.

This should only be initially surprising. For, as Andrew Piper argues compellingly, Goethe had already in the early nineteenth century configured the literary space made available through novel writing to be much larger than just what appears in black and white in the printed book, effectively drawing a large part of his literature network into the actual text. His *Wilhelm Meisters Wanderjahre* (1821, *Wilhelm Meister's Travels*), for example, is fed by multiple publications and presents multiple networks, both material and intellectual, that are constituted in and around recording and sharing stories. Indeed, in 1832, Goethe was moved to comment that he had become so omnipresent in contemporary thought and culture, and his work so vast, that his oeuvre might best be understood as 'that of a collective being who bears the name Goethe'. Such a statement hovers on the cusp between total

---

[57] Antonius Weixler writes very much in this vein, stressing how in 'de-authorising' her own authority across the text, Hoppe writes the authentic biography of her authorial persona: '"Dass man mich nie für vermisst erklärt hat, obwohl ich seit Jahren verschollen bin": Autorschaft, Autorität und Authentizität in Felicitas Hoppe', in Frank & Ilgner, eds, *Ehrliche Erfindungen*, pp. 359–88.

self-aggrandizement and absolute humility.[58] Literally given an authorial voice and means of dissemination by the material and media support of the Goethe Institute, Hoppe's text has a similarly diverse set of sources and tributaries. It incorporates passages from Ilf and Petrow's book, stories from contemporary America about both the present and the past relayed to the group as they recreate the Russian journey, as well as flights into fiction, such as when Hoppe claims to be carried off by a tornado and parts company from the rest of the group for several days. Like Goethe's text, parts of it are published elsewhere – on the website or relayed in interviews and readings held at the Goethe Institutes. And just as Goethe's interests ranged well beyond the linguistic component of creative practice to include visual and scientific representations as well as material culture, the expertise of two of the other group members – Foma's background in landscape gardening and Jerry's study of photography – inform not just the kinds of exchanges that they will have along the way, but also, in the work of the real-life plastic artist Alexej Meschtschanow and photographer Jana Müller, the accompanying outputs from the project. These notably include an exhibition inspired by their travels, entitled 'Europa verlassen / Leaving Europe', which is featured on the project's website as well as having been physically displayed for a time in Germany.

Embracing multiplicity of time and place does not, however, map onto creating a totally unfettered text. Despite its multiple literary intertexts and deliberate creation of literary spaces that are both marked out as such in the book and go significantly beyond the book in the form of open-ended exchanges and encounters across continents supported by digital media, *Prawda* stands out for being rooted in the political reality of twentieth- and twenty-first-century global capitalism. Hoppe's tendency to escape into tangential worlds that open up alongside their real journey, while never less than entertaining, is held in check by acknowledging the parameters of this journey and repeatedly returning to them. Thus, for example, she will both wilfully turn Ford factory workers into imaginary swallows that fly up from the factory floor to send her hidden signs, and at the same time point to the realities of blue collar workers trying to retain their dignity in a system that mechanizes the service industry and wears people out like replaceable spare parts.

Given the underlying commitment to real people acting in real time, both in 1935 and 2015, it is worth pausing over the broader network

---

[58] Piper provides a stunning reading of how to move from the former to the latter when interpreting Goethe's work and broader significance for our understanding of Romantic authorship: *Dreaming in Books: The Making of the Bibliographic Imagination in the Romantic Age* (Chicago: U. of Chicago P., 2009), pp. 21–52.

After the Death of the Author 227

that can be immediately traced within and around the self-confessedly literary space staked out by Hoppe's project. The team's activities at the time are captured photographically as part of a blog and dedicated web space that was set up by the German Goethe Institute: http://blog.goethe.de/little-golden-america-revisited/. This (now defunct) site makes available a wealth of material about the trip which Hoppe shared as she travelled – alongside transcripts from interviews she gave at the Goethe Institutes, a brief blog reports on each stage of the journey, accompanied by photographs of both the team travelling today and of the historic journey undertaken by Ilf and Petrow. While this site is primarily a historic record, put together at the time and not updated since, the dedicated website http://www.3668ilfpetrow.com uses some of this material, but as part of an 'ongoing' project (the English word is used in the top banner, demarcating the contemporary project materials from those of the 1935 archive; figure 5.1). The web domain is officially copyrighted to Hoppe herself, although she elsewhere refers to the

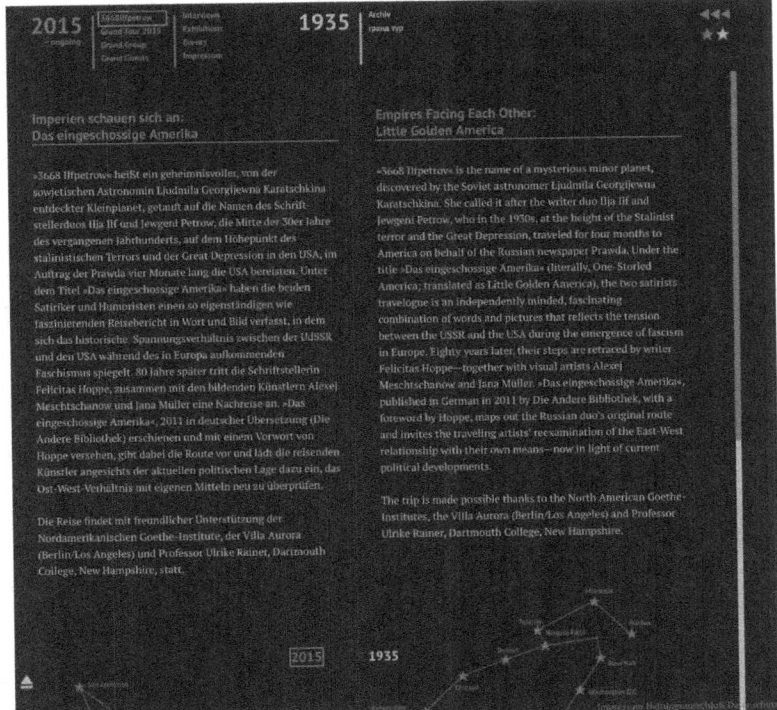

Figure 5.1 Main home page of the website www.3668ilfpetrow.com. Reproduced courtesy of Daniela Weirich and Felicitas Hoppe.

website managers.[59] The main difference between it and the Goethe blog is the significantly greater space made available to show not just the work of the other people involved in both journeys (including Russian and German-language excerpts from Ilf and Petrow's work, as well as pictures of the accompanying installation artist's resultant exhibition in 2017), but also to re-present the travel blog as guided far less by people and more by objects and concepts that are inspired by both everyday and literary culture. This is achieved by including many more photographs of things encountered along the way (drawing on the work of the accompanying photographer), as well as interspersing throughout the extended, at times bilingual, prose travelogue spontaneous poems and hyperlinks to local newspapers or points of information thrown up by the journey (figure 5.2).

This second website scopes out a far larger network than the first by focusing much less on the sponsored author and her set of practices and experiences, and much more on what the whole venture itself has to tell. In this, it could be seen as a twist on Ransmayr's literary heterotopia: it is a really-existing reflection of the world but held within the binary code of the internet and with no commitment to yielding any overarching meaning from its disparate parts. Significantly, 'Empires Facing Each Other' is the title introducing its home page, as if the West and East themselves are being held in static opposition through the diverse material signs of their cultural and political history that the troupe of travelling authors, artists, and academics have been able to record, from 1935 to the present. The website's name – 3668ilfpetrow – is the name given to the distant planet that was discovered by a Soviet astronomer and deliberately named after the literary duo. This therefore further spins the seemingly known world encapsulated in the website away from our own. It underscores the notion that, as we proceed from the (space-themed) landing page through to the rest of the site, we are accessing a different realm; one that really does exist and which shares in encapsulated form all the core elements of the known world outside it, but which will nevertheless make us feel different and reflect differently on our world as a result (figure 5.3)

Extending the utopian mode of authorship from the literary text through to the website, Hoppe thus replays the kind of textual self-reflexivity we discerned in Ransmayr. However, the different affordances of the media involved – the internet compared to the book – spin the results in a markedly different direction. Where Ransmayr's literary heterotopia folds in on itself to become a literary pedagogical message about reading and writing and effectively consuming both reader and

---

[59] In the acknowledgements of *Prawda* she thanks 'den Betreibern von 3668. Ilfpetrow.com'.

After the Death of the Author 229

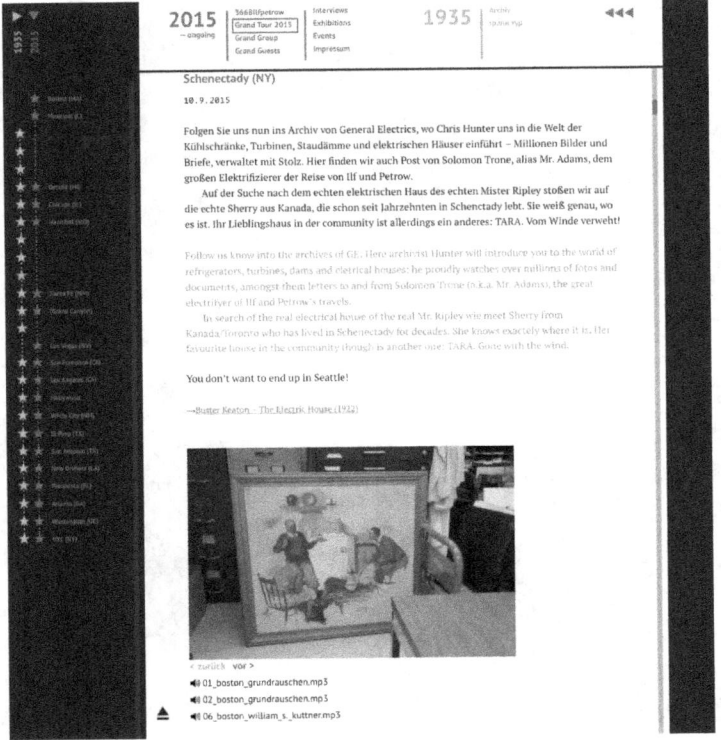

Figure 5.2 Detail from the multi-media blog on www.3668ilfpetrow.com, including a photograph by Jana Müller. Reproduced courtesy of Jana Müller and Felicitas Hoppe.

author in its textual fabric as it does so, Hoppe's internet heterotopia opens ever outwards. In this, it develops Müller's cautious hope in connecting up objects and perspectives differently into a confident and highly generative, really-existing bank of resources. It not only spins out diverse creative outputs – *Prawda* the book, the art exhibition, photography, diary entries, newspaper reports, blogs – it is also at pains to make time-bending, place-shifting dialogue and exchange into its founding mode. The build of the website emphasizes timelines and geographies in such a way that the user is encouraged to shuttle back and forth between them, collapsing realms onto one another in a way that is not possible in real life but is wholly the terrain of literary texts. Clicking on the 'Grand Tour 2015' tab, for instance, takes the reader to a blog that merrily mixes extracts from Ilf and Petrow's text, photographs taken on the road in 2015, North American newspaper headlines, extracts from *Hoppe*, diary entries, links to other websites, and poetry by others

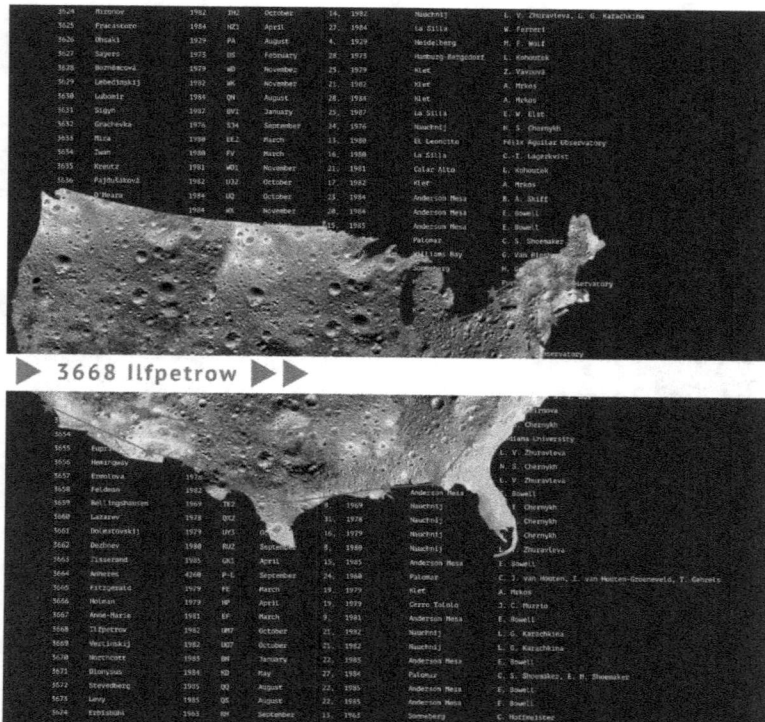

Figure 5.3 Landing page of the website www.3668ilfpetrow.com. Reproduced courtesy of Daniela Weirich and Felicitas Hoppe.

that are in one way or another relevant to the trip. Unlike in Ransmayr's text, however, there is no danger of disappearing and, unlike in Müller's text, objects do not evoke a traumatic or otherwise destabilizing past that might knock either author or reader substantially off course. Rather, multiple authors have created their work in dialogue with many other people and things; each web user remains in control of how she interacts with the different components, each time creating her own journey through the material and piecing it together as her interests dictate. There is not one compelling text to weave any more, but rather multiple different threads to pick up that belong to multiple different worlds.

Staying Alive

In her 2017 biopic, Hoppe proposes that one of her motivations for writing might be to help both people and the German language 'die well'. Although it is tempting to equate her comments on authorship and death with statements from Barthes and Foucault about the individual subject slipping away within the post-structuralist text, such a reading loses sight of her commitment to sharing something meaningful with her readers. With some affinities to Heinrich Böll's search in 1964 for ways of making Germany 'inhabitable' in and through its literature, her *Sieben Schätze* (Seven Treasures) lecture series from 2008 stresses that literature allows us to know well because the approach to knowledge that it offers is profoundly different to the empirical approaches underpinning scientific and historical research. Literary space, with its often multiple worlds and clashing perspectives and chronology, can appear a logical impossibility in the time–space continuum of conventional research, yet it does allow both subjective and objective experiences and connections between people and things to be explored in ways that are not preconditioned by their assumed position within time and space. Furthermore, precisely because it cannot be reduced to facts and figures that support any clear overarching causality, the literary space into which Hoppe invites her readers naturally does not lend itself to the commodity fetishism of first capitalism and then neoliberalism. Nor indeed can it be directly grafted onto any one ideological model of positioning individuals within a certain social structure or understanding their experiences solely as part of a particular historical constellation, as was common in Germany's post-war period. It favours instead the surprise of finding our lives brought into dialogue with those from very different places and times, and this happens through associative chains of objects and circumstances that we might not expect.

As the idea of individual authorial exemplarity thereby becomes ever more relativized, Hoppe's texts take their distance from the celebratory and commemorative modes of authorship, but they do not lose sight of them entirely. The satirical way in which her own authorial persona is deconstructed and reconstructed through past models of literary greatness, not least Goethe himself, in fact urges readers to reflect back on what is worth preserving from German culture for use in their own lives and, when it comes to it, deaths. In so doing, assumptions around the individual writer's authority in and ownership of this culture are clearly being broken down. The website that accompanies the *Prawda* project literally makes this orientation towards an expanded, more deliberately egalitarian authorship tangible, as it embeds Hoppe's German text into a network of other sources, each of which point as much away from her writing as towards it.

The new adaptation of the utopian mode of authorship that we have already seen partially unfolding in Ransmayr's and Müller's work thus gains ever more in contour. Echoed in the work of other authors since the turn of the millennium such as Ulrike Almut Sandig, Ulrike Draesner and the three Ingeborg Bachmann prize-winning authors discussed in my next chapter, this new, oftentimes multi-media adaptation of the utopian mode is increasingly clearly underpinning a new foundational model of authorship that we might tentatively call the transnational model of authorship. The trend is towards opening up both real and imagined networks to be more deliberately inclusive as the old post-war world orders shift around the late twentieth- and early twenty-first-century experience of being in the world. In all three cases discussed here, a clear sense of what an author is and how he or she might be positioned in respect of the wider world is present. At the same time, it is also actively undone by the distinctly literary space of each text, as the protagonists use language and literary traditions to question where power and authority are held, both within the text and within the world. In each case, a dialogic dispersal of authorship across, at the very least, author, readers, significant objects and geographical locations, is the result. True to the etymology of 'utopia', the author figure is accordingly both everywhere and nowhere and points to both a 'good' life and 'no' life in the space of the literary text, as other perspectives on both literature and the world with which it engages – what these are and why they matter – come to prevail within it. Pursued to this kind of paradoxical extreme, such a positioning of authorship can no longer serve an exemplary function in the manner of the earlier models that played on notions of placeness and placelessness that were put forward by Seghers or Grass and harnessed more directly to a celebratory and/or commemorative mode. The life and death of the authorship in evidence within the space of these literary texts is simply too ambiguous to carry this kind of pedagogical brief for society.

However, where the earlier expansion of authorship across multiple narrators (Grass) or peer groups (Seghers) always also pointed back to the heroism of the individual author taking a stance against the odds and coordinating the impossible whole in a way that ended up being exclusive, these recent iterations of authorship both within and around the literary text allow for new ethical directions that explicitly require inclusivity and cut across conventional notions of 'Germanness'. Because it is more self-effacing, the kind of authorship pursued by Ransmayr, Müller and Hoppe is more inherently interested in profiling different voices, experiences and materials from alternative times and places. This in itself can carry significant political weight. My final chapter and the appended conversations further explores the significance of this, both in terms of what gets written in the very contemporary moment and how the German literature network has evolved to support different models of authorship. Specifically, I ask whether a more open-ended and inclusive model of transnational authorship has finally helped German-language literature break out of the national frame – the move Goethe so boldly proclaimed was on the cusp of happening almost two hundred years ago.

Six New Collaborations: Models of Transnational Authorship in Contemporary German-speaking Europe

The transnational as both a socio-economic and a cultural phenomenon has been debated across a range of cognate disciplines since the turn of the millennium. Studies of transnationalism have branched out from primarily economic understandings of contemporary global trade to include intercultural encounters happening at scale that are linked to experiences of mass migration in an uncertain world order affected by growing global inequalities and climate change.[1] My interest in the transnational is less directly political. As I argue with Benedict Schofield, if 'trans' is glossed as meaning 'across, through, between, before and beyond', then the 'transnational' is premised on multiple conceptual paradoxes that must be held in view: it presumes the ongoing significance of the nation, but it also goes beyond that concept. Historically speaking, German transnational experiences pre-date the political formation of a nation state even as they also post-date it now. And although the German language has for many centuries been a form of shorthand for defining the German nation, a wealth of very different speaker experiences lies behind this apparent linguistic uniformity, linking German-language lives and cultures to many different other ones around the world.[2] The transnational, then, inherently opens up a trans-period and trans-lingual approach to capturing the wider significance of cultural activity even as it also encourages us to think about both the challenges and opportunities of contemporary globalization. In this very dispersal across multiple time periods and speaker positions, as well as in the

---

[1] For examples of the former see Stephen Vertovec, *Transnationalism* (London and New York: Routledge, 2009). On the latter, see Stuart Taberner, *Transnationalism and German-Language Literature in the Twenty-First Century* (Basingstoke: Palgrave Macmillan: 2017)

[2] Rebecca Braun & Benedict Schofield, eds, *Transnational German Studies* (Liverpool: Liverpoool U. P., 2020).

fundamental conceptual incompatibility of being both in and beyond the national frame at the same time, the transnational is a natural ally of the utopian mode of authorship.

The significance of these paradoxical conceptual positionings for how authorship plays out in the world can be grasped through the attempts made by the Austrian city of Klagenfurt, the place of Ingeborg Bachmann's birth, to capitalize on the author's literary legacy as both an Austrian writer and more broadly a canonical figure in the German literature network. Bachmann's own well-documented dislike of the small, provincial city, as well as the fact that she spent much of her creative life outside of Austria altogether, have made little to no impression on either local cultural politics or the machinations of the wider literary industry in Austria, which remain determined to celebrate the author as a spearhead for its cultural capital and associated tourism activities.[3] The clearest example of this is the state-funded Ingeborg Bachmann Prize, which has been annually awarded in Klagenfurt as the culmination of a three-day literary competition open to public spectatorship since 1977. Although the three-day competition is officially marketed as the 'Days of German-Language Literature' and includes other smaller prizes with their own sponsors, Bachmann is the event's main 'brand' with serious money and multiple vested interests attached to it, as even a cursory glance at the festival website, run through the TV channel ORF, shows.[4] That Bachmann's name carries wider emotional cultural value as well was shown when ORF threatened to pull its support for the prize (which requires a total annual budget of about €750,000) in response to cuts to its funding in 2013. This triggered the Austrian Chancellor, Werner Feymann, to reassure the public that the prize would continue to exist.

The annual media focus on Klagenfurt that inevitably results from such a significant media investment in the prize thus repeatedly re-inserts one of the country's most famous non-resident authors into her native place of memory in the Austrian provinces as a matter of national pride and part of a broader narrative about Austrian literature and culture. This happens in spite – or perhaps precisely because – of

---

[3] See also, Frauke Meyer-Gosau's popular book, *Einmal muss das Fest ja kommen: Eine Reise zu Ingeborg Bachmann* (2008) that also structures its narrative around the act of seeking an author in a place. For an in-depth discussion of how Bachmann's authorial persona has been re-created in TV portrayals linked to German and Austrian cultural politics, see Rebecca Braun, 'Wandelnde Mythen: Zur populären Darstellung Ingeborg Bachmanns und der Gruppe 47', in W. Hemecker & M. Mittermayer, eds, *Mythos Bachmann: Zwischen Inszenierung und Selbstinszenierung* (Vienna: Zsolnay, 2011), pp. 110–30.
[4] https://bachmannpreis.orf.at/ (last accessed 19 July 2019).

the fact that the Bachmann Prize was conceived as a direct successor to the Gruppe 47 Prize, the only other German-language literary prize to have enshrined live competition in its award structure and directly linked to the foundational model of authorship that would take hold in West Germany (and which Bachmann also famously won in 1953). Accordingly, the Bachmann Prize has become the most open manifestation of a shared competitive German-language literature network with fuzzy national boundaries and where considerable economic and symbolic capital is at stake. With the large German publishing houses of Suhrkamp, Piper, Fischer, Hanser and Rowohlt often the most immediate beneficiaries of this national Austrian event, the extent to which diverse national, cultural, economic and political interests are entangled in the exemplary use made of one author is particularly apparent.[5]

As we have already seen in chapter four, such systematic multi-modal appropriation of an author for regional and national identity politics has its wellsprings in the increasingly media-friendly literary sector in West Germany of the later 1960s and 1970s, and it unfolds both alongside and at least partly at odds with writers' own attempts to stake out an intellectual space for literature and themselves as producers of this literature that is not beholden to contemporary geopolitical boundaries. Neither the phenomenon nor the paradox it entails is in itself new to my examination of the evolving contexts of German-language authorship. Unlike the ritualistic celebratory and commemorative appropriations of Goethe, Thomas Mann and the Gruppe 47 in East and West Germany, however, Bachmann is more resistant to being directly incorporated into normative narratives about a region's cultural landscape. While much of her poetic work revolves around haunting evocations of non-specific places and apodictic statements tinged with the universal, her prose work focuses on extended metaphors of physical not-belonging and ideological exclusion from society. Common to both, and in contrast to the otherwise similar case of Christa Wolf explored in chapter three, is a difficulty in pinning down any definitive authorial standpoint, either within or surrounding the work. Where Wolf encourages associations to be drawn between herself and her characters and codes instructions into her texts as to how they should be read, Bachmann deliberately obscures the gender of the majority of her lyric subjects and uses symbolic structures across her prose writing that encourage multiple readings. The immediate result in Bachmann's lifetime was that her writing was

---

[5] For extensive discussion of the prize in these broader terms, see Doris Moser, *Der Ingeborg-Bachmann-Preis: Börse, Show, Event* (Vienna: Böhlau, 2004).

attributed quasi-visionary power, as it seemed to come from somewhere beyond any one obvious biography, such that the author was quickly mythologized in contradictory ways, and at times even equated with the German language itself, attractively packaged for broad consumption.[6]

The result of Bachmann's ubiquity as both a famous twentieth-century female author and a place-bound, institutionalized way of valuing literary aesthetics is that later authors with a similar interest in pushing at the norms of German literature, particularly if they also have a biography that goes beyond the straightforward (West) German norm, are very likely to find themselves incorporated into such frames of reference. As I shall argue below, however, none of the authors who find themselves more or less directly cast in Bachmann's mould are interested in re-creating either her authorial mystique or the content of her work, elegiacally or otherwise, for their readerships. Yet while they do not tend her legacy in any literal sense, they often do operate within a particular space for a more inclusive model of authorship that her work helped open up. In particular, they exemplify an openness towards reconsidering how much agency non-human actors may exert within the process of authorship – the language that underpins it, the places in which it unfolds, the objects that give it tangible shape and form – and therefore promote a distinctly relative understanding of their own agency within the broader literature network: ways of being both central and marginal at the same time. This relativization of individual authorship continues the observations I made about Christoph Ransmayr, Herta Müller and Felicitas Hoppe's use of the inherently dialogic utopian mode in chapter five. Spreading amongst diverse groupings of authors from the mid-1990s onwards, a move towards dispersing authorship across multiple forms, media and transnational relationships has led to a shift in literary practice, as particularly women and minority authors have sought to prise open where and how they can relate to the world through writing. The resulting places and practices of authorship that have asserted themselves ever more clearly in the second decade of the twenty-first century act as a counterweight of sorts to the stifling normative

---

[6] For extended consideration on this both during and after Bachmann's life, see Karen Leeder, 'Ingeborg Bachmann as Poet and Myth: A Case Study in Cultural Impact', in Rebecca Braun and Lyn Marven, eds, *Cultural Impact in the German Context: Studies in Transmission, Reception, and Influence* (Rochester, NY: Camden House, 2010), pp. 260–77. Also Constance Hotz, *"Die Bachmann": Das Image der Dichterin: Ingeborg Bachmann im journalistischen Diskurs* (Konstanz: Faude, 1990).

structures in which post-war German publishing had become ossified by the mid-1990s.

This chapter accordingly considers and significantly broadens out the ongoing legacy of an iconic female author whose own literature networks extended from Berlin to the Black Sea and from Vienna to Venice, whose work ranged across multiple media (notably incorporating music and musical structures into prose writing as well as radio plays), and whose modes of authorship routinely tinged the commemorative with the satirical and the celebratory with the utopian in striking combinations. My emphasis is not, however, on Bachmann and her work directly – these have been amply studied elsewhere and my modes can be readily applied to the excellent readings of her texts offered by, for example, Sigrid Weigel, Georgina Paul, Sara Lennox and Katja Krylova.[7] Rather, I wish to give space to the contemporary authors from across Germany and Central Eastern Europe who have been incorporated into the dominant German literature network of the twenty-first century, but whose work gains a particular contour when it is examined for the way in which it also puts the dynamics of this network into question. This location both in the literary mainstream and on its margins, both in the German language and beyond it, is one that Bachmann particularly cultivated in her work, and it is in developing this model of co-location at both the centre and the periphery, rather than presenting a certain authorial posture, erecting a physical monument or enacting a media ritual to the world, that her legacy is most meaningfully tended. In this sense, her work and person serve as a base reference point for an emerging model of transnational authorship, one that goes both through and beyond questions of the German cultural canon and develops particular means, both practical and poetic, to do so.

In what follows, I therefore set out how the work of three recent female Bachmann prize laureates, Maja Haderlap (born in 1961 in Slovenian-speaking Carinthia, Austria), Olga Martynova (born in 1962 in Russia, moved to Germany in 1991) and Katja Petrowskaja (born in 1970 in Ukraine, moved to Germany in 1999), can be read as part of a wider movement towards profiling a diversity of experience in and

---

[7] Sigrid Weigel, *Ingeborg Bachmann: Hinterlassenschaften unter Wahrung des Briefgeheimnisses* (Munich: DTV, 2003); Georgina Paul, *Perspectives on Gender in Post-1945 German Literature* (Rochester, NY: Camden House, 2009); Sara Lennox, *Cemetery of the Murdered Daughters: Feminism, History, and Ingeborg Bachmann* (Amherst, Boston: U of Massachusetts P, 2006); Katya Krylova, *Walking through History: Topography and Identity in the Works of Ingeborg Bachmann and Thomas Bernhard* (Oxford: Lang, 2013).

through German literature that both builds on and shifts how the core modes of authorship function within well-established textual forms. In the subsequent section I then broaden my discussion to reflect on the insights provided by the three conversations, with Ulrike Draesner (b. 1965), Ulrike Almut Sandig (b. 1979) and Olga Martynova, reproduced after this chapter. These conversations, held in the summer of 2019, actively demonstrate how differently calibrated models of authorship to those seen in chapter four are being developed both in conventional literary forms and in new collaborative undertakings – in some cases circumventing from within some of the core problems that have hitherto determined the dynamics of German literature. The necessary purchase for this comes from a continuing turn towards the utopian mode that goes hand in glove with an emergent model of transnational authorship for the twenty-first century.

Ghostings: On Commemorating What Cannot be Heard and Celebrating What Cannot be Seen

Maja Haderlap, Olga Martynova and Katja Petrowskaja were each brought to wider public attention when they won the Ingeborg Bachmann Prize in 2011, 2012 and 2013 respectively. Each author shares with the prize's namesake a biography that embraces multilingualism, multiple border crossings and a textual aesthetics that routinely experiments with literary space, this latter as understood in the terms developed in my previous chapter. Each has in many ways been 'brought into' German-language literature through the institutional structures of the celebratory prize mechanism, with the result that collectively they also stand for a kind of authorship that foregrounds the view from beyond the German language and narrowly German postwar experiences.[8] From a historical West German perspective, these authors represent a starting position of placelessness in the extreme. The question of how they both make this into a feature of writing as well as the way they position themselves in quite practical terms within the German-language literature network therefore logically determines the model of authorship they can enact. Indeed, as I will go on to show in depth, all three of the authors reflect on how to tell socially meaningful stories in a world that is characterized by too much – too much

---

[8] On the vocabulary used around writers who take up German as a second language or otherwise make their way into the German canon with a migration background, see Dirk Weissmann, 'German Writers from Abroad: Translingualism, Hybrid Languages, "Broken Germans"', in Rebecca Braun & Benedict Schofield, *Transnational German Studies* (Liverpool: Liverpool U. P., 2020), pp. 57–76.

history, too many connections, too many voices clamouring to be heard. Against this background, their concern is to give a voice to the lives and things that have tended to get drowned out or gone unnoticed, and they do so by marshalling the innate ability of the literary text to hold multiple intangible things in view. In so doing, the utopian mode of authorship is harnessed to a critical reconsideration of how dominant celebratory and commemorative modes have unfolded up to now and how they should be oriented for the future.

Haderlap, winner of the 2011 prize, reflects on the challenges of multiple places and languages directly in her work. *Engel des Vergessens* (2011, Angel of Forgetting) deliberately stakes out the 'no-man's-land' traversed by an aspiring author who has grown up in Slovenian-speaking Carinthia in Austria in terms that emphasize the hiding and silence imposed by the dominant social structures upon minorities who might challenge or otherwise qualify normative post-war memory narratives:

> Zwischen der behaupteten und der tatsächlichen Geschichte Österreichs erstreckt sich ein Niemandsland, in dem man verloren gehen kann. Ich sehe mich zwischen einem dunklen, vergessenen Kellerabteil des Hauses Österreich und seinen hellen, reich ausgestatteten Räumlichkeiten hin- und herpendeln. Niemand in den hellen Räumen scheint zu ahnen oder vermag es sich vorzustellen, dass es in diesem Gebäude Menschen gibt, die von der Politik in den Vergangenheitskeller gesperrt worden sind, wo sie von ihren eigenen Erinnerungen attackiert und vergiftet werden.[9]

> [Between the purported and the actual history of Austria there stretches a no-man's-land where it is easy to get lost. I see myself shuttling back and forth between a dark, forgotten cellar compartment in the House of Austria and its bright, richly furnished quarters. Nobody in the bright quarters seems to guess or is able to imagine that there are people in this building whom politics have banished to the cellar of history, where they are attacked and poisoned by their own memories.]

The proud upholder of a minor language at a historically contested political border on the one hand, her autobiographically-informed protagonist is also educated and becomes professionally active in the major

---

[9] Maja Haderlap, *Engel des Vergessens* (Munich: btb, 2013), pp. 185–6.

language of German on the other. Her experiences of growing up in a rural area delineated by poverty dovetail with her gradual discovery of the violence inflicted on the Slovenian-speaking community by National Socialist troops, often with local militia support. This violence has severely traumatized many of the surviving members of her family and their close friends (notably her father and his peers, many of whom take their own lives) or otherwise decisively marked the life stories that unfold within the Carinthian hills. The grandmother, for example, who is a key formative person in the young girl's life, repeatedly returns to her experiences as an intern at the Ravensbrück labour camp, having drawn many of the life lessons she wishes to impart to her granddaughter from this period. By the end of the novel, the first-person narrator reflects on how, in learning of all these stories and weaving them into her own life, she has been visited by the 'angel of history'. This well-known trope developed by Walter Benjamin conjures up another form of no-man's-land, one delineated now not by space but time, as the angel looks in horror at the past but moves towards the future.[10] Alongside it, the narrator places the 'angel of forgetting', who, by in turn forgetting to ensure the narrator fully forgets the past, becomes aligned with the ethical thrust of literature itself and the story that this narrator will now be able to write. This angel is also positioned between the past and the future, and it is out of this space that her narrative ensues in markedly Benjaminian terms:

> Der Engel des Vergessens dürfte vergessen haben, die Spuren der Vergangenheit aus meinem Gedächtnis zu tilgen. Er hat mich durch ein Meer geführt, in dem Überreste und Bruchstücke schwammen. Er hat meine Sätze auf dahintreibende Trümmer und Scherben prallen lassen, damit sie sich verletzen, damit sie sich schärfen. [. . .] Er wird in den Büchern verschwinden. Er wird eine Erzählung sein.[11]

> [The angel of forgetting must have forgotten to erase the traces of the past from my memory. He guided me through a sea in which remnants and broken pieces swam. He let my sentences crash against the ruins and shards drifting by, so that they would be damaged, so that they would grow sharp. [. . .] He will disappear in the books. He will be a narrative.]

---

[10] Walter Benjamin, *Über den Begriff der Geschichte*, in *Werke und Nachlass: Kritische Gesamtausgabe*, vol. 19 ed. by Gérard Raulet (Berlin: Suhrkamp, 2010).

[11] Haderlap, *Engel des Vergessens*, pp. 286–7.

Written otherwise in the present tense throughout, Haderlap's narrative thus consciously stakes out a space where these unheard but 'unforgotten' stories and fragments of experience are publicly voiced for the first time. They are shared first with the young girl as she hears them from her Slovenian-speaking relatives, but also with the German-language readers who are implied in the reference above to the occupants of the large, bright rooms of the House of Austria and are the presumed readers of this text. The challenge for the narrator is to align herself with the language and the stories of those who have been largely overlooked by the march of history and now need her voice, whilst at the same time not 'getting lost' – sucked down into the metaphorical cellar where people cast off as marginal by Austria's ongoing politics are delivered into the hands of their own despair. In order to achieve this, the author must manage a delicate balance between the commemorative and the celebratory modes of authorship.

With regard to the former mode, the motif of the angel places a commemorative stance squarely at the centre of the text. It invokes not just Benjamin's horrified angel of history, with whom the gestus of the whole narrative is implicitly aligned as the narrator calls out the betrayals that were visited upon the minority community by the German-speaking majority, but also the 'Schutzengel'[12] (guardian angel) that appears to have watched over all those who have survived and thus ensured that commemoration across the generations is possible. Significantly, in this novel and unlike in Petrowskaja's slightly later *Vielleicht Esther* (2014, Maybe Esther), the subjects of the stories are still alive and able to tell their stories. All that is needed is a way of connecting them in time and space to the people who need to listen. Accordingly, the narrator, who stems from this community but is educated in Klagenfurt and Vienna, goes on to work in the creative arts in Austria, and also profits from professional stays in Slovenia, becomes the nodal link between the different rooms in the imagined house above. Throughout all of these experiences, she finds herself balancing an excess of Carinthian-Slovenian phrases and sentences with the realization that she must find ways of reconciling them with the rather different norms and expectations of the majority communities in Austria on the one hand and Slovenia on the other. Yet as she tries to convey the historical-political narratives that she feels compelled to represent, she finds herself caught in another kind of no-man's-land, this time as much linguistic as political in nature. Settling on one language over the other entails crossing a border that means you immediately lose some of the context, the life-blood of the story, the

---

[12] Haderlap, *Engel des Vergessens*, p. 15.

excess of experience born of a particular time and place that keeps it alive, or, as she puts it in a soul-searching question-and-answer session to herself while considering her German-language work at the Klagenfurt Theatre:

> Hätte ich vorher das unbestimmte, ungesicherte Land zwischen den Sprachen verlassen sollen, das mich lange herumstreunen ließ, das keine Unbedingtheit voraussetzte wie das Schreiben in einer Sprache mit seinem alles entscheidenden Entweder-oder? Äußerlich wird alles unverändert bleiben [...] Nur etwas Luftdurchlässiges, Ungreifbares wird zerbrochen sein. [...] Die Sehnsucht nach dem Schreiben wird erlahmen. Meine schwärmerischen Pläne zerbrochen sein. Um mich verstreut werden Wörter liegen, als hätte ich sie in einem Anfall von Verzweiflung zu Boden geschleudert und wäre nicht mehr imstande, sie aufzuheben.[13]

[Should I have left that indefinite, insecure land between languages earlier, which had given me plentiful freedom to wander here and there and which did not demand any absolutes, quite unlike writing in just one language with its all-deciding either-or? Externally everything will remain unchanged (...) Only something airy, intangible will be broken (...) The desire to write will wilt. My dreamy plans will be broken. Words will lie scattered around me, as if I had cast them on the ground in an act of desperation and were no longer able to pick them up.]

While it is clear that commemorative work needs to happen in such a way that it will reach the majority German-speaking audience of Austria, officially affiliating herself with this language takes an emotional toll on the narrator, as it forces a distance between her and those for whom she wants her narrative to speak. The counter, however, that can prevent this vision of writerly despair becoming reality – the narrator's vision of being left exhausted on a rubble heap of words – also lies within the very act of authorship she finds so problematic. Throughout the text, the power of marshalling language to bring about positive interventions in people's lives has been a recurrent theme. The grandmother not only stands for a quasi-shamanistic belief in the power of words to heal and ward off evil, but also equips herself with two books about the Ravensbrück camp so that she is able to dispel her daughter-in-law's incredulity as well as ensure the broader context of

---

[13] Haderlap, *Engel des Vergessens*, pp. 231–2.

her story is accurately relayed to her granddaughter, the narrator, 'wenn es so weit sein wird'[14] ('all in due course'). Along with the historical information, this inherent belief in the power of language and literature to draw other, more spiritual worlds beyond any one language into our own, is imparted to the narrator. At the formative period just before she leaves secondary school, she has the time and space both to daydream through poetry and to recognize what she needs to be able to do with this literary discipline in future, echoing her grandmother's underlying optimism in the healing march of time: 'Das Gedachte und Gefühlte, das Empfundene und Befürchtete soll erst später zur Sprache kommen, in einem Satz zusammentreffen oder zusammengeführt werden, hoffe ich, irgendwann, wenn es so weit sein wird'[15] (thoughts and feelings, impressions and fears won't be put into words until later, I hope, sharing a sentence or being otherwise brought together in it, sometime later, all in due course).

The fact that the narrative of *Engel des Vergessens* exists in spite of all the misgivings expressed within it about occupying a spatial, temporal and linguistic no-man's-land is testament to her successful realization of this ambition. It is therefore also a quiet celebration of her own accession to authorship, drawing out the things, experiences and places that need to be voiced from her world, expressly celebrated in the final dream scene with her grandmother. Here, her grandmother has unexpectedly returned and designed a giant woven apparatus to capture the voices from the landscape all around them – an apparatus that metaphorically mirrors the text the narrator herself has created, out of all the material and immaterial links she has been able to trace through the stories told to her, to ensure these very voices are heard.

If Haderlap's text, with its emphasis on passing stories, objects, words and beliefs down the female line celebrates a particularly female ability to amplify voices and experiences from downtrodden communities and indeed other submerged ways of life beyond language, Olga Martynova's novel, *Mörikes Schlüsselbein* (2013, Mörike's Collarbone), which won the Bachmann Prize in the subsequent year, unfolds ideas of authorship across an even more expansive understanding of historical time and geographical place. Itself part of a loose trilogy (to-date) that is bookended by *Sogar Papageien überleben uns* (2010, Even Parrots Outlive Us) and *Der Engelherd* (2016, Ensnaring Angels), its guiding conceit is one of trickery conflated with excess. The collarbone of the Romantic poet and novelist, Eduard Mörike (1804–1875) is spotted on display in the seminary in Tübingen where he

---

[14] Haderlap, *Engel des Vergessens*, p. 45.
[15] Haderlap, *Engel des Vergessens*, p. 168.

studied, supposedly on loan from a cemetery in Stuttgart. It becomes a point of reference across the narrative for the principle protagonists, a Russian-German patchwork family. Marina is urged by her stepson, the aspiring author Moritz, to get to the bottom of what Mörike's collarbone is doing divorced from the rest of his remains. She eventually uncovers the prosaic reason (the whole thing is a student prank), but not before Moritz has fabricated a Romantic story of literary lineage: the poet Friedrich Hölderlin (1770–1843) rips out his collarbone to pass his creative spirit on to Mörike, causing Mörike to fling his own into the river.[16] However, Mörike's collarbone is equally endowed with creativity, something Mörike himself later realizes, causing him to return and (unsuccessfully) look for it. It is thus waiting to be found and put to use by the next creative spirit – Moritz himself being the obvious would-be-Romantic-author-in-waiting. The novel ends with him ceremonially throwing a replica collarbone into the river and buying another to put on the grave of Fjodor Stern, a family friend and celebrated Soviet underground poet. In so doing, he is both perpetuating the (male) chain and tying himself and his ambition into it.

This notion of literary inspiration as an excess accompanied by repeat gestures of search and return spreads throughout the text. It follows the twists of fiction on the one hand, as Moritz rewrites the lives of people around him as genre fiction (a spy thriller and a teenage romance), and those of reality on the other: as a Russian émigré working for a German cultural foundation, Marina is plugged into multiple networks of authors, translators and professional literary critics covering North America, Europe and Russia, all of whom rely on an innate ability to harvest language and tell different stories for different audiences. While the narrative overtly follows the multiple perspectives of a diverse range of people from within these overlapping real and fictional networks ('real' and 'fictional' within the fiction), its covert focus is on the unspoken elements of human relations that bring life and meaning to a world that can seem otherwise on course for political and personal stasis in the stifling context of neoliberalism. The gesture of too much – too many collarbones, too many mothers and fathers, too many lovers, too many apartments, and multiple spies and magic blankets – calls out for a mediator figure who can make sense of how such a kaleidoscope of abundance fits together. The Russian poet Fjodor

---

[16] Hölderlin spent the latter half of his life deemed by his contemporaries to have gone mad and living a radically confined existence in a tower overlooking the river in Tübingen. Mörike is known to have visited Hölderlin during this period and to have included a character based on him in his novel *Maler Nolten* (1832, *The Painter Nolten*).

Stern, who succumbs to his own stereotype and drinks himself to death but whose life and work touches those of all the other characters, leaves a clear statement on the role of the author in this respect:

> Wozu man uns braucht? Wozu wir gut sind? Nachdem ein Gedanke entsteht, sucht er nach den Wörtern, um verkörpert zu werden. Sie ihrerseits kommen dienstbereit herbei, und da lauert die Gefahr, dass der Gedanke in einen falschen Körper hineinspringt. Die fertigen Sätze sind jederzeit bereit, einen frischen Gedanken zu verschlingen. Und eben darin besteht die Arbeit eines Dichters, die verbrauchten Schemen aufzuscheuchen. Sonst würden wir Gedanken denken, die nicht unsere sind; uns Gesetzen unterwerfen, die nicht unsere sind; Gefühle empfinden, die nicht unsere sind.[17]

> [Why are we needed? What are we good for? Once a thought has formed, it looks for words to embody it. These dutifully show up for work, and there's the danger, lurking, that the thought will jump into the wrong body. Those ready-made sentences are always ready to swallow up a fresh thought. And there's the author's task: to shake up those worn-out moulds. Or else we might think thoughts that are not ours, obey laws that are not ours, feel emotions that are not ours.]

Each in their own way, all three of Martynova's novels articulate this ethical sense of authorship being a case of marshalling the tangible and intangible aspects of the wider world into literary form so that we can collectively come to the right stories for the right time and place. Her first novel does this in respect of the disintegration of the Soviet Union, capturing a set of semi-underground literary relations and the formative years of a Cold War love story before they disappear from living memory, while her most recent novel picks up the story of National Socialist experimentation on vulnerable children and gives it new impetus amidst contemporary concerns around the rise of artificial intelligence. Located between the two, *Mörikes Schlüsselbein* dedicates considerable space to reflecting on the authorial gesture that underpins such rewritings, focusing in particular on the question of how to capture intangible influences and make visible things that cannot ordinarily be seen.

At the most obvious level, this move is represented typographically, with some sections of the text presented in greyscale: things that the characters think, but do not say, or, in the case of the multiple

---

[17] Olga Martynova, *Mörikes Schlüsselbein* (Munich: btb, 2015), p. 282.

chapter sub-headings, things that are happening simultaneously but are not currently the focus of the narrative. The explicit effect of this is visually to underscore the multiple times, spaces and perspectives that co-exist within the text, while implicitly pointing to the utopian mode that both provides access to an alternative world and at the same time requires a loosening of conventional forms of subjecthood and authority if this access is to be realized. The reader has to divide her reading attention between the multiple strands, effectively being in multiple places simultaneously, while the very notion of authorship has become recursive and collaborative, as all the main characters are involved in writing and re-writing shared texts that condition what they see in the world around them. This stretches from Marina's idle translation of an advertising pamphlet promoting courses in tolerance that will later reappear unexpectedly in both Moritz' fiction and in the apartment block of her childhood artistic mentors, to Moritz' dramatic re-casting of Fjodor's American translator as a Cold War spy stuck in the Siberian Boreal forest and his sister Franziska's temporary disappearance in Berlin. In all of these cases, we witness thoughts being put into language, semi-articulated, but then discarded, so that they are both there and not there, carrying agency and forging links, but also abandoned as dead ends or idle musings. These largely unheard and unseen intangible structures guide human experience just as much as the more obvious events and spoken interactions between the characters, and the narrative is structured accordingly, giving the tangible and the intangible elements within it equal weight.

There is a certain pathos to this utopian mode of authorship when it intersects with the underlying celebratory mode of any text that is deliberately drawing attention to itself as a crafted, literary artefact. This is compounded by the fact that all of the intangible, semi-articulated connections that draw together the multiple experiences of the characters also more or less directly point back to Fjodor Stern. His symbolic role in representing the intangible aspects of literary activity is underscored by the fact that for much of his life he operated as an underground, Samizdat author. His death therefore carries the weight of a tragedy that ricochets throughout the worlds that his literal and symbolic presence connected. The question of how a new constellation will form that can continue to give a tangible expression to these sub-structures is perhaps the biggest unvoiced question around which the narrative revolves, and it risks both reproducing dominant gender tropes of the 'great' author and tipping the spirit with which the utopian mode was introduced into the text in the first place, from one of open-endedness and inclusivity to a rather more closed-off sense of self-regard: literature mourning the passing of the literary, celebrating its own canon, and thereby implicitly limiting who has access to it.

This charge is mitigated to a certain extent by the satirical mode that predominates at certain key junctures – notably at the commemorative event held for Fjodor on the first anniversary of his death, and at which the passage above underscoring the importance of the author is read out. Here, in the manner of Gisela Elsner or Thomas Bernhard, the cynicism with which the Russian state is trying to avail itself of the new-found cultural capital vested in former dissident poets is also placed centre stage: the event organizer, who sees in Marina the chance to further her career connections, is at the same time more concerned to please the Russian Orthodox oligarch who has funded the evening than develop a compelling cultural frame for the proceedings, and leaves without listening to any of the readings from Fjodor's work. A more meaningful way of commemorating the author's work by literally providing access to the places and networks from which it sprang – his widow wants to establish a 'Museum für die inoffizielle Dichtung'[18] (museum for unofficial poetry) in their former large apartment – fails on account of ongoing Soviet legacies within cultural politics. Fjodor himself has already foreseen all this and speaks like a voice from beyond the grave in pointing out a possible way forward. In the third posthumous piece that is read out at his commemorative event, the deficiencies of the post-Soviet literary scene that remains subject to political power-play are merged with the deficiencies of technocratic neoliberalism more generally:

> Ein guter Roman muss heute eine mühsame Lektüre sein, unberechnet, vom Geschmack des Publikums nichts wissend. Das war nicht immer so. Aber vieles war früher nicht so. Ein genialer Schachspieler heute muss ein Verlierer sein. Nicht die Züge und Kombinationen durchrechnen, die genauso gut von einem Rechner berechnet werden können, sondern seinen Gegner gewinnen lassen, aber ihn dabei mit Wagemut und scheinbarem Unsinn der Kombinationen irritieren, ihm eine Vorstellung von der unbegreifbaren Welt geben, die Grenzen des (Un)Denkbaren und des zu Denkenden weiter hinausschieben.[19]

> [Today a good novel must be hard work, not calculated, not knowing anything about its public's taste. That wasn't always the case. But many things weren't always the case. A great chess player today has to be a loser. Not working through the moves and combinations that can just as well be calculated by a computer,

---

[18] Martynova, *Mörikes Schlüsselbein*, p. 287.
[19] Martynova, *Mörikes Schlüsselbein*, p. 283.

but rather letting his opponent win. Upsetting him along the way with his risky play and apparently daft combinations, giving him a sense of the incomprehensible world, pushing out ever further the limits of the (un)thinkable and what is still to be thought.]

Relinquishing control over the final outcome – arranging things so that you can 'win', whether this is on the literary market or in a chess competition – becomes the necessary sacrifice in a world where algorithms are increasingly outclassing human performance, if you want to remain capable of playing the game in any meaningful sort of way. What can be retained and championed instead is the innately human ability to stray from the rules, operate within grey zones, embrace an unpredictable line of action and, in so doing, indicate just how much of the imaginary is far beyond the reach of artificially intelligent machines and technocratic systems. The value of a complicated novel that perhaps never shakes down into a clear picture of the world resides in a way of seeing precisely all those things that cannot be captured and monetized or otherwise programmed into a system of control. The '(un)thinkable and what is still to be thought', are part of that utopian world where humans, thanks to the multiple affordances of literature for carrying multiple perspectives, times and places simultaneously, can still take pride in humanity's ability to discern so much more in the world around us – if only we take the time to look. Throughout the text, this authorial focus on seeing more and seeing better is repeatedly allied with Moritz' ability to spin both real objects and hypothesized situations into stories, and, in so doing, weave narratives along the edge of the uncanny, with E.T.A Hofmann's tales – hinted at through stray cats or night-time streets in historic towns – coming temporarily into focus. The result is the promotion of a model of authorship that both advances and shies away from the overtly pedagogical, as a fundamental belief in literature is splintered across the multiple, partially contradictory perspectives offered by the different practitioners within the novel.

If Martynova sets out a poetics that champions literature's ability, for those who care to perceive it, to make the case for humanity's intangible values and experiences in a post-Soviet but also increasingly post-human age, the next Bachmann Prize laureate grounds this discussion once more in actual lives that have been brutally extinguished. 'Geschichte ist, wenn es plötzlich keine Menschen mehr gibt, die man fragen kann, sondern nur noch Quellen'[20] (history is when suddenly

---

[20] Katja Petrowskaja, *Vielleicht Esther* (Berlin: Suhrkamp, 2015), p. 30.

there are no more people for you to ask, only sources), writes the autobiographical narrator in Katja Petrowskaja's *Vielleicht Esther*, who will work outwards from scraps of recipes and half-remembered labels on jars to try to piece together a picture of who her ancestors were. The resulting text tells the story of how what started out as simple research into her Jewish family history quickly revealed multiple lives that had been lost, as well as unexpected connections across an extended network that stretched from Vienna and Warsaw through to Kiev and further into small provincial towns in Ukraine, Poland and Russia, as well as France and North America. Strikingly, one of the recurring connections is her maternal family's work in establishing schools for deaf and mute people: literally giving a voice to those who would otherwise routinely not be heard in society. In this respect, her task becomes one of hearing those who have been doubly not heard, or, as she puts it: 'Unser Judentum blieb für mich taubstumm und die Taubstummheit jüdisch. Das war meine Geschichte, meine Herkunft, doch das war nicht ich'[21] (Our Jewishness remained for me deaf and mute, and to be deaf and mute was to be Jewish. It was my history, my origins, but it wasn't me). Thus, although she shares with Haderlap's narrator a direct familial association with the people and stories she wishes to have heard, these lives and stories have been multiply erased from her background: she is not a practising Jew herself, the stories she wishes to uncover are mostly of those who did not survive the Soviet and National Socialist regimes, and many of these characters were even in their own day intricately allied with people whose voices and experiences were pushed to the margins of society.

Bearing all this in mind, Petrowskaja's narrative takes an even more direct aim at official memory narratives than Haderlap's, as the main ethical thrust of her text is to write against the fact not that commemoration of her community has not happened, but that it has happened in such a way as actively to silence them. Writing about the official commemoration of the siege of Leningrad that would take one million lives, she observes, 'man rief uns dazu auf, niemanden und nichts zu vergessen, damit wir vergaßen, wer und was vergessen war'[22] (we were called upon to forget no-one and nothing, so that we would forget who and what had been forgotten). This sense of how the commemorative mode can itself cast a shadow is particularly clearly set out when she attempts to look at the house in Warsaw where her grandmother was born in 1905. The only information she can access compels her to look at the area through the lens of the Jewish ghetto:

---

[21]   Petrowskaja, *Vielleicht Esther*, p. 51.
[22]   Petrowskaja, *Vielleicht Esther*, p. 40.

> Ich versuchte, mich dagegen zu wehren, ich wiederholte, dass das Ghetto natürlich das Wichtigste sei, ich hier aber meine Geschichte suche, die viel früher anfange, meine Großmutter sei 1905 in Warschau geboren, mein Urgroßvater habe hier bis 1915 eine Taubstummenschule gehabt und Schluss. Aber mein Gesprächspartner, mein Gegenüber, die Warschauer Geschichtsschreibung und ihre gut gerüsteten Vorposten in Internet und Wissenschaft – sie waren in der Überzahl, und sie alle sagten Ghetto. Ghetto dort! Ghetto hier! Ghetto da! Ghetto oben! Ghetto unten![23]

> [I tried to defend myself against this, I repeated that of course the ghettos was the most important thing, but I was looking for my history here, and this began much earlier, my grandmother was born in Warsaw in 1905, my great grandfather had a deaf-and-mute school here up to 1915, and that was that. But my conversant, my opposite number, Warsaw historiography and its well-equipped outposts on the internet and in academe – there were more of them, and they all said 'ghetto'. Ghetto up! Ghetto down! Ghetto here! Ghetto there! Ghetto everywhere!]

The rhetorically cacophonous repetition of the word 'ghetto' conveys the sense of being drowned out, with the narrator forced to allow her own perspective, which does not fully mesh with the well-known narrative of trauma and loss, to be submerged. She will counter this by doggedly piecing back together what she can and, in so doing, challenging what exactly is remembered: 'Man sagt jüdisch, weiß aber nicht, womit das Wort gefüllt ist'[24] (people say Jewish, but don't know what that word contains), she observes, and it is clear that her narrative is designed to change this as far as her own family experiences are concerned. In fact, the whole thrust of her text becomes one of filling in the very considerable blank space on the metaphorical map of memory narratives that draw on the lives and experiences of millions of people right across Central and Eastern Europe, but all too frequently treat them as a homogenous mass. Precisely because it has become so difficult to trace individual family members with any certainty, she finds herself taking on the fates of all the people she finds listed who share the more common names in her family tree. However, in recognizing 'dass ich alle Aufgelisteten zu den Meinigen zu zählen hatte'[25] (that I must count

---

[23] Petrowskaja, *Vielleicht Esther*, p. 102.
[24] Petrowskaja, *Vielleicht Esther*, p. 103.
[25] Petrowskaja, *Vielleicht Esther*, p. 27.

all those who were listed as part of my family), Petrowskaja is also determining that she must provide a qualitatively different kind of commemorative mode to that which has hitherto guided the kind of monolithic memory narratives that she encounters online and in various social and scholarly exchanges. She wants to know not how these people were deported and died, but how they lived, and how those lives that were lived still shape the world today. She wants to include them in her unfolding of authorship.

With this in mind, the entirety of Petrowskaja's text is underpinned by her deliberate performance of her particular kind of commemorative mode against the backdrop of the German-inflected norm that she finds so lacking. Indeed, the preface 'Google sei Dank'[26] (Thank Google) explicitly shows her wildly fabricating a story to explain to a puzzled Iranian-American tourist how it can be that the main railway station in Berlin is displaying the oversized sign, 'Bombardier Willkommen in Berlin', from its roof[27] (literally: Bombardier Welcome to Berlin, but, as it turns out actually the name of a Canadian rail and aircraft manufacturer, Bombardier). Her fanciful tale of how Bombardier is a hugely successful French musical that has brought significant tourism to the city raises ethical questions around how the arts are seen and heard amidst the hustle and bustle of the everyday in a globally leading developed nation. Pretending that the one-word advertising strategy for this musical caused controversy with the unfortunate associations it triggered in the historic locations where it was being displayed and led to a high-profile court case, she sets out the normative frame for German memory narratives, which, since the turn of the millennium have increasingly shifted to consider the extent to which Germans are victims. This backdrop then contrasts all the more starkly with the rest of her text, which will repeatedly uncover the ways in which officially sanctioned acts of commemoration and dominant narratives of victimhood tend to erase the actual experiences of those lives lived.

Yet in critiquing the shadow cast by dominant memory narratives, Petrowskaja is not interested in some kind of nationalist or ethnically-led tally of relative suffering or ethical oversight. In fact, central to her endeavour is the ability to step outside any one linguistic or political frame. Having learned German as an adult, she is particularly positive about how researching and writing through this language makes it easier to see and hear the untold stories that run through her extended family in Russian, Polish and Yiddish. Drawing on Russian etymology, she explains how 'German' in Russian, 'nemeckij', literally means the

---

[26] Petrowskaja, *Vielleicht Esther*, p. 7.
[27] Petrowskaja, *Vielleicht Esther*, p. 7.

language of the mute, 'nemoj nemec'.[28] Unexpectedly, then, the German language itself places her in a similar situation to those deaf-mute children to whom her ancestors would give a voice, and, as also the 'Sprache des Feindes'[29] (language of the enemy) it provides her with both an escape route from and a way back in to her family history. Where for Haderlap writing in this language causes some considerable emotional difficulty, for Petrowskaja it sets the whole creative process of research and writing in motion: 'Ich dachte auf Russisch, suchte meine jüdischen Verwandten und schrieb auf Deutsch. Ich hatte das Glück, mich in der Kluft der Sprachen, im Tausch, in der Verwechslung von Rollen und Blickwinkeln zu bewegen'[30] (I thought in Russian, was searching for my Jewish relatives, and wrote in German. I was lucky to be moving in that chasm between languages, in the exchange and in the swapping of roles and perspectives).

The idea that a multiplication of languages, roles and perspectives might be helpful when trying to establish how one should live in the world takes us back to the insights provided by Olga Martynova's work. Petrowskaja will repeatedly be overwhelmed by the unexpected signifiers she will encounter in her family's past – the newspaper reports from 1932 that disintegrate in her hands as she tries to find out the truth about her great-uncle, shot by the Soviet state for apparently attempting to assassinate the German ambassador, for example, or the perfect horror of the paradise apple trees that link her long-lost grandfather and suspected beneficiary of early Stalinist purges with Nazi atrocities that, when the narrator learns about them, cause her to rewrite some of the happiest memories of her childhood. Even her own German-language authorial persona seems eerily prefigured in the place of her birth, as she reflects on how she is the product of two streets in Kiev, the Uliza Engelsa (Engels Street) and Uliza Liebknechta (Karl Liebknecht Street), birthplaces of her father and mother respectively. But this sense that material objects, places and language itself also have agency that can seriously undermine the individual's attempt to orient herself in the world is also distinctly liberating. If the author can stop trying to control and order the narrative around what she can immediately perceive and thinks she knows, and instead lets the deaf and mute connections between people, places and things come to the fore, then she is also able to create a text that has many more points of access for many different people.

The diverse linguistic, ethnic and geopolitical perspectives informing Haderlap, Martynova and Petrowskaja's authorship of their texts, ranging

---

[28] Petrowskaja, *Vielleicht Esther*, p. 79.
[29] Petrowskaja, *Vielleicht Esther*, p. 80.
[30] Petrowskaja, *Vielleicht Esther*, p. 115.

from the different languages and ethnic experiences they incorporate to the many miles and different political regimes their narratives cover, automatically places the German-language cultural canon, whether invoked by Mörike or the Berlin railway station, into dialogue with broader transnational currents. Yet this is not a respectful knocking on the door of a historically and economically dominant language on the part of authors who might have chosen to write in Slovenian or Russian. It is an urgent reconfiguration of that language and narrowed-down, post-war canon from without, indicating just how much more of the world there is to be seen and heard, both at the literal and metaphorical borders of German-speaking Europe, but also much further afield. Telling these stories requires a location that is constantly in-between, and thus an authorial positioning that looks and moves in multiple directions at once. In rewarding these authors, the Ingeborg Bachmann Prize has thus given significant institutional and cultural backing to a new kind of German-language author who knows how to see and defend German culture from both within and well beyond its own terms and, in so doing, relativize both its achievements and its failings. Marina, Martynova's Germanophone Russian protagonist, brings this to a point. On a visit to the United States, in response to the suggestion that anti-Muslim propaganda is sweeping through contemporary Germany in a re-run of the Nazi treatment of the Jews, she is captured hovering between thoughts and words:

> *Nicht aufregen!*, sagt sich Marina, die, um sich auf diese Reise vorzubereiten, eine TV-Serie in der hiesigen Sprache angeschaut hat [. . .], die sie allerdings mit einem völlig undienlichen Wortschatz ausgerüstet hat. Unter dem Einfluss dieser linguistischen Erfahrung entstehen Sätze wie, dass der Kollege ihres freundlichen Gegenübers ein Cocksucker sei, der sich diesen fucking Vergleich up his ass sticken könne, aber sie sagt, die richtigen Wörter zusammenkratzend:
> "Das ist genau das, was die Deutschen über die Amerikaner erzählen"[31]

> [*Don't get annoyed!*, Marina says to herself. She has prepared herself for this journey by watching a TV series in the local language [. . .], but unfortunately it has provided her with a totally unserviceable vocabulary. Under the influence of this linguistic experience, she finds herself coming up with sentences like, the colleague of her friendly partner-in-conversation is a cocksucker

---

[31] Martynova, *Mörikes Schlüsselbein*, p. 59.

who can stick this fucking comparison up his ass, but she says, scratching together the right words:
"That's exactly what Germans say about Americans"]

The Parallel Worlds of Contemporary German Authorship

In raising the profile of work by Maja Haderlap, Olga Martynova and Katja Petrowskaja, the Ingeborg Bachmann Prize has also significantly raised the profile of a growing number of writers who have been giving expression to non-German backgrounds and experiences from the late 1980s onwards and, in so doing, opening up what it means to be a German-language writer in the wider world. What began as the well-documented 'Turkish turn' and gained a particular figurehead in the writer Feridun Zaimoğlu with the publication of his *Kanak Sprak* (Kanak Tongue) in 1995, broadened into an 'Eastern turn' with the arrival across the 1990s and early 2000s of writers such as Maxim Biller, Terézia Mora, Wladimir Kaminer and Saša Stanišić from the former Eastern bloc.[32] This has since taken an even more transnational turn, with authors, for example, from the Middle East (Tomer Gardi, Abbas Khider), post-colonial Britain (Sharon Dodua Otoo) and Japan (Yoko Tawada) all gaining a readership precisely for the way they add to a body of German-language writing from a position both within and beyond it. The kind of literature these authors are producing is valued both on account of the different perspectives they bring – writing from the point of view of political migrants or ethnic minorities, for example (Biller, Khider, Otoo) – and for the startling use of language and literary form with which they do this (Gardi in particular experiments with 'imperfect' language in a manner reminiscent of Zaimoğlu's *Kanak Sprak*, while Otoo and Tawada bring Afrofuturism and Japanese literary forms into German respectively). Coupled with the Adelbert-von-Chamisso Prize, which was awarded up to 2017 for German-language writing by authors whose first language was not German (see Martynova's comments on this in our conversation after this chapter), the Ingeborg Bachmann Prize has increasingly underscored the literary and socio-political significance of a kind of writing that is inherently in-between languages and cultures in a way that its namesake herself sought to achieve in vain during her lifetime.[33]

---

[32] On both phenomena, see Brigid Haines, ed., *The Eastern European Turn in Contemporary German-Language Literature*, special issue of *German Life & Letters*, 68.2 (2015), 145–333.

[33] On how the Chamisso Prize fits into a chain of support for writing in German as a second language, see Chantal Wright, 'Before Chamisso: The role played by the Munich DaF writing competitions and anthologies in the promotion of a "deutsche Literatur von außen", 1979–1987', *Oxford German Studies*, 43.1 (2014), 20–36. On the Bachmann Prize, see Moser, *Der Ingeborg-Bachmann-Preis*.

However, it is also far more inclusive than any attempt to reward direct emulation of her work would have made possible. This is not least because the particularly German pedagogic and/or creative models that drew so heavily on the commemorative and celebratory modes of authorship and are also highly formative of Bachmann's work have begun to recede a little from view. What instead unites such a diverse set of writers, beyond the simple fact of their diversity, is a distinct propensity towards the open-ended utopian mode of authorship, whether it is coupled with satire in Khider's bestselling provocation on the German language that is reborn as a mixture of Bavarian and Arabic (*Deutsch für Alle*, 2019, German for Everyone) or directly explored in the quietly hopeful reimagining of race, gender and class relations in German society of Otoo's work (2014, *Synchronicity*).

On a practical level, these writers are quite open about the networks that have supported them, including the fact that they routinely work with translators and proof readers, whether these come from professional or personal circles. They often also enjoy other platforms entirely for different forms of cultural experimentation that both complement that of their authorial persona and enhance a certain celebrity status that the commercial end of the literature network is always keen to deploy to its advantage. Kaminer is the foremost example in this respect, as he has benefited significantly from his penetration of the Berlin music scene, both in live venues and on radio. However, almost all of them, including the three authors studied in the previous section, also routinely work as journalists or otherwise contribute frequently to essay columns and online blogs, often laying out their day-to-day experiences for multiple diverse audiences. Collectively, they give us a different way in to making tangible the networks within which authorship unfolds, regardless of the individual authors' principal language(s) or set of cultural experiences. This shared gestus of locating a visibly expanded understanding of authorship both at the heart of German cultural activity and to the side of it allows it to connect in a fundamentally different way with transnational publishing practices. This, in turn, allows new forms of Germanness to be seen, and suggests a new and distinct model of transnational authorship with foundational force for the German twenty-first-century cultural experience.

At the same time, deep sub-structures persist within the publishing industry. These are not always conducive to reversing long-standing patterns of exclusionary behaviour – notably in the areas of gender and ethnicity, as Ulrike Draesner discusses at length in her conversation after this chapter. Equally, some more conservative approaches to authorship – especially the celebratory mode – unsurprisingly continue to be valued by a wide range of writers, including those who also represent different voices and experiences to the historical mainstream. Feridun Zaimoğlu's deep dialogical engagement with key figures of German Romanticism and European Humanism, which we also find in Martynova's work, represents a form of the utopian mode that remains much more aligned with conservative cultural values than the work of, for example, Gardi or Kaminer, who are both quite ambivalent about the cultural value routinely attached to German-language authorship.[34] Equally, throughout the same period broadly described by this chapter, older models of authorship stressing now pedagogy and now exemplary creativity, as represented by Günter Grass, Martin Walser, Christa Wolf, Elfriede Jelinek and Ingo Schulze, amongst others, have remained clearly in evidence. And while the model of transnational authorship I have described above may be a new development in our day, it should also be apparent that it draws on a particular weighting of historically conditioned modes of authorship that have changed over time and most certainly thrown up models in earlier centuries that bear comparison to the contemporary moment. It is no coincidence that Goethe's concept of world literature and actual practice of world authorship provided me with a starting point for my own work, for example, and I would encourage a return to them looking specifically now through the lens of the utopian mode to consider how the model of world authorship gleaned from Goethe may be a natural parallel to the contemporary transnational one.

Closing with the very contemporary moment of German authorship and therefore without the benefit of hindsight makes the task of sorting and categorizing these different yet co-existing models difficult. However, it also opens up the possibility of highlighting the circumstantial network information that is so difficult to piece together from archival sources, as well as to explore particular views and experiences before they are forgotten or otherwise overridden by dominant cultural trends. Bearing all this in mind, I have elected to capture the very contemporary worlds of German-language authorship, both in their practical network circumstances and in the abstract values and beliefs that shape them, in a series of open-ended conversations with three female authors. Ulrike Draesner, Olga Martynova and Ulrike Almut Sandig each spoke with me individually and at length about their working practices in the early summer of 2019 and then assisted in

---

[34] On Zaimoğlu's conscious appropriation of humanist discourse and traditions, see Frauke Matthes, '"Ich bin ein Humanistenkopf": Feridun Zaimoğlu, German Literature, and Worldness' in *Seminar*, 51.2 (2015), 173–90; on Tomer Gardi's challenge to literary conventions, see Weissmann, 'German Writers from Abroad'.

the subsequent editing of the printed conversations that follow this chapter. By birth a West German, a Russian and an East German respectively, at different career stages, and living in Berlin (Draesner, Sandig) and Frankfurt (Martynova), they operate in networks that are quite distinct from one another and collaborate with others across genres and media in very different ways. At the same time, recurrent similarities crop up across the three conversations that, seen in the round, provide a rich and multi-layered perspective on what it means to be an author writing in German at the end of the second decade of the twenty-first century. The extent to which the authors either directly volunteered ideas that chimed with the modes and models of authorship developed in my study, or indirectly spoke in similar terms to my understanding of authorship as an inherently collaborative activity that includes the agency of non-human actors, provides a 'proof of concept' for the guiding approach I have taken throughout this book. Against the attempts to manage literary legacy with which this chapter started, therefore, I leave my readers not with a monument to important German authors that demands we tend them in a certain way, but with a new way of hearing their voice: in their own terms, and as part of a literature network that continues to thrive off multiple forms of interaction with the wider world.

In Conversation Ulrike Draesner: On Creating Contexts for Literature

Ulrike Draesner (b. 1962 in Munich, West Germany) has been writing poetry, stories, essays and novels as well as translating from English and French since the early 1990s. Today she is considered one of the foremost women writing in German. She has won multiple awards for her work and been invited to hold poetics lectures in Bamberg and Frankfurt, amongst other places. In 2018 she took up a post as Professor of German Literature and Creative Writing at the German Literature Institute in Leipzig. We got to know one another during her extended stay in England, 2015–17, when Ulrike came to Lancaster to research Kurt Schwitters, the subject of a pair of novels in German and English (the German *Schwitters* appeared with Penguin in 2020). The conversation reproduced below took place in English in the summer of 2019 in her apartment in Berlin.

* * *

RB In the poetics lectures published in *Grammatik der Gespenster* (2018, The Grammar of Ghosts) you talk about the hidden structures that guide meanings.[1] Your work is really driven by how structures within language, etymologies, can write your text. Obviously, you're working with them, but there's something about language that controls the way the text is unfolding. I'm wondering if this might be a good place for us to start thinking about how the act of writing relates to the world and how you understand authorship within this frame?

UD I don't think that we're talking about hidden structures in this case. The structures you mentioned are used in ordinary speech. In

---

[1] Ulrike Draesner, *Grammatik der Gespenster: Frankfurter Poetikvorlesungen* (Stuttgart: Reclam, 2018).

most cases we wouldn't pay much attention to them, because we concentrate on getting a 'message' or some specific meaning across. But that's different in literature: literature for me is this very space where you can start to dig into and develop these structures. Because structures, linguistic structures, form and inform how we perceive the world. As a writer I experience 'meaning' as a process, interpersonal, multi-layered and recursive. Having learnt several languages and having lived in England for a while, it's become obvious to me that who you are, what you see and what you say depends on the language you are using, because language and the cultural codes held within it, literally 'make' our thoughts. Some idioms, images and connections between sentences or words come easily in one language but wouldn't occur at all in another. These affinities and subtle connections resemble the sub-texts literary texts create and use: currents of rhythms, sound clusters, the use of and play with idioms and metaphors, the creation of (new) images. These 'patterns' or structures make up as much, if not more, of the meaning of a literary text as what is signified by the signs. This double-layering, or this working with various currents of signification is where literature is at home, at least for me. I quite like the idea of the author as someone who translates ordinary linguistic structures into something more tangible than they would be in a day-to-day conversation. Including bodily messages – the presence of a heartbeat, of posture, of facial expression, into the cadences of a sentence or paragraph.

RB I was wondering whether you can also talk about that through this idea of control, that language is the attempt to control your world. When you name something you've got it, you know what it is, you've got it on your radar. Whereas perhaps there are these large areas of life which you just cannot control.

UD Control is an illusion. I don't want to control. You name the 'thing' – and what have you got? You've shrunk it. That's nice for daily communication. Literature is the opposite. It means expansion. Fuzzy fringes, ambivalence, and Musil's 'Möglichkeitssinn' – an enhanced sense of possibilities.[2]

RB But those areas of life may nevertheless be quite controlling and formative and shaping of us?

---

[2] Robert Musil, *Der Mann ohne Eigenschaften*, ed. Adolf Frisé, (Hamburg: Rowohlt, 1988), vol. 1, p. 16.

UD Let's take emotions as an example. Most notions for emotions are fairly huge and general, big bags containing almost anything like 'love' or 'anger'. They come alive by the way they are translated into the representation of bodily reactions, intellectual manoeuvres, discussions between characters, these characters' actions and so on. This is for me the core of what literature can do or what can be done through narration: you invent characters, using all your knowledge about 'the world', set them going and re-transform concepts. You transform given words into dynamic, interpersonal processes.

RB Which is what you said in your third Frankfurt poetics lecture, on *Sieben Sprünge vom Rand der Welt* (2014, Seven Leaps from the Edge of the World). You talked about how here we encounter people trying to express the things they cannot express.

UD The novel hinges on the liminality of silence and utterance. It explores the borderland between the ability to express 'oneself' (to know, to remember, to formulate) and intergenerationally transmitted spaces of silence (because of traumatization or strong social taboos inhibiting speech). Characters start to stutter because there are no adequate words, because they are unable to remember things, because remembering would be too harmful even twenty years after the event in question. Alternatively, they start to talk too much in order to cover up the emptiness of their minds or hearts. They split themselves into an 'I' and a 's/he', in order not to become crazy. By the way, expressing joy or happiness can be equally difficult.

RB But in your writing you also flip this whole idea around, so that the things express themselves in other ways. You've talked elsewhere, for example, about the boy with the limp, where a very physical thing manifests itself. Without any words, and without the person who has the limp even knowing, that experience is expressed and can be made tangible.[3] So, it seems like one of the ways you work with language is like an archaeologist: you're digging out the meanings from language. On the one hand that's a very language-focused understanding of how you capture reality. But on the other hand, you are also interested in all the non-language areas and how you can bring those into literature as well. So, you're getting everything out of language, but you are also looking at all these non-linguistic areas. Isn't that a bit of a paradox?

---

[3] Draesner, *Grammatik der Gespenster*, p. 93.

UD Only if you think that language is nothing else but what you hear or read. Utterance. Without the silence. Which is wrong. There is no meaning at all without the pause. The fraction. The full stop and the comma, the breathing in between. But I think you meant something else. We perceive a difference between language (as a verbal communicative act) and non-language (things, emotions, experiences) because we need it. It's useful. Sometimes it reminds me of the relationship between the net and the fish. You need language to be there and I've always been affected by it as a wonderful, flexible, diverse, historically immense, collectively wise tool. I need many aspects of it in order to catch any fish. Fish are silent and slippery. Sometimes, especially when writing a poem, I feel like standing on the bank of a pool or a small lake, quite muddy, holding fast onto a net that I threw into the water. I start to pull and pull, it's hard work, you need to concentrate, it's bodily work and you never know what you get. Sometimes you just find an old boot in the net. More often the net comes back empty. If you're lucky this reminds you of the nature of your net: it is nothing but some metres of thread (words) artfully slung around holes.

RB And maybe sometimes you're not pulling the net at all, but a fish jumps up and hits you in the face?

UD Or it comes from behind, turns out to be a frog and takes you down into the mud flat on your face! Kafka came up with a very nice simile for that: There's someone sitting in his, or let's say her, room when there is a knock on the door. The person opens the door and faces a dragon. It's an enormous, impressive animal, pressing into the room, telling its surprised owner: 'You called me. Here I am.' The person addressed, the writer, doesn't remember having called for anybody at all, but the dragon insists: 'I've come all this way because of you. Look at my belly, it's scratched and torn from my journey, dragging myself to you.' Saying this, the animal pushes further into the room which is far too small to contain it. This is exactly what it sometimes feels like to be hit by a 'Stoff', which in German means subject, topic, matter, material, drugs, tissue and cloth. It combines matter, language and transformation of perception into one word. I like its sound, too: 'Stoff'. There's something tangible and bodily about it, just listen: 'Stoff, Stoff, Stoff', and if you read it backwards it almost turns into one of the German words for the female genital. So 'Stoff' is wonderful 'Stoff' to develop new ways of thinking about inspiration and creativity.

RB Let's delve a little further into those issues of language and (the) material and how you work with them. I'm thinking again about *Sieben Sprünge* because it's one of the instances where you've been very generous in sharing how you went about writing the novel, and that has included a lot of going and listening to other people, gathering their stories, going to parts of Poland and keeping those available, through the website.[4] Was that a very different kind of authorship experience, or was it just making tangible something that you would say is always part of the literary process?

UD It was both. Sorry, if this sounds confusing! But the journey of writing a novel needs to be unique each time. I had written a historic novel about the Olympic games in Munich in 1972, but I used autobiographical or family-related materials for the first time when writing *Sieben Sprünge*.[5] Yet, the concept of bringing different voices to life has been at the centre of my writing ever since *gedächtnisschleifen*, my first book.[6] I think this brings us back to me being fascinated by language and its double nature as a collective and an individual device. *Sieben Sprünge* renders the collective space of language more tangible, more visible, and even audible on the website. I decided to share my research because the story of *Sieben Sprünge* itself – talking about the forced migration of a Polish and a German family, telling basic aspects of mid-Eastern European history in the twentieth century – all of this 'Stoff', grew out of a collective experience in the first place. This is important because it also means that national borders are transcended. And it is where the novel started in the writing and as a concept, or where my most valuable sources lay hidden. The entire emotional make-up of the families who are forced to migrate to the West in *Sieben Sprünge* grew out of my actual memories of my paternal grandparents' living room in Munich. My grandparents would invite other East-European migrants around for a visit. All of them had met in their new 'home' in Munich, but they met in order to talk about their old homes and what they might still mean to them. I witnessed these meetings as a child and marvelled at how these old people talked about their life situations now and what had happened to them. I was intrigued by their languages, they used their East-German dialects, Silesian for example, sang traditional songs and ate Streuselkuchen (crumble cake). Remembering the tensions of my childhood in a world where nobody would talk about 'the flight' and where I felt that I didn't fit into the Bavarian environment I grew up in but didn't really know why, it's these voices that come back to me, their stutters and flaws, sudden gaps, false laughs, silences. To me, as

---

4   Ulrike Draesner, *Sieben Sprünge vom Rand der Welt* (Munich: Luchterhand, 2014); www.der-siebte-sprung.de (last accessed 4 July 2019).
5   Ulrike Draesner, *Spiele* (Darmstadt: Luchterhand, 2005).
6   Ulrike Draesner, *gedächtnisschleifen* (Frankfurt a.M.: Suhrkamp, 1995).

the child amongst them who couldn't be burdened with 'knowledge', meaning was basically conveyed through emotions in the words, the cadences, the lines of the songs. The novel started in this collective space that perished long ago in the seventies, and ends in the internet, opening up a collective space in its contemporary form. The last chapter of the website invites readers to contribute their own stories and experiences of forced migration and intergenerational traumatization.

RB You yourself are not only subject to the play of language and these intangible influences, but also to the play of other people in the publishing industry, and things and places; these all affect what you do. One of the things I'm looking to find a way of exploring is the things that go missing. And in a way, writing the history of German authorship across the twentieth century is to constantly come up against the things that were excluded, or the structural reasons as to why things went one way. We can see all of the institutions and the glory and the prizes and the support that means a certain type of authorship can thrive. But how do you go about finding the other kinds of authorship that didn't?

UD That's quite an issue, touching on a long story of suppression of various aspects of writing for commercial and general reasons. That's been the case in many Western societies. Even looking just at the books that were published and then, in a second step, counting those that have survived up to today, makes you aware that we are facing the tip of the iceberg of what has been and still is being written. I remember how on entering the literary scene as an author in 1995, I felt quite shocked that for those who came to my poetry readings the only point of reference seemed to be Ingeborg Bachmann. She was of the generation of my mother and quite far away from me and what I was trying to do in poems. Of course, I felt flattered as well, but it also struck me as wrong. It was partial, and patriarchal. The context supplied by the iceberg was that I should write love poems and die young.

RB Did you say 'flattened' or 'flattered'?

UD Both! Absolutely flattened, too. After the readings people asked me how I wrote my poems, and when I said I that I typed them on my computer they would look aghast. Obviously, this was not what a young, blonde, female poet should be doing in 1995. I should have been writing in ink, at least! Ideally with a quill. My volume of poems was widely reviewed, very enthusiastically, but almost everybody concentrated on the love poems. My poems about the Middle Ages, science and organ transplants were hardly ever mentioned, because obviously there was a strong gender bias. I am glad to say that expectations and contexts have been considerably transformed since then. We, the generation of poets born in the 1960s, were lucky in a way. We were just about to publish our first books when 1989 happened. It took some time, but, slowly, in the nineties, things accelerated and changed. Partly because everybody expected change. And partly because we emphasized performance and the oral aspects of poetry and really worked on them, moving from a rather static understanding of meaning to more performative formats.

In 1996 I moved to Berlin where I found circles of authors that had formed in West Berlin during the seclusion. They had generated some figureheads of political writing in the 1960s and 1970s, e.g. Hans Christoph Buch and Peter Schneider, who still seemed to dominate the West Berlin authorial scene at the time. There was the Tunnel über der Spree, organized by the LCB (Literary Colloquium Berlin) where authors would meet and discuss new texts. But since the event was officially organized by a literary institution, dependant on money from the cultural senate of Berlin, it needed to be public. And journalists were invited to report on 'our' development. The authors sat around a huge table, like thirty to forty of us, and we were supposed to talk about new and unfinished writing, which of course hardly anybody did since you would read about it in a newspaper the next day. Shows of vanity immediately started, people were picking at each other and became highly competitive. Eventually, these kinds of meetings died, because everybody was longing either for silence or for some real exchange.

When you're a young writer, you know you need to improve, you want to sharpen your point of view and you need people who are really competent to talk about contemporary literature and who are benevolent in a constructive way. Quite soon after I had moved to Berlin, I ended up in a circle with four other emergent poets, Florian Voss, Hendrik Jackson, Monica Rinck and Daniel Falb. We met every four weeks, and everybody read his or her new texts and we talked about them. This really worked; we knew we could trust each other's judgements and secrecy – nothing of what we said would leave the room. These meetings went on for about ten years or longer. At the same time, the internet was on the rise and new channels of exchange could be explored. Brigitte Oleschinski and I founded the website www.neuedichte.de in 2004.[7] We invited various authors from Germany and Austria and of different generations to write about their poetics, the situation of poetry and how they thought about their work with language, trying to create a

---

[7] This web domain is no longer active. Basic information is provided on Ulrike Draesner's current website: http://www.draesner.de/intermediale-projekte/ The German Literature Archive in Marbach has archived the entire project.

multilateral, interdiscursive space. This might seem quite natural today, but it was new at the time – we were practising talking multilaterally and dealing with divergent sets of meanings, developing a polylogue. Partly, the experiment worked – I suspect that in hindsight now one might detect a lot of practising how to communicate on the internet.

In a way I feel that there are two main areas when it comes to testing your writing. On the one hand there is the professional and public reception of your work. On the other hand, there is feedback that you organize for yourself in a private or half-private space, where you control access. I've done this for years, at least with my novels. I invited people to my flat and read out the entire, almost finished novel to them. An hour of reading each night. Whoever had time would come and listen, like neighbours in my house, artists, friends. I would serve wine, bread and cheese, and after the reading we would talk about the text. It was important for me to create this semi-public reading space. Sharing the room with a real audience also changes how I listen to myself. It creates a distance to my text. By reading out loud from the manuscript, I am enabled to feel the flow of concentration and emotions with the audience. In addition, things came up in the discussions afterwards, questions, ideas, shortcomings, preferences. These were really valuable contributions, uttered in a more direct, spontaneous way than those of the next level of working on the text where you confer with the editor from the publishers.

RB It's interesting, it might sound a bit crazy but what you're describing is that the bread and wine and cheese, the building that you're in, in some ways contribute to the writing of the book.

UD In my experience the instruments used for writing are at least partly formative of what is being written. The author Georg Christoph Lichtenberg, well known for his pointed aphorisms, allegedly said, 'das Schreibwerkzeug schreibt an den Gedanken mit' (the instrument used for writing partly manufactures the thought), and I would like to extend the notion 'instrument' to comprise the writer's body. To me a book, even a printed book, is almost alive. All its actual lif-icity – sorry, I'm just making up this word, I should say vitality – comes to it through me, at least in a first step: I breathe life into it, bringing my imagination, my emotions, my history as a living being to it. As I enact this, two different kinds of communication develop. This links back to our talk about silence and the spaces of silence and non-communicability. Reading out an unpublished text I force the audience to listen. They don't see anything. I see the text, I hear my own voice, and I read the audience. They don't talk, but after twenty years on stages and more than 1,000 readings, I fairly often know what's happening to them. You feel when people are distracted, and you feel when you've got them. I feel their imagination and their concentration, and I painfully feel when I lose them. Reading aloud elucidates my own text's architecture to me. This is what I mean if I talk about 'enacting' the text: the flow of tensions. These silent communications with the audience during a reading are a very specific and beautifully intense form of exchange: I talk to my audience, and they talk back to me in silent mode, just by their degrees of presence. Sometimes for me the mute information is at least as important as anything communicated verbally.

RB It seems in some ways you have always also been translating your body into language, that this has been an integral part of your authorship as a holistic literary process: to embody your literature to other people, sometimes by writing what you physically experience, sometimes by speaking what is ordinarily written.

UD In a way that separation of orality and the written word is artificial. It's therefore quite rewarding not to follow it in all respects. Last year I published the book *Eine Frau wird älter* (A Woman Gets Older). It grew out of a spoken text, created in a long 'interview'.[8] Klaus Sander, the publisher of supposé Verlag who exclusively specialize in audio books, asked me about my experiences with and thoughts concerning age, wanting to entice me to freely talk about the topic and tell stories. There is this wonderful essay by Heinrich von Kleist, 'Über die allmähliche Verfertigung der Gedanken beim Reden' (*c*. 1805, On gradually finalizing thoughts whilst speaking). I read it at school and found it amazing and awe-inspiring in equal measure. I was a very shy child and young person and could never have imagined doing anything as bold as getting up in front of a class or group of people and starting to speak without a concept or even the faintest idea of what I wanted to say. Kleist describes a scene from the French Revolution: A man opens his mouth and finds himself saying words he didn't know he had within himself. I never dared to do that in a discussion, but there, with Klaus at the kitchen table, I finally managed to 'let go' and tell memories and thoughts about what it means to be a woman in her fifties, 'winging it' – talking while thinking. It felt like climbing a huge swing and making body and thought move in unison. After the CDs had been published, people asked for 'the book'. I wrote it, using the talk as its basic line of reference, adding and editing. But still the writing came from the spoken text.

---

8   Ulrike Draesner, *Eine Frau wird älter* (Munich: Penguin, 2018). Ulrike Draesner, *Happy Aging: Ulrike Draesner erzählt ihre Wechseljahre* (Wyk auf Föhr: supposé, 2016).

RB   And lives on with you speaking about it. You still go on radio talking about it and it's not just about the written text, that really is just one part of how you are managing to translate your body and the realities of all of our bodies, but rather the text is one thing, one part of a set of things, and that whole set is the literature. I suppose I'm encouraging you to think about how all of these performances, whether it's in your own flat or whether it's a public reading or whether it's going on air, is also part of that text that you are authoring in a broader sense than simply writing.

UD   It definitely is, and also the translations would be part of the text. I encourage my translators to ask me any questions they like, I try to tell them as much as I can about the German poem, but I also tell them that it will be theirs in the end: a poem in their language. I can't and wouldn't want to interfere. The text needs to live a life of its own – including being transformed into a different tongue and performed by different voices. To me any translation or (oral) recreation of the text is a function, in the mathematical sense of this word, of the so-called original. A function, stretching across time and space.

RB   I'm interested in your role in the Deutsches Literaturinstitut in Leipzig (Leipzig Institute for German Literature) and how you understand the potential for transformation there. One point of reference for me is what Walter Höllerer did in Berlin in the early 1960s. He was brought into the Technische Universität (Technical University), which was all new and exciting at the time, and he was young and exciting too. He set up all sorts of things, including the linguistic journal, *Sprache im technischen Zeitalter*, and in some ways it seems to me that there's something parallel going on here: the way you've come into Leipzig as the first female professor there and you've got this forensic interest in language. You've got your own ways of networking which we were talking about earlier, different kinds of spaces to the ones Höllerer was looking for. I'm interested to hear more about how you have found working in Leipzig and how you think you can shape a network, or not, or what you might like to achieve.

UD   Given the variety of media everybody uses and is surrounded by today, it is vital for literature that we teach reading, reading complexity, and that we train schoolteachers in how to approach and understand literary techniques and how to perceive linguistic beauty. I try to teach writing to aspiring writers by teaching them how to talk about literature and how to interpret, rethink and rewrite literary texts. Our students at Leipzig may or may not become professional writers, but I am sure to endow each of them with a valuable gift: the ability to read any text whatsoever, to write as clearly as possible and as intricately as necessary about controversial topics and characters, and to pass on this knowledge, playing an important part in cultural transfers. Teaching people to enjoy reading and to teach literature as an active combination of reading and writing skills is one of the networks we are creating and extending in Leipzig.

Yet, sometimes I find with my students that it might be equally important to talk about all the non-things, the negatives. How does it feel not to be able to write? How do you do your work not knowing how to proceed? How do you survive a year of writing and writing and throwing it all away and being stuck with nothing, with an idea that won't go away because this dragon in your room, there it is, complaining? How do you change a character's voice? What do you need to read and how do you research for a novel? It's quite different from any academic research.

RB We're back to, how do we find the things that can't be seen? Speaking of academic research, one of the shortcomings of German as an academic discipline has surely been that it's tended towards the canonical and its tended towards reinforcing what's already there and a way of doing things that is quite exclusionary. That's why I'm wondering if in your role in Leipzig you see yourself really able to effect change by creating a different space where you talk about the things that aren't visible and then perhaps put different things on the map as a result.

UD I would hope so. I encourage my students not to think in preconceived formats. We don't enforce distinctions, such as, 'this is fiction', 'this is poetry'. Each text needs to find its form and it is fascinating to jointly migrate into hybrid spaces. We also encourage mixed media approaches, some of our students bring either artistic or musical backgrounds to the Institute. They organize their own readings and presentations, even workshops, and from time to time we teach seminars on these topics, too. Currently there is an exhibition on with the HGB, Hochschule für Graphik und Buchkunst (College of Graphic Design and Book Art), it's just next door to the Literature Institute. It comprises paintings, texts, installation, and a printed catalogue. But there is one thing we cannot do: change the literary market. We can't change the situation in publishing.

RB Well you can't change it immediately, but over time?

UD It will change because different formats are developing. Who knows what's going to happen on the internet and with the publication of texts anyway? The process has been going on now for two decades and more. Smaller new publishing houses have come up. They might not be commercially very successful but earn just enough money to survive. Wonderful texts have been published there and the canon has become a bit less homogenous. I would encourage any development enhancing variety and divergence as a teacher and as the female writer that I am myself. Things have changed since I started out, but discriminatory sub-structures and 'habits' of unequal pay have survived. So, looking at the roles and positions of women writers in Germany makes me feel quite ambivalent. Numbers are appalling in some fields, e.g. the predominantly male membership in German academies.

RB What about the major prizes? The German Book Prize is fairly even handed, deliberately so I think.

UD Most prizes seem to be fine, and I am not talking about number-counting and female/male rates. The stories tend to become more meaningful if you follow up the events after the prize: how many books were sold? How did the reputation of the writer develop afterwards? I remember Marlene Streeruwitz saying how she only felt that she was considered a writer after she had turned fifty. Before, she had always been a 'female writer'.

RB So, there's a ghost of a grammatical structure?

UD Of a patriarchal structure, definitely. If you look at publishing houses, although structures have been improving there as well over the last ten years, you just encounter what seems to be 'normal' in Germany: a dwindling proportion of female employees as you move towards the top. Press agents still tend to be young, good-looking, female. And the CEO? Male. There are some female publishers now, but when I started out there weren't any besides Antje Kunstmann. It will be quite a journey till anything like an equal ratio in real power will be reached. This is important, because it influences our ideas about entitlement and authority, about scope and renumeration, about the value of authors as well. Who is allowed to do what? We talked about canons and texts, be they primary or secondary, that I use in teaching. Of course, I take care to come up with reading lists where half of the texts was written by a female author, but this is difficult given the history of German literature: our nineteenth century just seems to be devoid of female writing. Women writers were suppressed. It's not that they wrote and then weren't published. They didn't even get to the writing. You have to make an effort to teach in a more equal way. Not everybody is willing to do this. It also challenges you to be inventive and again think about what is lacking and how it could be made audible and visible. Here writing literature and teaching literature share a common purpose, at least for me.

RB You'd like to think things have changed a little in how visible women writers are now?

UD Friederike Mayröcker told me that once she took part in a dinner after someone had been given a literary prize. I don't remember where it took place, but she described how she sat next to Ernst Jandl, her husband, and Reich-Ranicki, who had usurped the role of 'I'm the most important literary critic Germany has ever seen.' He had placed himself between Jandl and Mayröcker and sat there for the entire dinner with his back turned to Mayröcker, exclusively talking to Jandl. On top of this, everybody taking part in the dinner could watch for hours how he humiliated her. I don't think that this would happen any longer, but I simultaneously don't believe that this kind of behaviour has vanished entirely. It occurs in more subtle form; you notice it in body language, time spans of attention and the like. We also find a lot of differences in, for example, the marketing setup for male or female writers, in the advances that are given to writers for their manuscripts. The book market is ridden by a gender gap as much as any other area of German life. And how should this not be the case? It's part of this society. Structures of discrimination have turned more subtle, especially discrimination by women against women can be quite elusive. This is where the metaphor of the glass ceiling comes in. You feel it, it's there, it's difficult to really touch it, but after having been around for more than twenty years, you definitely know that it does exist.

RB I was just thinking of a female writer who might help us think slightly differently about this issue of a glass ceiling and women who are made invisible by the literary establishment: Gabriele Wohmann, was really very well-known and very popular in her day, in the 1970s and 1980s. She worked in all sorts of different registers and genres, from commissioned pieces for radio and TV, through to complex novels that won important prizes and were highly regarded. People really liked her work, it spoke to readers' interests, particularly because she often wrote about middle-class marriage problems, and that had a real reach. But she's been forgotten, and she actually foresaw this in quite an early interview, where she humorously said she was a 'Vielschreiberin', a woman who writes a lot, and this is a category doomed to be disregarded by the academic and literary establishment. And I wondered about your own experience. You've also done all sorts of things. Some things have been commissions where you've been asked by a local region to write something that would fit in, for example *Mein Hiddensee* (2015, *My Hiddensee*) came from that sort of exchange.⁹ Or *Eine Frau wird älter* began as a surprise request, and it's turned out that there are lots of people who wanted to have that kind of story told. How do you feel about those pieces which could at some level turn you into a 'Vielschreiberin'?

UD I'm not a Vielschreiberin. This word is a devastating and deprecatory label, which I fiercely refute. I don't produce quantity, but quality. Vielschreiberin implies that you just scribble down some mediocre lines – and publish them. I don't know Wohmann's case. But while you were talking, I remembered Marlene Streeruwitz about ten years ago, giving a short talk on the occasion of a literary prize exclusively for women. She told us about a then recent incident at the Literaturhaus (literature centre) in Munich where the director had introduced her. He entered the stage obviously entirely unprepared, but with some sheets of paper in his hands, at which he glanced only to flippantly remark: 'Oh, such a long list of writing. You are a very 'fleißig Autorin' – an industrious female author. She told us that a good friend, sitting next to her, had had to calm her down about this 'fleißig'. She gave the reading and went off to do some research on literary reviews in magazines and newspapers, checking out the use of adjectives and their gender-specific attribution.

RB What did she find?

UD There is an image in Germany, the 'fleißig Lieschen' (industrious little Liesel), used as a role model to turn girls into good wives and mothers. Here they are, silently bent over needlework. 'Text' literally means fabric, but these fleißig Lieschen produce it from wool not words, and, more importantly, they follow strict rules and produce objects which serve a practical purpose. I remember the fleißig Lieschen from textbooks in my childhood in the sixties and early seventies. Streeruwitz found that in literary criticism the word 'fleißig' was almost exclusively applied to female writers. Male authors were called productive, creative, wonderful, figureheads of literary development, brilliant and ingenious, instead of 'fleißig'. A female mastermind still is a very foreign concept in the German context.

RB I know for Wohmann, some of it was just a case of doing the work that would bring in some money, and she was quite OK with that. She

---

⁹ Ulrike Draesner, *Mein Hiddensee* (Hamburg: mare, 2015).

was quite pragmatic. So, to move away from Wohmann but stick with the basic question: You get asked to do things and some of them are quite handy because they bring in money. Other things you're going to do, whether it brings in money or not. Do you differentiate, or do you find that actually one thing can become more of a pet project for you than you had thought it would do?

UD   If someone suggests a certain topic to me or format, I usually wait and see. I need a genuine point of interest in order to get started at all. If I cannot find one, I decline the offer, never mind the money. This may sound heroic, but it isn't – since the sums offered usually aren't that big anyway. I've been asked to do many things, translations, editing jobs, all of which I declined, write literary criticism, which I also don't do, contribute to anthologies, write a libretto for an opera, which I enjoyed, write lyrics for songs. When mare publishers asked me whether I wanted to write a book for their series on islands, I immediately said yes. I have been interested in nature writing right from my beginnings as an author, so the book about Hiddensee island provided me with the perfect occasion to make a serious effort in that field and even get paid for it. I also wrote a kind of travel guide about London, which I did for two reasons. First, because I was invited to provide the photographic material as well. I love to take pictures and combine text and image.[10] And second, because I was able to be my own master: I could choose the places and topics I wanted to include. The book made me explore London, it made me think about urban spaces, their developments, and ways of representing them. I needed to invent the form as well, which made the entire enterprise attractive as an artistic project. That's why I said yes, not because of the money, which covered a fairly professional camera and a few trips to London but nothing else. Sometimes I'm mistaken, too, I agree to write about a certain topic because it sounds interesting and I might even have a first idea how to tackle it. But then it doesn't work out. Yet, all of this is only true of prose. It never worked for me in poetry. I can't write poems to order: 'Write a poem on the birthday of . . .'. Of course, I could produce a text, and it might even look like a poem. Probably most people would even believe it to be a poem. But it would just be sham. And I would know. I absolutely don't do this. My work is my work, and I need to protect it.

---

[10]   Ulrike Draesner, *London* (Berlin: Insel, 2016).

In Conversation Olga Martynova: On Living in Multiple Literary Worlds

Olga Martynova (b. 1962 in Siberia) grew up in Leningrad (Saint Petersburg) and did not learn German until she was an adult, when she moved to Germany in 1991. Her debut novel, *Sogar Papageien überleben uns* (Even Parrots Outlive Us), was longlisted for the German Book Prize and shortlisted for the Aspekte Prize in 2010, while her next novel, *Mörikes Schlüsselbein* won the Ingeborg Bachmann Prize in 2013. She has published five volumes of poetry in Russian, as well as collections of essays in both languages, and routinely collaborates with other poet-translators in moving both her own work and that of her husband, Oleg Jurjew, between the two languages. I became interested in Martynova's work when I began researching authors writing in German as a second language for this study, and Ulrike Draesner was able to put us in touch. We met in the German Film Museum in Frankfurt am Main in the summer of 2019. An English translation follows the German original.

RB Wir sind im Deutschen Filmmuseum, wo hervorragend alles gezeigt wird, was in einen Film hineinkommt. Es gibt ja nicht nur die Story und die Schauspieler, sondern die verschiedensten Objekte, Techniken, Geräusche, eine Farbpalette, das kommt alles zusammen und bildet einen Film. In diesem Museum wird das erfahrbar gemacht. Bei der Literatur ist es vielleicht auch ähnlich, aber dieses Netzwerk von Objekten, Blickwinkeln, von mir aus Geräuschen, Erfahrungen, alles, was in eine literarische Welt hineinfließt, kann man in diesem Fall schwerer erfahrbar machen. Wie denkt man als Autor über solche Sachen nach?

OM Das ist schwierig, das sind verschiedene Medien, aber jede Kunst macht das Gleiche. Letztendlich auch ein Musikstück oder ein Bild. Sie alle schaffen etwas, was es gibt, und was es auch autonom gibt, ohne Betrachter oder Leser. Aber wenn ein Betrachter oder Leser vorhanden ist, da ändert einfach ein Kunstwerk etwas im Kopf, oder in der Art der Wahrnehmung, das ist ganz egal. Mit welchen Mitteln der Film oder die Literatur das macht, ist, glaube ich, nicht die hauptsächliche Frage, weil innerhalb des Films oder innerhalb der Literatur es auch so verschiedene Arten zu schreiben oder zu filmen gibt. Und die Unterschiede können innerhalb eines Genres größer sein.

RB Trotzdem meine ich, dass Sie uns einen großen Einblick in diesen kreativen Prozess erlauben. Ich denke an den Roman *Mörikes Schlüsselbein*, wo man das ganze Netzwerk schon zu Augen bekommt, wie Leute zusammen Literatur schaffen. Und zum einen ist das eine Art Bildungsroman für den Moritz, der ja Schriftsteller werden will, und also alles Mögliche aus seinem Alltag in verschiedene Geschichten hineinverwebt. Das sind nicht nur seine Gedanken, oder eine gewisse Vorstellung von Sprache, es ist wirklich alles, was er sieht. Zum Beispiel diese Übersetzung, die seine Mutter macht, und die dann in einem Schriftstück von ihm wiederauftaucht, sowie tatsächlich in Russland, wo Marina später ein Stockwerk über ihrem ursprünglichen Auftraggeber zu Besuch ist. Also denke ich mir schon, dass dieser Roman versucht, ein Netzwerk für den Leser erfahrbar zu machen, ja konkret zu zeigen, wie Literatur aus persönlichen Beziehungen, aber eben auch aus Objekten, Welterfahrungen und zum Teil auch wirklich aus Sachen, die jenseits der Sprache liegen, wie Literatur aus diesen Eindrücken entsteht.

OM Aber denken Sie nicht, dass eigentlich jedes oder fast jedes literarische Werk das macht, das ist genauso wie im Film, das ist eine Auswahl von Objekten, die ins Bild kommen oder erwähnt werden, da wird etwas gebaut, genau wie im Film.

RB Ja, aber was ich an Ihrem Werk besonders schön finde, ist, wie Sachen, die sich nicht so leicht fassen lassen, auch herausgearbeitet werden. Die Stimmen, die Engel in *Engelherd* zum Beispiel, machen etwas erfahrbar, was man nicht sehen kann.

OM Ja, das finde ich auch, dass es Aufgabe auch eines jeden Kunstwerks ist, egal ob das Musik, Bild oder Literatur ist, etwas erfahrbar zu machen, sichtbar zu machen, was davor nicht sichtbar war. Ich glaube, dass Kunst überhaupt unsere Wahrnehmung immer erweitert – dass Malerei uns lehrt zu sehen, zum Beispiel. Wir sehen dank der bildenden Kunst Dinge, die wir ohne sie nicht merken würden. Und ich glaube genauso, dass das mit der Literatur und der Dichtung auch so ist. Das ist – eine Schule der Formulierung, wie die Malerei eine Schule des

Sehens ist. Lesen erweitert unsere Möglichkeiten, wahrzunehmen und unsere Gedanken für uns zu fassen und zu formulieren. Deshalb diese Mühe, die jeder, der schreibt, auch auf sich nimmt, etwas erfahrbar und sichtbar zu machen.

Seit einigen Tagen denke ich, dass das folgende Bild für mich eine Visualisierung der Stille und Ruhe ist: Ein mit Mull bedeckter Eimer mit Wasser, der auf einem Holzhocker in einem von der Mittagssonne gefüllten, aber mit Tüllvorhängen gedämpften Zimmer steht, ein Krug zum Schöpfen daneben. In einem Film (in der Ästhetik von, sagen wir, Tarkowski) zeigst du den Eimer und brauchst nichts zu erklären. In der Literatur ist das bloße Zeigen des Eimers, ohne weitere Erklärungen, ein minimalistischer Vorgang, wie etwa jener berühmte Frosch, der beim japanischen Dichter Bashô einfach mit einem 'Plumps' im Teich verschwindet und uns eine Stimmung hinterlässt, die von einem Leser des Gedichtes zum anderen verschieden sein kann.

Wenn wir einen Schwimmkäfer in diesem Eimer von Rand zu Rand rudern lassen, wird er einige von uns an Hofmannsthals Käfer erinnern. Manche von uns kommen nicht darauf. Manche haben von Hofmannsthals Käfer nie gehört. Stört mich das, dass mein Leser diesen Käfer eventuell nicht so einordnet, wie ich es meine? Nicht im Geringsten. Er wird ihn anders einordnen. Genau wie der Eimer, der vermeintlich in der Ästhetik Tarkowskis präsentiert wird, ganz anders eingeordnet werden könnte: Nicht Ruhe und Stille, sondern: Opa erzählt vom Krieg, wie scheiße es war, als sie Wasser vom Brunnen am Ende der Straße holen mussten.

Also besteht meine Aufgabe so gesehen nicht einmal darin, die Idee der Stille und Ruhe zu vermitteln, sondern darin, den Eimer sichtbar zu machen.

RB Und wie lassen Sie sich dann inspirieren, wenn das Sachen sind, die nicht da sind? Wie findet man sie, die Sachen, die nicht da sind, die man nicht sehen kann, die man nicht irgendwie anfassen kann?

OM Das ist eine nicht so einfache Frage. Weil wenn man nichts anderes als das das ganze Leben lang macht, ist das schon keine Inspiration, sondern eine Lebensart. Und das ist natürlich eine Konzentration, die notwendig ist, wahrscheinlich. Jemand hat mir vor kurzem gesagt – heute kann man alles messen –, dass Wissenschaftler Gehirnwellen von meditierenden Mönchen und von Dichtern, die gerade dichten, gemessen haben. Und sie sind gleich, diese Gehirnwellen. Das sind die gleichen Frequenzen. Das sind, denke ich, Frequenzen einer Konzentration, man kann auch sagen, einer Konzentration eigentlich auf Nichts. Sowohl westliche als auch östliche Philosophien setzen sich mit Begriffen wie Nichts oder Stille auseinander, aber diese Stille ist nicht Abwesenheit von

Geräuschen, sondern etwas, das auch inspirierend sein kann. Das klingt etwas abgehoben, aber dazu gehört alles, die ganze Welt, auch der ganze Schmutz der Welt, die Pein der Welt, die durch die Filter dieses angeblichen Nichts und dieser angeblichen Stille sichtbar werden. Man hat einerseits Eindrücke des Lebens und gibt sie in einem Kunstwerk weiter, andererseits gibt es das Wissen, dass ein Kunstwerk nur scheinbar das Leben widerspiegelt, dass es die Vorstellung der Wahrnehmenden vom Leben auch formt. Es gibt eine Grenze zwischen dem Leben und dem Kunstwerk, das Leben wiedergibt. Was passiert, wenn diese Grenze passiert wird, ist entscheidend. Das ist tatsächlich ganz technisch, das gehört zum Beruf, dass man als Künstler immer auf der Suche ist nach den Möglichkeiten, das zu erfassen, was in dieser Grenze steckt.

RB Es wäre interessant, mal die Gehirnwellen von einem Leser auch mal zu messen. Denn, wenn der Roman wirklich gelungen ist, dann muss sich der Leser auch in diese Welt hineinfinden, wo man eben über das Nichts meditiert.

OM Bestimmt. Ich stehe momentan in einem Briefwechsel mit einem österreichischen Autor, der in Japan lebt, Leopold Federmair, für ein Projekt über die Zukunft des Romans. Also verschiedene Autoren tauschen ihre Gedanken dazu aus. Und er hat mich an eine Szene in Tolstois *Anna Karenina* erinnert, wo Anna im Zug sitzt und ein Buch mit einer Taschenlampe liest. Und sie ist damit von der ganzen Welt losgelöst. Und natürlich ist sie in derselben Welt und wahrscheinlich auf derselben Frequenz wie der Autor des Buches, aber auch Tolstoi, der das beschreibt. Dieselbe Anna Karenina im Roman, jemand hat sie gefragt, was Liebe ist. Und sie hat gesagt – tja, auf Russisch ist das sehr einfach gesagt und auf Deutsch sehr umständlich. In der neuesten Übersetzung von R. Tietze heißt es z. B.: „wenn es gilt: so viele Köpfe, so viele Geister, dann gilt auch: so viele Herzen, so viele Arten der Liebe". Eigentlich ist das ein lateinischer Spruch: „Quot capita, tot sensus" – So viele Köpfe, so viele Meinungen. Vielleicht ließe das sich so umschreiben: Wenn es stimmt, dass es so viele Meinungen wie Köpfe gibt, dann stimmt auch, dass es so viele Arten der Liebe wie Herzen gibt. Und wir können dann auch sagen, dass es so viele Varianten eines Buches gibt wie Leser. Weil natürlich jeder Leser das Buch aufs Neue schafft. Das ist nicht dasselbe Buch, das geschrieben wurde. Das ist eine kreative Zusammenarbeit zwischen dem Buch und dem Leser. Und deshalb glaube ich, Sie haben völlig Recht, diese Gehirnwellen sind auch bei dem Leser wie bei einem kreativen Akt.

RB Jetzt auch mal ganz praktisch gedacht, wir sprechen von Autoren und von Lesern. Bevor der Leser zum Buch kommt, gibt es auch verschiedene andere Literaturvermittler. Sei es beim Verlag die Leute, die das Cover designen, oder vermarkten, oder eben, wenn das Buch übersetzt wird, der Übersetzer, der dazukommt. Und jedes Mal haben diese Personen einen gewissen Einfluss auf den Text. Also kann man das immer weiter auffächern?

OM Nein, ich glaube nicht, dass Cover oder Vermarktung einen Einfluss auf den Text haben; Übersetzung ja, selbstverständlich. Bei Übersetzung wird etwas anderes geschaffen, etwas anderes als das Original. Natürlich alles, was Sie jetzt erwähnt haben, kann das Schicksal des Buches sehr stark beeinflussen, aber ich glaube, das Buch bleibt dasselbe.

RB Egal, wie das Cover aussieht?

OM Ich glaube ja.

RB Aber mit den Übersetzern ist es doch eine andere Arbeit. Und Sie arbeiten ja auch stark mit Elke Erb zusammen?

OM Ja, in der letzten Zeit weniger, aber wir haben sehr viel zusammen übersetzt. Wir haben zwei Romane von Oleg Jurjew übersetzt und wir haben viele, viele Gedichte übersetzt.

RB Und wie ist dann diese Erfahrung? Also Sie schreiben die Gedichte auf Russisch, und Elke Erb übersetzt sie dann ins Deutsche. Aber Sie sind natürlich des Deutschen sehr mächtig. Also, inwiefern waren Sie dann an diesem Prozess beteiligt?

OM Wissen Sie, wenn Elke meine Gedichte übersetzt, dann mische ich mich überhaupt nicht ein. Ich schreibe seit einiger Zeit Gedichte nur auf Deutsch, seit dem Tod meines Mannes, Oleg Jurjew, schreibe ich nur auf Deutsch. Er war genau wie ich russischer Dichter. Und wir waren so eng zusammen als Dichterpaar, nach seinem Tod fühle ich mich nicht mehr in der Lage, Gedichte auf Russisch zu schreiben. Aber damals dachte ich, Elke macht jetzt ihr Werk aus meinem, und ich habe mich nicht eingemischt. Anders, wenn wir zusammen andere Autoren übersetzt haben. Da haben wir unser gemeinsames Werk geschaffen, als zwei Übersetzer. Da haben wir sehr, sehr viel, man kann sagen, gestritten, aber das war nicht gestritten im eigentlichen Sinne, wir haben einfach alles besprochen. Wir konnten stundenlang über eine Zeile diskutieren, oder ein Wort. Das war sehr intensiv und sehr interessant, das war für mich eine große Bereicherung. Man erfährt sehr viel, wenn man übersetzt. Ich übersetze jetzt fast nicht, aber das fehlt mir ein bisschen. Man wird klüger durch die Übersetzung. Niemals wird ein Buch so gründlich gelesen, wie von einem Übersetzer, und ich glaube, kein Lektor merkt so viele Unstimmigkeiten in einem Buch wie ein Übersetzer. Das ist wirklich die gründlichste Art zu lesen. Und das hat mir unglaublich viel gebracht, diese Zusammenarbeit.

RB Da kommen wir eigentlich auf diese Idee zurück, dass man mehr sehen muss, als auf den ersten Blick zu sehen wäre. Übersetzer sind sozusagen berufsmäßig darin wirklich gut trainiert. Könnte man weiter gehen und sagen, dass Autoren auch in einer gewissen Weise alle Übersetzer sind, weil sie eine Realität in Sprache übersetzen?

OM Ja, selbstverständlich, natürlich. Ich glaube jeder Akt des Schreibens ist eine Übersetzung. Entweder Realität in Sprache zu übersetzen, oder auch einen Gedanken zu formulieren ist auch Übersetzung. Weil der Gedanke dann ganz frisch und unformuliert kommt, und man muss das fassen und sehr fein ausarbeiten, um dann tatsächlich diesen Gedanken auszuformulieren und nicht einen anderen.

RB Der Fjodor Stern in *Mörikes Schlüsselbein* sagt so etwas Ähnliches über Gedanken: die Gedanken entstehen und sie brauchen dann die richtigen Worte und man muss aufpassen, dass die Falschen nicht den Gedanken schnappen. Das fand ich richtig gut formuliert.

OM Das ist wie gesagt auch eine Übersetzung, der Vorgang des Denkens. So gesehen ist jeder Sprechakt eine Übersetzung. Wenn ein Übersetzer das Original so präzise, wie es nur geht, wiederzugeben hat (und die Genauigkeit ist keine wortwörtliche Übersetzung), dann hat jeder Sprechende eigentlich eine ähnliche Aufgabe: seine Gedanken so präzise wie möglich wiederzugeben.

RB In zwei Büchern deuten Sie auf diesen Satz von Alexander Wwedenskij hin, dass jede Beschreibung falsch sei. Dass man genauso gut sagen kann, ein Schiff hängte über dem Kopf als dass man ein Buch läse. Das kommt dann im Text von *Sogar Papageien überleben uns* und auch als Epigraph in *Mörikes Schlüsselbein* vor. Das wäre dann auch beinahe eine Art Liebeserklärung an eine literarische Welt, wo man einfach anders denkt. Also dass Literatur einfach andere Wahrnehmungsräume aufschließt, in die man hineinversinken kann. Oder wie haben Sie das gemeint?

OM Wissen Sie, das ist keine andere Wahrnehmung, das ist eine sehr realistische Beschreibung. Diese Stelle aus Wwedenskij:

In einem Roman wird das Leben beschrieben, da läuft angeblich die Zeit, aber sie hat nichts gemeinsam mit der wirklichen Zeit, da gibt es keine Ablösung des Tages durch die Nacht, da entsinnt man sich spielerisch beinah des ganzen Lebens, während du dich in der Wirklichkeit kaum an den gestrigen Tag erinnern kannst. Und überhaupt: Jede Beschreibung ist falsch. Der Satz: 'Ein Mensch sitzt, über seinem Kopf ist ein Schiff' ist doch vielleicht richtiger als 'Ein Mensch sitzt und liest ein Buch'.

Was beschreibt das? Dass jemand sitzt, und wenn er gerade an ein Schiff denkt, beschreibt das, dass über seinem Kopf ein Schiff ist, seinen inneren Zustand genauer, als wenn wir sagen, er hätte das Buch in der Hand. Aber Wwedenskij war ein radikaler Absurdist, und ich glaube, er wäre nicht zufrieden, wenn man sagen würde, man könne tatsächlich das, was er sagt, interpretieren. Generell bleibt in jeder Kunst einiges unerklärbar. Stellen wir uns viele Menschen in einem Raum vor, jeder hat seine eigene Welt um sich. Jeder hat seine eigenen Gedanken und Probleme, und seinen eigenen Gedankenfluss. Wenn wir das visualisieren, was jeder Mensch, der im selben Raum ist, momentan denkt und fühlt und spürt und vielleicht vor seinem inneren Auge hat, dann wird es ein Gedränge sein aus sehr chaotischen Bildern und Ideen und Problemen und Erinnerungen und Erwartungen. Und das ist auch Realität, das ist eine unsichtbare, aber für jeden Menschen in diesem Raum oft die wichtigere Realität als das, was sich in diesem Raum abspielt. Nicht immer, aber oft. Das kann passieren, dass jemand so intensiv mit seinen momentanen Problemen beschäftigt ist, dass das, was gerade vor ihm ist, nicht mehr so viel Bedeutung hat wie das, woran er denkt. Und natürlich, wenn man diesen Raum als Schreibende beschreibt, dann muss man auswählen, welche Figuren, welche Gedanken, welche Gefühle, und welche Bilder er wiedergibt oder nicht wiedergibt. Oder man kann auch verschieden daran arbeiten, man kann denselben Menschen mit denselben Problemen entweder über Beschreibung dieses Menschen zeigen, oder das erzählen, was gerade passiert, oder über einen Dialog zwischen ihm und noch jemandem, oder über die Beobachtung einer dritten Person und so weiter. Oder sagen: 'Ein Mensch sitzt, über seinem Kopf ist ein Schiff'.

RB Und wenn ich das richtig verstehe, in *Mörikes Schlüsselbein* haben Sie versucht, das auch visuell erfahrbar zu machen, durch die graue Schrift, die zeigt, dass das Eine oder das Andere jetzt zum Vorschein kommt, aber eigentlich muss man alles schon irgendwie gleich im Kopf behalten.

OM Ja, ich wollte auch ein bisschen mit den Schriften spielen, in der Zeit, wo das Buch als physisches Objekt gefährdet ist. Das ist auch ein bisschen eine Hommage an das Buch. Die Entwicklung des Buches ähnelt der Entwicklung der modernen Technik. Es gibt etwas, das zuerst nicht so bequem ist, dann entwickelt man es, perfektioniert es, das wird immer handlicher und irgendwann haben wir das bequemste Gerät seiner Art, aber danach entwickelt man es weiter und plötzlich ist es nicht mehr so bequem, und nicht mehr so benutzerfreundlich, der Fortschritt beginnt, sich selbst ad absurdum zu führen. Ich glaube, dass die Menschheit jahrtausendelang auf dem Weg zu diesem Gegenstand, zum Buch war, und irgendwann hatten wir das perfekte Buch. Danach begann man, diesen Gegenstand weiter zu perfektionieren, was nicht nötig war. Das E-Book ist ein Schritt zurück zu einer Schriftrolle, ohne Gliederung von Seiten und so weiter. Und ich wollte unbedingt in *Mörikes Schlüsselbein* polygraphisch auch ein bisschen spielen. Bezeichnenderweise ist das in der E-Book-Ausgabe misslungen, es gab ein technisches Problem, das die anders gedruckten Stellen unlesbar machte.

RB Dann kann man davon abstrahieren und sagen, das Physische an dem Buch ist auch Teil der Geschichte.

OM Nicht unbedingt. Ich glaube nicht, dass das tatsächlich etwas ausmacht. Genauso wenig wie bei dem Cover. Ich glaube nicht, dass das eine große Bedeutung hat. Man hätte den Text auch normal setzen können.

RB Um weiterhin beim Erfahrbaren zu bleiben: eine Sache, die mich wirklich interessiert, ist, dass Sie schon Teil an mindestens zwei, wenn nicht mehr, unterschiedlichen literarischen Welten oder Netzwerken haben. Sie haben ja natürlich eine russische Schriftstellerpräsenz und auch eine deutschsprachige. Und das würde mich interessieren, ob diese Welten völlig verschieden sind, ob sie sich überschneiden, ob Sie große Unterschiede zwischen den beiden erfahren?

OM Nicht völlig verschieden, sie überschneiden sich. Groß sind die Unterschiede nicht, auch wenn es natürlich verschiedene Literaturbetriebe sind, und die Autoren, die dort involviert sind, sind mit verschiedenen Problemen konfrontiert. Aber ganz verschieden sind sie wiederum nicht, jeder, der als Dichter lebt, ich meine als Lyriker, der nur Gedichte schreibt, muss auch einen Brotberuf haben, der Buchmarkt wird immer mehr von Konzernen geprägt, die keinen Sinn darin sehen, gute Literatur zu verlegen, sondern nur an Umsätzen interessiert sind, die wirklich literarischen Verlage entwickeln verschiedene

Überlebensstrategien, der Buchhandel ist bedroht usw., wie überall. Ich bin jetzt regelmäßig im Kontakt mit russischen Kollegen und Verlagen. Als Oleg Jurjew lebte, schrieb er ebenso auf Russisch und auf Deutsch und war genau wie ich in beiden Literaturwelten präsent. Aber er war eher in der russischen, und ich war eher in der deutschen. Jetzt, nach seinem Tod, verwalte ich seinen Nachlass mit Hilfe von Freunden und Kollegen in Russland. Wir sind dabei, Werkausgaben vorzubereiten und Archivarbeit zu leisten. Deshalb kommuniziere ich jetzt viel enger mit der russischen literarischen Welt, weil dort momentan mein Hauptinteresse, Oleg Jurjews Nachlass, ist. Ich bin im Kontakt mit Oleg Jurjews Verlag in St. Petersburg und mit den Kollegen, die mir bei dieser Arbeit helfen. Andererseits sind natürlich meine deutsche literarische Welt und mein Freundesnetzwerk dort nach wie vor präsent. Ich schreibe momentan kaum, weil ich meine Trauer verarbeiten muss. Das ist jetzt das Hauptthema meines Lebens, Verlust und Trauer, ich kann nicht einfach so weiterschreiben, als wäre es nichts. Wenn ich mich frage, wie es vor Oleg Jurjews Tod war, das war, wie ich gesagt habe, ich war sehr stark im deutschen Literaturleben und Literaturbetrieb und er eher im russischen. Obwohl das sich in unserem Fall nicht einfach überschnitten hat, sondern alles bildete eine völlige Einheit. Wir hatten innerhalb einer Familie eine volle Übereinstimmung zwischen der deutschen und der russischen Literatur. Unser Sohn, Daniel Jurjew, hat bereits vor einigen Jahren angefangen, russische Literatur ins Deutsche zu übersetzen, er brachte einige sehr gute Bücher heraus, so wird diese Vermittlungsarbeit und das Leben in zwei Kulturen weitergeführt.

RB Also im deutschen Kontext, ist das auch schon vorgekommen, dass Sie dann immer wieder als die russische Schriftstellerin dargestellt worden sind. Und das war Ihnen recht? Ich meine, Sie haben ja gewählt, auf Deutsch zu schreiben.

OM Das ist mir mehr oder weniger egal. Gerade jetzt in diesen Tagen hat man immer wieder aufgelistet, wer schon irgendwann den Bachmannpreis gewonnen hat, und 2012 die 'russische Autorin Olga Martynova', was ziemlich absurd ist, weil ich natürlich als deutsche Autorin dort mit meinem deutschen Text war.

RB Sie sind 1990/91 nach Deutschland übergesiedelt. Ich stelle mir vor, zu der Zeit wäre es schon ziemlich unvorstellbar gewesen, dass man einfach so davon spricht, dass eine russische Schriftstellerin den Bachmannpreis gewonnen hat. Die deutsche Literatur war schon deutsch. Inzwischen hat sich die ganze Szene doch ziemlich aufgelockert. Sie müssen da einige Veränderungen erlebt haben?

OM Nein, wie jeder Autor kann natürlich auch ich sehr viel Schlechtes über den Literaturbetrieb sagen, aber nicht das. Von Anfang an hatten weder Oleg Jurjew noch ich irgendein Problem der Ausgrenzung, man war sehr offen und sehr interessiert und sehr neugierig uns gegenüber. Kein einziges Mal haben wir gefühlt, dass man uns als Fremde behandelt hätte.

RB Und das Leben in Frankfurt? Das war mal über Siegfried Unseld ein Ort besonders der westdeutschen Literaturszene, aber in den frühen 2000er Jahren ist Suhrkamp nach Berlin weggezogen. Inzwischen spricht man beinah ausschließlich von der Szene in Berlin. Ist das fair? Oder gibt es noch in Frankfurt eine gute literarische Szene?

OM Ja. Es gibt gerade in Frankfurt eine Szene von jungen Autoren – das ist ein sehr blödes Wort, wenn man über Künstler jung sagt, das bedeutet nichts. Aber junge Autoren, die vergleichsweise jung sind, viel jünger als ich zum Beispiel. Und sie haben ein Buch oder zwei Bücher, oder noch überhaupt kein Buch, aber es gibt eine Gruppe, auch mein Sohn gehört zu dieser Dichtergruppe, sie nennen sich ‚Fluchtentiere'. Sie bilden eine Literaturszene in Frankfurt, das ist gut und angenehm, in einer Stadt zu leben, wo so eine neue Literaturszene entsteht. Geschichtlich war natürlich nicht nur Suhrkamp prägend, im Frankfurt der 60er, wahrscheinlich schon Ende der 50er gab es auch eine andere Literaturszene. Es gab die satirische Zeitschrift *Pardon*, ihr Nachfolger ist, glaube ich, *Titanic*. Und da gab es die Szene von Autoren wie Wilhelm Genazino, der im letzten Jahr gestorben ist, oder Robert Gernhardt, und das war auch ein reges literarisches Leben.

RB Also wirklich dann auf Witz aufgebaut, das ist interessant.

OM Ja, und sie sind dann sehr verschiedene Wege gegangen, diese Autoren, aber es gab das auch. Und auch Suhrkamp, selbstverständlich. Es gibt auch den S. Fischer Verlag, meinen Verlag in Frankfurt, und es gibt auch, nicht als Teil irgendeiner Szene, aber es gibt viele gute Autoren in Frankfurt. Sie schreiben, sie leben hier. Ebenso im letzten Jahr ist im Alter von 82 Jahren Paulus Böhmer gestorben, ein Dichter, den diese jungen Lyriker sehr geschätzt haben. Oleg Jurjew und ich haben sie manchmal zusammen eingeladen, den alten Paulus Böhmer und diese ziemlich jungen Dichter, und wir dazwischen. Übermorgen ist ein Jahr vergangen seit dem Tod meines Mannes, und wir haben einen Abend zusammen mit Lydia Böhmer, der Frau von Paulus Böhmer, und diesen jungen Dichtern. Ich fühle mich doch in einer literarischen Stadt und in einer freundlichen literarischen Stadt.

RB Meinen Sie, dass diese Stadt dann auch irgendwo einen Einfluss auf das Werk hat, oder kann man das nicht so sagen?

OM Ich glaube, Einfluss auf das Werk hat alles, egal, was passiert, jede Busfahrt.

RB Also das macht dann schon was aus, dass Sie hier in Frankfurt leben und eben nicht in Berlin?

OM Wahrscheinlich. Frankfurt ist auch eine sehr kleine, überschaubare, ruhige und freundliche Stadt. Das ist eine Stadt, wo ich gerne lebe. Vielleicht weil ich aus St. Petersburg stamme, und St. Petersburg ist eine sehr große Stadt mit einem sehr ausgeprägten Charakter, und eigentlich eine schwierige Stadt. Frankfurt ist im Vergleich mit St. Petersburg eine einfache Stadt.

RB Lassen Sie uns zum Abschluss hin über Preise reden. Sie haben bereits mit Ihrem Debüt viel Aufsehen bei den verschiedenen Jurys erregt, 2011 den Adelbert-von-Chamisso-Preis bekommen und dann eben 2012 den Ingeborg-Bachmann-Preis. Diese Preisstiftungen und -verleihungen bauen natürlich auch ihre eigenen Netzwerke auf. Der Adelbert-von-Chamisso-Preis wurde ja in den 80er Jahren mit der Absicht gegründet, zuerst die deutschsprachige Literatur von Nichtmuttersprachlern und dann, etwas breiter ausgelegt, die deutschsprachige Literatur, die aus einem starken Kulturwechsel zustandekommt, zu ehren. Dieser Preis wurde 2017 eingestellt, weil man das Gefühl hatte, dass man im Grunde dieses Netzwerk, diese Gruppe, die dadurch geformt wurde, nicht mehr explizit brauchte, weil sich diese Autoren auch im sozusagen normalen deutschsprachigen Raum profilieren konnten. Wie haben Sie dann den Chamisso-Preis empfunden, als eine Art Einbindung in eine Gruppe?

OM Ich glaube nicht, dass man diesen Preis zu Recht abgeschafft hat. Ich bin sowieso der Meinung, dass je mehr Preise es für Künstler gibt, desto besser. Man sagt, dass dieser Preis wahrscheinlich einen ghettobildenden Effekt gehabt habe, aber das stimmt nicht. Bevor sie diesen Preis abgeschafft haben, die Robert-Bosch-Stiftung, haben sie sehr viel für die Preisträger gemacht, sie haben auch Lesungen gefördert. Das hieß, dass dadurch die Autoren präsent und sichtbar waren. Eigentlich bin ich nach Deutschland mit fast 30 Jahren gekommen, ohne Deutsch zu sprechen, und ich finde, dass das tatsächlich eine Leistung ist, dass ich inzwischen auf Deutsch schreibe, und warum nicht das auch als Leistung anerkennen? Ich sehe da keine Beleidigung darin. Allerdings wird ein neuer Chamisso-Preis gegründet. Jemand hat das fortgesetzt, eine andere Stiftung, andere Menschen.

RB Mit demselben Namen dann?

OM Mit demselben Namen, ja. Es gab kein Copyright für den Namen, anscheinend. Also wird es fortgesetzt. Aber sie hatten, bevor sie das abgeschafft haben, tatsächlich ein Netzwerk gebildet, und das war für den Status des Preises entscheidend.

RB Also praktische Förderung im Grunde, nicht nur das Geld, sondern dann auch das Profilieren.

OM Ja, das stimmt. Und der Bachmann-Preis, da gibt es wirklich eine sehr große Medienpräsenz dadurch, dann wird mehr Aufmerksamkeit auf Bücher gelenkt. Ich bin überhaupt ein großer Freund von allen Preisen, ich bin jetzt zum Beispiel in der Jury von einem neuen Preis: dem Gertrud-Kolmar-Preis. Das ist ein Preis für Frauen, die Gedichte schreiben. Man kann auch sagen, dass das eine Ausgrenzung sei, oder dass Frauen heute ohnehin präsent seien (die Idee ist, dass eben Frauen unterrepräsentiert sind). Darüber kann man verschiedene Meinungen haben, aber so oder so finde ich das toll, dass das ein Preis ist, der Getrud Kolmar ehrt. Auch die Möglichkeit, einigen Lyrikerinnen einen Preis zu geben, ist hervorragend. Egal welche Idee, ich finde, dass das gut ist, weil das Leben eines Dichters nie leicht ist. Man ist als Schreibender sowieso ziemlich einsam, man kann sehr gute Kollegen und Freunde haben, aber das ist eigentlich eine Einsamkeit fördernde Arbeit. Weil man wirklich immer auf die eigene Arbeit konzentriert ist, und das ist nicht einfach. Und so lukrativ ist das auch sehr oft nicht, deshalb finde ich, wie gesagt, jeden neuen Preis gut. Ich meine jetzt nicht für mich persönlich, sondern überhaupt.

RB Sie haben am Anfang erwähnt, dass Sie an einer vermittelten Briefkorrespondenz arbeiten, zum Thema Zukunft des Romans. Das Projekt interessiert mich sehr, auch weiterhin mit Blick auf die kreative Zusammenarbeit und den Austausch – den materiellen sowie den intellektuellen – über ein gewisses Netzwerk.

OM Es gibt in Wien einen sehr guten literarischen Ort, der heißt 'Alte Schmiede'. Und sie machen ab und zu solche Projekte, mit sehr spannenden Ideen. Es gab letztes Mal, da habe ich nicht teilgenommen, das Thema 'Was ist gute Literatur?' Das haben sie dann als Buch herausgegeben: den Briefwechsel zwischen Autoren, die die Frage diskutieren, was gute Literatur ist. Das Buch ist wirklich gut geworden. Und vor einigen

Jahren zum Beispiel haben sie Autoren aufgefordert, zum Thema 'Das Schreiben und das Geld' zu schreiben, wie das Leben eines Schreibenden von dieser Seite aus aussieht. Das war auch spannend. Und jetzt haben sie diese neue Sache. Ich freue mich darüber, ich schätze österreichische Kollegen, ich liebe Wien, ich mag diesen Ort, die Alte Schmiede.

RB Ja, dann auf der einen Seite haben wir von der Einsamkeit des Schriftstellerlebens gesprochen, auf der anderen Seite sind Sie schon natürlich in diesen verschiedenen Netzwerken eingebunden. Und ich nehme an, dadurch schaffen Sie auch Inspiration, aus diesem Austausch?

OM Ja natürlich, selbstverständlich, das ist wichtig. Aber Tatsache bleibt, dass man als Schreibender eigentlich allein ist, und auf sich selbst angewiesen. Mein Mann und ich waren 38 Jahre zusammen, und das war eine Luxussituation: zwei Schreibende, die einander gut verstehen, sich jederzeit gegenseitig unterstützen, durch menschliche Nähe und gegenseitige Wertschätzung als Dichter. Ich bin meinem Schicksal dafür dankbar.

* * *

RB We are in the German Film Museum where you can get a great sense of everything that goes into making a film. There's more than just the story and the actors, the most varied of objects, technology, sounds, a colour palette, all these things come together to make a film. This museum makes all that tangible. Perhaps it is a similar case when it comes to literature, however this network of objects, points of view, sounds, experiences, all the things that a literary world encompasses, can be harder for people to grasp. How much do you think about these things as an author?

OM That's difficult, they are different media, but all art does this in its own way, music and visual art included. They all create something that exists, and that also exists independently of any observer or reader. But when an observer or a reader is present, a work of art changes something in their head or in the way they perceive things, it doesn't matter which. The means by which film or literature does this is not the main question as far as I'm concerned, because even within the artforms of film or literature there are so many different styles of writing or composition. And the differences within a genre can be greater.

RB Yes, and you provide us with great insight into this creative process. I'm thinking about your novel *Mörikes Schlüsselbein* where we get to see this whole network with our own eyes, how people create literature together. And firstly, it's a kind of Bildungsroman for Moritz who wants to become a writer and interweaves anything he can from his everyday life into the various stories. It's not just his thoughts or a certain take on language, it really is everything that he sees. For example, this translation that his mother does which then reappears in something he writes, and then again in Russia, where Marina is visiting friends who live just one floor above her original client. I really think that this novel tries to make a network tangible for the reader, to show it concretely, how literature is produced from personal relationships, but also simply from objects, experiences of the world and really, in part, from the things that lie beyond language, how it is produced from these impressions.

OM But don't you think that actually every, or nearly every, literary work does that, it is just like a film: we have a selection of objects that come into shot, or are mentioned, and something is made there, exactly like in a film?

RB Yes, but what I find particularly great about your work is how things that aren't so easy to grasp are depicted too. The voices, the angels in *Engelherd* for example, make something that you can't see tangible.

OM Yes, I agree that the task of a work of art, regardless of whether it is music, a picture or literature, is to make tangible, make visible, what wasn't visible before. I think that art always enhances our perception – that painting teaches us to see, for example. Thanks to the visual arts, we see things that we wouldn't notice without them. And I also believe that it is exactly the same with literature and poetry. They are a school of expression – like painting is a school of seeing. Reading expands our opportunity to perceive things and helps us to collect and formulate our thoughts. That's why everyone who writes goes to such efforts to make something tangible and visible.

For some days I've been thinking that the following image is a visual representation of peace and quiet for me: a gauze-covered bucket of water standing on a wooden stool in a room filled with the midday sun muted by tulle curtains, a jug for ladling next to it. In a film (in the style of Tarkowski, let's say) you show the bucket and don't need to explain anything. In literature, the simple depiction of the bucket without further explanation is a minimalistic image, not unlike the famous frog which, according to the Japanese poet Bashō, simply disappears with a plop into a pond and leaves us with a mood that can differ from one reader of the poem to the next.

If we have a water boatman in this bucket, rowing from side to side, some of us will be reminded of Hofmannsthal's beetle. Some of us won't think of that. Some of us have never heard of Hofmannsthal's beetle. Does it bother me that my reader potentially won't interpret this beetle as I intend? Not in the slightest. He will interpret it differently. Just like the bucket, which is supposed to reference Tarkowski's style, could be interpreted completely differently: not 'peace and quiet', but rather 'Grandpa talking about wartime and how rubbish it was when they were forced to collect water from the fountain at the end of the street'.

So my job, when seen like this, isn't to convey the idea of peace and quiet, but rather to make the bucket visible.

RB And where do you get your inspiration from, considering these are things that aren't there? How do you find them, the things that are not there, that you can't see, that you can't somehow touch?

OM That isn't such a simple question. Because when you do nothing other than that your whole life it's not really a question of inspiration anymore, but rather a way of life. And that presumably requires a high degree of concentration. Someone recently told me – anything can be measured nowadays – that scientists have measured the brainwaves of monks meditating and of poets writing. And they are the same, these brainwaves. They have the same frequencies. They are, I reckon, the frequencies of concentrating, of concentrating, in fact, on nothing. Both Western and Eastern philosophies have engaged with such concepts as nothingness or silence, but this silence isn't the absence of noise, rather it is something that can inspire. That sounds a bit abstract, but it includes everything, the whole world, as well as all the corruption of the world, the pain of the world, made visible through the filters of this so-called nothingness and this so-called silence. On the one hand, you have impressions of life and communicate them through a piece of art, on the other, we know that an artwork only seems to reflect life; actually it shapes how people perceive life as well. There is a boundary between life and the work of art that portrays life. What happens when this boundary is crossed is crucial. That is actually very technical, that's part of your job as an artist: to be always on the hunt for the opportunity to capture what's there, in this boundary.

RB Yes, and it would be interesting to measure the brainwaves of a reader too. Because if a novel is really successful, then the reader also has to find their way into this world where one meditates on nothingness.

OM Definitely. I am currently in correspondence with an Austrian author who lives in Japan, Leopold Federmair, on a project about the future of the novel. Lots of authors are collaborating on this. And he reminded me of a scene in Tolstoy's *Anna Karenina*, where Anna is sat on a train reading a book by the light of a torch. And she is transported away from the whole world. And she must, of course, be in the same world, and probably on the same frequency, as the author of the book, but also Tolstoy as he is describing it. The same Anna Karenina in the novel is asked by someone what love is. And she says – well, it is very succinctly expressed in Russian and very long-winded in German. In the newest translation by R. Tietze, for example, it goes, 'wenn es gilt: so viele Köpfe, so viele Geister, dann gilt auch: so viele Herzen, so viele Arten der Liebe'. Actually, that is a Latin phrase: "Quot capita, tot sensus" – as many heads, so many opinions. Perhaps best paraphrased like this: if it's true that there are as many opinions as there are heads, then it must also be true that there are as many kinds of love as there are hearts. And we could then also say that there are as many versions of a book as there are readers. Because naturally every reader creates the book anew. It is not the same book as was written. It is a creative collaboration between the book and the reader. And I believe, therefore, that you're totally right, these brainwaves are the same in a reader as they are in the process of a creative act.

RB Let's just think in totally practical terms, we're talking about authors and about readers. Before the reader gets to the book, there are also various other people involved in making the work of literature. So, for example, the people at the publishers who design the cover or market the book, or, if the book is translated, then of course a translator is involved. And each time these people have a certain influence on the text. Can this be extended ever further?

OM No, I don't think that the cover or marketing has an influence on the text; translation, yes, of course. Something different is created through translation, something different to the original. Naturally everything that you've mentioned can have a very strong influence on the fate of the book, but I believe the book remains the same.

RB Regardless of what the cover looks like?

OM I believe so.

RB But with translators you agree it's actually another piece of work. And you yourself work very closely with Elke Erb?

OM Yes, less so recently, but we have translated a great deal together. We've translated two novels by Oleg Jurjew and many, many poems.

RB   And what is this experience like? I mean, you write your poems in Russian, and Elke Erb then translates them into German. But you are of course totally fluent in German. So to what extent did you get involved in this process?

OM   You know, when Elke translates my poems, I don't interfere at all. I've been writing my poems purely in German for some time now, since the death of my husband, Oleg Jurjew, I write only in German. Just like me, he was a Russian poet. And we were so close as a pair of writers that after his death I haven't felt able to write poems in Russian any more. But at the time my perspective was that Elke makes her work out of mine and I shouldn't interfere. It was different when we were translating other authors together. Then we created our work collaboratively as two translators. We've had many, very many, arguments you could say, but they weren't arguments in the usual sense of the word, we simply discussed everything. We could spend hours discussing one line or one word. That was very intensive and very interesting, it was a real pleasure for me. You learn a great deal when you translate. I barely ever translate now but I do miss it a bit. Translating makes you cleverer. Never is a book so thoroughly read as it is by a translator, and I believe that no editor picks up on as many mistakes in a book as a translator. It really is the most thorough form of reading. And I got an unbelievable amount out of it, this collaboration.

RB   We've actually come back to this idea that you have to see more than appears at first glance. Translators are really well trained in that on the job, so to speak. Could you go one step further and say that all authors are translators to some extent, because they translate reality into language?

OM   Yes, of course, naturally. I believe that every act of writing is a translation. Either translating reality into language, or even to put a thought into words is also a translation. Because thoughts come totally raw and unformulated, and you have to capture them and carefully work them through in order fully to express that thought and not another.

RB   In *Mörikes Schlüsselbein* Fjodor Stern says something similar about thoughts: thoughts arise but then they need the right words, and you have to be careful the wrong ones don't snatch the thought away. I thought that was really well articulated.

OM   That, like I said, is a translation too, the process of thinking. When you look at it that way, every speech act is a translation. If a translator reproduces the original as precisely as possible (and by precision I don't mean word-for-word translation), then every speaker actually has a similar task: to convey their thoughts as precisely as possible.

RB In two of your books, you mention this sentence by Alexander Wwedenski, that no description is right. That you can just as well say there is a ship hanging above someone's head as you can say someone is reading a book. It appears in the text of *Sogar Papageien überleben uns* and also as an epigraph in *Mörikes Schlüsselbein*. That could almost be a kind of declaration of love for a literary world that just allows us to think differently. I mean, that literature unlocks different realms of perception in which we can immerse ourselves. Or what did you mean by that?

OM You know, that isn't a different perception, it is a very realistic description. This passage from Wwedenski:

> When life is described in a novel, time appears to pass but it has nothing to do with real time. Night doesn't follow day, you almost playfully remember your entire life – whereas in reality you can barely remember what happened yesterday. And moreover: no description is right. The sentence: 'a person is sitting with a ship above their head' may even be more accurate than 'a person is sitting reading a book'.

What is that describing? That someone is sitting and when they think about a ship the inner workings of their mind are more accurately described by saying that there is a ship above their head than by saying that there is a book in their hand. But Wwedenski was a radical absurdist and I don't believe he would have been satisfied with the suggestion that you can actually interpret the things he said. In general, every art practice remains inexplicable to a certain extent. If we imagine lots of people in a room, everyone is in their own world. They each have their own thoughts and problems and their own stream of consciousness. If we visualize that, what every person in that room is thinking and feeling in that moment and what they see in their minds' eye, then there would be a maelstrom of chaotic images and ideas and problems and memories and expectations. And that is also reality, that is an invisible but often more important reality for every person in that room than what is actually taking place around them. Not always, but often. That can happen, that someone is so intensely occupied with their current problems that what is directly in front of them doesn't hold as much importance as what they're thinking about. And of course, if you describe this room as a writer, then you have to decide which figures, which thoughts, which feelings, and which images you want it to portray, and which you don't. Or you could also approach it differently, you could show the same person with the same problems by either describing this person, or by explaining what's happening in the present moment, or by creating a dialogue between them and someone else, or by having a third person observe them, and so on. Or say: 'A person is sitting with a ship above their head'.

RB   And if I understand correctly, in *Mörikes Schlüsselbein* you've also tried to make it visibly discernible through the grey font which shows when one thing is in focus and then the other, but actually you somehow have to keep both things in mind.

OM   Yes, I also wanted to play around with the font a little, in a time when the book as a physical object is in danger. It is also something of an homage to the book. The development of the book was similar to the development of modern technology. You have something that's not so convenient, then it gets developed, perfected, it keeps getting easier to use and at some point we have the most convenient gadget of its kind, but then it continues getting developed and suddenly it's not so convenient anymore, not so user-friendly, progress continues to the point of absurdity. I think that humanity was on its way to this object, the book, for thousands of years, and eventually we had the perfect book. Then we started to perfect this object further when we didn't need to. The e-Book is a regression to the scroll, without the division into discrete pages and such like. So I really wanted to play around with *Mörikes Schlüsselbein* polygraphically. Funnily enough, this was unsuccessful in the e-Book, there was a technical issue that made the differently formatted lines impossible to read.

RB   Is it possible to abstract from that and say that the physical make-up of the book is also a part of the story?

OM   Not necessarily. I don't think that matters, actually. As little as the cover. I don't think that it holds any great significance. The text could just as well have been conventionally formatted.

RB   To continue on with the topic of experiencing things: something that really interests me is that you're part of at least two, if not more, different literary worlds or networks. You have, of course, a Russian authorial presence and also a German-speaking one. And I'm interested in whether these worlds are completely different, whether there's a crossover, whether you experience significant differences between the two?

OM Not completely different, there's overlap. The differences aren't significant, although, of course, they are different literary industries, and the authors that are involved in each are faced with different problems. But they're not really very different; anyone who lives as a poet who writes only poetry has to have another job to put food on the table; the book market is increasingly shaped by big companies who see no sense in publishing good literature, they are only interested in sales; the real literary publishers develop various survival strategies; the book trade is under threat etc. – it's the same everywhere. I am now in regular contact with Russian colleagues and publishers. When Oleg Jurjew was alive, he wrote in Russian as well as in German and was present in both literary worlds, just like me. But he was more in the Russian sphere, and I was more in the German one. Now, after his death, I manage his estate with the help of my friends and colleagues in Russia. We are in the process of preparing editions of his work and doing archival work. Therefore, I communicate a lot more closely with the Russian literary world, because that's where my main interest lies at present, with Oleg Jurjew's estate. I'm in contact with Oleg Jurjew's publisher in St Petersburg and with the colleagues who help me with this work. On the other hand, my German literary world and my network of friends are still there, just as before. I'm barely writing at the moment, because I need to work through my grief. That's the main topic of my life now, loss and grief, I can't simply go on writing as though it's nothing. When I think about what it was like before Oleg Jurjew's death, it was, as I've said, the case that I was very firmly in the German literary scene and industry and he more so in the Russian. Although we didn't just overlap, rather everything fitted together as a whole. Within one family we had complete harmony between German and Russian literature. Our son, Daniel Jurjew, started translating Russian literature into German some years ago, he's brought out a few very good books; and that's an example of how this life in two cultures and the mediation between them continues.

RB In the German context it's repeatedly been the case that you are portrayed as a Russian author. Are you okay with that? I mean, you have of course chosen to write in German.

OM That's more or less irrelevant to me. Right at the moment there's been a lot of talk about who won the Bachmann Prize when, and in 2012: 'the Russian author Olga Martynova', which is rather absurd because, of course, I was there as a German author with my German text.

RB You moved to Germany in 1990/91. I imagine that at the time it would have been quite unimaginable that you'd be speaking about an author from Russia winning the Bachmann Prize. German literature was rather German. Since then the whole scene must have opened up a bit. You must have experienced a few changes?

OM No, like any author I could obviously say a lot of negative things about the literary industry, but not that. From the outset neither Oleg Jurjew nor I experienced any issues with being excluded, people were very open and very interested and very curious about us. Not once did we feel that people were treating us as foreigners.

RB And your life in Frankfurt? For a long time, thanks not least to Siegfried Unseld, it was the place for the West German literary scene, but in the course of the 2000s Suhrkamp relocated to Berlin. Since then, people speak almost exclusively about the scene in Berlin. Is that fair? Or is there still a good literary scene in Frankfurt?

OM Yes. There's a scene of young authors right in Frankfurt – 'young' is a very silly word when you're referring to artists, it means nothing. But young authors, who are comparatively young, much younger than me, for example. And they have one or two books, or no books at all, but they form a group, my son belongs to this group of writers too, they call themselves 'Fluchtentiere' (animals of flight). They're creating a literary scene in Frankfurt, it's nice and pleasant to live in a city where this new kind of literary scene is forming. Of course, it wasn't just Suhrkamp which was influential historically, in the Frankfurt of the 1960s, probably even at the end of the 1950s, there was a different literary scene. There was the satirical newspaper *Pardon*, its successor, I believe, is *Titanic*. And there was the group of authors around Wilhelm Genazino, who died last year, or Robert Gernhardt, and that was a lively literary scene as well.

RB So really built on wit then, that's interesting.

OM Yes, and they all went in very different directions, these authors, but that was also there. And Suhrkamp too, obviously. There's also S. Fischer Verlag, my publisher in Frankfurt, and there are many good authors in Frankfurt as well who aren't part of any particular scene. They write, they live here. Just last year, Paulus Böhmer, a writer who was really treasured by these young authors, died aged eighty-two. Oleg Jurjew and I invited them all round together sometimes, old Paulus Böhmer and these rather young writers, and us in the middle. The day after tomorrow is a year since my husband's death and we have an evening with Lydia Böhmer, the wife of Paulus Böhmer, and these young writers. I do feel like I'm in a literary city and in a friendly literary city.

RB Do you think that this city has some kind of influence on the work that gets written here, or wouldn't you say that?

OM I believe everything has an influence on the work, no matter what happens, every bus journey.

RB So that counts for something then, that you live here in Frankfurt and not in Berlin?

OM Most likely. Frankfurt is also a very small, manageable, calm, and friendly city. That is a city where I want to live. Maybe because I come from St Petersburg and St Petersburg is a very big city with a very distinctive character; it is really rather a complicated city. Frankfurt, in comparison to St Petersburg, is very straightforward.

RB To conclude let's talk about prizes. Your debut was already highly regarded by various juries, you received the Adelbert-von-Chamisso Prize in 2011, and then the Ingeborg Bachmann Prize in 2012. The prize funds and awards ceremonies are of course also building their own networks too. The Adelbert-von-Chamisso Prize, for example, was set up in the eighties specifically to support people writing in German as a second language and then recast a little more broadly later on to support literature that has been shaped by moving between cultures. It was stopped in 2017 because there was a feeling that the network, this group that it formed, was no longer explicitly needed; the kinds of authors it profiled were also perfectly able to make a name for themselves in the mainstream German-speaking realm, so to speak. What was your experience of the Adelbert-von-Chamisso Prize, in terms of how it facilitated a kind of group belonging?

OM I don't think it was right to abolish this prize. I think the more prizes there are for artists the better. People speculate that the prize had some kind of 'ghettoizing' effect, but that's not true. Before the Robert-Bosch Foundation got rid of this prize they did an awful lot for the prize-winners, they also sponsored readings. This helped authors be present and visible. I was actually nearly thirty when I came to Germany, without speaking any German, and I consider it an achievement that I now write in German, so why not also recognize it as an achievement? I don't take that as an insult. Mind you, a new Chamisso Prize is being established. Someone is reviving it, another foundation, other people.

RB With the same name then?

OM With the same name, yes. There was no copyright for the name, apparently. So it's being revived. But, before they abolished it, they really had built up a network and that was paramount for the status of the prize.

RB So it gave practical support; not just the money, but real help with raising your profile too.

OM Yes, that's right. And as for the Bachmann Prize, that really does have a big media presence, so you get more attention for your books. I am a big supporter of all prizes. For example, I am now on the jury for a new prize: the Gertrud-Kolmar Prize. This is a prize for women who write poetry. You could say that this is exclusive, or that women are present nowadays anyway (the idea is that women are still underrepresented). You can have different opinions about that, but either way I think it's great that there's a prize which honours Gertrud Kolmar. Also, the chance to give a prize to some female poets is amazing. Whatever the ideas behind it, I think it's a good thing because the life of a writer is never easy. You're pretty lonely as a writer, you can have very good colleagues and friends but it's actually a lonely job by nature. Because you really are always focused on your own work and that isn't easy. And it isn't often that it's especially lucrative, therefore, as I said, I consider every new prize to be good. I don't mean for me personally, but in general.

RB At the beginning you mentioned that you're working on a mediated letter correspondence on the theme of the future of the novel. I'm really interested to hear more about that project, also particularly with a view to creative collaboration and exchange – both material and intellectual – across a certain network.

OM There's a really good literary place in Vienna called 'Alte Schmiede' (Old Smithy). From time to time they do projects like this with very exciting ideas. Last time that I took part in it the theme was 'What is good Literature?' Then they published that as a book: the exchange of letters between authors discussing the question of what good literature is. The book turned out really well. And, for example, a few years ago the authors were invited to write on the topic 'Writing and Money', what the life of a writer looks like from that perspective. That was exciting too. And now they have this new thing. I am excited about it, I treasure my Austrian colleagues, I love Vienna, I like this place, Alte Schmiede.

RB Yes, so on the one hand we have spoken about the loneliness of the writers' life, on the other hand you're connected to this diverse network. And I imagine you're inspired by that, by this exchange?

OM Yes of course, obviously, that is important. But the fact of the matter remains that as a writer you are really alone and rely on yourself. My husband and I were together for thirty-eight years and that was a luxury: two writers who understand one another well, always offering mutual support to one another through human closeness and mutual respect as writers. I am thankful for my good fortune with that.

In Conversation Ulrike Almut Sandig: On Collaborating across Media, Genres and Countries

Ulrike Almut Sandig (b. 1979 in Großenhain, East Germany) has been writing and performing poetry since the turn of the millennium and now routinely attracts international attention for her multi-modal performances combining poetry, film, music and vocals. She has published four volumes of poetry, including *Leuchtende Schafe* (Shining Sheep) in 2022, as well as two highly-regarded collections of short stories and a novel. I first met Ulrike Almut on one of her tours to England in 2016, where she performed a selection of her work in Lancaster alongside her English translator, Karen Leeder. This was the beginning of a series of repeat visits to work with both students and researchers at the university as well as perform publicly, most recently on 29 March 2019, the date the UK was originally set to leave the European Union. The conversation reproduced below took place in a café in Berlin in early summer 2019. An English translation follows the German original.

* * *

RB Als du vor kurzem in Lancaster warst, haben wir über Schwellen gesprochen, Schwellen zwischen Ländern im Sinne von *borders* oder Grenzen, aber auch abstrakter gedacht, als Schwellen zwischen der Kunst und der Welt. Dabei hast du bemerkt, dass du deinen Körper nicht unbedingt als Schwelle wahrnimmst, sondern wirklich auch als Teil sowohl deiner Kunst als auch der weiteren Welt, und das wäre auch politisch gemeint. Kannst du dich in diesen Gedanken wieder hineinfinden?

UAS Also, ich weiß auf jeden Fall, dass ich oft darüber nachdenke, in Bezug auf den letzten Gedichtband.[1] Und auch eben beim Schreiben

---

[1] Ulrike Almut Sandig, *ich bin ein Feld voller Raps verstecke die Rehe und leuchte wie dreizehn Ölgemälde übereinander gelegt* (Frankfurt a.M.: Schöffling, 2016).

des Gedichtbandes habe ich für mich versucht das zu untersuchen: was ich als schreibende, weibliche Person des beginnenden 21. Jahrhunderts für eine Rolle spiele. Das ist zum einen mit der Frage nach dem Ich im Gedicht verbunden. Weil die Leser und Leserinnen, wenn jemand 'ich' im Gedicht sagt, ja sehr häufig denken, dass es tatsächlich um den Autor selber oder die Autorin geht, und ich glaube, dass diese Auffassung noch stärker vorherrscht, wenn das eine Frau ist, die diese Gedichte schreibt. Und dann habe ich halt beim Schreiben dieses Gedichtbandes viel damit rumgespielt. Und eigentlich auch schon bei den Erzählungen davor, dass ich beim Schreiben der Texte, und auch später beim Vortragen oder Vertonen der Texte, mit dieser Unsicherheit des Publikums ein bisschen spiele.[2] Und zum anderen sage ich Dinge, die eigentlich über meine Person als Autorin hinausgehen, aber gleichzeitig interessiert mich das natürlich, welche Verantwortung ich ja auch habe; zum Beispiel, ich als Frau mit einer sozialen Verantwortung, weil ich eine Stimme habe. Es gibt eben diese zwei Aspekte. Und das empfinde ich nicht als eine Schwelle, über die ich nicht hinwegkomme, als eine Grenze, die ich nicht überschreiten kann, sondern als ein wundervolles Spielgerät, mit dem ich arbeiten kann. Was aber auch eine gewisse Verantwortung mit sich bringt, und diese Verantwortung nehme ich mal an, und mal weise ich sie von mir.

RB Zum Teil bringst du auch die Sprache selbst zum Sprechen, vor allem eben in der Art und Weise deiner Performance. Dann stehst du körperlich da und sagst: ich. Aber machst doch klar, dass du es nicht bist, eben weil das Ganze so multimedial gestaltet wird, dass man gezwungen wird, anders auf die Worte selbst einzugehen.

UAS Genau. Oder ich mache auch viele schlichte A-cappella Lesungen. Und dann besteht die Herausforderung eben darin, das jetzt nicht von mir zu weisen. Ich habe diesen einen Text, 'Nachricht von der deutschen Sprache', wo die Sprache aus der Zukunft heraus spricht.[3] Und mir ist natürlich klar, dass wenn man diesen Text liest, man vielleicht in der Lage ist, mal kurz das auszuschalten, dass es eine Autorin ist, dass ich als Frau das geschrieben habe. Aber wenn ich da auf der Bühne stehe, bringt es ja nichts, meinen Körper zu verstecken und zu sagen: 'Und jetzt nur die Sprache'. Sondern ich muss es ja auch ein bisschen annehmen, dass das Publikum mich da stehen sieht und mich mit meiner zudem auch eher höheren, fast so einer mädchenhaften,

---

[2] Ulrike Almut Sandig, *Buch Gegen das Verschwinden* (Frankfurt a.M: Schöffling, 2015), *Flamingos* (Frankfurt a.M.: Schöffling, 2010)

[3] Sandig, 'Nachricht von der deutschen Sprache, 2026 AD', *ich bin ein Feld*, p. 59.

Stimmlage hört. Und dann besteht die Kunst in einer Gratwanderung für mich. Das ist sozusagen meine Präsenz, also dass ich mich selbst nicht über das Gedicht stülpe und trotzdem den Text sein lasse, wie er ist, aber jetzt auch nicht so tue, als hätte ich keinen Körper.

RB Und das Ganze findet auch in einem Kontext statt. Es ist ja immer ein physischer Raum da, nicht jetzt nur metaphorisch ein öffentlicher Raum, sondern wenn du live vorträgst, findet das ja immer in einem tatsächlichen Ort statt. Heißt das für dich, dass der Text dann jedes Mal auch anders wirkt, weil natürlich das Publikum und der Raum und das ganze Physische, das spielt dann alles auch mit in deine Performance und in das, was der Text eigentlich bedeuten kann?

UAS Also, ich hatte letzte Woche in Münster vor einem geplanten Konzert mit Grigory Semenchuk, meinem Partner in der Band *Landschaft*, eine relativ unvorbereitete Lesung, weil ich nicht wusste, dass ich vorher noch eine Lesung machen sollte. Und zu dem kam, dass ich das Publikum nicht sehen konnte. Und normalerweise brauche ich eigentlich viel Blickkontakt, weil ein Vortrag natürlich immer ein Geben und Nehmen ist. Ich ballere ja nicht das Publikum zu, sondern ich gucke, wie muss ich sprechen, damit die Verbindung entsteht. Das hält mich am Laufen, dass ich die Leute sehen kann, und ich konnte das Publikum überhaupt nicht sehen. Und dann habe ich mich da hingesetzt, und hab unter anderem diesen Text gelesen, 'Nachricht von der deutschen Sprache'. Ich habe dann beim Sprechen gemerkt, dass der total anders ist, als ich ihn jemals sonst gelesen habe. Also das ist auch oft was, was ich nicht vorhersagen kann, aber es ist ganz klar, der Text gehört mir nicht. Selbst im Buch ist es ja eigentlich so, dass der Text eigentlich nicht auf der Seite stattfindet, und auf jeden Fall auf einer Lesung oder im Vortrag, findet der Text nicht auf der Bühne statt, sondern er findet zwischen dem Rezipienten und mir statt. Also, dass es eigentlich eine gemeinschaftliche Tätigkeit ist, von einem Schweigenden und einer Sprechenden, aber der Schweigende hat genauso viel Teil daran.

RB Du hast auch mit Übersetzern gearbeitet. Und dann wird der Text natürlich noch weiter gemeinschaftlich gestaltet, in noch einem Zwischenraum rezipiert und zugleich neu produziert. Kann man das mit einer Performance gleichsetzen? Ist die Übersetzung nur noch eine andere Performance des Textes?

UAS Es ist auf jeden Fall immer eine Lesart. Also ich habe mit Karen Leeder, meiner Übersetzerin ins Englische, oft die Situation, dass sie sich für eine bestimmte Richtung eines Textes entscheiden muss. Und danach, wenn Karen erstmal eine Übersetzung abgeschlossen hat, dann findet eigentlich eine Aneignung statt. Ich hole den neuen Text irgendwie so ein bisschen näher an mich ran. Es gibt dann so Texte, die fühlen sich fremder an, und manche näher, und manche kann ich einfach nicht vorlesen, weil z.B. für meine deutsche Zunge da unglaubliche Zungenbrecher drin sind, so dass ich die einfach nicht vortrage, um mich nicht zu blamieren. Und dann gibt es aber Texte, deren Originalversion zum Beispiel ich kaum vortrage, wo ich aber bei deren Übersetzung feststelle, die Nachdichtung ist eigentlich hörbarer, stärker ein Hörtext als die Vorlage. Und die baue ich dann ganz anders in meine Lesungen ein, für die entwickle ich dann einen ganz anderen Tonfall, einen Tonfall, den ich nicht von Karen übernehme, weil ich das gar nicht kann, sondern die entwickeln dann für mich eine ganz eigene Hörbarkeit.

Und natürlich gibt es auch Texte, die vor einem englischsprachigen Publikum anders funktionieren. Also ganz viele Texte funktionieren vollkommen anders, also nicht nur englischsprachige. Zum Beispiel habe ich einen Text, 'Hans im Glück' heißt der, und der schlägt immer unglaublich ein, wenn ich den in Indien vorlese.[4] Obwohl dieses Märchen dort nicht bekannt ist. Es gibt so ein ähnliches Märchen, ein altes Märchen auch, aber doch mit anderen Bildern. Und es schlägt aber immer total ein, und das hat mit verschiedenen Aspekten zu tun. Ich glaube, dass es erstens damit zu tun hat, dass es eine hervorragende Übersetzung zweier indischer Dichterkollegen ins Kashmiri gibt davon. Diese Übersetzung ist sehr zart und melodiös, während mein deutsches Original eher rhythmisch ist. Zweitens hat der Frontmann der indischen Band ALIF, mit der ich zusammenarbeite, dieses Gedicht 'Hans im Glueck' in einer vollkommen unironischen Art vertont, obwohl ich den Text total ironisch meine. Der hat halt wirklich nur den Aspekt der Sehnsucht darin vertont. Und dann gibt's diesen Aspekt auch noch, dass in Indien die Älteren der Mittelschicht, vor der ich eben oft da vorlese, natürlich die ganze Zeit eine große Sehnsucht nach ihren Kindern haben, weil viele von denen in Europa oder in den USA oder Kanada studieren. Und das heißt, die verbinden damit diese Geschichte. Das heißt, der Text hat sich losgelöst von seinem Ursprung, transportiert aber immer noch die Sehnsucht einer Mutter nach ihrem Sohn. Dieser Text arbeitet ja mit so Abkürzungen, von mir gemeint als, 'ich will was aussprechen, aber ich spreche es doch nicht aus, aber dann spreche ich es doch aus'. Und dort ist dieses Element jetzt aber rhythmusgebend, also so ein Strukturelement, was eigentlich nur noch so Rhythmusfunktion erfüllt, aber diese Wiederholungen sind auch Suchbewegungen. Diese Texte,

---

[4] Sandig, 'Hans im Glück', *ich bin ein Feld*, p. 77.

die lösen sich vollkommen von ihrem Original ab einem bestimmten Punkt. Und das ist für mich dann ja eigentlich ein Zeichen, dass der Text selbst funktioniert. Ob er als Übersetzung funktioniert, das kann ich nicht beurteilen, sondern dass die Übersetzung als Text an sich gut funktioniert.

RB Ich würde gerne über das Stoffliche reden. Besonders wenn du Videos machst, sind häufig ausgefallene Objekte dabei. Da ist zum Beispiel in deiner Zusammenarbeit mit Hinemoana Baker mal ein aufblasbarer Globus da.[5] Welche Rolle haben solche Objekte, entweder im kreativen Prozess selber oder als Darstellungsform? Man hat das Gefühl, wenn man sich das anschaut, dass das sehr wohl Teil eines kreativen Dialogs wäre.

UAS Ja, diese Objekte sind Teil des kreativen Dialogs. Aber sie kommen erst nach dem Text dazu. Der Dialog ist ja nicht beendet, nur weil der Text geschrieben ist. Der Text in unserem Kurzfilm 'It wasn't me und du warst es auch nicht', dieser Text selbst ist ja schon ein Dialog mit Hinemoana Baker. Weswegen ich den ja eigentlich wie so eine Art Brief formuliert habe: 'meine Liebe' geht es los und endet mit 'Deine Hinemoana'.[6] Also, ich hatte diese Briefform, ein Ansprechen ihrer Person, schon beim Schreiben im Kopf, obwohl ich sie damals kaum kannte, ich kannte nicht mehr als eine Handvoll Texte von ihr, und sie als Person kannte ich kaum. Klar ist, der Text steht immer am Anfang. Also habe ich sozusagen erst diesen Text, und der Text ist ein Dialog und arbeitet natürlich mit der Idee der zwei Hemisphären, und der Ähnlichkeit der Hemisphären und der kompletten Umgekehrtheit. Und das fasziniert mich in Texten, im Sprechen, im Denken eigentlich, dass alles sein Gegenteil haben könnte. Du schreibst was, und dann merkst du, du kannst eigentlich genau das Gegenteil von dem sagen, was geschrieben ist, und es ist genauso richtig. Ich merke, dass darin eigentlich was Typisches liegt, was ich für sehr menschlich halte, dass alles in seinem Gegenteil umschlagen kann, wie diese Kippbilder, die entweder eine Vase sind oder zwei Gesichter. Dass, um sich einem Thema anzunähern, es eigentlich Sinn macht, es sich über die Schattenrisse genau anzuschauen, also das Gegenteil sich anzugucken.

Als ich dann mit Hinemoana was machen wollte, war relativ klar, welche Texte in diesen Dialog dazugehören. Denn sie hatte in derselben Zeit für dasselbe Projekt einen Text geschrieben, der eigentlich auch ein

---

[5] Hinemoana Baker, Beate Kunath, Ulrike Almut Sandig, 'It wasn't me und du warst es auch nicht', available on YouTube: https://youtu.be/-syWM_TMKCM (last accessed 6 July 2019).

Dialog mit mir ist. Der heißt, 'The fifteen paces between my socks and my shoes'.[7] Und dann ist der Rest eigentlich Spiel. Du brauchst was Visuelles, du brauchst was, was nicht von vornherein festgeschrieben ist, sondern sich verändern kann, während wir da sind. Und dann verändert sich es halt auch wirklich so, dass du nicht damit rechnest. Also zum Beispiel, als wir das gefilmt haben, war es ziemlich windig, und wir hatten diese Bälle dabei, und die sind uns ständig weggeflogen. Und das war total schwierig, die alle an einem Ort zu halten. Und genau das war eigentlich das, was am Ende Sinn gemacht hat für den Film, weil das eigentlich die Denkbewegung illustriert hat. Dass du versuchst, deine Gedanken zusammenzukriegen, und du hast ein grobes Bild, und in diesem Versuch, es auf den Punkt zu bringen, eigentlich der Text entsteht, ohne jemals auf den Punkt zu kommen. Weil die Suchbewegung der Text selbst ist und nicht der Punkt, auf den du kommen willst. Und dadurch hat das total Sinn gemacht. Da gibt's so eine Stelle, wo sie so versucht zu balancieren, und ständig fliegt ihr irgendwas weg.

RB Das war also nicht von Anfang an gedacht, dass ihr den Ball nehmt, um den Punkt zu illustrieren. Insofern hat der Ball den Punkt vielleicht selbst rausgebracht?

UAS Also es war wirklich so ähnlich wie eine klassische Performance, mit dem Unterschied, dass die nicht für ein analoges Publikum vor Ort gedacht war, aber schon in der Hinsicht, dass du was machst mit Elementen, die du mit einbeziehst, die mit dem Text zu tun haben, aber du weißt nicht, was rauskommt. Und dann kommt sozusagen das Element Wind dazu, dann kam glaub ich auch dazu, über unsere Schuhe hatten wir so weiße Überschuhe gezogen, und die sind uns kaputt gegangen, während wir da gelaufen sind. Und es war sehr schwer, darin zu laufen, weil der Boden nass war, und die sind uns immer mehr kaputt gegangen, und die haben eigentlich zu diesem komischen Geräusch geführt. Und dieses Geräusch haben wir dann aufgenommen und dann weitergezogen durch den ganzen Band. Also was wie ein Rhythmus wirkt, ist eigentlich am Anfang nur ein Laufgeräusch und das haben wir immer weitergezogen, und das war vorher nicht klar.

---

[6] Sandig, 'Hinemoana', *ich bin ein Feld*, p. 16.
[7] Hinemoana Baker, 'The fifteen paces between my socks and my shoes' in *Transit of Venus. Poetry Exchange*, (Wellington: Victoria U. P., 2016), p. 28. Available online: https://www.lyrikline.org/de/gedichte/hinemoana-baker-i-fifteen-paces-between-my-socks-and-my-7801 (last accessed 6 July 2019).

RB In diesem Sinne wollte ich dich auch zu diesem Video mit den Bluescreens fragen, das eins der ersten Gedichte des Gedichtbandes *ich bin ein Feld voller Raps* verbildlicht und vertont.[8] Inwiefern hast du hier versucht, das Ganze im Voraus so zu gestalten, dass du deinen Text in einem anderen Medium wiederfindest?

UAS Da war eigentlich klar, dass der Filmemacher gleichwertig ist. Also bei dem Film mit Hinemoana, da hatten wir auch zwar eine Filmemacherin dabei, aber die hat wirklich gesagt, 'ich stell die Kamera nur auf, und ihr macht, was ihr wollt, ihr entscheidet auch über den Schnitt, ihr macht den Film, nicht ich. Ich drücke nur auf den Auslöser'. Und bei ihm war aber klar, er ist vollwertiges künstlerisches Mitglied der Angelegenheit. Und er wollte gerne diese Projektion auf den Klamotten machen, und wollte was mit Textprojektion, es sollten ursprünglich nur Texte sein, während ich unbedingt meine Tochter drin vorkommen lassen wollte, was er am Anfang ein bisschen cheesy fand, weil ja am Anfang die Zeile kommt, 'ich bin die Mutter, ich bin die Tochter', und ich wollte auch diesen Hasen drin vorkommen lassen und die Cellistin, was dann in eins gekommen ist. Also alles andere hat sich rein spontan entwickelt, weil wir eben nicht wussten, was am Ende rauskommt, und das sollte auch so sein, dass du sozusagen interagierst mit dem, was dich umgibt, und was entstehen lässt, was sich vom Text auch lösen kann, oder von der Vertonung auch lösen kann.

RB Also aus meiner Sicht beschreibst du da eine sehr kollaborative Autorschaft, die die verschiedensten Elemente miteinbezieht und mitwirken lässt.

UAS Total, vollkommen. Also wirklich, dass es mein Text ist, steht nicht über allem, sondern das ist sozusagen ein Teil der Aktion, also ein Teil der Urheberschaft ist halt, dass ich zufällig diesen Text geschrieben habe. Da ist es dann auch gar nicht mehr so wichtig, wer ich gewesen bin, und dass ich eine Frau bin zum Beispiel. Es wird zwar damit gespielt, aber es geht dann in ein Anderes über, was größer ist.

RB Was ja überhaupt mit den Themen deiner Arbeit sehr eng zusammenhängt. Dass man Teil eines größeren Universums ist, ist überhaupt

---

[8] Sandig, 'ich bin ein Feld voller Raps / ich bin der Schatten zum drunter Verstecken', *ich bin ein Feld*, p. 13; The version of this performed by Landschaft with the visuals discussed here is freely available on YouTube: https://youtu.be/J7V1ViKz3CU (last accessed 6 July 2019). Filmed by Sascha Conrad, Produktion Waldstrasse.

wiederkehrendes Thema bei dir. Insofern hast du bestimmt auch für deine eigenen Themen die richtigen Formen gefunden. Also: nicht nur geschriebene Texte.

UAS   Ich kann mir einfach nicht vorstellen, und das war von Anfang an eigentlich so, dass ein Text nur in einem Buch stattfinden soll, oder dass der überhaupt eine Endform hat, dass ein Text überhaupt irgendwann fertig geschrieben ist. Das finde ich so ein relativ künstliches Denken. Und als ich meinen ersten Gedichtband geschrieben habe, danach habe ich den ersten Literaturpreis gewonnen, und dann war plötzlich diese winzige Auflage ausverkauft.[9] Und dann sollte ich das in eine zweite Auflage geben, und dann hab ich halt wie fast alle Autoren mit dem Buch schon wieder meine Schwierigkeiten gehabt, weil das mein erstes war, und ich ja erst mit dem Publizieren angefangen hatte, und dann hab ich das komplett nochmal ganz stark eigentlich umgeschrieben, so dass einige Texte sich von dem Text in der Erstauflage so fundamental unterschieden, dass nur noch ein paar Kernwörter, irgendwie die Grundideen, dieselben waren. Und so ist es eigentlich heute noch, dass ich denke, ein Text ist nicht beendet in dem Sinne. Schon allein, weil er gelesen wird, ist er nicht beendet. Gerade wenn man sich so für akustische oder für hörbare Literatur interessiert, ist man natürlich relativ schnell an dem Punkt, dass man feststellt, wie alt dieses Erbe ist. So alt, wie Religion ist, so alt, wie der Mensch ist, so alt ist hörbare Literatur. Und dass die Zeit der Schriftlichkeit, oder überhaupt des Buchdrucks nur ein Teil davon ist. Wenn ich jetzt nur Bücher schreiben würde, da hätte ich das Gefühl, ich würde in so einer Gegenwart feststecken, ich käme aus meiner Zeit nicht heraus.

RB   Es ist aber interessant, wie du das hörbare Literatur nennst, denn man könnte auch sagen sprechbare. Aber du betonst ja denjenigen, der hört, nicht denjenigen, der spricht. Und das betont noch einmal eigentlich diese Community, die sich mit einem Text oder einer Idee auseinandersetzt und gleich vielleicht mitproduziert?

UAS   Weil eben das Publikum ein nicht wegzudenkender Bestandteil ist, aber natürlich auch um mich ein bisschen abzugrenzen, gegenüber Slam, um mich eher in einer Ars-Acustica-Richtung einzuordnen. Weil natürlich Texte, die wirklich fürs Sprechen geschrieben sind, mit anderen Stilmitteln arbeiten. Und während ich einen Text schreibe, denke ich eigentlich nicht ans Sprechen, ich denke ans Denken.

---

[9]   Ulrike Almut Sandig, *Zunder* (Leipzig: Connewitzer Verlagsbuchhandlung, 2005; 2nd rev. edn 2009).

RB Das kann man bei dir dann hören, aber auch sehen, weil du halt auch so viele visuelle Arbeiten aus deinen Texten machst. Diese Filme und auch die Performances, die sind alle sehr visuell. Ein visuelles Denken?

UAS Jetzt gerade haben wir tatsächlich für die Poetry-Band *Landschaft visuals* entwickeln lassen, in Zusammenarbeit wieder mit einer Filmemacherin und einer Illustratorin.[10] Also es ging anfangs nur darum, Karens englische Übersetzungen einzubauen, so dass wir auch außerhalb von Deutschland oder der Ukraine auftreten können und die Leute verstehen, worum es gerade geht. Das war der Anfang, und dann haben sich die beiden da komplett reingekniet, die Illustratorin und die Filmemacherin, und jetzt haben wir da kleine Filme, die zu jedem Song mitlaufen, die aber eigentlich über klassische Band-*visuals* schon wieder weit hinaus gehen. Weil es eigentlich schon wieder kleine Poesiefilme sind, die auch wieder eigene Interpretationen geben. Aber ich merke, dass du dich ja nicht für eine Art von Literatur entscheidest, sondern macht man ja das, was man versteht, also zu was man geistig und emotional und intellektuell in der Lage ist. Und ich stelle natürlich fest, dass meine Herangehensweise beim Schreiben eines Textes – erst mal wirklich nur auf den Denkvorgang zu achten und jetzt weniger darauf, wie sich das anhört -, dass man wegen dieser Herangehensweise deutlich schon spürt, dass das eben Texte sind, die halt z.B. keine Liedtexte sind, und dass ich erst nachher die Sachen verbildliche oder vertone. Für Songtexte sind diese Sachen viel zu kompliziert. Das führt dazu, dass ich mit einem Notenständer auf der Bühne bin, weil die Texte so kompliziert sind, dass ich die gar nicht in dem Sinne zusätzlich zu den ganzen Audioeffekten, die von Wort zu Wort teilweise wechseln, einbauen kann, in so einen Song, so ein körperliches Songgedächtnis. Und natürlich bespielen wir so auch gar nicht die Musikszene, weil das viel zu kompliziert ist, was wir machen. Und das ist manchmal ein bisschen schade, weil es mir ja um eine Kommunikation mit dem Publikum geht, aber ich kann es eben nur so, ich kann es nicht anders.

RB Vorhin hast du von Hinemoana Baker gesprochen, und am Anfang kanntest du sie kaum, nur die Texte, und inzwischen ist deutlich mehr aus eurer Zusammenarbeit geworden. Wie kommt das

---

[10] Clips from the band as well as options to purchase recordings can be accessed on the publisher's website: https://www.schoeffling.de/buecher/ulrike-almut-sandig-grigory-semenchuk/landschaft-cd but the poetry-songs are also on Spotify, iTunes, bandcamp, SoundCloud.

zustande, ist das wirklich einfach Zufall, oder suchst du, oder gibt es Vermittler?

UAS Alles ja, eigentlich. Es ist Zufall und es ist Absicht, es gibt Vermittler und es entsteht von alleine. Hinemoana habe ich kennengelernt, die wurde mir vermittelt. Zum einen durch die Literaturwerkstatt Berlin, was heute das Haus für Poesie ist, und zum anderen durch einen neuseeländischen Verlag. Und die beiden haben zusammengearbeitet für ein Dichtungsübersetzungsprojekt, in dessen Zusammenhang wir eben auch Texte schreiben sollten. Und diese Texte, über die wir vorher sprachen, sind in diesem Zusammenhang entstanden, und erst war das quasi wirklich nur meine '*sparring Partnerin*' und dann ist sie nach Berlin gezogen, und es hat sich eine Art Freundschaft entwickelt. Uns interessieren privat und künstlerisch ähnliche Themen. Sie interessiert sich ähnlich wie ich für Fragen des Geschlechts, sie kommt aus der Queer-Szene eigentlich, sie interessiert sich auch für Vortragskultur im weitesten Sinne, schreibt und singt. Und dann war irgendwie relativ klar, da kann man jetzt auch was draus machen.

Und ähnlich auch bei Grigory, der ist mir zuerst vermittelt worden über das Goethe-Institut. Ja, ich kriege sehr oft Leute vermittelt, aber die Frage ist dann immer, wie gehst du damit um? Ich habe oft vorher mit Leuten auch mal literarisch oder musikalisch improvisiert, und danach habe ich die nie wieder getroffen. Bei Grigory war das aber so, dass wir total geflasht waren von diesem ersten Auftritt, weil wir nicht damit gerechnet hatten, dass es so einen Spaß miteinander machen würde. Und wir haben gute Rückmeldungen bekommen, und direkt danach gleich ein paar Clips auf YouTube eingestellt, die mir fast peinlich sind inzwischen, weil wir inzwischen so viel weiter gegangen sind, aber es war einfach, weil wir so begeistert waren voneinander. Und dann haben wir eigentlich ohne uns wirklich persönlich zu kennen einfach gesagt, wir machen weiter damit. Und irgendwann bist du natürlich dann auch miteinander befreundet, und das intensiviert dann auch das künstlerische Arbeiten, weil dann andere Energien für mich nochmal reinkommen. Ich war eigentlich immer mit meinen Bühnenpartnern auch sehr eng privat. So ist es jetzt auch, dass er eigentlich wie mein kleiner Bruder ist. Also quasi am Anfang eine Vermittlung und dann gehst du so weiter.

Oder gerade mit der Filmemacherin, die diesen Hinemoana Film gemacht hat, die hat jetzt aber auch die *visuals* gemacht, die kannte ich eigentlich eher erst privat und sie hat aber vor vielen Jahren schon mal eine Verfilmung von einem Gedicht von mir gemacht, mit einem ziemlichen technischen Aufwand. Die hat eine ganze Wohnung gebaut dafür, eine gute Schauspielerin engagiert, und der Film ist sehr gut angenommen worden, ist über Festivals weitergereicht worden. Und mich hatte das damals aber nicht besonders interessiert, ich war irgendwie mit meinen Sachen beschäftigt. Und dann irgendwann, weil wir uns immer wieder hier in Berlin gesehen haben, hat sich eine Freundschaft draus entwickelt, und über die Freundschaft eigentlich erst dieses Herumspinnen. Und da ist es eigentlich auch immer die Frage, ich kann sie natürlich nicht so bezahlen, wie so eine Arbeit bezahlt werden müsste, das wären dann so 2000 Euro, die ich locker machen müsste. Stattdessen machen wir es dann halt so, ich texte dann für ihren nächsten Dokumentarfilm, oder ich mache ein Textlektorat für sie, und sie gibt mir dafür einen Freundschaftspreis. Oder ich unterstütze ihr nächstes Crowdfunding-Projekt, und sie weiß dann über die Unterstützung schon, welche Art von ihren Filmen mich interessiert, weil ich genau das unterstütze und was anderes nicht. Und dann sitzen wir zusammen bei einem Essen und fangen dann an, herumzuspinnen. Und dann spinnt sich so die nächste Idee zurecht. Das ist für mich eine total schöne Arbeit, weil der Text nicht im Zentrum steht, sondern es ist eine Arbeit auf Augenhöhe, also der Film hat sozusagen genauso viel Gewicht wie mein Text, aber dadurch, dass ich diejenige bin, die quasi auch Schriftstellerin ist, bin ich diejenige, die es dann nach außen bringt, es läuft über meinen Namen, aber intern bin nicht ich die Chefin, sondern es ist eine Arbeit auf Augenhöhe.

RB Die Institutionen, die hier zum Teil alles erstmal einleiten, das Goethe-Institut und die verschiedenen Literaturhäuser, sie sind traditionell schon ziemlich mit Kanons beschäftigt, also einer gewissen Form von Literatur, einer gewissen Art Autor, die man vermitteln will. Hast du das Gefühl, du müsstest irgendwas da repräsentieren, dass du aus gewissen Gründen dann zur Vertretung gewählt worden bist?

UAS Die Goethe-Institute ordnen mich ganz klar ein. Das sind dann natürlich manchmal Einordnungen, die mich auch ärgern, zum Beispiel als Vertreterin der jungen Szene, was ich fast schon eine Beleidigung finde inzwischen. Also nicht nur mir gegenüber, sondern auch der wirklich jungen Szene gegenüber ist das eine Beleidung, die dann für null und nichtig damit erklärt wird, als ob es die nicht geben würde. Ich weiß nicht, ob das immer noch so ist, aber als ich angefangen habe, war es lange für die Leute wichtig, dass ich aus dem Osten komme. Jetzt wo ich in Berlin bin, ist es nicht mehr so stark, aber als ich noch in Leipzig gelebt habe, wurde das immer wieder betont. Da hast du einfach gemerkt, die brauchten jetzt noch eine Frau aus dem Osten. Und damit kann ich OK leben, weil es sich ja nicht leugnen lässt. Und jetzt inzwischen ist es häufig so, dass ich, glaub ich, so einen Ruf weghabe, genreübergreifend zu arbeiten, mit dem Fokus auf hörbare Literatur, und dennoch keine Slammerin bin. Klar, du hast halt so eine Einschätzung dann, und die trifft mal zu, und es ist immer eine Vereinfachung. Und ich versuche, mich darum nicht zu kümmern. Weil es natürlich ganz klar ist, dass ich auf dem freien Markt – also jetzt freier Markt auch im Sinne von freier Szene, auch freier Untergrundszene – dass ich komplett untergehen würde. Weil es hier so viele gibt, also ehrlich gesagt auch die genreübergreifenden Sachen: ich bin einfach eine von ganz vielen. Hier in Berlin unter den Künstlern werde ich eigentlich gar nicht so wahrgenommen. Und dadurch habe ich natürlich das Schwein, dass ich dank des Goethe-Instituts oder bestimmter Literaturhäuser irgendwie aus der Szene rausgehoben werde, und irgendwie Honorare bekomme für das, was ich mache, im Gegensatz zu den meisten anderen.

RB Ist das dann problematisch? Du hast natürlich auch mit diesen anderen zu tun. Fühlst du dich dabei unwohl?

UAS In Leipzig war das problematischer, und hier in Berlin ist die Schwemme so groß, dass die Leute gar nicht wirklich vergleichen. Hier in Berlin geht man dann so unter, dass es schon wieder OK ist. Aber in Leipzig war das ein richtiges Problem. Da gibt's ja auch sehr gute Autoren, und auch sehr gute unbekannte Autoren, die einfach andere faktische Entscheidungen in ihrem Leben getroffen haben, die sich für einen Hauptberuf entschieden haben. Und das ist natürlich dann schwierig geworden.

RB Du hast im Leipziger Literaturinstitut studiert. Inwiefern kann so ein Institut etwas an der Literaturszene ändern? Es könnte weiterhin selbst Teil einer Kanonbildung bleiben: man unterrichtet Literatur so, dass dann auch die nächste Generation so erzogen wird, wie die, die erziehen. Oder siehst du da neue Räume, neue Möglichkeiten sich entfalten?

UAS Also, als ich am Literaturinstitut studiert habe, hatte das noch einen stärkeren Alleinstellungswert, als es das heute hat. Weil, außer uns gab es eigentlich nur die Hildesheimer, die ja aber auch nicht das Gleiche unterrichtet haben. Wien entstand gerade, und Biel war auch noch nicht so bekannt. Und die FU in Berlin unterrichtete auch, das war aber auch noch nicht so bekannt. Das bedeutet, der Blick von der Öffentlichkeit wie auch von der Verlagsszene war stärker auf uns gerichtet. Das hat sich, glaub ich, aufgelöst.
   Aber natürlich ganz klar ist, egal wo du das studierst, wenn du so eine öffentliche Legitimierung hast, dich drei Jahre lang mit Literatur hauptberuflich beschäftigen zu dürfen, bevor du wieder in den Arbeitsmarkt hinaus musst, oder überhaupt in den Arbeitsmarkt

hinaus musst, dann hast du natürlich eine ganz andere Möglichkeit, dich zu professionalisieren und auch künstlerisch zu entwickeln als jemand, der von vornherein in der freien Szene ist und sich von Job zu Job hangelt, um zu überleben. Und ich merke, dass diese große Konzentration auf etwas, ob das in Leipzig ist, oder woanders, dass das schon Qualität auch bringt.

Und natürlich gibt es halt immer noch, heute und damals, diesen Ruf der Kanonbildung durch Institute, und das ist damals schon Blödsinn gewesen, das war schon Blödsinn, als das so in den Nullerjahren diskutiert worden ist. Bloß weil da ein paar Romane in einem ähnlichen Stil geschrieben worden sind. Zu meiner Zeit war diese Diskussion des Fräuleinwunders, und obwohl das mit Judith Hermann anfing, wurden auch wir Jüngeren ständig mit Judith Hermann verglichen, ob es gepasst hat oder nicht. Das ist totaler Blödsinn, und ich habe das nicht besonders ernst genommen, das wurde auch damals im Institut unter uns Studierenden nicht ernst genommen, wir haben da drüber gelacht und jeder hat sein Ding gemacht. Und natürlich ist es ja so, dass die allerwenigsten, die bei uns studiert haben, tatsächlich hauptberuflich Schriftstellerinnen werden, es sind ja ganz wenige, die das wirklich sowohl schaffen, als auch wollen. Viele bleiben im Dunstkreis und arbeiten dann in Redaktionen oder kulturellen Einrichtungen, oder viele veröffentlichen dann auch alle Jubeljahre mal ein Buch, arbeiten aber hauptsächlich als Lektorin zum Beispiel, aber so wirklich freiberufliche Schriftsteller und Schriftstellerinnen, die nur das machen, sind wirklich ganz wenige. Es sind immer so eine Handvoll pro Jahrgang. Oder weniger als eine Handvoll eigentlich.

RB Mit Blick auf die Entwicklung des genreübergreifenden Elements deiner Arbeit, siehst du die Zukunft der Literatur auch weiterhin so? Immer mehr genreübergreifend? Ist das der Raum, in dem sich die Literatur bewegen sollte?

UAS Ich glaube eher, dass es das immer gab. Jetzt wird da gerade im Moment ein bisschen mehr drauf geguckt, weil natürlich auch digitale Medien ein Teil der Sache geworden sind. Aber eigentlich gab es das ja immer, ob das jetzt Stefan George war oder Thomas Kling. Und allein schon in der bildenden Kunst, die ganzen Leute, die mit Text arbeiten, das gab's die ganze Zeit immer. Und das wird auch immer so sein. Ich wunder mich immer so ein bisschen, dass genreübergreifendes Arbeiten als so etwas Modernes wahrgenommen wird, weil das eigentlich für mich eher traditionell ist.

RB Es geht ja mindestens bis ins Mittelalter zurück.

UAS Ja, und wenn man da genau guckt, die Autoren, die genreübergreifend arbeiten, sind auch oft tatsächlich Kenner alter Textformen. Also wenn ich jetzt an Tristan Marquardt denke, Ulrike Draesner, auch ein super Beispiel, weil sie sich ja in dieser Schnittstelle zwischen Akademischem und Literarischem sich bewegt. Die genreübergreifenden Künstler sind nicht die Leute, die sagen, das poppt so aus dem Nichts heraus, und ist in nichts als der Gegenwart gefußt. Das sind doch oft Leute, die sich mit Geschichte, mit Kunst oder Literaturgeschichte auskennen. Also ich glaube, es wird immer alles geben, und je nachdem, mit welchen Medien du ohne Geld arbeiten kannst, darum geht es. Dass das natürlich immer die Medien sind, die inspirierend sind, weil du dann halt rumspinnen kannst. Für mich ist YouTube zum Beispiel, obwohl ich wenige Abonnenten habe, und keine großen Klickzahlen habe, ist das für mich ein nicht wegzudenkender Teil meiner Arbeit. Beim Einpflegen und überhaupt Pflegen der Videos geht sehr viel Zeit für mich drauf, weil ich das toll finde, dass ich sozusagen nicht mehr an Sender gebunden bin, die auf meinen Rechten sitzen. Deswegen bin ich vom Hörspiel weggegangen. Am Anfang habe ich ja ein paar Hörspiele gemacht, und zwei davon waren große Skripthörspiele, und daran habe ich lange und intensiv gearbeitet, und bin sehr stolz auf diese Hörspiele, aber ich kann sie nirgendwo präsentieren, weil die Sender wie die Glucken auf unsere Rechte achten. Und das fasziniert mich persönlich an Formen, eben wie YouTube oder Soundcloud oder Bandcamp, dass ich da was machen kann. Ich muss nur mit den Kollegen, mit denen ich was entwickle, sprechen, und dann machen wir eine Verabredung und stellen das drauf. Und dann kann ich das mal schnell nach Neuseeland an einen Kollegen schicken, ohne, dass ich mir über Rechteverletzung Gedanken machen muss. Und das ist natürlich auch was, was mich inspiriert, weil ich mich darin frei fühle. Es ist natürlich auch beim Verlag so, so eine tolle Unterstützung wie das ist, dass ich ja natürlich auch meine Textrechte an den Verlag verkaufe. Ich habe viele Vorteile davon, aber wenn ich nur im Buchbereich arbeiten würde, würde ich mich immer wieder gegängelt fühlen, weil ich jeden Mist mit denen absprechen müsste, was ich jetzt hochladen darf. Und dann müssten ständig irgendwelche Lizenzen ausgestellt werden, bloß damit ein tasmanisches Literaturfestival was machen kann.

Und diese Freiheit im Internet wird sich wahrscheinlich in Zukunft ändern, die Entwicklung geht ja in die Richtung, wir sind ja jetzt in den letzten Ausläufern dieser Anarchie eigentlich. Ich springe sozusagen auf einen Zug auf, aber wirklich auf den allerletzten Waggon. Und jetzt ist halt die Frage, wie geht es weiter? Welches Genre bietet sich in Zukunft an? Und die Genres, die halt eine geringe finanzielle und technische Hürde bieten, das sind natürlich die, wo Kunst und Kultur erstmal passiert, weil die freie Ausübung der Kunst erstmal nicht auf Förderung und auf Rechte angewiesen ist.

RB When you were recently in Lancaster we spoke about thresholds; thresholds between countries in terms of borders, but also in a more abstract sense, as thresholds between art and the world. In relation to that you commented that you don't necessarily perceive your body as a threshold but rather as a real part of your art as well as the wider world, and you meant that politically too. Can you delve back into that train of thought?

UAS Well, I know that I certainly think about that often in relation to my most recent volume of poetry.[11] Even while I was writing the volume that's what I was trying to explore: what role I play as a woman writing at the beginning of the twenty-first century. On the one hand that's tied up with the question of the 'I' in the poem. Because when someone says 'I' in a poem, the reader very often thinks that it's actually about the author themselves, and I think that this perception dominates even more strongly when it's a woman. And so when I was writing this volume of poetry I played around with that a lot. And also with the stories before it actually, whilst writing those texts, and later when performing or recording them too; I like to play around a bit with the audience's uncertainty.[12] On the other hand, I'll say things that transcend my person as an author but at the same time I do still care of course about where my responsibility lies; for example, as a woman I have a social responsibility because I have a voice. So there are these two aspects. And I don't perceive that as a threshold that I can't overcome, as a border that I can't cross, but as a wonderful device that I can play with. And that brings with it a certain responsibility which sometimes I take on and sometimes I reject.

RB You also partly get the language to speak for itself, above all in the way you perform. You stand there physically and say: I. However, you make it clear that it is not you, especially because the whole thing is put together with such a focus on multi-media that the audience is forced to approach the words themselves differently.

---

[11] Ulrike Almut Sandig, *ich bin ein Feld voller Raps verstecke die Rehe und leuchte wie dreizehn Ölgemälde übereinander gelegt* (Frankfurt a.M.: Schöffling, 2016).
[12] Ulrike Almut Sandig, *Buch Gegen das Verschwinden* (Frankfurt a.M: Schöffling, 2015), *Flamingos* (Frankfurt a.M.: Schöffling, 2010)

UAS Exactly. I do a lot of simple acapella readings too. And then the challenge is precisely not to distance myself from the text. I have this one text, 'Message from the German Language' ('Nachricht von der deutschen Sprache'), where the language speaks from the future.[13] And of course it's clear to me that when someone reads this text they might be able simply to ignore that it's a female author, that I have written it as a woman. But when I'm stood up there on stage it's no use hiding my body and saying: 'and now pure language speaks'. Instead I do have to take a bit into account that the audience will see me standing there and, moreover, hear me with my fairly high-pitched, almost girlish voice. And so my art is a kind of balancing act. That's my presence, so to speak, that I don't thrust myself on to my poetry but rather let the text be as it is, and yet at the same time I don't pretend I don't have a body.

RB And it's not like the whole thing takes place in a vacuum. There is always a physical space there, not just the metaphorical public space, but when you perform live it always takes place in a real space. Does that mean that the text has a different effect for you every time, because naturally the audience and the room and the whole corporeality of it contribute to your performance and to what the text can actually mean?

UAS Well, last week I had a relatively unrehearsed reading before a concert in Münster that I'd planned with Grigory Semenchuk, my partner in the band *Landschaft*, because I didn't know that I would also be doing a reading beforehand. And then it transpired that I couldn't see the audience. And normally I need a lot of eye contact because, of course, a performance always relies on give and take. I don't bombard the audience but rather I judge how I need to speak to form a connection. That's what keeps me going, that I can see people, and I couldn't see the audience at all. And so I sat there and read this text, 'Message from the German Language', amongst other things. I noticed while I was talking that the text was totally different to any time I'd ever read it before. That's generally something that I can't predict, but it's very clear that the text doesn't belong to me. Even in a book the text doesn't really take place on the page, and certainly during a reading or a performance it doesn't take place on the stage – rather it takes place between me and the audience. It's actually a collaborative activity between the person who is silent and the person who is speaking, but that silent person is just as much part of it.

---

[13] Sandig, 'Nachricht von der deutschen Sprache, 2026 AD', *ich bin ein Feld*, p. 59.

RB You've also worked with translators. And then of course the text is even more collaboratively shaped, received and, at the same time made anew, in yet another in-between space. Is that comparable with a performance? Is the translation just yet another performance of the text?

UAS It's always an interpretation at any rate. The situation often arises with Karen Leeder, my English translator, where she has to decide on a particular direction for a text. And after that, once Karen has completed a translation, an appropriation takes place. I take the new text and bring it a bit closer to me. Some of the texts feel further from me, and some closer, and some I simply can't read aloud because, for example, there are unbelievable tongue-twisters in there for my German tongue, so I simply don't perform them to save embarrassing myself. And then there are texts whose original version I barely ever perform, but where I determine that, in translation, they are actually better to listen to, a stronger aural text than the original. And I work them into my readings totally differently, I develop a completely different tone of voice for them, not an intonation that I adopt from Karen, because I really can't do that, rather they develop a sound completely of their own for me.

And naturally there are also texts that work differently in front of an English-speaking audience. Lots of texts work completely differently, not just English-language ones. For example, I have a text, 'Hans im Glück' it's called, and it's always unbelievably well received when I read it in India – even though the fairy tale isn't well known there.[14] There is a similar fairy tale, an old fairy tale too, but with different imagery. And it's always a total hit, and there are various reasons for that. I think that's firstly because there is an exciting translation of it by two Indian poets in Kashmiri. This translation is delicate and melodious, whereas my German original is more rhythmic. Secondly, the frontman of the Indian band ALIF whom I work with has put this poem, 'Hans im Glück', to music in a completely unironic way, even though I mean the text to be totally ironic. He's only really emphasized the aspect of longing in it. And then there's the fact that the older, middle-class Indians in front of whom I often perform feel this great yearning for their children all the time, because many of them study in Europe or in the USA or Canada. And that means they relate to this story. That means that the text has detached itself from its origin but continues to convey a mother's longing for her son. My original text works with abbreviations, which I use to say something that I want to say without really having to say it. But in the new, Kashmiri context this element

---

[14] Sandig, 'Hans im Glück', *ich bin ein Feld*, p. 77.

provides rhythm, so it's a structural element that really just serves a rhythmical function, but the repetitions are also searching movements. These texts, they separate themselves completely from their originals after a certain point. And that's actually a sign for me that the text itself works. Whether it works as a translation I can't judge, but certainly if the translation works well as a text or not in its own right.

RB I'd like to talk about material things. Particularly when you make videos, there are often unusual objects present. For example, in your collaboration with Hinemoana Baker there's an inflatable globe there.[15] What role do objects like this have, either in the creative process itself or as an expressive device? You get the impression when you watch it that it's very likely that it's part of the creative dialogue.

UAS Yes, these objects are part of the creative dialogue. But they enter into the mix only after the text. The dialogue isn't over just because the text is written. The text in our short film, 'it wasn't me and it wasn't you either' ('It wasn't me und du warst es auch nicht'), is itself a dialogue with Hinemoana Baker. Which is actually why I put it together as a kind of letter: it begins with 'my dear' and ends 'your Hinemoana'.[16] So by the time I started writing, I already had this letter-form, a response from her, in my head, even though I barely knew her at the time. I was familiar with no more than a handful of her texts and I barely knew her as a person. What's clear is the text always comes first. So first I have this text as it were, and the text is a dialogue and works, of course, with the idea of the two hemispheres and the similarity of the hemispheres, and the idea of complete inversion. And that fascinates me in texts, in speaking, in thought actually, that everything could be expressed as its opposite. You're writing something and then you realize that you can actually be saying the exact opposite of what is written and it works just as well. I find that there's something typical in that, something I consider very human, that everything can be illustrated as its opposite, like these optical illusions that either look like a vase or like two faces. That, to get close to a topic, it actually makes sense to take a close look at the silhouettes, that is, to take a look at its opposite.

Then when I wanted to make something with Hinemoana it was relatively clear which texts belonged in this dialogue, since she had written a text at the same time and for the same project which is also a dialogue with me. It's called 'The fifteen paces between my socks and my shoes'.[17] And then the rest is really a game. You need something

---

[15] Sandig, 'Nachricht von der deutschen Sprache, 2026 AD', *ich bin ein Feld*, p. 59.
[16] Sandig, 'Hinemoana', *ich bin ein Feld*, p. 16.

visual, you need something that isn't fixed from the outset, but rather can evolve in front of you. And then the whole thing really changes in ways that you don't expect. So, for example, when we were filming, it was quite windy and we had these balls and they were constantly flying away from us. And it was really difficult to keep them all in one place. And that was actually exactly what made sense for the film in the end because it had really illustrated the way thoughts fly around. That you try to gather your thoughts together and you have a rough picture and, in the attempt to get to the point, the text emerges without ever once actually getting to the point. Because the act of exploration is the text itself and not the point you want to get to. And in this way it made total sense. There's a moment just like that where she's trying so hard to balance but something is always flying away from her.

RB So, it wasn't decided at the outset then, that you would use the ball to illustrate the point. Would it be fair to say the ball itself revealed the point?

UAS Well, it was really something akin to a classical performance with the difference that it wasn't conceived for a live audience *in situ*, but in the sense that you're making something and including elements which have something to do with the text, but you don't know what else will emerge. And then the element of wind arrives on the scene, so to speak, and then when we had these white shoe-covers on over our shoes which fell apart while we were walking. And it was very hard to walk in them because the ground was wet, and they kept falling apart even more and they were the cause of this funny noise. And we recorded this noise and used it throughout the whole soundtrack. So, what gives the effect of rhythm actually began as just the sound of us walking which we developed; that wasn't planned from the start.

RB On that note, I wanted to ask you about this video with the blue screens that illustrates one of the first poems from the volume *I am a Field Full of Rapeseed* (*ich bin ein Feld voller Raps*) and sets it to music.[18] To

---

[17] Hinemoana Baker, 'The fifteen paces between my socks and my shoes' in *Transit of Venus. Poetry Exchange*, Victoria U. P., Wellington 2016, p. 28. Available online: https://www.lyrikline.org/de/gedichte/hinemoana-baker-i-fifteen-paces-between-my-socks-and-my-7801 (last accessed 6 July 2019).

[18] Sandig, 'ich bin ein Feld voller Raps / ich bin der Schatten zum drunter Verstecken', *ich bin ein Feld*, p. 13; The version of this performed by Landschaft with the visuals discussed here is freely available on YouTube: https://youtu.be/J7V1ViKz3CU (last accessed 6 July 2019). Filmed by Sascha Conrad, Produktion Waldstrasse.

what extent did you try to shape the whole thing from the outset so that you would recognize your text in another medium?

UAS Here we were clear that the film-maker must have an equal say. In the film with Hinemoana we had a film-maker with us too, but she really told us, 'I'm just setting up the camera and you can do whatever you want, you can also decide on the cut, you're making the film, not me. I'm just pressing record.' But with the other film-maker it was clear that he would be an equal artistic collaborator on the project. And he was really keen on doing this projection on the clothes and wanted some kind of text-projection, originally it was only going to be text, whereas I definitely wanted my daughter to appear in it, something he found a bit cheesy to begin with because at the start there's the line, 'I am the mother, I am the daughter' ('ich bin die Mutter, ich bin die Tochter'), and I also wanted this hare to appear in it and the cellist, which we were then able to combine in one. But everything else evolved completely spontaneously because we didn't know what the final product was going to be, and that's how it should be as well, that you interact with your surroundings, so to speak, and allow something to arise that can become quite separate from the text or from the music.

RB From my perspective, you're describing a very collaborative kind of authorship here that draws in the most varied of elements and allows them to play a part.

UAS Absolutely, completely. Yes, really, the fact that it's my text doesn't trump everything else, it's just one part of the action, so to speak. It's just one part of the original creative act that I happen to have written this text. The circumstances of my life, or the fact that I am, for example, a woman, are really not that important. These details come into play, of course, but they also merge into something else, something bigger.

RB Which is something that's very closely connected with the topic of your work in general: that we're part of a bigger universe is a recurring theme for you. In this respect, you have definitely found the right forms for your own themes. That is: not purely written texts.

UAS I simply cannot imagine, and this has always been the case actually, that a text should only exist in a book or that it even has an ultimate form, that a text can ever finish being written at some point. I find that to be a relatively artificial way of thinking. I won my first literary award after I had written my first volume of poetry and then suddenly this tiny little print run was sold out. And so I had to release a second edition and then, like almost all authors, I had my difficulties with the book when I looked at it again, because it was my first, and I had only just started publishing, and so I rewrote it completely, so that some texts differ so fundamentally from those in the first print run that only a couple of key words, the key concepts ostensibly, remain the same. And it's still the same today, that I don't think a text is over in that sense. The very fact that it is read means that it is not over. When you're interested in acoustic or aural literature, it doesn't take long to see how old this tradition is. As old as religion, as old as humanity, that's how old aural literature is. And the age of literacy or even the printing press is just one part of it. If I were only to write books now, I would feel as though I were so stuck in just one present that I couldn't get beyond my own time.

RB It's interesting that you call it 'aural' literature because you could also say 'oral' literature. But you put the emphasis on those who listen not those who speak. And that emphasizes once again this community that engages with a text or an idea and perhaps therefore also co-creates it.

UAS Yes, because the audience is an integral component, but also of course in order to distance myself a little from slam and place myself more in the direction of *Ars Acustica* (acoustic art). Because of course texts that are really written to be spoken work with different stylistic devices. And when I'm writing a text, I don't really think about speaking, I think about thinking.

RB You can hear that in your work, but also see it, because you make so much visual work out of your texts. These films and also the performances, they're all very visual. A visual way of thinking?

UAS As a matter of fact, we have just developed some visuals for the poetry-band *Landschaft*, again in collaboration with a film-maker and an illustrator. To start with it was just about incorporating Karen's English translation so that we could venture outside of Germany or Ukraine and people would understand what was going on. That was how it started, and then the two of them completely knuckled down, the illustrator and the film-maker, and now we have little films that go with every song, but they actually go far beyond classic band-visuals. Because they are little poetry-films they leave themselves open to further interpretation. But I don't feel that you just decide on a type of literature, rather you make what you understand, what you are spiritually and emotionally and intellectually capable of, that is. And I find, of course, that my approach to writing a text – only really to pay attention to the thought process in the first instance and less to how it will sound – that this approach means you can clearly feel that they are texts, not lyrics for example, and that I only illustrate them or bring music into play afterwards. These things are much too complicated for song lyrics. That means that I need a music stand on stage for my notes, because the texts are so complicated that I just can't make a memorable song out of them with its own structure, not on top of all the auditory effects that change from one word to the next. And, of course, we don't play the music scene at all because what we do is way too complicated. And sometimes that's a bit of a shame because it's all about communication with the audience for me, but I can only do it this way, I can't help it.

RB You spoke about Hinemoana Baker before and at the beginning you hardly knew her, only her work, and clearly more has become of your collaboration since then. How does this happen, is it really just coincidence, or do you look for it, or are mediators involved?

UAS Yes to all, actually. It is coincidental and intentional, there are mediators and it happens of its own accord. I got to know Hinemoana through an official introduction. Through, on the one hand, the Berlin Literature Workshop (Literaturwerkstatt Berlin), which is now the House of Poetry (Haus für Poesie), and, on the other, a New Zealand publishing house. The two of them collaborated on a poetry translation project that we both ended up working on. So, these texts that we've already spoken about came out of this, and at first she was really only something of a 'sparring partner' for me but then she flew to Berlin and a kind of friendship developed. We are interested in similar topics both personally and creatively. Like me, she is interested in questions of gender – she comes from the queer scene, as it happens –, she is interested in performance culture in the broadest sense, she writes, and she sings. And then somehow it was pretty clear, we could make something of this.

And it was the same with Grigory too, he was first introduced to me through the Goethe Institute. Yes, I often get these introductions, but then the question is always, what do you do with them? I have improvised with many people through music or writing and then never met them again. But with Grigory we were both totally blown away by the first gig because we didn't expect to have so much fun together. And we got a good reaction and uploaded a couple of clips to YouTube straight afterwards, which almost make me cringe now because we've come so far since then, but it was simply because we were so enthused by each other. And then, without really knowing each other personally, we just agreed we would keep going with it. And then at some point, of course, you become friends with one another and that intensifies the artistic work too because then other energies come into it. I have actually always also been very close privately with my stage partners. And it's no different here either, it's like he's my little brother. So, an introduction to begin with and then you take it from there.

Or in the case of the film-maker who did the film with Hinemoana and who has also done the recent visuals, with her it was the other way around. I actually knew her privately first and she'd already made a film of one of my poems many years ago which was technically pretty complex. She had an entire flat built for it, hired a decent actress, and the film was really well received, it was screened at festivals. And at the time that didn't particularly interest me because I was preoccupied with my own things. And then at some point, because we were always seeing each other in Berlin, our friendship grew, and from the friendship came this playing around with ideas. And then there is always the matter of payment, because I can't very well afford the amount you'd normally need to pay for that kind of work, I'd have to find about 2,000 Euros. Instead, we swing it so that I'll write for her next documentary film or do copy-editing for her and in return she'll give me mates' rates. Or I support her next crowdfunding project and from this support she knows which type of film I'm interested in because that's the one I'll support over something else. And then we'll sit down with some food and start to mess about. And so we conjure up the next idea. For me, it's really wonderful work because it doesn't all revolve around the text but is rather work amongst equals: the film is every bit as important as my text. But because I'm the one who is the author, as it were, I am the one who takes it to the world and it runs under my name. Behind the scenes, though, I'm not the boss, it's work amongst equals.

RB The institutions which play a part in initiating everything here, the Goethe Institute and the various centres for literature, are traditionally quite preoccupied with canons, that is, a certain style of literature, a certain type of author, that they want to promote. Do you get the feeling that you have to stand for something, that you're chosen to represent something for certain reasons?

UAS The Goethe Institutes definitely have me categorized. Naturally some of the ways I am categorized annoy me, for example being a representative of the young scene, something which I find almost insulting nowadays. And not just to me, it's really an insult to the actual young scene, which is consequently declared null and void, as though it doesn't exist. I don't know if this is still the case but for a long time when I was starting out it was really important to people that I come from East Germany. Now that I live in Berlin it's not as bad, but when I was still living in Leipzig it was always emphasized. You could just tell, now they needed a woman from the East. And I'm OK with that because there's no denying it. And meanwhile I seem to have a reputation for working across genres with a focus on aural literature, but without being a poetry slammer. Evidently you're always going to be put in some kind of category, and that's sometimes accurate enough but it's always a simplification. And I try not to worry about that. Because it's clear, of course, that on the free market – by which I mean the free market as in the freelance scene, including the freelance underground scene – that I would get lost completely. Because there is so much here, even the stuff that mixes genres to be honest: I am simply one of a great many. Here in Berlin I am barely noticed at all. And in that sense I am really very lucky: thanks to the Goethe Institute or certain literature centres, I have somehow been plucked out of this scene and get paid for what I do, in contrast to most others.

RB Is that problematic then? You also hang out with some of these other artists of course. Does it make you uncomfortable?

UAS It was more problematic in Leipzig, and here in Berlin there are just so many of us that people don't even tend to make comparisons. Here in Berlin you blend in so much that it's fine. But in Leipzig that was a real problem. There are very good authors there too, including some very good undiscovered authors, who have simply made alternative, practical decisions in their lives, to have full-time jobs, for example. And that's difficult, of course.

RB You studied at the Leipzig Literature Institute. To what extent can an institute like that have an influence on the literary scene? It has the potential to remain part of the canonization process: by people teaching the next generation just as they were taught themselves. Or can you see new spaces, new possibilities opening up?

UAS Well, when I was studying at the Literature Institute it was even more unique than it is today. Because, other than us, there were really only the folk in Hildesheim, and they didn't teach the same thing. Vienna had only just come into being, and Biel wasn't so well known either. And the FU in Berlin did teach creative writing but that also wasn't quite as well known yet. That meant that the eye of the public, as well as that of the publishing scene, was trained more strongly on us. That has, I believe, lessened over the years.

But it's very clear that no matter where you study, when you have the official legitimation of studying literature for three years full-time before you have to go back out onto the job market, or go out onto the job market full stop, then of course you have a completely different chance of becoming a professional and of developing creatively compared with someone who has been on the freelance scene from the outset and relies on going from job to job to survive. And I think this chance to focus intensively on something, whether that's in Leipzig or somewhere else, really does produce quality.

And, of course, there has always been this notion, both nowadays and at the time, that institutes create the canon, and that's stupid; it was stupid when it was being discussed in the noughties. Merely because a couple of novels were written in a similar style. In my time there was this discussion about the fräulein-miracle ('Fräuleinwunder') and, although that began with Judith Hermann, us young writers were constantly compared with Judith Hermann, whether it made sense or not. That is complete nonsense and I didn't take it especially seriously, it wasn't taken very seriously by any of the students at the institute at the time, we laughed about it and everyone carried on doing their thing. And, of course, very few who have studied with us will actually go on to become an author as their career, there are very few who want to do this and who actually succeed. Many stay in the field and work in editing or cultural organizations, or a lot of them publish a book once in a blue moon but work predominantly as an editor in a publishing house, for example. But people who genuinely work as authors on a freelance basis are really very rare. It's always only a handful per year. Or less than a handful to be honest.

RB Given the direction your own work has taken, do you see the future of literature as residing in working even more across genres? Is that the direction literature should go in?

UAS I'm more inclined to think that it has always been that way. It's receiving a bit more attention at the moment because digital media have become more of a thing, of course. But it's actually always been there, whether it's Stefan George or Thomas Kling. And within the visual arts alone there have always been all those people who work with text. And that'll always be the case. It always surprises me a bit that working across genres is perceived to be such a modern thing, because for me it's really rather traditional.

RB It must date back to at least the Middle Ages.

UAS Yes, and when you take a closer look, those authors whose work cuts across genres tend to be experts on old texts. Take Tristan Marquardt; Ulrike Draesner is another example because she occupies this middle-ground between the academic and the literary. Artists who work across genres aren't the ones saying this is popping up out of nowhere and is only rooted in the present. They are usually well-versed in history, or art, or the history of literature. So, I believe all approaches will always exist, and much will depend on which media people are able to work with for free, that's what it comes down to. Those will always be the media which are the most inspiring, of course, because you're able to play around with them. For example, YouTube is an integral part of my work, even though I don't have that many subscribers or a huge click count. I spend a lot of my time editing and uploading videos because I love how I'm no longer hampered by broadcasters sitting on the rights to my work. That's why I've moved away from radio plays. When I started out, I wrote a few radio plays, and two of them were big, scripted radio-plays, and I worked intensively on them for a long time. I am very proud of these radio plays, but I can't present them anywhere because the stations hold the rights for them. And that's what fascinates me about platforms like YouTube or Soundcloud or bandcamp, that I can do something there. I just have to speak to the people I'm working with and then we come to an agreement and upload it. And then I can send it to a colleague in New Zealand without having to think about rights infringement. And, of course, this is what inspires me because I don't feel restricted by it. It's also the case with publishers, of course, as good as this support is, I am also selling the rights to my texts to the publishers. There are many advantages in this, but if I were only to work in the book sector, I would always feel tied because I'd have to discuss every little thing with them, whenever I wanted to upload something. And then some licence or other would constantly have to be drawn up, just so that a Tasmanian literature festival can use something.

This freedom offered by the internet will probably change in the future, things seem to be moving in that direction, we are really in the final throes of this anarchy now. I'm jumping on the bandwagon, so to speak, but really on the very last wagon. And so that raises the question of what next? What genre will the future offer? And, of course, it'll be the genres that offer the least financial and technical hurdles where art and culture happen first, because this is where people can make art freely in the first instance, without worrying about funding or about rights.

Bibliography

Please note: editions listed are the ones used for referencing purposes in this book. Dates of publication, particularly for primary sources, do not necessarily reflect the original date of publication.

Primary Sources – Printed
[n.a.], *Welt als Sprache: Auseinandersetzung mit Zeichen und Zeichensystemen der Gegenwart* (Akademie der Künste: Berlin, [1972])
Baker, Hinemoana, et al, *Transit of Venus. Poetry Exchange* (Wellington: Victoria U. P., 2016)
Becher, Johannes R., *Gesammelte Werke*, 18 vols, ed. Johannes-R.-Becher-Archiv (Berlin: Aufbau, 1966–1981)
Bernhard, Thomas, *Goethe schtirbt: Erzählungen* (Berlin: Suhrkamp, 2010)
―― *Meine Preise* (Frankfurt a.M: Suhrkamp, 2009)
―― *Erzählungen / Kurzprosa*, ed. Hans Höller, Martin Huber & Manfred Mittermayer (Frankfurt am Main: Suhrkamp, 2003)
―― *Der Stimmenimitator* (Frankfurt a.M: Suhrkamp, 1978)
Bichsel, Peter, et al., *Das Gästehaus: Roman* (Berlin: Literarisches Colloquium, 1965)
Bloch, Ernst, *Werkausgabe*, Vol. 5 (Frankfurt am Main: Suhrkamp, 1993), p. 1628
―― *The Principle of Hope*, trans. Neville Plaice, Stephen Plaice & Paul Knight, 3 vols (Oxford: Blackwell, 1986)
―― *Das Prinzip Hoffnung*, in Ernst Bloch, *Gesamtausgabe*, 17 vols (Frankfurt a.M.: Suhrkamp, 1959–1978), vols 5.1 and 5.2 (1959)
Boettiger, Helmut with Lutz Dittrich, *Elefantenruden: Walter Höllerer und die Erfindung des Literaturbetriebs* (Berlin: Literaturhaus Berlin, 2005), p. 7.
Böll, Heinrich, *Frauen vor Flußlandschaft* (Cologne: Kiepenheuer & Witsch, 1985).
―― *Frankfurter Vorlesungen* (Cologne: Kiepenheuer & Witsch, 1966)
Calvino, Italo, *Invisible Cities*, transl. William Weaver (London: Vintage, 1997)
Draesner, Ulrike, *Schwitters* (Munich: Penguin, 2020).
―― *Grammatik der Gespenster: Frankfurter Poetikvorlesungen* (Stuttgart: Reclam, 2018)
―― *Happy Aging: Ulrike Draesner erzählt ihre Wechseljahre* (Wyk auf Föhr: supposé, 2016)
―― *London* (Berlin: Insel, 2016)
―― *Mein Hiddensee* (Hamburg: mare, 2015)

—— *Sieben Sprünge vom Rand der Welt* (Munich: Luchterhand, 2014)
—— *Spiele* (Darmstadt: Luchterhand, 2005)
—— *gedächtnisschleifen* (Frankfurt a.M.: Suhrkamp, 1995)
Eckermann, Johann Peter, *Gespräche mit Goethe in den letzten Jahren seines Lebens*, ed. Christoph Michel (Berlin: Deutscher Klassiker Verlag, 2011)
Elsner, Gisela, *Versuche, die Wirklichkeit zu bewältigen: Gesammelte Erzählungen, 1*, ed. Christine Künzel (Berlin: Verbrecher, 2013)
—— *Die Riesenzwerge* (Berlin: Aufbau, 2001)
Enzensberger, Hans Magnus 'Gemeinplätze, die Neueste Literatur betreffend', *Kursbuch*, 15 (1968), 187–96
—— *Einzelheiten I: Bewußtseins-Industrie* (Frankfurt a.M.: Suhrkamp, 1964
—— *Blindenschrift* (Frankfurt a.M.: Suhrkamp, 1964)
—— *Landessprache* (Frankfurt a.M.: Suhrkamp, 1960)
—— *Verteidigung der Wölfe* (Frankfurt a.M.: Suhrkamp, 1957)
Goethe, Johann Wolfgang von, *Conversations of Goethe with Johann Peter Eckermann*, trans. John Oxenford, ed. J.K. Moorhead, intr. Havelock Ellis (United States of America: da Capo, 1998)
Grass, Günter, *Werkausgabe*, 19 vols, ed. Volker Neuhaus & Daniela Hermes (Steidl: Göttingen, 1997–2015)
Haderlap, Maja, *Engel des Vergessens* (Munich: btb, 2013)
Hasenclever, Walter, ed., *Prosaschreiben* (Berlin: Literarisches Colloquium Berlin, 1964)
Heidegger, Martin, 'Sprache und Heimat', in Martin Heidegger, *Gesamtausgabe*, vol. 13 (Klostermann: Frankfurt a.M., 1983), pp. 155–80.
Höllerer, Walter, ed., *Autoren im Haus: Zwanzig Jahre Literarisches Colloquium Berlin* (Berlin: Galerie Wannsee, 1982)
—— *Die Elephantenuhr* (Frankfurt a.M.: 1973); rev. shortened edn 1975.
—— *Ein Gedicht und sein Autor: Lyrik und Essay* (Berlin: Literarisches Colloquium Berlin, 1967)
—— *Gedichte: Wie entsteht ein Gedicht?* (Frankfurt a.M.: Suhrkamp, 1964)
—— *Der andere Gast: Gedichte* (Munich: Hanser, 1952)
Hoppe, Felicitas, *Prawda: Eine amerikanische Reise* (Frankfurt a.M.: Fischer, 2018)
—— *Hoppe* (Frankfurt a.M.: Fischer, 2012)
Janka, Walter, *Schwierigkeiten mit der Wahrheit* (Reinbek bei Hamburg: Rowohlt, 1989)
Kramberg, K. H., ed., *Vorletzte Worte: Schriftsteller schreiben ihren eigenen Nachruf* (Berlin: Goldman, 1985)
Mann, Thomas, *Gesammelte Werke*, 13 vols (Frankfurt a.M.: Fischer, 1960–1974)
—— [Antwort auf die Umfage] 'Wie soll das Goethe-Jahr 1932 gefeiert werden?', *Die literarische Welt: unabhängiges Organ für das deutsche Schrifttum*, 7 (1931), Issue 38, p. 2
Martynova, Olga, *Mörikes Schlüsselbein* (Munich: btb, 2015)
More, Thomas, *Utopia*, trans. and ed. Dominic Baker-Smith (London: Penguin, 2012)
Müller, Herta, *Reisende auf einem Bein* (Frankfurt: Fischer, 2010)
—— *Der König verneigt sich und tötet* (Munich: Hanser, 2003)
—— *Der Fremde Blick oder Das Leben ist ein Furz in der Laterne* (Göttingen: Wallstein, 1999)
Musil, Robert, *Der Mann ohne Eigenschaften*, 2 vols, ed. Adolf Frisé (Hamburg: Rowohlt, 1988)

Petrowskaja, Katja, *Vielleicht Esther* (Berlin: Suhrkamp, 2015)
—— *Maybe Esther*, trans. Shelley Frisch (London: 4th Estate, 2019)
Raddatz, Fritz J., *Jahre mit Ledig: Eine Erinnerung* (Hamburg: Rowohlt, 2015)
—— *Unruhestifter: Erinnerungen* (Munich: Propyläen, 2003)
Ransmayr, Christoph, *Die letzte Welt* (Frankfurt a.M: Fischer, 1988)
Richter, Hans Werner, *Briefe*, ed. Sabine Cofalla (Munich: Hanser, 1997)
—— *Im Etablissement der Schmetterlinge: 21 Portraits aus der Gruppe 47* (Munich: Hanser, 1986)
—— ed., *Almanach der Gruppe 47: 1947–1962* (Reinbek: Rowohlt, 1962)
Sandig, Ulrike Almut, *Leuchtende Schafe* (Frankfurt a.M.: Schöffling, 2021)
—— *Buch Gegen das Verschwinden* (Frankfurt a.M: Schöffling, 2015)
—— *Flamingos* (Frankfurt a.M.: Schöffling, 2010)
—— *Zunder* (Leipzig: Connewitzer Verlagsbuchhandlung, 2005; 2nd rev. edn 2009)
Seghers, Anna, *Werkausgabe*, 21 vols, ed. Helen Fehervary and Bernhard Spies (Berlin: Aufbau, 2000 -), V/2, *Tage wie Staubsand: Briefe 1953–1983*, ed. Christiane Zehl Romero and Almut Giesecke (Berlin: Aufbau, 2010)
—— *Hier im Volk der kalten Herzen: Briefwechsel 1947*, ed. Christel Berger (Berlin: Aufbau, 2000)
—— *Das Vertrauen* (Berlin: Aufbau, 1975)
—— *Die Entscheidung* (Berlin: Aufbau, 1975)
Unseld, 70 Siegfried, *Chronik*, 2 vols, ed. Raimund Fellinger (Berlin: Suhrkamp, 2014)
—— *Briefe an die Autoren* (Frankfurt a.M..: Suhrkamp, 2004)
—— *Der Autor und sein Verlger* (Frankfurt a.M.: Suhrkamp, 1985)
Walser, Martin, *In Goethe's Hand: Szenen aus dem 19. Jahrhundert* (Frankfurt a.M.: Suhrkamp, 1982)
Wohmann, Gabriele, *Schreiben müssen: Ein Arbeitstagebuch* (Frankfurt a.M.: Luchterhand, 1991)
Wolf, Christa, *Nachdenken über Christa T.* (Neuwied: Luchterhand, 2002)
—— *Die Dimension des Autors: Essays und Aufsätze; Reden und Gespräche, 1959–1985*, 2 vols, (Berlin: Aufbau, 1986)
—— *Der geteilte Himmel* (Munich: dtv, 1981)
—— *Kein Ort. Nirgends* (Neuwied: Luchterhand, 1979)
Wolf, Christa & Anna Seghers, *Das dicht besetzte Leben: Briefe Gespräche und Essays* (Berlin: Aufbau, 2003)

Primary Sources – Films / TV Material / Audio Material

Ammer, Andreas (director), *Vom Glanz und Vergehen der Gruppe 47*, ARD / 3Sat / SW3, 2007
Baker, Hinemoana, Beate Kunath, Ulrike Almut Sandig, 'It wasn't me und du warst es auch nicht', available on YouTube: https://youtu.be/-syWM_TMKCM (last accessed 6 July 2019)
Bechert, Hilde, & Klaus Dexel (directors), *Der Verleger oder Die Lust am Buch*, ARD, 1987
Draesner, Ulrike, *Happy Aging: Ulrike Draesner erzählt ihre Wechseljahre* (Wyk auf Föhr: supposé, 2016)
Held, Oliver, Thomas Henke (directors), *Felicitas Hoppe sagt*, Germany / Switzerland 2017, available online at https://www.felicitas-hoppe-sagt.de (last accessed 20 November 2019)

Landschaft, 'Landschaft: Official Video', available on YouTube: https://www.youtube.com/watch?v=J7V1ViKz3CU&feature=youtu.be (last accessed 19 November 2020)

Müller-Hanpft, Susanne & Martin Bosboom (directors), *Wie sie wurden, was sie sind. Gruppe 47: eine Schriftstellergeneration schreibt Geschichte*, ZDF, 1987

Palzer, Thomas (director), *Wie wird man Bestseller?*, SWR, 2009

Ramsbott, Wolfgang & Walter Höllerer (directors), *Das literarische Profil von Berlin*, Literarisches Colloquium Berlin, 1970/71

Reich, Gisela, & Barbara Bronnen (directors), *Dichter und Richter: Die Gruppe 47, vorläufiges Schlußbild nach 30 Jahren*, ARD, 1978

Wohmann, Gabriele (director), *Schreiben müssen: Ein elektronisches Tagebuch*, ZDF, 1990

Secondary Sources

Adelson, Leslie A., 'Literary Imagination and the Future of Literary Studies', *Deutsche Vierteljahresschrift*, 89.4 (2015), pp. 675–83

Adorno, Theodor, 'Kulturkritik und Gesellschaft', in *Schreiben nach Auschwitz? Adorno und die Dichter*, ed. Petra Kiedaisch (Stuttgart: Reclam, 1995), pp. 27–49

Amslinger, Tobias, *Verlagsautorschaft: Enzensberger und Suhrkamp* (Göttingen: Wallstein, 2018)

Ankum, Katharina von, *Die Rezeption von Christa Wolf in Ost und West: Von Moskauer Novelle bis "Selbstversuch"* (Amsterdam / Atlanta: Rodopi, 1992)

Ansel, Michael, Hans-Edwin Friedrich, Gerhard Lauer, eds, *Die Erfindung des Schriftstellers Thomas Mann* (Berlin: de Gruyter, 2009)

Apter, Emily, *Against World Literature: On the Politics of Untranslatability* (London: Verso, 2013)

Arnold, Heinz Ludwig, *Die Gruppe 47* (Reinbek: Rowohlt, 2004)

Aron, Paul, & Jérôme Meizoz, 'Littérature, histoire et sciences sociales: travailler "par cas". Un échange entre Paul Aron et Jérôme Meizoz', *Revue italienne d'études francaises* (online), 7 (2017)

Ashton, Rosemary, 'Carlyle's Apprenticeship: His Early German Criticism and His Relationship with Goethe (1822–1832)', *The Modern Language Review*, 71:1 (1976), 1–18

Assmann, Aleida, *Cultural Memory and Western Civilization: Functions, Media, Archives* (Cambridge: Cambridge U. P., 2011)

Assmann, David-Christopher, *Poetologien des Literaturbetriebs: Szenen bei Kirchhoff, Maier, Gstrein und Händler.* (Berlin: de Gruyter, 2014)

Augé, Marc, *Non-Places: Introduction to an Anthropology of Supermodernity*, trans. John Howe (London: Verso, 1995)

Barthes, Roland, 'The Death of the Author', in Roland Barthes, *Image, Music, Text*, trans & ed. Stephen Heath (London: Fontana, 1977), pp. 142–8

Bathrick, David, 'Die Intellektuellen und die Macht. Die Repräsentanz des Schriftstellers in der DDR', in Sven Hanuschek, Therese Hörnigk and Christine Malende, eds, *Schriftsteller als Intellektuelle: Politik und Literatur im kalten Krieg* (Tübingen: Niemayer, 2000), pp. 235–48

―― *The Powers of Speech: The Politics of Culture in the GDR* (Lincoln: U. of Nebraska P, 1995)

Becker, Howard, *Art Worlds* (Berkeley: U. of California P., 2008)

Benjamin, Walter, *Werke und Nachlass: Kritische Gesamtausgabe*, 21 vols, ed. Christoph Gödde & Henri Lonitz (Berlin: Suhrkamp, 2008–), vol. 19, *Über den Begriff der Geschichte*, ed. Gérard Raulet (Berlin: Suhrkamp, 2010)

Bering, Dietz, *Die Intellektuellen. Geschichte eines Schimpfwortes* (Stuttgart: Klett-Cotta, 1978)

Biendarra, Anke, *Germans Going Global: Contemporary Literature and Cultural Globalization* (Berlin: de Gruyter, 2012)

Boes, Tobias, *Thomas Mann's War: Literature, Politics, and the World Republic of Letters* (Ithaca, NY: Cornell U. P., 2019)

—— *Formative Fictions: Nationalism, Cosmopolitanism, and the Bildungsroman* (Ithaca, NY: Cornell U. P., 2012)

—— 'Thomas Mann, World Author: Representation and Autonomy in the World Republic of Letters', in 'World Authorship', ed. Rebecca Braun & Andrew Piper, special issue of *Seminar*, 51.2 (2015), 132–47

Boes, Tobias, Rebecca Braun & Emily Spiers, eds, *World Authorship* (Oxford: Oxford U. P., 2020)

Böttiger, Helmut, *Elefantenrunden: Walter Höllerer und die Erfindung des Literaturbetriebs* (Berlin: Literaturhaus Berlin, 2005)

Boorstin, Daniel J., *The Image, or What Happened to the American Dream?* (New York: Athenaeum, 1962)

Bourdieu, Pierre, *The Rules of Art* (Cambridge: Polity, 1996)

—— *The Field of Cultural Production: Essays on Art and Literature*, ed. Randal Johnson (Cambridge: Polity, 1993)

Bowie, Andrew, *Introduction to German Philosophy: From Kant to Habermas* (Cambridge: Polity, 2003)

Bradley, Laura, *Cooperation and Conflict: GDR Theatre Censorship, 1961–1989* (Oxford: Oxford U. P., 2010)

Braun, Rebecca, 'World Author: On Exploding Canons and Writing Towards More Equitable Literary Futures', in Joel Evans, ed., *Cambridge Critical Concepts: Globalization and Literary Studies* (Cambridge: Cambridge U. P., forthcoming 2022), pp. 226–43.

—— 'The World Author in Us All: Conceptualising Fame and Agency in the Global Literary Market', *Celebrity Studies*, 7.4 (2016), 457–75

—— 'Prize Germans? Changing Notions of Germanness and the Role of the Award-Winning Author into the Twenty-First Century', *Oxford German Studies*, 43.1 (2014), 37–54

—— 'Embodying Achievement: Thomas Bernhard, Elfriede Jelinek, and Authorship as a Competitive Sport', in *Austrian Studies* (2014), 22, special issue on 'Elfriede Jelinek in the Arena', ed. A. Fiddler & K. Jürs-Munby, 121–38

—— 'Wandelnde Mythen: Zur populären Darstellung Ingeborg Bachmanns und der Gruppe 47', in Wilhelm Hemecker & Manfred Mittermayer, eds, *Mythos Bachmann: Zwischen Inszenierung und Selbstinszenierung* (Vienna: Zsolnay, 2011), pp. 110–30

—— 'Fetishizing Intellectual Achievement: The Nobel Prize and European Literary Celebrity', *Celebrity Studies*, 2.3 (2011), 320–34

—— 'Daniel Kehlmann, *Die Vermessung der Welt*: Measuring Celebrity Through the Ages', in S. Taberner and L. Marven, eds, *Emerging German-Language Novelists of the Twenty-First Century* (Rochester, NY: Camden House, 2011), pp. 75–88

—— '1967–2007: The Gruppe 47 as a Cultural Heimat', *German Quarterly*, 83:2 (2010), 212–29

―― 'Cultural Impact and the Power of Myth in Popular Public Constructions of Authorship', in *Cultural Impact in the German Context: Studies in Transmission, Reception and Influence*, ed. by R. Braun and L. Marven (Rochester, NY: Camden House, 2010), pp. 78–96

―― *Constructing Authorship in the Work of Günter Grass* (Oxford: Oxford U. P., 2008)

―― '"Sticks and Stones may break my Bones": The Aesthetic Enactment of Violence in the Work of Elfriede Jelinek', in H. Chambers, ed., *Violence, Culture and Identity in Germany and Austria* (Oxford: Lang, 2006), 343–58

Braun, Rebecca & Lyn Marven, eds, *Cultural Impact in the German Context: Studies in Transmission, Reception, and Influence* (Rochester, NY: Camden House, 2010)

Braun, Rebecca & Benedict Schofield, eds, *Transnational German Studies* (Liverpool: Liverpool U. P., 2020)

Briegleb, Klaus, *Mißachtung und Tabu: Eine Streitschrift zur Frage "Wie anti-semitisch war die Gruppe 47?"* (Berlin: Philo, 2003)

Brockmann, Stephen, *German Literary Culture at the Zero Hour* (Rochester, NY: Camden House, 2004)

Carlyle, Thomas, *The Cornerstone of a New Social Edifice / Der Grundstein eines neuen geselligen Gebäudes*, ed. Horst Pöthe & Norbert Miller (Berlin: de Gruyter, 1981/82)

Cepl-Kaufmann, Gertrude, 'Verlust oder poetische Rettung? Zum Begriff Heimat in Günter Grass' Danziger Trilogie', in Hans-Georg Pott, ed, *Literatur und Provinz: Das Konzept 'Heimat' in der neueren Literatur* (Paderborn: Schöningh, 1986), pp. 61–83

Dahnke, Hans-Dietrich, 'Humanität und Geschichtsperspektive: Zu den Goethe-Ehrungen 1932, 1949, 1982', in *Weimarer Beiträge*, 28/10 (1982), 66–89

Dambacher, Eva, *Literatur und Kulturpreise 1859-1949: Eine Dokumentation* (Marbach: Deutsche Schillergesellschaft, 1996)

Damrosch, David, *What is World Literature?* (Princeton: Princeton U. P., 2003)

Davies, Peter, *Divided Loyalties: East German Writers and the Politics of German Division 1945–1953* (Leeds: Maney, 2000)

Drescher, Angela, ed., *Dokumentation zu Christa Wolf "Nachdenken über Christa T."* (Hamburg: Luchterhand, 1992)

Dücker, Burckhard, Dietrich Harth, Marion Steinicke & Judith Ulmer, special issue, 'Literaturpreisverleihungen: ritualisierte Konsekrationspraktiken im kulturellen Feld', *Forum Ritualdynamik*, 11 (2005), 19

Durzak, Manfred, *Die deutsche Kurzgeschichte der Gegenwart: Autorenporträts, Werkstattgespräche, Interpretationen* (Stuttgart: Reclam, 1980) [a third updated and expanded edition was printed in 2002]

Dwars, Jens-Fietje, *Abgrund des Widerspruchs: Das Leben des Johannes R. Becher* (Berlin: Aufbau, 1998)

Eigler, Friederike, '"Könnte nicht alles auch ganz anders sein?" Hoppe zwischen Autofiktion und Metafiktion', in Holdenried, ed., *Felicitas Hoppe*, pp. 145–59

Emmerich, Wolfgang, *Kleine Literaturgeschichte der DDR*, rev. edn (Berlin: Aufbau, 2005)

Foucault, Michel, 'What is an Author?', in Michel Foucault, *The Essential Works of Foucault 1954–1984*, vol 2, ed. James Faubion (London: Penguin, 2000), pp. 205–22

―― 'Of Other Spaces', trans. Jay Mickowiec, *Diacritics*, 16.1 (1986), pp. 22–27

Frank, Svenja, 'Ikonisches Erzählen als Einheit von Realität und Imagination: Zum Verhältnis von ästhetischer Reflexion und narrativer Realisation im Werk von Felicitas Hoppe', in Frank & Ilgner, eds, *Ehrliche Erfindungen*, pp. 207–36
—— 'Inzest und Autor-Imago im Marionettentheater: Zum Identitätskonzept in Felicitas Hoppes *Paradiese, Übersee*, in Michaela Holdenried, ed., *Felicitas Hoppe: Das Werk* (Berlin: Schmidt, 2015), pp. 49–68
Frank, Svenja, & Julia Ilgner, eds, *Ehrliche Erfindungen: Felicitas Hoppe zwischen Tradition und Transmoderne* (Bielefeld: transcript, 2017)
Fuchs, Anne, *After the Dresden Bombing: Pathways of Memory, 1945 to the Present* (Basingstoke: Palgrave MacMillan, 2012)
—— 'A Heimat in Ruins and the Ruins as Heimat: W.G. Sebald's Luftkrieg und Literatur', in Cosgrove, Fuchs, Grote, eds, *German Memory Contests*, pp. 287–302
Fuchs, Anne, Mary Cosgrove & Georg Grote, eds, *German Memory Contests: The Search for Identity of Literature, Film, and Discourse since 1990* (Rochester, NY: Camden House, 2006)
Gahl, Christoph, 'Literatur im technischen Zeitalter', in *Colloquium: eine deutsche Studentenzeitung*, (1962) 16:3, 11–13
Geisenhanslüke, Achim, and Michael Peter Hehl, eds, *Poetik im technischen Zeitalter: Walter Höllerer und die Entstehung des modernen Literaturbetriebs* (Bielefeld: transcript, 2013)
Goll, Thomas, *Die Deutschen und Thomas Mann: Die Rezeption des Dichters in Abhängigkeit von der Politischen Kultur Deutschlands 1898–1955* (Baden-Baden: Nomos, 2000)
Goodman, Jessica, 'Between Celebrity and Glory: Textual After-Image in Late Eighteeenth-Century France', *Celebrity Studies* (2016), 7.4, special issue on 'Literary Celebrity', ed. R. Braun and E. Spiers, 545–60
Grimm, Reinhold, ed., *Hans Magnus Enzensberger* (Frankfurt a.M.: Suhrkamp, 1984)
Grunau, Skott, 'Gruppe 47. Nachkriegsliteratur zwischen Poesie und Politik', (Amt für kulturelle Freizeitgestaltung der Stadt Nürnberg, 'Kooperation Freizeit und Schule', July 1987)
Hagestedt, Lutz, 'Sinn für Überholtes: Aspekte der Repräsentationssemantik in Thomas Manns "Deutschlandreden"' in Michael Ansel, Hans-Edwin Friedrich, Gerhard Lauer, eds, *Die Erfindung des Schriftstellers Thomas Mann* (Berlin: de Gruyter, 2009), pp. 351–70
—— 'Das Glück ist eine Pflicht: Der Suhrkamp Verlag wurde fünfzig Jahre alt', 01.07.2000, published in *literaturkritik.de*, 7/8, July 2000 and available online at: http://www.literaturkritik.de/public/rezension.php?rez_id=1261&ausgabe=200007 (last accessed 19 July 2019)
Hahn, Hans-Joachim, 'Günter Grass's Hundejahre: Ein Beitrag zur Erinnerungskultur in der Bundesrepublik der Sechziger Jahre', *German Life & Letters*, 72.2 (2019), 187–203
Haines, Brigid, ed., *The Eastern European Turn in Contemporary German-Language Literature*, special issue of *German Life & Letters*, 68.2 (2015)
Haines, Brigid, & Lyn Marven, eds, *Herta Müller* (Oxford: Oxford Univeristy Press, 2013)
Hall, Katharina, *Günter Grass's 'Danzig Quintet': Explorations in the Memory and History of the Nazi Era from 'Die Blechtrommel' to 'Im Krebsgang'* (Bern: Lang, 2007)
Hammer, Manfried, Edelgard Abenstein, Daniel Danisch et al., eds, *Das Mauerbuch: Texte und Bilder aus Deutschland von 1945 bis heute* (Berlin: Oberbaum, 1986)

Hammermeister, Kai, 'Heimat in Heidegger and Gadamer', *Philosophy and Literature* (2000), 24.2, 312–26

Häntzschel, Günter, Jürgen Michael Benz, Rüdiger Bolz & Dagmar Ulbricht, *Gabriele Wohmann* (Munich: Beck, 1982)

Harscheidt, Michael, *Günter Grass: Wort-Zahl-Gott: Der 'phantastische Realismus' in den Hundejahren* (Bonn: Bouvier, 1976)

Hayot, Eric, *On Literary Worlds* (New York: Oxford U. P., 2012)

Hehl, Michael Peter, 'Vom "Spießbürger" zum "flexiblen Menschen": Überlegungen zum Verschwinden und Wiederauftauchen Gisela Elsners, in Hehl & Künzel, eds, *Ikonisierung, Kritik, Wiederentdeckung: Gisela Elsner und die Literatur der Bundesrepublik* (Munich: text + kritik, 2014), pp. 11–28

—— 'Berliner Netzwerke: Walter Höllerer, die Gruppe 47 und die Gründung des Literarischen Colloquiums Berlin', in *Poetik im technischen Zeitalter: Walter Höllerer und die Entstehung des modernen Literaturbetriebs*, ed. by Achim Geisenhanslüke and Michael Peter Hehl (Bielefeld: transcript, 2013), pp. 155–89

—— 'Poetik der Institutionen: Walter Höllerers institutionelles Engagement und die Literatur der Moderne', *kultuRRevoltion*, 63 (2012), 45–53

Hehl, Michael Peter, & Christine Künzel, eds, *Ikonisierung, Kritik, Wiederentdeckung: Gisela Elsner und die Literatur der Bundesrepublik* (Munich: text + kritik, 2014)

Hemecker, Wilhelm, & Manfred Mittermayer, eds, *Mythos Bachmann: Zwischen Inszenierung und Selbstinszenierung* (Vienna: Zsolnay, 2011)

Hermand, Jost, & Wigand Lange, *"Wollt ihr Thomas Mann wiederhaben?": Deutschland und die Emigranten* (Hamburg: Europäische Verlagsanstalt, 1999)

Hodenberg, Christina von, *Konsens und Krise: Eine Geschichte der westdeutschen Medienöffentlichkeit, 1945–1973* (Göttingen: Wallstein, 2006)

Holdenried, Michaela, ed., *Felicitas Hoppe: Das Werk* (Berlin: Schmidt, 2015)

Homscheid, Thomas, & Esbjörn Nyström, eds, *Geschichten des Reisens – Reisen zur Geschichte: Studien zu Felicitas Hoppe* (Uelvesbüll: Der andere Verlag, 2012)

Hotz, Constance, *"Die Bachmann": Das Image der Dichterin: Ingeborg Bachmann im journalistischen Diskurs* (Konstanz: Faude, 1990)

Hutchinson, Ben, *Lateness and Modern European Literature* (Oxford: Oxford U. P., 2016)

Innerhofer, Roland, 'Die Polfried AG: Satirisches Kabarett von Egon Friedell und Alfred Polgar', in Wendelin Schmidt-Dengler, Johann Sonnleitner & Klaus Zeyringer, eds, *Komik in der österreichischen Literatur* (Berlin: Erich Schmidt, 1996), pp. 179–88

Inwood, Michael, *Heidegger: A Very Short Introduction* (Oxford: Oxford U. P., 1997)

Jones, Sara, *Complicity, Censorship and Criticism: Negotiating Space in the GDR Literary Sphere* (Berlin: de Gruyter, 2011)

Jurgensen, Manfred, *Deutsche Frauen der Gegenwart: Bachmann, Reinig, Wolf, Wohmann, Struck, Leutenegger und Schwaiger* (Bern: Francke, 1983)

Knapp, Gerhard, & Mona Knapp, *Gabriele Wohmann* (Königstein: Athenäum, 1981)

Koch, Manfred *Weimaraner Weltbewohner: Zur Genese von Goethes Begriff "Weltliteratur"* (Tübingen: Niemeyer, 2002)

Koebner, Thomas, 'Goethe im bundesdeutschen Fernsehen', *Jahrbuch für internationale Germanistik* (1983), XV/2, 90–96

Krylova, Katya, *Walking through History: Topography and Identity in the Works of Ingeborg Bachmann and Thomas Bernhard* (Oxford: Lang, 2013)

Kuhn, Anna, *Christa Wolf's Utopian Vision: From Marxism to Feminism* (Cambridge: Cambridge U. P., 1988)

Künzel, Christine, ed., *Die letzte Kommunistin: Texte zu Gisela Elsner* (Hamburg: konkret, 2009), pp. 23–28
—— 'Eine "schreibende Kleopatra": Autorschaft und Maskerade bei Gisela Elsner', in Christine Künzel & Jörg Schönert, eds, *Autorinszenierungen: Autorschaft und literarisches Werk im Kontext der Medien* (Würzburg: Königshausen & Neumann, 2007), pp. 177–90
Lamping, Dieter, *Die Idee der Weltlitertur: Ein Konzept Goethes und seine Karriere* (Stuttgart: Kröner, 2010)
Latour, Bruno, *Reassembling the Social: An Introduction to Actor-Network-Theory* (Oxford: Oxford U. P., 2005)
Lechner, Stefanie, 'The Making of the "Suhrkampkrise": Oedipus, Dame Fortune and the Power of the Tropes. How Language Shapes Business Reality', published online at https://www.yumpu.com/en/document/view/20707029/the-making-of-the-suhrkampkrise-oedipus-dame-fortune-and-the- (last accessed 20 November 2020)
Leeder, Karen, 'Ingeborg Bachmann as Poet and Myth: A Case Study in Cultural Impact', in Rebecca Braun & Lyn Marven, eds, *Cultural Impact in the German Context: Studies in Transmission, Reception, and Influence* (Rochester, NY: Camden House, 2010), pp. 260–77
Lennox, Sara, *Cemetery of the Murdered Daughters: Feminism, History, and Ingeborg Bachmann* (Amherst, Boston: U of Massachusetts P, 2006)
Leser, Joachim, & Georg Guntermann, eds, *Brauchen wir eine neue Gruppe 47? 55 Fragebogen zur deutschen Literatur* (Bonn: Nenzel, 1995)
Maertz, Gregory, 'Carlyle's Critique of Goethe: Literature and the Cult of Personality', *Studies in Scottish Literature*, 29.1 (1996), 205–26
Magenau, Jörg, 'Freunde fürs Lesen', *die tageszeitung*, 13 Oct 2007
Manthey, Jürgen, '*Die Blechtrommel* wiedergelesen', in Heinz Ludwig Arnold, ed, *Günter Grass*, 1 (Munich: Text + Kritik, 1988), pp. 24–36
Marven, Lyn, 'Life and Literature: Autobiography, Referentiality, and Intertextuality in Herta Müller's Work', in Brigid Haines & Lyn Marven, eds, *Herta Müller* (Oxford: Oxford Univeristy Press, 2013), pp. 204–223
—— *Body and Narrative in Contemporary Literatures in German: Herta Müller, Libuše Moníková, and Kerstin Hensel* (Oxford: Oxford University Press, 2005)
Mason, Ann, *The Skeptical Muse: A Study of Günter Grass's Conception of the Artist* (Bern: Lang, 1974)
Massey, Doreen, *For Space* (London: Sage, 2005)
Matthes, Frauke, '"Ich bin ein Humanistenkopf": Feridun Zaimoğlu, German Literature, and Worldness' in *Seminar*, 51.2 (2015), 173–90
Mayer, Sigrid, & Martha Hanscom, *Critical Reception of the Short Fiction by Joyce Carol Oates and Gabriele Wohmann* (Rochester NY: Camden House, 1998)
McGowan, Moray, '"Stadt und Schädel", "Reisende", and "Verlorene": City, Self, and Survival in Herta Müller's Reisende auf einem Bein', in Haines & Marven, eds, *Herta Müller*, pp. 664–83
Meizoz, Jérôme, *La littérature "en personne" : Scène médiatique et formes d'incarnation* (Geneva: Slatkine, 2016)
—— *La Fabrique des Singularités: Postures Littéraires II* (Geneva: Slatkine, 2011)
—— *Postures littéraires: Mises en scène modernes de l'auteur* (Geneva: Slatkine, 2007)
Meyer-Gosau, Frauke, *Einmal muss das Fest ja kommen: Eine Reise zu Ingeborg Bachmann* (Munich: Beck, 2008)

Micke, Marina, & Matthew Philpotts, 'Irreconcilable Differences: The Troubled Founding of the Leipzig Institute for Literature', in 'Post-War Literature and Institutions', ed. Seán M. Williams and W. Daniel Wilson, special issue of *Oxford German Studies* (2014), 43:1, 5–19

Minden, Michael, '"Grass auseinandergeschrieben": Günter Grass's *Hundejahre* and Mimesis', *German Quarterly*, 86.1 (2013), 25–42

Mittermeyer, Manfred, *Thomas Bernhard: Eine Biografie* (Vienna: Residenz, 2015)

Moltke, Johannes von, *No Place Like Home: Locations of Heimat in German Cinema* (Berkeley: U. of California P., 2005)

Morgan, Ben, *On Becoming God: Late Medieval Mysticism and the Modern Western Self* (New York: Fordham U. P., 2013)

—— 'Understanding the Cultural Impact of Popular Film', in Rebecca Braun & Lyn Marven, eds, *Cultural Impact in the German Context: Studies in Transmission, Reception, and Influence* (Rochester, NY: Camden House, 2010), pp. 58–77

Moser, Doris, *Der Ingeborg-Bachmann-Preis: Börse, Show, Event* (Vienna: Böhlau, 2004)

Nägele, Rainer, 'Die Goethefeiern von 1932 und 1949', in *Deutsche Feiern*, ed. Reinhold Grimm and Jost Hermand (Wiesbaden: Athenaion, 1977), pp. 97–122

Noyes, John K., 'Writing the Dialectical Structure of the Modern Subject: Goethe on World Literature and World Citizenship', *Seminar* 51.2 (2015), 100–14

Obermeier, Stephanie, '"Im beweglichen Umgang mit den störrischen Fakten": Attitudes to Genre in Felicitas Hoppe's *Prawda: Eine amerikanische Reise*', *German Life & Letters*, 72.3 (2019), 378–98

Oster, Sandra, *Das Autorenfoto in Buch und Buchwerbung: Autorinszenierung und Kanonisierung mit Bildern* (Berlin: de Gruyter, 2014)

Palmowski, Jan, *Inventing a Socialist Nation: Heimat and the Politics of Everyday Life in the GDR, 1945-1990* (Cambridge: Cambridge U. P., 2009)

Parker, Stephen, 'Brecht and *Sinn und Form*: The Creation of Cold War Legends', *German Life and Letters* (2007), 60.4, 518–33

Parkes, Stuart, 'Martin Walser's *Tod eines Kritikers*: A "Crime" of Anti-Semitism?', in *German Text Crimes: Writers Accused from the 1950s to the 2000s*, ed. Tom Cheesman (Amsterdam & New York: Rodopi, 2013), pp. 153–74

—— *Writers and Politics in Germany, 1945–2008* (Rochester, NY: Camden House, 2009)

Parr, Rolf, 'Walter Höllerers Neuakzentierung der Intellektuellenrolle im Literaturbetrieb', in Achim Geisenhanslüke & Michael Peter Hehl, eds, *Poetik im technischen Zeitalter: Walter Höllerer und die Entstehung des modernen Literaturbetriebs* (Bielefeld: transcript, 2013), pp. 192–211

—— *Autorschaft: Eine kurze Sozialgeschichte der literarischen Intelligenz in Deutschland zwischen 1860 und 1930* (Heidelberg: Synchron, 2008)

—— 'Kein universeller, kein spezifischer Intellektueller: Walter Höllerer im Literaturbetrieb der 1950er und 1960er Jahre', *kultuRRevolution*, 61/62 (2011), 76–85

Paul, Georgina, *Perspectives on Gender in Post-1945 German Literature* (Rochester, NY: Camden House, 2009)

Paul, Ina Ulrike, 'Autorfunktion, Autorfiktion: Schriftstellerfiguren bei Daniel Kehlmann', *Gegenwartsliteratur* 16 (2017), 77–99

Philpotts, Matthew, and Stephen Parker, *The Modern Restoration: Rethinking German Literary History, 1930–1960* (Berlin: de Gruyter, 2004)

Pietsch, Timm Niklas, *"Wer hört noch zu?" Günter Grass als politischer Redner und Essayist* (Essen: Klartext, 2006)

Piper, Andrew, *Dreaming in Books: The Making of the Bibliographic Imagination in the Romantic Age* (Chicago: U. of Chicago P., 2009)
Pizer, John, *Imagining the Age of Goethe in German Literature, 1970–2010* (Rochester, NY: Camden House, 2011)
Plachta, Bodo, *Dichterhäuser: Mit Fotografien von Achim Bednorz* (Darmstadt: Theiss, 2017)
Preece, Julian, *Günter Grass* (London: Reaktion, 2018)
Raddatz, Fritz J., *Zur deutschen Literatur der Zeit 2: Die Nachgeborenen. Leseerfahrungen mit zeitgenössischer Literatur* (Reinbek bei Hamburg: Rowohlt, 1987)
Reddick, John, *The Danzig Triology of Günter Grass: A Study of The Tin Drum, Cat and Mouse, and Dog Years* (London: Secker & Warburg, 1975)
Redmond, Sean, & Su Holmes, eds, *Stardom and Celebrity: A Reader* (London: Sage, 2007)
Relph, Edward, *Place and Placelessness* (London: Pion, 1976)
Robertson, Ritchie, *Goethe: A Very Short Introduction* (Oxford: Oxford U. P., 2016)
Rojek, Chris, *Celebrity* (London: Reaktion, 2001).
Rüther, Günther, *"Greif zur Feder, Kumpel": Schriftsteller, Literatur und Politik in der DDR 1949–1990* (Düsseldorf: Droste, 1991)
Sayad, Cecilia, *Performing Authorship: Self-Inscription and Corporeality in the Cinema* (London: Tauris, 2013)
Schaper, Benjamin, *Poetik und Politik der Lesbarkeit in der deutschen Literatur* (Heidelberg: Winger, 2017)
Schaub, Christoph, *Proletarische Welten: Internationalistische Weltliteratur in der Weimarer Republik* (Berlin: de Gruyter, 2019)
—— 'Internationalist Montages: World-Making in Interwar Germany's Labor Movement Literature', in Chunjie Zhang, ed, *Composing Modernist Connections in China and Europe* (New York: Routledge, 2019), pp. 50–69
Scheidgen, Ilka, *Gabriele Wohmann: Ich muss neugierig bleiben: Die Biografie* (Lahr: Kaufmann, 2012)
Scheuffeln, Thomas, ed., *Gabriele Wohmann: Materialienbuch* (Darmstadt: Luchterhand, 1977)
Schirrmacher, Frank, ed., *Die Walser-Bubis-Debatte* (Frankfurt a.M.: Suhrkamp, 1999)
Segeberg, Harro, *Literatur im Medienzeitalter: Literatur, Technik und Medien seit 1914* (Darmstadt: Wissenschaftlich Buchgesellschaft, 2003)
Silbermann, Marc, 'Schreiben als öffentliche Angelegenheit: Lesestrategien des Romans Hundejahre', in Manfred Durzak, ed., *Zu Günter Grass: Geschichte auf dem poetischen Prüfstand* (Stuttgart: Klett, 1985), pp. 80–95
Smith, Colin, *Tradition, Art and Society: Christa Wolf's Prose* (Essen: die blaue Eule, 1987)
Sonntag, Bärbel, 'Unser aller Unseld', *die tageszeitung*, 23.06.2000
Stamp Miller, Ann, *The Cultural Politics of the German Democratic Republic: The Voices of Wolf Biermann, Christa Wolf, and Heiner Müller* (Bock Ration: Brown Walker, 2004)
Steiner, George, 'Adorno: Love and Cognition', *The Times Literary Supplement*, 09 March 1973
Stephenson, Barry, *Ritual: A Very Short Introduction* (Oxford: Oxford U. P., 2015)
Summers, Caroline, *Examining Text and Authorship in Translation: What Remains of Christa Wolf?* ([n.p]: Palgrave, 2017)

Taberner, Stuart, *Transnationalism and German-Language Literature in the Twenty-First Century* (Basingstoke: Palgrave Macmillan: 2017)

—— *Aging and Old Age Style in Günter Grass, Ruth Klüger, Christa Wolf, and Martin Walser: The Mannerism of a Late Period* (Rochester, NY: Camden House, 2013)

Tatlock, Lynne, ed., *Publishing Culture and the "Reading Nation": German Book History in the Long Nineteenth Century* (Rochester, NY: Camden House, 2010)

Tautz, Birgit, *Translating the World: Toward a New History of German Literature around 1800* (University Park, PA: Penn State U. P., 2018)

Thesz, Nicole, *The Communicative Event in the Works of Günter Grass: Stages of Speech, 1959–2015* (Rochester, NY: Camden House, 2018)

—— 'Illusions of Return: City and Memory in Günter Grass's Danzig Novels', *Seminar*, 45/1 (2009), 64–81

Tommek, Heribert, & Klaus-Michael Bogdal, eds, *Transformationen des literarischen Feldes in der Gegenwart: Sozialstruktur – Medien-Ökonomien – Autorpositionen* (Heidelberg: Synchron, 2012)

Töteberg, Michael, '"Das wärs, lieber Herr Verleger, für diesmal": Eine Hausautorin wird verramscht: Gisela Elsner und der Rowohlt-Verlag', in Künzel & Schönert, eds, *Ikonisierung, Kritik, Wiederentdeckung: Gisela Elsner und die Literatur der Bundesrepublik* (Munich: text + kritik, 2014), pp. 54–71

Vandenrath, Sonja, *Private Förderung zeitgenössischer Literatur: Eine Bestandsaufnahme* (Bielefeld: transcript, 2006)

Vees-Gulani, Susanne, & Laurel Cohen-Pfister, eds, *Generational Shifts in Contemporary German Culture* (Rochester, NY: Camden House, 2010)

Vertovec, Stephen, *Transnationalism* (London and New York: Routledge, 2009)

Wagenbach, Klaus, Winfried Stephan & Michael Krüger, eds, *Vaterland, Muttersprache: Deutsche Schriftsteller und ihr Staat von 1945 bis heute* (Berlin: Wagenbach, 1979)

Wagener, Hans, *Gabriele Wohmann* (Berlin: Colloquium, 1986)

Weigel, Sigrid, *Genea-Logik: Generation, Tradition and Evolution zwischen Kultur- und Naturwissenschaften* (Munich: Fink, 2006)

—— *Ingeborg Bachmann: Hinterlassenschaften unter Wahrung des Briefgeheimnisses* (Munich: DTV, 2003)

Weissmann, Dirk, 'German Writers from Abroad: Translingualism, Hybrid Languages, "Broken Germans"', in Rebecca Braun & Benedict Schofield, eds, *Transnational German Studies* (Liverpool: Liverpool U. P., 2020), pp. 57–76

Weixler, Antonius, '"Dass man mich nie für vermisst erklärt hat, obwohl ich seit Jahren verschollen bin": Autorschaft, Autorität und Authentizität in Felicitas Hoppe', in Frank & Ilgner, eds, *Ehrliche Erfindungen*, pp. 359–88

Wichert, Adalbert, *Goethefeiern: Ein Rückblick auf 150 Jahre Dichterverehrung* (Augsburg: Katholische Akademie Augsburg, 1983)

Will, Wilfried van der, 'The embattled intellectual' in *The Narrative Fiction of Heinrich Böll*, ed. by Michael Butler (Cambridge: Cambridge U. P., 1994), pp. 21–48

Wilson, W. Daniel, *Der Faustische Pakt: Goethe und die Goethe-Gesellschaft im Dritten Reich* (Munich: dtv, 2018)

Wood, Michael, *Heiner Müller's Democratic Theatre: The Politics of Making the Audience Work* (Rochester, NY: Camden House, 2017)

Wright, Chantal, 'Before Chamisso: The role played by the Munich DaF writing competitions and anthologies in the promotion of a "deutsche Literatur von außen"', 1979–1987', *Oxford German Studies*, 43.1 (2014), 20–36

Zehl Romero, Christiane, *Anna Seghers: Eine Biographie, 1947–1983* (Berlin: Aufbau, 2003)

Index

Academy of Arts 29, 58, 122, 125, 134
  see also Akademie der Künste
Actor-Network-Theory (ANT) 10, 152–6
  network(s) 5, 9, 10, 11, 14, 15, 16, 19, 20, 21, 22, 23 24, 26, 27, 28, 33, 34, 36, 37, 45, 65, 67, 68, 74, 102, 105, 106, 107, 111, 115, 151–6, 158, 159, 161, 164, 165, 166, 167, 168, 169, 170, 171, 172, 173, 174, 175, 176, 177, 181, 184, 185, 187, 190, 191, 194, 197, 215, 217, 223, 225, 226, 228, 231, 232, 234, 235, 236, 237, 238, 244, 247, 249, 255, 256, 257, 268, 269, 287, 288, 293, 294, 296, 297, 298
  mediator(s) 10, 12, 14, 25, 32, 37, 65, 105, 107, 152, 154, 155, 156, 161, 165, 167, 170, 172, 173, 175, 185, 190, 193, 244, 320
  actor(s) 5, 10, 14, 16, 18, 25, 28, 34, 36, 66, 67, 68, 73, 74, 107, 110, 152, 154, 165, 171, 172, 173, 175, 181, 183, 287
    human 26, 151, 156, 174, 185
    non-human 15, 32, 35, 151, 155, 160, 173–6, 177, 185, 191, 236, 257
  node(s) 20, 156, 164, 173
Adelson, Leslie 4, 213, 215, 221
Adorno, Theodor W. 4, 79, 80, 86, 95, 96, 97, 98, 100, 145, 156, 183, 186, 190
  'Kulturkritik und Gesellschaft' 76–8
agency 5, 34, 44, 104, 111, 154, 155, 164, 173, 174, 175, 204, 205, 206, 210, 236, 246, 252, 257
Akademie der Künste 122
  see also Academy of Arts
America 127, 130, 132, 157, 159, 161, 167, 169, 221, 222, 223, 224, 226, 227, 229, 244, 246, 249, 251, 254
Andersch, Alfred 44, 63, 65, 71, 78, 85, 88, 175
Anniversary(ies) 27, 28, 29, 40, 50, 58, 61, 116, 247
Assmann, Aleida 42, 43, 44, 48, 49, 75, 77, 85, 95, 175, 210
  memory of place 41, 43, 44, 76, 94, 95, 175, 176, 177
  places of commemoration 41, 44, 49, 85
  places of generational memory 41, 43, 44, 48, 175

Index

audience(s) 21, 23, 38, 39, 44, 62, 82, 99, 133, 134, 159, 161, 177, 180, 185, 190, 197, 215, 242, 244, 255, 266, 267, 313, 314, 315, 317, 319, 320
Augé, Marc 94
Austria 19, 37, 167, 193, 234, 237, 239, 241
    Austrian 19, 23, 24, 50, 54, 55, 56, 68, 88, 169, 177, 178, 193, 224, 234, 235, 289, 297
author
    body of 37, 38, 44, 51, 101, 266, 267, 268, 313, 314
    female 9, 22, 23, 68, 100, 137, 167, 168, 188, 236, 237, 243, 256, 264, 268, 270, 271, 272, 297, 314
    male 20, 21, 23, 33, 62, 105, 107, 114, 145, 168, 169, 172, 177, 181, 182, 188, 189, 211, 244, 270, 271, 272
    minority 11, 12, 15, 23, 189, 236, 254
    persona 11, 26, 33, 34, 37, 38, 41, 44, 87, 106, 169, 193, 194, 215–16, 231, 252, 255
    woman 7, 8, 12, 15, 102, 189, 196, 267, 271, 313, 314, 318, 322
authority 5, 50, 97, 122, 151, 155, 166, 185, 191, 196, 208, 224, 231, 232, 246, 270
authorship
    biographical 5, 9, 11, 13, 37, 88, 126, 129, 132, 135, 146, 147, 195, 199, 204, 217, 218, 219, 220, 222, 239, 249, 263
    collaborative 5, 109, 162–3, 165, 167, 170, 181, 238, 246, 257, 291, 314, 315, 318

    collective 32, 34, 43, 44, 57, 58, 72, 125, 151, 153, 154, 162, 165, 168, 176–82, 184, 225, 238, 264
    dispersed 50, 68, 97, 98, 193, 197, 232, 233, 236
    extended 100, 106, 152–6, 184, 228, 266, 290
    in literary theory 1–2, 5, 27, 30, 35, 196
    mode(s) of 5, 6, 7, 9, 10, 12, 13, 15, 17, 18, 20, 21, 23, 25–69, 77, 78, 81, 83, 85, 87, 88, 92, 94, 96, 97, 98, 101, 102, 103, 104, 105, 106, 107, 114, 115, 116, 117, 118, 119, 120, 121, 126, 127, 128, 129, 130, 134, 137, 138, 140, 141, 142, 143, 145, 146, 148, 149, 151, 170, 173, 177, 180, 182, 187, 190, 193–232, 234, 236, 237, 238, 239, 241, 246, 247, 249, 251, 255, 256, 257
    celebratory 6, 9, 10, 12, 13, 15, 28, 36–41, 43, 44, 45, 50, 53, 56, 57, 59, 61, 63, 64, 65, 67, 68, 78, 83, 87, 98, 101, 102, 106, 107, 114, 116, 117, 118, 119, 131, 138, 141, 143, 147, 149, 170, 177, 179, 182, 187, 190, 191, 196, 198, 199, 202, 215, 231, 232, 235, 237, 238, 239, 241, 246, 255
    commemorative 6, 27, 28, 34, 36, 41–4, 50, 57, 58, 59, 61, 63, 64, 65, 66, 67, 68, 78, 81, 85, 87, 88, 92, 94, 95, 97, 98, 114, 116, 117, 118, 119, 121, 122, 127, 128, 130, 131, 134, 137, 140, 141, 142, 143, 145, 177,

180, 196, 198, 199, 202,
205, 206, 208, 2019, 210,
211, 213, 214, 215, 231,
232, 235, 237, 239, 241,
242, 247, 249, 251, 255
  satirical 6, 10, 28, 36, 50–7,
    66, 67, 78, 85, 94, 96, 97,
    98, 102, 103, 104, 105, 196,
    215, 237, 247
  utopian 6, 28, 36, 44–50, 57,
    59, 60, 61, 63, 65, 66, 67,
    68, 77, 78, 81, 85, 87, 97,
    98, 102, 114, 118, 119, 120,
    121, 128, 130, 131, 138,
    141, 145, 148, 193–232,
    234, 236, 237, 238, 239,
    246, 255, 256
  models of 6, 7, 15, 17, 18, 20, 21,
    22, 23, 24, 32, 33, 36, 37,
    48, 50, 57, 58, 61, 63, 66–9,
    71–111, 113–49, 151, 154,
    156, 160, 161, 193, 194,
    196, 197, 202, 214, 215,
    217, 225, 231, 232, 233–57
  exemplary creator 21, 66, 67,
    71–111, 115, 149, 155, 256
  exemplary pedagogue 21,
    113–49
  transnational 23, 24, 69, 197,
    232, 233–57
  multi-media 196, 223, 229, 232,
    313
  national 8, 12, 19, 23, 29–30, 37,
    50, 68, 155, 175, 197, 232,
    234, 235, 263
  ontology of 5, 7
  open ended and inclusive 48,
    68, 148, 232, 236, 255
  romantic 6, 17, 27–8, 31, 36–7,
    56, 217, 243–4, 256
  transnational 23, 24, 69, 197,
    232, 233–57
  world 14, 15, 33, 44, 53, 68,
    77, 256

Bachmann, Ingeborg 22, 159, 211,
    234, 235, 236, 237, 255, 264
  Malina 211–12
Barthes, Roland 1, 3, 5, 12, 34, 195,
    196, 202, 215, 231
  'Death of the Author' 1, 193,
    195, 196, 215
Becher, Johannes R. 21, 67, 73,
    115–26, 132, 133, 134, 135,
    136, 138–40, 141, 144, 145,
    146, 148, 216
  'Auf andere Art so große
    Hoffnung' 139–40
  'Der Befreier' 116–26
  Kulturbund zur
    demokratischen
    Erneuerung
    Deutschlands 73, 122
  'Rede zur Verleihung des
    Goethe-Nationalpreises
    an Thomas Mann' 116–26
belonging 6, 31, 32, 43, 47, 49, 50,
    78, 80, 81, 82, 83, 84, 85,
    87, 113, 117, 121, 123, 124,
    125, 126, 128, 129, 135,
    136, 138, 146, 147, 149,
    156, 158, 165, 180, 182,
    197, 204, 296
  not- 84, 141, 144, 149, 182,
    203, 235
Berlin 13, 21, 29, 58, 88, 124, 125,
    134, 152, 156, 157, 158,
    159, 162, 167, 173, 176,
    177, 178, 179, 180, 181,
    182, 183, 184, 203, 212,
    237, 246, 251, 253, 255,
    257, 259, 265, 268, 284,
    285, 295, 296, 299, 308,
    309, 310, 320, 321, 322
  Literarisches Colloquium
    (LCB) 21, 157
  Literary Colloquium (LCB) 21,
    58, 160, 161, 162, 167, 169,
    173, 176, 265

Technical University 21, 156, 158, 169, 173, 268
Technische Universität 21, 268
Wall 99, 110, 113, 147, 203
  see also Wall, Berlin
West 58, 136, 157, 177, 203, 209, 212, 265
Berlin Literary Colloquium 21, 58, 160, 161, 162, 167, 169, 173, 176, 265
  see also Literarisches Colloquium Berlin
Bernhard, Thomas 50–7, 84, 186, 188, 189, 247
  Goethe schtirbt 51–7
Bewohnbar 81, 82, 84, 167
  -keit 165, 168
Biermann, Wolf 20
Biller, Maxim 62, 64, 65, 254
biopic 7, 184, 185, 186, 187, 188, 190, 214, 215, 216, 230
Bloch, Ernst 4, 47–8, 50, 79, 82, 84, 97, 132, 179, 189, 190, 213
  Das Prinzip Hoffnung 47–8, 189
body, physical 37, 38, 44, 51, 101, 120, 130, 212, 245, 266, 267, 268, 271, 313, 314
Böll, Heinrich 20, 21, 45, 60, 67, 71, 78, 79, 81–7, 89, 92, 95, 97, 99, 105, 107, 129, 165, 183, 212, 216, 231
  Frankfurter Vorlesungen 81–7
  Erkenntnis 78, 82, 86, 95, 97, 106, 165, 166, 168
Bourdieu, Pierre 1, 3, 14, 26, 35, 55, 76, 155, 197
  cultural field 26, 33, 156
  habitus 35
Brecht, Bertolt 126, 134, 177, 179

canon(ical) 3, 8, 9, 20, 21, 51, 84, 87, 102, 106, 117, 145, 148, 180, 184, 187, 190, 234, 237, 246, 253, 269, 270, 321, 322, 323
celebrity 7, 13, 17, 29, 36, 38, 39, 51, 66, 101, 124, 132, 216, 255
celebrification 39, 50, 65, 142
Christian, religion 186, 200
Cold War period 21, 109, 110, 114, 156, 157, 195, 215, 245, 246
collaboration(s) 5, 134, 161, 196, 214, 225, 233, 290, 291, 297, 316, 319, 320
collective(s) 41, 57, 58, 72, 117, 125, 128, 130, 154, 160, 161, 162, 164, 165, 177, 179, 181, 184, 263
cultural
  heritage 43, 48, 60, 115, 120, 122
  institutions 34, 123, 124, 132
  landscape 3, 17, 18, 20, 32, 36, 45, 51, 56, 61, 62, 79, 88, 120, 121, 165, 169, 235
  value 28, 39, 50, 59, 64, 151, 234, 256

Danzig 87, 88, 89, 90, 92, 94, 96
Deutsches Literaturinstitut in Leipzig 157, 259, 268, 269, 310, 311, 322, 323
diary(ies) 8, 12, 13, 14, 15, 106, 133, 139, 140, 144, 229
Draesner, Ulrike 8, 22, 69, 216, 231, 238, 255, 256, 257, 259–73, 275, 312, 323
  Eine Frau wird älter 267–8
  gedächtnisschleifen 263
  Grammatik der Gespenster 259
  London 273
  Mein Hiddensee 271–2
  Schwitters 259
  Sieben Sprünge vom Rand der Welt 261, 262–3, 263–4
Durckheim, Émile 26, 32, 35

Eckermann, Johann Peter 13, 14, 15, 20, 224
editor(s) 78, 100, 106, 107, 109, 134, 266, 291, 323
Elsner, Gisela 20, 21, 67, 99–106, 108, 109, 110, 111, 247
  'Die Auferstehung der Gisela Elsner' 100–2
  Die Riesenzwerge 102–6
Enzensberger, Hans Magnus 20, 21, 45, 67, 78–81, 85, 87, 98, 99, 109, 110, 153, 160, 181, 183, 184, 191, 216, 222
  'Die Sprache des Spiegel' 79–81
  'Journalismus als Eiertanz: Beschreibung einer Allgemeinen Zeitung für Deutschland' 79–81
Erb, Elke 279, 290, 291
Erkenntnis 76, 78, 79, 82, 86, 95, 97, 106, 165, 166, 168, 206, 207
ethics 44, 63, 66, 77, 78, 81, 85, 87, 97, 100, 110, 114, 118, 119, 121, 128, 129, 130, 149, 151, 174, 196, 232, 240, 245, 249, 251
Europe 2, 3, 11, 12, 13, 16, 17, 19, 26, 33, 46, 67, 71, 84, 87, 97, 102, 106, 113, 114, 115, 116, 130, 160, 175, 176, 178, 180, 181, 182, 187, 193, 194, 195, 200, 221, 226, 233, 237, 244, 250, 253, 256, 263, 299, 315

film 7, 11, 13, 15, 16, 18, 57, 59, 60, 61, 62, 63, 64, 65, 66, 83, 157, 18, 159, 160, 176, 177, 178, 180, 181, 188, 189, 200, 216, 275, 276, 277, 287, 288, 299, 303, 304, 305, 307, 308, 309, 316, 317, 318, 319, 321

Foucault, Michel 1, 4, 5, 29, 34, 46–7, 55, 157, 195 196, 199, 200, 221, 231
  heterotopia 46–7, 50, 59, 60, 61, 63, 111, 127, 128, 129, 131, 135, 140, 141, 144, 157, 196, 199, 200, 201, 202, 205, 214, 221, 228, 229
France 3, 113, 128, 132, 186, 249
Frankfurt 21, 40, 51, 52, 55, 60, 64, 81, 85, 89, 127, 151, 154, 156, 182–4, 212, 257, 259, 261, 275, 284–5, 295–6
Frisch, Max 20, 45, 159, 164
future(s) 17, 18, 32, 44, 46, 48, 50, 51, 57, 58, 65, 67, 73, 82, 87, 93, 117, 120, 121, 127, 129, 131, 136, 137, 145, 178, 193, 206, 211, 213, 214, 216, 239, 240, 243, 290, 297, 314, 323, 324

genealogy(ies) 9, 92, 174, 175, 176, 177, 182, 184
generation(s) 22, 41, 43, 44, 45, 48, 59, 60, 71, 81, 84, 85, 93, 98, 114, 117, 118, 120, 122, 130, 135, 138, 140, 141, 142, 143, 145, 147, 152, 153, 154, 156, 158, 164, 174, 175, 176, 180, 181, 182, 183, 184, 191, 241, 264, 265, 310, 322
genius 17, 27, 28, 30, 31, 36–9, 51, 52, 55, 56, 119
Gentile 33, 110, 114, 169, 181, 182
Germanness 20, 23, 30, 43, 44, 96, 232, 255
Germany 2, 6, 7, 9, 14, 18, 19, 20, 22, 23, 24, 25, 28, 39, 40, 41, 43, 44, 46, 48, 51, 58, 59, 61, 62, 64, 67, 68, 71, 72, 73, 74, 77, 79, 80, 81, 83, 85, 88, 90, 92, 96, 97,

102, 107, 110, 113, 116, 117, 119, 120, 122, 123, 124, 124, 126, 127, 129, 132, 145, 148, 156, 157, 160, 167, 180, 185, 190, 197, 203, 204, 206, 209, 212, 215, 221, 222, 226, 231, 235, 237, 253, 259, 265, 270, 271, 272, 275, 294, 296, 299, 319, 321
East 19, 61, 67, 68, 88, 113–49, 180, 215, 257, 263, 299, 321
Federal Republic (FRG) 7, 12, 19, 21, 24, 45, 61, 66, 79, 103, 105, 107, 109, 110, 111, 131, 153, 162, 178, 179, 184, 197
German Democratic Republic (GDR) 19, 21, 100, 106, 110, 111, 113–49, 157, 161, 178, 179
post-war 3, 6, 12, 16, 19, 20, 21, 23, 33, 36, 39, 43, 45, 54, 59, 62, 63, 64, 65, 66, 67, 71–111, 115, 122, 127, 130, 137, 141, 142, 145, 160, 175, 184, 190, 191, 225, 231, 232, 237, 239, 253
Second World War 36, 39, 42, 66, 67, 71, 84, 127, 143, 179
West 12, 19, 20, 39, 40, 41, 61, 66, 68, 71–111, 113, 114, 115, 117, 122, 126, 127, 129, 132, 134, 144, 148, 149, 152, 156, 157, 158, 169, 171, 172, 184, 185, 191, 193, 198, 203, 206, 209, 212, 235, 236, 238, 257, 259, 295
reunified 6, 12, 21, 122, 147, 194
Goethe, Johann Wolfgang von 1, 2, 3, 4, 7–16, 17, 19, 44, 45, 64, 68, 73, 77, 83, 84, 110, 130, 151, 160, 189, 190, 197, 216, 225, 232, 235, 256
  in Johannes R. Becher's work 116–22, 124, 132, 133
  in Thomas Bernhard's work 50–7
  in Johann Peter Eckermann's work 13–15
  in Felicitas Hoppe's work 222–8, 231
  in Thomas Mann's work 28–36, 37–41, 42
Institute 223, 226, 227, 308, 309, 310, 320, 321, 322
Gruppe 47 11, 44–50, 57–66, 71, 72, 78, 83, 88, 99, 100, 123, 142, 153, 154, 156, 157, 159, 160, 167, 168, 175, 182, 187, 235
  Dichter und Richter: Die Gruppe 47, vorläufiges Schlußbild nach 30 Jahren 57–66
  Wie sie wurden, was sie sind. Gruppe 47: eine Schriftstellergeneration schreibt Geschichte 57–66
  Vom Glanz und Vergehen der Gruppe 47 61–6
Günter Grass 20, 21, 45, 62, 63, 65, 67, 71, 79, 86, 87–99, 100, 103, 105, 106, 110, 113, 114, 115, 117, 128, 143, 159, 161, 176, 177, 183, 191, 194, 216, 219, 232, 256
  Danzig Trilogy 87–99
  Hundejahre 89, 90–9

Habermas, Jürgen 86, 87, 96, 99
Haderlap, Maja 22, 68, 237–43, 249, 252, 254
  Engel des Vergessens 237–43
Handke, Peter 20, 153, 166, 194
Hayot, Eric 4

Index 343

Heidegger, Martin 4, 47, 48–50, 64, 73, 82, 92, 116
   'Sprache und Heimat' 48–50
Heimat 3, 31, 32, 33, 34, 35, 41, 47, 48, 49, 50, 57, 59, 60, 61, 62, 63, 64, 5, 66, 71, 72, 78, 81, 82, 83, 84, 88, 94, 97, 116, 120, 121, 122, 124, 132, 142, 177, 179, 180, 213
   cultural 3, 33, 34, 47, 57, 63, 65, 66, 78, 94, 124, 142, 177, 179, 180
   heimatlos 60, 72, 142
Hermlin, Stephan 114, 115, 134
Höllerer, Walter 21, 68, 152, 154, 156–73, 174, 176, 182, 190, 191, 268
   Das Gästehaus 162–9
   Das literarische Profil von Berlin 176–84
   Der andere Gast 169–70
   Die Elefantenuhr 170–3
   Gedichte: Wie entsteht ein Gedicht? 169–70
Holocaust 3, 88, 114, 122
Hoppe, Felicitas 20, 22, 68, 196, 214–32, 236
   Felicitas Hoppe sagt 215
   Hoppe 214, 217–22
   Johanna 214, 218, 224, 225
   Paradiese, Übersee 214, 224, 225
   Prawda 222–30
   Sieben Schätze 231
   www.3668ilfpetrow.com 223, 227–30

India 315
institution(s); 9, 21, 29, 34, 35, 39, 45, 56, 68, 78, 116, 122, 123, 124, 125, 132, 133, 134, 135, 147, 149, 151, 152, 153, 154, 156, 167, 169, 171, 173, 174, 223, 236, 238, 253, 264, 265, 309, 321

intellectual(s) 2, 6, 12, 13, 32, 44, 47, 54, 57, 58, 61, 76, 77, 81, 84, 87, 113, 114, 115, 122, 126, 145, 147, 161, 170, 176, 190
   public 6, 57, 58, 81, 87, 126, 176
internet 228, 229, 250, 264, 265, 266, 269, 312, 324

Jelinek, Elfriede 104, 219, 256
Jens, Walter 45, 62, 63, 152, 212
Jew(ish) 11, 47, 62, 64, 76, 88, 96, 127, 168, 249, 250, 252, 253
Johnson, Uwe 20, 71, 88, 100, 179, 180, 183
journalism 18, 57, 79, 81, 85, 156, 167, 218
journalist(s) 21, 40, 100, 106, 107, 110, 154, 182, 255, 265
Jurjew, Oleg 275, 279, 283, 284, 290, 294, 295

Kehlmann, Daniel 20, 194, 216
Klagenfurt 234, 241, 242
Kracht, Christian 20, 194, 216
Kulturnation 2, 117, 176

Latour, Bruno 10, 11, 12, 14, 32, 35, 104, 152, 155, 164, 165, 171, 173, 175, 181
   see also Actor-Network-Theory (ANT)
Ledig-Rowohlt, Heinrich Maria 100, 106, 107, 109
Lektor 280, 309, 311
   see also editor(s)
Lenz, Siegfried 71, 86, 87, 88, 100
Literarisches Colloquium Berlin 21, 17
   see also Berlin Literary Colloquium
Literaturbetrieb 26, 282, 283, 284
literature network(s) 15, 16, 20, 21, 22, 23, 24, 26, 27, 28, 33, 36,

37, 65, 67, 68, 102, 105, 106, 107, 111, 151, 154, 15, 156, 166, 10, 171, 172, 173, 176, 177, 181, 184, 185, 187, 190, 191, 194, 197, 215, 217, 223, 225, 232, 234, 235, 236, 237, 238, 255, 257
Literaturhaus(häuser) 2, 158, 272, 309, 310

Mann, Thomas 28–36, 37–41, 42–3, 44, 45, 51, 52, 56, 79, 116, 117, 118, 121, 235
  'Goethe als Repräsentant des bürgerlichen Zeitalters' 28–36, 42
  'Goethes Laufbahn als Schriftsteller' 37–41, 42
Mannheim, Karl 174–5
market 3, 18, 19, 24, 68, 173, 183, 193, 203, 248, 269, 271, 290, 294, 322
Martynova, Olga 22, 28, 68, 69, 237, 238, 243–8, 252, 253, 254, 256, 257, 275–98
  Mörikes Schlüsselbein 243–8, 275, 276, 280, 281, 282, 287, 291, 292, 293
  Sogar Papageien überleben uns 243, 275, 280, 292
Massey, Doreen 73–6, 77, 93, 128, 148, 200
media 7, 9, 10, 19, 21, 26, 39, 43, 45, 56, 58, 59, 61, 62, 63, 65, 79, 81, 83, 99, 100, 109, 110, 152, 153, 154, 156, 158, 159, 160, 161, 169, 170, 176, 185, 194, 196, 208, 223, 226, 228, 229, 232, 234, 235, 236, 237, 257, 268, 269, 287, 297, 299, 300, 313, 323, 324
Meizoz, Jérôme 1, 3, 14, 29, 34, 35, 149
  posture 1, 29, 34, 35, 237

memory 42, 45, 49, 64, 92, 96, 197, 199, 209, 239, 240, 245, 249, 250, 251
culture 34
generational 41, 43, 44, 48, 93, 117, 118, 122, 142, 143, 175, 180
of place(s) 41, 43, 44, 76, 94, 95, 175, 176, 177
place of 44, 50, 63, 97, 121, 202, 210, 213, 234
money 86, 101, 234, 265, 270, 272, 273, 297
More, Sir Thomas 46, 84, 98, 121, 217
  Utopia 46, 84, 121, 217
Müller, Herta 22, 68, 194, 195, 197, 203–14, 215, 226, 229, 230, 231, 232, 236
  Reisende auf einem Bein 195, 203–14
  'Der Fremde Blick oder Das Leben ist ein Furz in der Laterne' 203–5
multilingualism 238
Munich 58, 259, 263, 272
music 62, 88, 237, 251, 255, 269, 287, 288, 299, 315, 317, 318, 320
Muslim, religion 188, 253

National Socialism 19, 72, 123
network(s) 5, 9, 10, 11, 14, 15, 16, 19, 20, 21, 22, 23, 24, 26, 27, 28, 33, 34, 36, 37, 45, 65, 67, 68, 74, 102, 105, 106, 107, 111, 115, 151–6, 158, 159, 161, 164, 165, 166, 167, 168, 169, 170, 171, 172, 173, 174, 175, 176, 177, 181, 184, 185, 187, 190, 191, 194, 197, 215, 217, 223, 225, 226, 228, 231, 232, 234, 235,

236, 237, 238, 244, 247, 249, 255, 256, 257, 268, 269, 287, 288, 293, 294, 296, 297, 298
literary 10, 74, 115, 167
literature 15, 16, 20, 21, 22, 23, 24, 26, 27, 28, 33, 36, 37, 65, 67, 68, 102, 105, 106, 107, 111, 151, 154, 15, 156, 166, 10, 171, 172, 173, 176, 177, 181, 184, 185, 187, 190, 191, 194, 197, 215, 217, 223, 225, 232, 234, 235, 236, 237, 238, 255, 257

performance(s) 22, 32, 33, 38, 56, 67, 158, 197, 203, 215, 216, 248, 251, 265, 268, 299, 300, 301, 304, 307, 314, 315, 317, 319, 320
Petrowskaja, Katja 22, 68, 237, 238, 241, 248–54
Vielleicht Esther 241, 248–54
place(s) 2, 3, 4, 5, 6, 10, 11, 18, 19, 21, 23, 26, 27, 28, 29, 32, 33, 34, 35, 41–50, 60, 63, 64, 65, 68, 71, 72, 73, 74, 75, 76, 78, 80, 81, 83, 85, 87, 88, 89, 90, 92, 93, 94, 95, 96, 97, 98, 100, 104, 105, 111, 115, 117, 119, 120, 121, 122, 127, 128, 129, 131, 137, 138, 140, 142, 143, 148, 151, 155, 16, 157, 158, 170, 171, 175, 176, 177, 179, 180, 182, 185, 190, 191, 195, 196, 197, 198, 199, 200, 201, 202, 203, 205, 206, 208, 210, 213, 214, 215, 216, 217, 220, 221, 226, 229, 231, 232, 234, 235, 236, 239, 242, 243, 245, 246, 247, 248, 252, 259, 264, 273, 295, 297, 317

of memory 44, 50, 63, 97, 121, 202, 210, 213, 234
memory of 41, 43, 44, 76, 94, 95, 175, 176, 177
placelessness 74, 75, 77, 84, 85, 87, 96, 97, 98, 100, 102, 105, 106, 115, 128, 140, 142, 144, 169, 180, 204, 206, 232, 238
placeness 49, 75, 80, 83, 84, 85, 96, 123, 126, 128, 129, 130, 131, 133, 134, 135, 137, 145, 146, 147, 148, 202, 204, 232
poem(s) 2, 22, 51, 59, 60, 62, 76, 139, 168, 169, 171, 178, 203, 204, 228, 262, 264, 268, 273, 288, 290, 291, 313, 315, 317, 321
poetry 16, 18, 22, 64, 85, 88, 134, 168, 169, 170, 204, 229, 243, 247, 259, 264, 265, 269, 273, 275, 288, 294, 297, 299, 307, 313, 314, 318, 319, 320, 322
poststructuralism 2, 30, 35, 194, 196, 198, 213, 231
posture 1, 29, 34, 35, 237
see also Meizoz, Jérôme
prize(s) 2, 7, 19, 22, 23, 24, 25, 26, 27, 42, 51, 103, 116, 117, 162, 204, 214, 231, 234, 235, 237, 238, 239, 243, 248, 253, 254, 264, 270, 271, 272, 275, 294, 295, 296, 297
literary 25, 26, 27, 235, 271, 272
Adelbert-Von-Chamisso Prize 254, 285, 286, 296
German Book Prize 270, 275
Gertrud-Kolmar Prize 286, 297
Ingeborg Bachmann Prize 19, 22, 23, 231, 234–7, 238,

243, 248, 253, 254, 275, 283, 285, 286, 294, 295, 296, 297
Prix Formentor 100, 102
province(s) 61, 63, 158, 234
provincial 45, 46, 47, 57, 61, 80, 140, 167, 171, 182, 222, 234, 249
publisher 13, 21, 26, 68, 100, 101, 105, 106, 107, 109, 130, 146, 176, 183, 185, 186, 187, 188, 189, 190, 193, 266, 267, 270, 273, 290, 294, 295, 324
publishing 5, 13, 16, 37, 65, 78, 102, 105, 109, 110, 111, 132, 153, 156, 157, 179, 181, 185, 190, 191, 222, 237, 255, 264, 269, 294, 319, 322
   house(s) 9, 21, 51, 100, 106, 108, 125, 154, 177, 178, 182, 183, 184, 187, 188, 197, 235, 270, 320, 323

Raddatz, Fritz J. 21, 67, 99, 100, 106–11, 154, 187
Ransmayr, Christoph 22, 68, 193–202, 203, 208, 214, 215, 228, 230, 231, 232, 236
   Die letzte Welt 193, 197–202, 204
reader(s) 8, 15, 16, 17, 23, 33, 37, 46, 55, 56, 68, 76, 78, 79, 80, 82, 87, 92, 95, 104, 109, 131, 134, 135, 138, 139, 143, 144, 145, 146, 148, 149, 160, 161, 162, 165, 166, 169, 171, 195, 196, 197, 198, 202, 203, 206, 210, 211, 212, 214, 214, 215, 216, 218, 219, 220, 221, 225, 228, 229, 230, 231, 232, 236, 241, 246, 254, 255, 257, 264, 271, 287, 288, 289, 290, 313

region 90, 96, 97, 235, 272
   -al 2, 12, 33, 35, 75, 91, 92, 100, 158, 235
Reich-Ranicki, Marcel 45, 144, 186, 271
Relph, Edward 74–5, 77
Richter, Hans Werner 44, 5, 46, 47, 58, 59–66, 71, 72, 74, 78, 85, 123, 142, 152, 153, 154, 157, 161, 167, 174, 175
ritual(s) 26, 27, 32, 34, 36, 56, 67, 104, 124, 235, 237
romantic 6, 28, 84, 120, 140, 143, 162, 181, 202, 217, 222, 225, 243, 244
   -ism 221, 256
   genius 17, 27, 28, 31, 36, 37, 56
Rowohlt Verlag 100, 105, 106, 107, 108, 109, 111, 153, 182, 183, 187, 235
Rühmkorf, Peter 109, 159, 161

Sandig, Ulrike Almut 22, 69, 196, 216, 231, 238, 256, 257, 299–324
   Buch gegen das Verschwinden 300, 313
   ich bin ein Feld voller Raps verstecke die Rehe und leuchte wie dreizehn Ölgemälde übereinander gelegt 299, 305, 313, 317–18
   Flamingos 300, 313
   Leuchtende Schafe 299
   Zunder 306
Schiller, Friedrich 2, 40, 42, 44, 171, 197
Schnurre, Wolfdietrich 60, 113, 114, 115, 181
school 46, 161, 288
Schriftstellerverband der DDR 125, 146
Schulze, Ingo 20, 256

Seghers, Anna 21, 67, 115, 124–34, 135, 136, 137, 138, 141, 145, 146, 147, 148, 216, 232
  Das siebte Kreuz 124
  Das Vertrauen 127, 129–31
  Die Entscheidung 127, 131, 136
S. Fischer Verlag 183, 235, 284, 295
Suhrkamp Verlag 21, 50, 51, 53, 54, 55, 78, 153, 154, 182, 183, 184, 185, 187, 188, 190, 235, 284, 29

Technical University Berlin 21, 156, 158, 169, 173, 268
  see also Technische Universität Berlin
Technische Universität Berlin 21, 268
  see also Technical University Berlin
technology 10, 287, 293
television (TV) 2, 7, 8, 16, 21, 46, 58, 59, 63, 71, 72, 109, 156, 158, 159, 160, 176, 177, 184, 185, 234, 253, 271
throwntogetherness 73, 93, 128, 129, 148, 200
  see also Massey, Doreen
tourism 101, 234, 251
translation 102, 152, 212, 259, 260, 261, 267, 268, 273, 288, 290, 291, 292, 294, 299, 315, 316, 319, 320
translator 16, 30, 244, 246, 255, 268, 275, 290, 291, 299, 315
transnational 4, 23, 24, 29, 68, 197, 232, 233, 234, 236, 237, 238, 253, 254, 255, 256
  authorship 233–57
trauma(s) 66, 85, 103, 116, 119, 127, 137, 143, 175, 200, 205, 206, 208, 211, 213, 240, 250, 261, 264
  traumatic 44, 63, 74, 77, 96, 109, 117, 128, 129, 131, 169, 179, 200, 230

unification 23
  post- 61
  re- 6, 12, 21, 122, 147, 194
university(ies) 2, 21, 51, 101, 138, 140, 156, 158, 169, 173, 268, 299
Unseld, Siegfried 21, 52, 68, 154, 156, 182–90, 284, 295
  Der Verleger oder Die Lust am Buch 184–90
utopia(n) 28, 33, 74, 78, 83, 84, 131, 132, 134, 135, 143, 144, 145, 171, 237, 248
  heterotopia 46–7, 50, 59, 60, 61, 63, 111, 127, 128, 129, 131, 135, 140, 141, 144, 157, 196, 199, 200, 201, 202, 205, 214, 221, 228, 229
  mode 6, 36, 44–50, 57, 59, 60, 61, 63, 65, 66, 67, 68, 77, 81, 85, 87, 97, 98, 102, 114, 118, 119, 120, 121, 128, 130, 138, 141, 148, 193–232, 234, 236, 237, 238, 239, 246, 255, 256
  More, Sir Thomas 46, 84, 121, 217

Von Arnim, Bettina 181
Von Günderrode, Karoline 140, 181

Wall, Berlin 99, 110, 113, 147, 203
Walser, Martin 8, 20, 45, 62, 86, 92, 100, 107, 164, 183–5, 188–9, 191, 256
Weber, Max 32, 38, 216
website 223, 224, 226, 227, 228, 229, 230, 231, 234, 263, 264, 265
Weigel, Sigrid 174–6, 237

Weimar 12, 13, 15, 29, 44, 51, 116, 118, 177
Weiss, Peter 88, 161
Welt-Literatur 4, 12, 14, 15
Wieland, Christoph Martin 12
Wiener, Oswald 177, 179
Wohmann, Gabriele 7–16, 19, 62, 65, 166, 271–3
  Schreiben müssen: Ein elektronisches Tagebuch 7–8

Wolf, Christa 21, 67, 133, 134–47, 148, 194, 216, 235, 256
  Der geteilte Himmel 136–7
  Nachdenken über Christa T. 137–47
world literature 1, 4, 12, 14, 1, 16, 17, 33, 36, 68, 73, 119, 130, 160, 215, 256
  see also Welt-Literatur

Zaimoğlu, Feridun 254, 256

New Directions in German Studies
Vol. 36

Series Editor:

IMKE MEYER
Professor of Germanic Studies, University of Illinois at Chicago

Editorial Board:

KATHERINE ARENS
Professor of Germanic Studies, University of Texas at Austin

ROSWITHA BURWICK
Distinguished Chair of Modern Foreign Languages Emerita,
Scripps College

RICHARD ELDRIDGE
Charles and Harriett Cox McDowell Professor of Philosophy,
Swarthmore College

ERIKA FISCHER-LICHTE
Professor Emerita of Theater Studies, Freie Universität Berlin

CATRIONA MACLEOD
Frank Curtis Springer and Gertrude Melcher Springer Professor in the College and the Department of Germanic Studies, University of Chicago

STEPHAN SCHINDLER
Professor of German and Chair, University of South Florida

HEIDI SCHLIPPHACKE
Associate Professor of Germanic Studies,
University of Illinois at Chicago

ANDREW J. WEBBER
Professor of Modern German and Comparative Culture,
Cambridge University

SILKE-MARIA WEINECK
Professor of German and Comparative Literature,
University of Michigan

DAVID WELLBERY
LeRoy T. and Margaret Deffenbaugh Carlson University Professor,
University of Chicago

SABINE WILKE
Joff Hanauer Distinguished Professor for Western Civilization and
Professor of German, University of Washington

JOHN ZILCOSKY
Professor of German and Comparative Literature, University of
Toronto

Volumes in the Series:

1. *Improvisation as Art: Conceptual Challenges, Historical Perspectives*
by Edgar Landgraf

2. *The German Pícaro and Modernity: Between Underdog and Shape-Shifter*
by Bernhard Malkmus

3. *Citation and Precedent: Conjunctions and Disjunctions of German Law and Literature*
by Thomas O. Beebee

4. *Beyond Discontent: 'Sublimation' from Goethe to Lacan*
by Eckart Goebel

5. *From Kafka to Sebald: Modernism and Narrative Form*
edited by Sabine Wilke

6. *Image in Outline: Reading Lou Andreas-Salomé*
by Gisela Brinker-Gabler

7. *Out of Place: German Realism, Displacement, and Modernity*
by John B. Lyon

8. *Thomas Mann in English: A Study in Literary Translation*
by David Horton

9. *The Tragedy of Fatherhood: King Laius and the Politics of Paternity in the West*
by Silke-Maria Weineck

10. *The Poet as Phenomenologist: Rilke and the* New Poems
by Luke Fischer

11. *The Laughter of the Thracian Woman: A Protohistory of Theory*
by Hans Blumenberg, translated by Spencer Hawkins

12. *Roma Voices in the German-Speaking World*
by Lorely French

13. *Vienna's Dreams of Europe: Culture and Identity beyond the Nation-State*
by Katherine Arens

14. *Thomas Mann and Shakespeare: Something Rich and Strange*
edited by Tobias Döring and Ewan Fernie

15. *Goethe's Families of the Heart*
by Susan E. Gustafson

16. *German Aesthetics: Fundamental Concepts from Baumgarten to Adorno*
edited by J. D. Mininger and Jason Michael Peck

17. *Figures of Natality: Reading the Political in the Age of Goethe*
by Joseph D. O'Neil

18. *Readings in the Anthropocene: The Environmental Humanities, German Studies, and Beyond*
edited by Sabine Wilke and Japhet Johnstone

19. *Building Socialism: Architecture and Urbanism in East German Literature, 1955–1973*
by Curtis Swope

20. *Ghostwriting: W. G. Sebald's Poetics of History*
by Richard T. Gray

21. *Stereotype and Destiny in Arthur Schnitzler's Prose: Five Psycho-Sociological Readings*
by Marie Kolkenbrock

22. *Sissi's World: The Empress Elisabeth in Memory and Myth*
edited by Maura E. Hametz and Heidi Schlipphacke

23. *Posthumanism in the Age of Humanism: Mind, Matter, and the Life Sciences after Kant*
edited by Edgar Landgraf, Gabriel Trop, and Leif Weatherby

24. *Staging West German Democracy: Governmental PR Films and the Democratic Imaginary, 1953–1963*
by Jan Uelzmann

25. *The Lever as Instrument of Reason: Technological Constructions of Knowledge around 1800*
by Jocelyn Holland

26. *The Fontane Workshop: Manufacturing Realism in the Industrial Age of Print*
by Petra McGillen

27. *Gender, Collaboration, and Authorship in German Culture: Literary Joint Ventures, 1750–1850*
edited by Laura Deiulio and John B. Lyon

28. *Kafka's Stereoscopes: The Political Function of a Literary Style*
by Isak Winkel Holm

29. *Ambiguous Aggression in German Realism and Beyond: Flirtation, Passive Aggression, Domestic Violence*
by Barbara N. Nagel

30. *Thomas Bernhard's Afterlives*
edited by Stephen Dowden, Gregor Thuswaldner, and Olaf Berwald

31. *Modernism in Trieste: The Habsburg Mediterranean and the Literary Invention of Europe, 1870–1945*
by Salvatore Pappalardo

32. *Grotesque Visions: The Science of Berlin Dada*
by Thomas O. Haakenson

33. *Theodor Fontane: Irony and Avowal in a Post-Truth Age*
by Brian Tucker

34. *Jane Eyre in German Lands: The Import of Romance, 1848–1918*
by Lynne Tatlock

35. *Weimar in Princeton: Thomas Mann and the Kahler Circle*
by Stanley Corngold

36. *Authors and the World: Literary Authorship in Modern Germany*
by Rebecca Braun

www.ingramcontent.com/pod-product-compliance
Lightning Source LLC
Chambersburg PA
CBHW052141300426
44115CB00011B/1472